The Last Escape

THE LAST ESCAPE

The Launching of the Largest
Secret Rescue Movement
of All Time

By Ruth Klüger and Peggy Mann

Doubleday & Company, Inc.
Garden City, New York
1973

ISBN: 0-385-00313-7
Library of Congress Catalog Card Number 72-92187
Copyright © 1973 by Ruth Aliav and Peggy Mann
All Rights Reserved
Printed in the United States of America

Acknowledgments

We wish to express our deep appreciation to the following for their generous help in supplying information for this book: Ehud Avriel, David Arnon, Josef Barpal (Kadmon), Adi Ben-Zvi, Joseph Blanchard, Yulik Braginski, Moshe Carmiel, Meir Cotic, Eliahu Dobkin, George Duca, Father F. M. Galdau, Arthur Gross, Ruth Gruber, David Hacohen, Teddy Kollek, Moshe Kones, Baron de Menasse, Joseph Nayer, Lili Nesher, Davidka N'meri, Jacob Padan (Polesiuk, Poli), David Polesiuk-Padan, Dasha Rittenberg, Gershon Rivlin, Alexander Shapiro, Moshe Sharett (Shertok), Arkadi Sloutski, Zvi Yechieli (Shechter), Shmarya Zameret and I. Zissu.

Our thanks also to the following for their help in checking facts and/or for editorial suggestions: Harry Alderman, Virginia Armstrong, Judy Baily Arnon, Miriam Chaikin, Ann Cutler, Erika Freeman, Dale Hackett, Fritz Levi, Harvey Mann, Dr. Ida Mayer, Lubtcho Mihaylov, Guenadi Pankin, Gershon Rivlin, Harry Steinberg, Hande Surmelioglu, Esther Togman and Mort Yarmon.

And our very special thanks to our brilliant editor Ken McCormick. And to William Houlton, for his valuable suggestions, and his steadfast encouragement and support during the years it took to write this book.

INTRODUCTION

THE STORY of the so-called "illegal immigration" into Palestine is one of the most dramatic in the four thousand-year-old history of the Jewish people.

If it had not been for the thousands of Jews smuggled into the country between 1938 and 1948 the infant state of Israel might well have lost her first war for survival.

During those years Eliahu Dobkin was the Jewish Agency representative in charge of the limited number of *legal* certificates allocated to European Jews desperate to enter Palestine. In Dobkin's words:

Of the four hundred thousand immigrants who came to Palestine in the years preceding our declaration of statehood, about half were illegals. If it were *not* for the illegals, instead of having over six hundred thousand people to fight off the invading forces of seven Arab states, we would have had only four hundred thousand; men, women and children. The population of the Arab nations who had declared war on us was over fifty million. *There is no doubt but that it would have been impossible for our nation to come to statehood, and to survive without the illegal immigration.*

Dobkin was one of the many Israeli Government officials I interviewed when gathering material for THE LAST ESCAPE. The statement he gave me on the *aliyah bet*—the illegal immigration—was expressed in similar words by everyone I spoke to in connection with this book.

There are, in fact, two separate aliyah bet stories. One concerns the *postwar* ships, which brought the holocaust survivors. That story is known.

This book concerns the other story, which is virtually unknown: the story of the first ships, the secret ships, which brought their passengers to Palestine's shores in the few years preceding and following the outbreak of World War II. If these "illegals" had not been rescued, they might never have lived to become survivors.

The early ships were organized by a network of Jews spread throughout the countries of Europe. A network of ten. Nine from Palestine, one from Vienna. Nine men, and a young woman named Ruth.

In researching this book I interviewed Ruth in over one thousand hours of tape-recorded sessions. I also interviewed most of the people still alive who played a role in this story. (Some whom I interviewed have since died: Josef Barpal [Kadmon], Shmarya Zameret, Arkadi Sloutski, Zvi Yechieli [Zvi Shechter], David Arnon, Davidka N'meri, Moshe Sharett [Shertok].)

In addition, I spent many hours in the Haganah Archives. There was not an abundance of documentation. For good reason. Many of the notes, letters and orders I found ended with the instructions: *Destroy after reading.* Ruth destroyed her papers when she fled from the Iron Guard in November 1940. Most of the scant documentation which exists today does so by negligence or accident. The Mossad members were not concerned with annotating an account of their ventures.

Consequently, much of the material in this book is based on the memories of those involved. At times I met with two people at once; interviewing them on a single event or phase of the operation. It became clear that two sets of memories can sometimes produce somewhat different versions of the same incident, facet or fact. But everyone I interviewed agreed on the basic accuracy of all that is written here. The entire manuscript has been further checked for factual accuracy by Colonel Gershon Rivlin, historian of the Haganah Archives, and by Ehud Avriel, one of the original ten Mossad members.

In addition, the main portion of the manuscript, set in Rumania, was checked for accuracy by George Duca, son of the Rumanian Premier Ion Duca, who was murdered by the Iron Guard. George Duca's fascinating day-by-day diary proved an invaluable research source. Mr.

Duca was in the Rumanian diplomatic service during the years with which this book deals, 1939–41.

All names are used as they were during those years. Only one name has been changed, that of Stefan Meta. The reason will be obvious to the reader.

Peggy Mann

New York City
March 1973

PART ONE

June 1939 to August 1939

ONE

IT WAS THE EMPTY TIME between darkness and the beginning of daylight. I started slowly down the gangplank, the last bridge between the safety of the ship and the unknown. Beyond the gray and glooming customs shed, the city of Constantza was hidden by mist.

I carried a small suitcase of papers, but my passport had been taken from me on the ship. A Jew, the old saying goes, is only an annex to his documents. And I sensed it then, the sodden fear of being a stranger, wandering without identity in a hostile land.

I was no stranger; I had grown up in Rumania. Part of my family still lived here. I had visited Bucharest often. But this time there was a difference.

"You must understand," Eliahu had said, "our work is considered illegal by every government in the world. Including our own. If you land in prison we'll have no way to get you out. You will disappear."

I stepped off the gangplank and started across the wet cobblestones to the customs shed.

The entryway was lit by a few bare light bulbs. The dimness was alive with voices. People stood about in bewildered groups clutching hand baggage. There was nothing, not a suitcase, a coat, an umbrella we would have trusted to the waterfront derelicts who swarmed through the shed claiming to be porters.

Then the crowd pressed forward and we came to a vast room jammed

3

with shouting, shoving passengers. Someone caught my arm; an official, his brass buttons open, his grimy shirt hanging out. "Watch your purse," he announced. "Here they steal even the whites of your eyes."

He drew me over to a table by the wall, took up a sheaf of papers. "These forms are complicated. I'll help you fill them out. Get you through customs." He sat down. "Most people consider such services to be worth a hundred lei."

I hesitated.

"It's not always so easy," he added, "to find your passport again. Unless you have help."

I opened my purse. At times, I assured myself, it pays to overpay.

He indicated a rickety chair. I sat stiffly.

His pen point scratched on the printed form. "Date. June nineteenth. One nine three nine. Name?"

"Ruth Klüger."

"With umlaut?"

I nodded.

He punctuated my name with two precise dots. "Date of birth?"

"April twenty-fourth. Nineteen fourteen."

"Why do you lie, Ruth Klüger with umlaut?"

I looked at him blankly.

"You are sixteen, seventeen. No?"

"Twenty-five." I had always looked young for my age. In the past this had been a source of humiliation. But in the future it might prove a protection. No one would suspect a schoolgirl of being a secret agent.

"Coming from?"

"Palestine."

"Proposed length of stay in Rumania?"

"A few months."

He moved the desk lamp closer toward me. His eyes went carefully over my face, then to my body. Rumanian men, I remembered, have a habit of looking. And the look they give seems always the same. It covers a woman in a single glance, and then, more lingeringly, uncovers her.

"Marital status?" he said.

It was a question which, in fact, I could not answer even to myself. I had been married for five years; a marriage which was never a mar-

4

riage. And this trip to Europe would, I felt, separate my husband and me in every way.

"Married," I said.

"Where is your husband?"

"Is that on the form?"

He smiled, revealing a black gap where two teeth were missing. "Purpose of visit? Tourism? In transit? Business? Other?"

"Business."

"What type?"

"To sell shares. Of land—in Palestine."

An explosive guffaw, smelling of garlic and stale wine. "Excuse me. But you don't look much like a real estate agent." Then his voice gentled. "I would like to invite you for a coffee. There's a nice cafe by the waterfront. Have you eaten breakfast?"

I shook my head, afraid to offend him until I had my passport again.

He filled out the rest of the form with dispatch. "Come!" And he erupted into a dynamo; shouting, shoving his bulk through the crowds as I tagged after him, clutching my small case of documents. My large valise, I'd been told, would be sent straight from the ship. I could reclaim it at customs.

It seemed impossible even to find a customs inspector in this melee; much less to locate one battered, brown valise. There was a high wall of luggage on the platform. Elegant suitcases. Packing boxes with metal rods around them. Cheap pressed-cardboard cases tied with rope. And the customs inspectors were busy bending back the rods, cutting the ropes, even at times breaking the locks on the fine valises.

Somehow, within minutes, my hundred-lei protector had my passport in his hands, had found my suitcase and had corralled an inspector. He then gave a brief flick of his fingers. At once my cases were marked as cleared, and we were on our way toward the oblong of daylight at the far end of the shed. We emerged into the pale sunlight of early morning.

"Now!" he exclaimed, setting down my valise. Again he awarded me his gap-toothed smile.

"The—passport."

He nodded, pulled it out of his pocket.

With the passport in my hand I felt I had been granted official re-entry into the human race. Then I looked at my watch and gasped. "I didn't know it was so late. My train leaves in a few minutes!"

His fingers were firm on my arm. "Take the next train."

"I can't do that. My family's meeting me at the station in Bucharest."

He gave me a sour look, as though I had betrayed him.

"Please," I said softly.

He released my arm. Let out a shrill whistle. Signaled a porter. Plunged back into the customs shed. And a uniformed station porter stood before me, his stiffly spread fingers gesturing into my face.

I paid his fee, said, "Bucharest." He picked up my cases and started running. I ran after him across row after row of railroad tracks. A train came toward me and I dodged in front of it, afraid of losing him if I let it go by.

Then we were on a piece of concrete pavement. To the left were the imposing doors of the station. Behind us, a sudden view of the water. The world was a light blue of sea and sky. The ships in the harbor were bright with flags flying.

I turned.

My porter had disappeared.

A train was emitting whistle shrills denoting imminent departure. It was on the track marked Bucureşti. I ran toward it, praying my valise might be somewhere on board.

I mounted the small iron steps, forced my way into a second-class carriage. People were climbing through the windows, were perched on the arms of seats, were sitting on suitcases clogging the aisles. I had a reservation, delivered to me aboard ship. But the number of reservations sold obviously had no relation to the number of seats on the train. There was, however, one vacant place; a single, backless bench near the door. I promptly sat down. Several passengers standing in the aisle spewed Rumanian at me, shaking their heads, gesticulating. I paid no attention.

With a lurch and a powerful blast from the engine the train began to move. The conductor came elbowing, shoving his way through the aisle, and he stood before me. The seat I had taken, he informed me in brusque Rumanian, was his.

I looked up at him, smiled and replied in French that I did not understand. At the same time I opened my purse, took out one hundred lei, and described my missing valise. He pocketed the tip; continued on his rounds.

As the gray baroque buildings of the city's skyline faded into distance, a miasma of despair swept through me. I had been sent on a mission to save human lives and I could not look after a single suitcase.

Vernichtung. Annihilation.

Berl had shown me the clipping from the S.S. newspaper *Das Schwarze Korps*. Words inserted in a rambling speech Hitler had made before the Reichstag.

"If the international Jewish financiers inside and outside Europe should again succeed in plunging the nations into a world war, the result will be the annihilation of the Jewish race throughout Europe." Annihilation! Vernichtung!

Words dredged from the hysteria of a madman.

Yet, Berl Katznelson believed those words. Eliahu Golomb believed those words. It was why they backed the efforts of the Mossad le Aliyah Bet: the Institute of the Illegal Immigration; the "Institute" that smuggled Jews out of Europe and into Palestine.

There were nine members of the Mossad operating in Europe. I would be the tenth. And the only woman.

It seemed impossible that they had chosen me.

I'd been sitting in the Café Storch; the long, narrow cafe opposite the Histadrut office in Tel Aviv, when Berl came in. Strode in. Took off the cap he always wore on his bushy hair. Looked around, saw me alone at a table, and walked over.

"May I sit? I'd like to have a chat."

I had nodded, overwhelmed. Berl Katznelson, one of the founders of the Histadrut.* Founder and editor of the influential newspaper *Davar*. Founder of much that was new and unique in Palestine.

Berl knew me, for I worked at the Histadrut. But he had never before joined me at a cafe table.

Then Eliahu Golomb entered. Golomb in his Russian blouse. Slightly stooped; carved lines in his thin aristocratic face. Straight, thick brows

---

* *See* Appendix One.

7

over penetrating eyes. Eliahu Golomb, commander in chief of the Haganah.†

Berl beckoned to him. And Eliahu came over to join us.

"This is the one I had in mind," Berl said.

And I found myself sitting in the Café Storch between two of the most honored men in Palestine.

"Well, I've been looking at your record," Berl announced. "It says you know eight languages."

I nodded.

"You're young to be such a linguist."

"I—started young."

Both men were watching me. I was obviously expected to say more. "I was born in Kiev; so I was born into Russian. And Yiddish."

They nodded, waiting.

"During the war—when I was two—I was sent to stay with my grandmother. She lived in a border town. Between Russia and Austria. The town was invaded. We were suddenly refugees. We had to keep running. And—" I shrugged—"I kept learning languages."

"Go ahead," said Berl. "Eat your sandwich."

I took a bite. I could scarcely swallow. What did they want of me?

"According to your record," Berl said, "you went to law school. The University of Vienna. Now why did a young lady lawyer who speaks eight languages take herself off to live in an isolated *kibbutz* in Palestine?"‡

"It was the kibbutz I've been training for, since I was a child. My mother always said you could milk cows better with a university degree."

Berl smiled. "And why did you leave the kibbutz? You didn't take to the cows, after all?"

"I'm afraid my husband didn't. It was either leave the cows. Or leave Emmanuel."

"Suppose *we* asked you to leave your husband," Berl said. "For an undetermined length of time. To go on a mission to Rumania."

"I'd go."

"You can say that before you even know what the mission is?"

† *See* Appendix Two.
‡ *See* Appendix Three.

8

"If you and Eliahu back it, I don't need to know."

"A trusting young lady," Eliahu remarked. Then, quite suddenly, he said, "Tell me about your trip from Rumania to Palestine. What made you decide to smuggle in those sixteen Polish Jews?"

I looked at him in pure surprise. I'd always been certain that the only Palestinian who knew of the matter was the Jewish immigration officer Dostrovsky. He certainly would say nothing. If he did he would lose his job, perhaps land in jail. And the sixteen Polish Jews would say nothing. Anyone who entered Palestine illegally kept very quiet about it.

"We know the whole story," Eliahu said with something of a smile. "Except for one small point. Why you decided to do it."

"Well, I don't quite know," I told him. "I mean—they were there. At the port in Piraeus. They wanted so desperately to be here. They had no papers. No one would help them. So I thought I might as well try."

"As good an answer as any," said Eliahu. He asked me more questions; about the years I'd lived in Rumania, the contacts I had there. Then he looked at Berl and nodded. "All right," he said. "If she wants to go."

They told me then something of the Mossad, but very little. They concentrated on the warnings.

"Every other so-to-say secret agent in the world," said Berl, "has at least *some* place of safety he can escape to. Return to. But not the members of the Mossad. Most of them have to go into hiding when they come back here. The British have a high price on their heads."

"If you join the Mossad," Eliahu warned, "you'll be giving up personal security. And your personal life. Even your husband must know nothing at all of your activities. Do you understand what that will mean?"

I nodded. "Please," I said. "I want very much to go."

Recalling that scene with Berl and Eliahu restored some faint sense of confidence.

I stared out the train window half hypnotized by the scenes flashing by. Cornfields and golden stretches of wind-brushed wheat flowing

9

out to the far horizon. Mud-brick huts with thatched roofs. Peasant women in long skirts, colored kerchiefs; men in pantaloons, knee-length tunics, bright cummerbunds. June in rural Rumania.

Vernichtung.

Looking out at the pastoral picture-book scene of spring, the word lost all meaning.

By the time we neared Bucharest the carriage had become stifling. The air was grayed with cigarette smoke, soot and dust. I was so hot that perspiration ran down my forehead, into my eyes. I felt like a heap of dirty wet laundry.

I opened my compact. My face was grimy. Since the aisle was clogged with people it was impossible to reach the washroom, but I had some cologne in my bag. I took out a handkerchief, tried to clean my dirt-streaked face. Then I put away the compact with an inward shrug. There was one advantage to being on a secret mission. No one would meet me at the station.

The mud-brick huts gave way to cottages of whitewashed stone, surrounded by neat flower gardens.

Then we arrived at the outskirts of the city. The houses were low, the shops small, the cobbled streets narrow. Gradually the buildings mounted higher. Their windows, edged by shutters, were balcony rimmed.

A shiver of excitement went through me. Bucharest: the Paris of the Balkans. I loved this city. But what sort of life would I lead here now? What had I come back to?

Cars, trams, people, buildings flitted backward as the train sped on. And suddenly we were drawing into the station.

People pulled their luggage from the racks; called out the windows for porters.

I sat there.

If I was ever to find my suitcase I would have to wait till the train cleared. I tried to console myself with the thought that no one would trouble to make off with that ancient brown valise. Yet, I was certain I would never see it again.

Then the conductor came striding down the aisle, my suitcase in his arms.

I jumped up; thanked him profusely. But before I could even lay hands on the valise he had handed it out the open window. And I found myself rushing after still another porter through the huge and gloomy station and out into the square.

A wall of muggy heat rose from the sidewalk. June in Bucharest, I remembered, can be as hot as the tropics.

The station square was jammed with taxis, trams, buses, even horse-drawn carriages. A taxi pulled up beside me. The porter threw my suitcase into the back seat. I paid him and climbed in. I had arrived—with my luggage. It seemed a small miracle.

"Hotel Continental," I said to the driver.

As we started down the Calea Griviței, he turned around. "Are you a governess?" he inquired in French.

I shook my head.

"You dress like a governess," he announced. "But of course you are too young to be one. Also," he added, "too young to dress like one."

Embarrassed, not knowing quite what to say, I looked in a business-like way at my watch.

"Perhaps you would like to take a tour of the city," he suggested. "My rates are reasonable." He awarded me a tobacco-stained smile. "For some my rates are very reasonable."

"Thank you," I said. "I'm just passing through. I'm afraid I won't have time for sightseeing."

We turned abruptly into the Calea Victoriei; street of elegant shops, restaurants, fine hotels. And the cab pulled up sharply before the entrance of the Continental. Years ago it had been one of the fashionable hotels on the street. It was now permitted its first-class status through the courtesy granted a faded has-been.

The lobby seemed vast; worn Persian carpets, red plush chairs, dark wood paneling, heavy chandeliers. Several men were lounging in arm-chairs, reading newspapers, smoking. Was one of them my contact? Josef Barpal—code name, Kadmon.

I registered, handed over my passport. And followed the bellhop to the elevator. As it rattled upward, the sound seemed a magnified echo of the nervousness knocking within me.

The room was large, hot, dusky. Then the bellhop flicked a switch. Feeble light from the chandelier lessened the dimness.

I tipped him. I'd been instructed that our living allowance was limited to one pound sterling per day. I had already spent more than that on tips.

The bellhop left. I went to the window, pulled back the heavy velvet drapes. There was a view of a gray stone wall several yards away. I opened the window wide. From the shaft of space outside rose a stale, muggy coolness, like air from a grave.

Then I started to wash. The cracked mirror above the sink cast back a rippled reflection.

The water was icy; hot water came on only at certain hours. But I think I have never scrubbed myself so hard, so long. The square of linoleum under the sink was wet with my splashings.

I was standing bare, glowing clean, when a ringing telephone startled the stillness.

I lifted the receiver, my heart thudding.

"*Shalom,* Ruth." The voice was deep, vibrant. "I'm in the lobby. Come down when you're ready."

That was all. I put the receiver back slowly. Then, galvanized, I started to dress. A skirt, creased from the suitcase, a white blouse, sandals.

I passed the brush through my hair, looked at my wavering face in the sink mirror. And I hurried from the room, closing the door hard behind me.

TWO

He was sitting in an armchair opposite the elevator. He got up as I entered the lobby, a gray-haired, heavy-set man with glasses. He gave me a nod, then turned.

I followed him to a table in the far corner of the lobby.

He settled himself on a small sofa. I sat in an armchair. As he leaned back and lit up a cigar he seemed the picture, almost the caricature, of a bourgeois businessman. It was hard to imagine him a leader of the underground Mossad.

"Well," he announced, "you look ridiculously young."

It was the last thing I wanted to hear, not the first.

"We're supposed to remain inconspicuous," he said. "So they send me a redhead who attracts attention when she walks through a hotel lobby."

A waiter passed by and Kadmon clapped his hands twice, sharply. The waiter came over.

I had not eaten all day and was about to request some rolls and coffee. But Kadmon merely said to the waiter, "Someone may ask for Monsieur Barpal. Please tell the front desk I'm over here."

The waiter nodded and left.

"Do you use your real name?" I asked.

"Whenever possible."

"Shall I call you Kadmon or—?"

"Call me what you wish."

"I'm sorry," I said. "Have I offended you in some way?"

After a moment he shrugged. "Not you. Those who sent you. I told them this isn't a job for a woman. I told them I would not be responsible."

"I assure you, no one need be *responsible* for me."

"If you're arrested I'm not responsible? Exactly the last thing we need is the added worry of looking after a woman!"

"All this 'woman' business," I said, "is strange talk from a kibbutznik."

"Yes! On a kibbutz a woman is equal. Equal to work in the fields. Equal to pick apples. But we are not picking apples here!"

"It's very simple," I told him. "Just stop thinking of me as a woman."

He smiled. Then he said, "Well, Berl and Eliahu seem to think you can be of some use. We will see what we will see." He took out his pocket watch. "How would you like to meet a man so fat he must buy two tickets for himself when he rides on an airplane? The fellow weighs well over three hundred pounds. He could be in the circus. Instead, he's in the shipping business. A Greek. But he also speaks French and English. Which I don't. According to your dossier you're something of a linguist. Suppose you come along as interpreter."

I nodded.

"But," he added quickly, "*just* as interpreter. You're to do nothing, say nothing on your own. Except hello. Good-by. And—we hope—thank you. Is that clear?"

"Quite clear."

"We meet to discuss a ship. There'll be some difficult bargaining. The Shamen—as he's always telling me—is a businessman. Not a philanthropist."

Shamen means "fat" in Hebrew. It seemed a rather obvious code name for a man who weighed over three hundred pounds.

Kadmon stubbed out his cigar carefully. "Our escort arrives."

Some people have a face which speaks against them. The man walking toward us was one of these. He was tall, in his mid-forties perhaps; his skin was olive-tinged, his hair sleek brown, his attire elegant.

"This fellow's a Jew," Kadmon said. "But never forget, he works for the Shamen. Not for us. The Shamen's court Jew."

14

As the man reached our table, Kadmon rose; performed a perfunctory introduction. "Ruth. Arkadi."

Elaborately Arkadi kissed my hand. As I looked down I was struck by his very small feet encased in patent-leather shoes.

"The car is waiting," he said.

It was a large black sedan, an American car. A liveried chauffeur held the door open for us. Arkadi sat in front, but throughout the ride he kept turning to us, offering comments as though he were leading a guided tour.

I felt also that he was trying to pigeonhole me. Was I merely, as Kadmon had told him, an interpreter? Or was I one of these so-called nieces or secretaries without whom certain middle-aged men seem unable to function when away from home?

He informed me that he had been a captain in the Russian Navy. But after the Revolution he had abandoned ship in Greece, where his wife later joined him. She was—he took pains to point out—still living in Greece.

He paused then, as if expecting me to reciprocate with items of my own biography.

Since Kadmon had warned me to say nothing at all, I merely smiled and looked out the window.

The Calea Victoriei, illuminated with sunlight, was alive with lunchtime strollers; women and men, a parade of fashion. And the numerous officers who strolled down the street or took their ease at a sidewalk cafe seemed to have come straight from an operetta chorus. A dashing specimen crossed the street in front of our car.

"Did you know," Arkadi remarked to me, "these splendid Rumanian officers often wear corsets laced as tight as a lady's?"

The car turned into a tree-shaded boulevard edged by fine stone buildings with elaborate wrought-iron fences. Some had national flags hung out before them.

"Boulevard Brătianu," Arkadi said. "One of our most famous streets. And the location, as you see, of many embassies and legations."

There was a young gypsy girl on the corner selling flowers. She had bare feet, long skirts, a bright carnation in her hair. She waved a bunch of flowers at our car as we went by. "These girls look a lot better than they smell," Arkadi informed me. "In the gypsy language there's no word for 'clean.' And," he added, "no word for 'honest.'"

We turned at last into a side street and stopped short between an old, shuttered, rundown dwelling which contrasted surprisingly with the splendor of the limousine in which we drove.

We followed Arkadi into the corridor; the stale air was heavy with cooking smells. He pulled a key from his pocket, unlocked the door of the small elevator.

We got off at the third floor.

"To the right," Kadmon said.

A woman's tinselly laughter came from the other side of the door. Arkadi rang the bell. A petite and beautiful girl let us in. She wore a maid's uniform and bedroom slippers. She looked me up and down carefully. Then nodded to Arkadi and disappeared.

Dust glinted and danced in the sunlight which slanted through the shutters. That seemed the keynote color of the room: dust. Grayish curtains hung sagging at the windows. The worn carpet was the color of footsteps. And a silvery layer of dust had settled on the heavy wooden furniture.

The intimate laughter of a woman was heard again; cut short by a man's words, abrupt as a slap.

Then the doors slid open. The Shamen stood in the double doorway. Though Kadmon had warned me about his weight, I was still not prepared for this walking mountain of fat. Yet, if his face were not bloated with jowls and chins, he would have had classic features. He came toward us, smiling, gracious; the nobleman in his palace. "I apologize," he said in impeccable French, "for appearing in shirtsleeves. I did not realize we would be joined by a lady."

Arkadi translated this opening into an awkward Russian-accented German. And Kadmon, speaking his own unique version of German, introduced me. "She's an excellent linguist," he added. "I thought this might help in our discussions."

"The presence of a lovely woman always helps discussions," said the Shamen. He led us into the adjoining room where a scent of perfume hung in the air, so thick I felt I could brush it off my skin. This room was long and luxurious. There was a massive sofa, two oversized armchairs, an immense coffee table. There was also a large mirror which the Shamen seemed to avoid, for his reflection looked even larger when encased in the elaborate gilded frame.

I sat in one armchair. Kadmon started toward the other. But a look from Arkadi stopped him, and the two men took their places on the sofa. The remaining armchair was therefore left for the Shamen. I wondered whether he preferred to confine his bulk; compressing the colossus of a body into the girdling chair, rather than spreading himself wide on the sofa.

The girl who had opened the door to us, re-entered. She had brushed her hair, and changed her bedroom slippers for high-heeled shoes.

The Shamen asked what we would like to drink. I requested turkish coffee; the men wanted brandy.

There were the customary amenities as the drinks were served. Remarks about the weather. Questions about Palestine. How long was I staying in Bucharest.

I translated dutifully, saying nothing on my own. Kadmon intercepted and answered even those questions directed at me.

Then the Shamen said to the girl, "Thank you, Mina. You may go now. And please, no telephone calls. I am not to be disturbed."

When she had gone, the Shamen leaned back in his armchair. The amenities were over. "*Alors*," he announced. "I've found a ship. It's taken me weeks of searching. But I've found you a fifteen hundred-ton cargo ship. The *Tiger Hill*. She can carry fifteen hundred of your illegals."

"Is the vessel seaworthy?" Kadmon asked.

"Seaworthy?" The word was an explosion. "Am I a criminal? Would I offer you a ship which might sink?"

"Others have done so."

"Exactly. Which is why you are fortunate in dealing at last with an honorable man."

Kadmon nodded. "It is certain we can have this ship?"

"If it is certain that you can meet the payments."

"And these are?"

"Ninety pounds sterling per head."

"That," said Kadmon flatly, "is three times the cost of a first-class passage from Constantza to Haifa."

"On a *legal* ship, monsieur."

17

"Yes, my friend. On a legal ship—a cruise ship. But a cruise ship supplies each passenger with a comfortable bed. Your ship will supply a slab of wood. With two feet of space between it and the berth above. A cruise ship the size of the *Tiger Hill* would carry a few hundred people. I suggest, therefore, that with fifteen hundred passengers you'd make an adequate profit by charging the rates asked by a luxury liner."

"Monsieur," the Shamen said, quite equably, "you forget the costs I incur in transforming a cargo ship into one which can *carry* fifteen hundred passengers. My price is a firm one. If your people prefer to pay the standard cruise fare, let them *go* on legal ships."

"They do go on legal ships," said Kadmon, "when they have legal certificates for entry into Palestine. But the number who have legal certificates would not, I assure you, cause a stampede at any shipping office. For example, my friend, after the *Anschluss* last March there were one hundred and seventy-six thousand Jews desperate to get out of Vienna.* Now, how many legal certificates do you suppose were available for the Jews of Vienna? Thirty-two! And that, of course, was a year before the British White Paper with its new restrictions on legal certificates."†

"Ah, yes," the Shamen exclaimed. "The White Paper. I was just about to mention this little matter. I understand that since the British White Paper was issued last month a dozen more British patrol boats have been parading up and down the coast of Palestine to apprehend cargoes of illegals."

Kadmon said nothing.

The Shamen spread his fat hands in a helpless gesture. "Which means, of course, that the *Tiger Hill* runs a very good chance of being impounded by the British. Therefore, I must insist that you deposit in a Swiss bank a sum equal to the value of the ship—to be paid to me if the *Tiger Hill* does not return. Then there is the matter of hiring a captain and crew, all of whom demand substantial bonuses for sailing on an illegal ship. Plus generous insurance guarantees for the seamen and their families. Plus the purchasing of a flag to sail under, which, as you know, sir, can cost—"

"All right," said Kadmon brusquely. "Your total figure?"

* *See* Appendix Four.
† *See* Appendix Five.

"Ten thousand pounds down payment to me. In cash. The remaining eighty thousand to be deposited in a Swiss bank of your choice. Forty to be rebated to you if the *Tiger Hill* returns."

"Ninety thousand pounds. An impossible figure," Kadmon said. "As you must realize."

The Shamen shrugged. "If it's impossible for you, monsieur, there are many other uses to which I can put a ship like the *Tiger Hill*."

"Are there any other uses which involve saving human lives?"

The Shamen swirled the brandy around in his glass. "Come, monsieur, we are involved in a business enterprise. Let us leave our emotions outside the door."

"Forgive me, my friend," Kadmon said. "I find that a difficult thing to do. Perhaps because I've just returned from a visit to Berlin and Vienna. I've seen people queuing up. Lines three blocks long. Jews waiting in front of embassies and legations they'd probably never heard of since they studied geography in school. Santo Domingo. Madagascar. Paraguay. They queue up night and day. Week after week. For what? To be told there are no visas. The borders are closed. The borders of the world are officially and unofficially closed to Jews."

"I see," the Shamen remarked blandly. "Then there are no Jewish refugees in the United States? None in France? England? South America?"

"Most of those," Kadmon said, "got out early when—as they say—the going was good. Oh, of course, if you happen to be a famous scientist, film director, professor—someone special—visas are still possible to come by. The Chosen People, you might call them. But what of those who are not so chosen? The Jewish bookseller. The tailor. The watch repairman. The furrier. The three hundred and fifty thousand Jews still trapped in Germany, Austria, Czechoslovakia. When war comes—as it surely will—those three hundred and fifty thousand may swell to millions. And when war comes, all roads out will be closed. Legal roads *and* illegal roads. The Jews still in Europe will remain in Europe. Will be trapped here. And will die here. Millions of Jewish men and women and children will die here."

The Shamen smiled. "I applaud your oratory, monsieur. I did not put you down as the speechmaking type. Of course, orators may be excused if, for added drama, they exaggerate. But, please, there is no need to go—as the English put it—overboard. To say the Jews who remain here will *die!*"

"That," said Kadmon flatly, "is what we believe will happen."

"And who," the Shamen inquired, "is *we?*"

"The members of the Mossad. And others. Including, for example, the director of the Central Office for Jewish Emigration. Adolf Eichmann. He has a simple one-sentence policy for Jews. *Sie verschwinden oder ich werde Sie verschwinden.* Either you disappear or I will make you disappear."

"Every nation has its madmen," the Shamen said, "vomiting insanities."

Kadmon nodded. "But in other nations the madmen do not rule." After a moment he added, "We believe that every Jew we can rescue from Western Europe will be one more Jew saved from extermination."

I opened my purse, took out a postcard, handed it to the Shamen. "For example, monsieur, if this boy had been on one of our ships, he would not be dead now."

"I am sorry," the Shamen said, "I don't read German."

"May I translate?" I asked the question of Kadmon. He had told me to say nothing.

He shrugged. It was answer enough.

"The card concerns a friend of mine," I said to the Shamen. "Gidon Katz. We met in Vienna. At the university. We spent a lot of time together. We sometimes spoke about getting married." For a moment I stared down at the delicate porcelain coffee cup. Then I went on. "I met Gidon's father last week in Tel Aviv. He showed me this postcard, forwarded from Vienna. 'We regret to inform you that your son, Gidon Katz, has died in Dachau of an unspecified illness. His ashes are available against the payment of postage.'"

The Shamen turned the card over and looked at the neatly typed address on the front.

"After the Anschluss," I said, "orders went out. All Jewish males between the ages of eighteen and forty-five were to be arrested. Gidon was twenty-four. He had blond curly hair," I added, for no reason.

"I'm—sorry," the Shamen said.

"The fact is," I told him, "many such postcards are being sent from the concentration camps. And many commandants are more mercenary. Some ask the equivalent of a hundred pounds for each container of ashes. Postcards like these can mean the beginning. Of mass murder."

The Shamen finished off his brandy. "It is the beginning of craziness. To sit here on a spring afternoon and listen to a beautiful girl talk about mass murder! This is the twentieth century, mademoiselle. We are no longer savages. You surely can't believe that the German Government intends to murder hundreds of thousands of human beings. For no crime at all. Except that their little boys have been circumcised. Or their grandfathers recite the Torah on Saturday afternoons. What, do you imagine the Germans will ask all Jews to line up in formation? And shoot them down like bowling pins? A million Jews, you say? Where would you bury a million bodies?"

I translated the grizzly question. And Kadmon answered. "The mechanics of the operation are less impossible than the concept. The Germans are an efficient people. As one small example, yesterday I was talking to a man who had spent a night in Buchenwald. He was lucky. He was able to buy himself out. But he told me about that night. It was freezing cold. The Jews were whipped, tortured in the open air. And all during the night a loudspeaker—a recorded voice—kept shouting over and over: 'Any Jew who wishes to hang himself is asked to first put a piece of paper in his mouth with his number on it, so that we may know who he is.'"

The Shamen frowned.

"An efficient means of bookkeeping," Kadmon said. He took a cigar from his pocket, and as he spoke, carefully sliced off the tip with a pocketknife. "I am convinced, my friend, that a people like the Germans, who have developed methods of mass production to such an art, can very easily develop methods of mass destruction."

There was a stiff silence.

Suddenly, I said, "Why *should* we expect him to understand? Why should we expect him to be any more humanitarian than all the great so-called countries of asylum of the world?" Though I spoke to Kadmon, I used French—which Kadmon did not understand. I turned then to the Shamen and Arkadi. "Have you gentlemen heard about the Évian Conference?"

Again, silence.

I hurried on. "Well, not many people *do* know about it. The Conference didn't exactly make world headlines. Though it should have. It was probably one of the most incredible conferences in world history. It was held last summer. In July. The official delegates of thirty-two nations met in the resort town of Évian. They met to discuss the Jews of Germany and Austria. The Jews who desperately wanted to get out. But had no place to go. Because no nation would let them in. For one week the delegates listened to speeches. To reports. To statistics. They agreed the situation was indeed very grave. And each distinguished delegate rose to announce that his country naturally wanted to help. But was, unfortunately, unable to do so."

I felt tears pressing behind my eyes; tears of rage, despair. "The Conference was called by President Roosevelt. Naturally, we assumed the United States would lead the way. But the United States has its quota system. Naturally, the quota was filled. So, naturally, there was nothing more the United States could do!

"France? Foreign Minister Bonnet announced that *she* could not take any more Jews. France had enough already. England? Chamberlain confessed they'd been quietly admitting five hundred Jews a week. To do any more might arouse anti-Semitic feeling in Great Britain.

"Switzerland? That little haven of freedom and democracy. *She* had several thousand of her own citizens stranded in Spain. She had to look after her own first!

"And so—it turned out—did all the other nations. Small and large. Peru. *She* had to help her Peruvian Indians. Integrate them into the life of the state. The Spanish, Latin—and Catholic life of the state.

"Bolivia? Unfortunately, their laws forbade the immigration of Jews. Brazil—had a new law. Every visa application must be accompanied by a certificate of *baptism*. Ecuador could only accept agricultural workers. Unfortunately, Jews of the Greater German Reich are forbidden by law to work in agriculture. So that got Ecuador off the hook.

"Nicaragua, Costa Rica, Honduras, Panama—*they* all classified intellectuals and merchants as undesirables. And, as it happens, monsieur, half the Jews of Germany and Austria fall into that totally useless category—intellectuals. Doctors, lawyers, professors; other such—types. Most of the rest are businessmen, merchants.

"And so it went. With thirty-two nations. Each had its own careful regulations—designed to keep out Jews!

"And then—to put double locks on the doors—the Évian delegates passed a *special* resolution. I remember the words. Quite clearly. 'The delegates of the countries of asylum are not willing to undertake any obligations toward financing involuntary emigration!' . . . No country would admit Jews unless they could support themselves. Yet, the German Government allows no Jew to leave the country with more than ten Reichsmarks. The equivalent of one pound. Less than five dollars. Therefore, by that one resolution, the Évian delegates made every Jew from Germany or Austria officially and automatically unacceptable to the countries of—" I choked on the word—"asylum."

"Perhaps," the Shamen said, "you would care for a brandy, mademoiselle."

I nodded. He motioned to Arkadi, who sprang up and filled a glass. The amber liquid seemed to burn and shrivel the words which clogged my throat. I glanced at Kadmon. He had told me to say nothing at all. And I was ranting on.

But Kadmon's eyes were on the Shamen.

"Tell me," the Shamen said, "this Évian Conference, did they accomplish anything at all?"

"Of course! Most certainly! They appointed a committee to study the matter! The Intergovernmental Committee on Refugees. The director was an American. George Rublee. A dedicated man. And after the pogroms of the *Kristallnacht*—when the world seemed, at last, to be somewhat concerned—Rublee put forth a plan. Each of the thirty-two Évian nations should agree to take twenty-five thousand refugees."

The Shamen nodded. "And how many *did* they agree to take?"

"None. Each of the thirty-two nations politely and diplomatically declined."

Again he nodded. And finished off his brandy.

"Oh," I went on, "some made helpful suggestions. Chamberlain proposed that Jews settle in Tanganyika. But Tanganyika didn't want them. America asked Portugal to let Jewish refugees into Angola. Portugal refused. So the United States—undaunted—suggested that Italy should let them settle in Ethiopia. Mussolini said if the United States had such sympathy for the Jews she should settle them in her own country; she had, after all, plenty of room. But the Congress of the United States unfortunately refused to increase the quotas."

I laughed suddenly. It was a strangled sound. "Quotas! Do you know what the quota is, for instance, for Rumania? Two hundred and eighty-nine a year."

"Two hundred and eighty-nine Jews?"

"Oh," I said, "the United States doesn't discriminate in their national quotas! How could you think that? Two hundred and eighty-nine Rumanians—Jew or Gentile. Naturally, there's quite a long waiting list. Did you hear about the Jew who went into the U.S. Embassy in Bucharest to apply for a visa? He was told to come back in the year two thousand and three. 'In the morning,' he said, 'or in the afternoon?'"

"That's funny," the Shamen said. "That's very funny," he repeated. Silence spread heavily in the room.

Finally, I went on, speaking calmly now. The brandy seemed to have burned the emotion from me. "There were other plans, other proposals, put forth by George Rublee. They were all rejected. So, finally, Rublee resigned. But first he issued a report. The situation was hopeless, he said. All doors were locked against the Jewish refugees. Yet, despite this fact, *more* official restrictions were being issued all the time by countries all over the globe!"

I stood up. I walked over to him.

"But there is one place, there is one small group of people in the world who *do* want the Jews of Europe. The *Yishuv*—the Jews of Palestine. Only now, because of the British White Paper, there are only five thousand legal certificates available every six months. Five thousand Jews will enter Palestine legally from July through next December."

I looked down at the mountainous man in the armchair. "With one voyage of the *Tiger Hill* we can increase this number—twenty per cent! We can, if you'll rent us the ship for a price we can afford to pay. We can pay. We can pay a reasonable amount. But our funds are limited. We can't pay what you ask!"

Suddenly, appalled at what I was saying, I looked at Kadmon. I had said too much. I had revealed our weakness. I had spoken out blindly when my orders had been to say nothing.

Kadmon was watching me. His eyes were like bullets.

I glanced at the Shamen. He was studying the postcard I'd given him. He turned it over. He read aloud the typewritten address on the front. "J. Katz. Seventeen Grunewaldstrasse. Vien." He looked up. "What does the J. stand for?"

"Jacob," I said.

"Jacob Katz and his son Gidon." He handed me the postcard. "I will think of this card—I will think of your friend Gidon Katz when I begin cursing myself for a bloody fool."

He shoved himself to his feet. Then he said to Kadmon, "I will let you have the *Tiger Hill* for thirty pounds sterling per head. But all the other expenses and guarantees must stand as I've stated them. And I must have the ten thousand down payment within one week's time."

Kadmon said nothing. He stared blankly at the Shamen. He had not understood, because I was staring at the Shamen and had forgotten to translate the words.

Arkadi filled in as interpreter.

Kadmon stood up. He shook the Shamen's hand. "You will have the deposit within a week."

The Shamen smiled at me. "So you see, mademoiselle, it turns out that one overweight Greek can have more compassion than thirty-two nations."

I smiled back. I felt drained.

Kadmon looked at his watch. "Well," he announced, "we know you are busy, my friend. And Ruth and I have many days and nights of work ahead of us, now that we are assured of a ship."

The Shamen chuckled. "You seem suddenly anxious to leave, monsieur. Are you afraid I may change my mind?"

I stood up. But the Shamen put a restraining hand on my arm. "I am impressed." Then he added, "By the things you told me." His heavy fingers moved slightly, stroking my skin. "Perhaps you would do me the honor of dining with me tonight? I would like to hear more."

I glanced at Kadmon. I felt helpless. The Shamen had spoken French; had spoken in an intimate tone. He would take offense if I translated his remarks. Yet, I needed guidance.

Kadmon slid back the doors.

The girl was there.

Quickly, the Shamen removed his hand from my arm. "Mina," he said, "please show my visitors out."

"Very good, monsieur." Her voice was icy. She turned and led us through the dusty foyer to the front door.

"Arkadi will see you back to your hotel," the Shamen said to me.

"Thank you, monsieur."

"It is I," he said softly, "who would like to thank you, mademoiselle. Or is it—madame?"

I nodded.

"I noticed your ring, of course," he said. "I assume your husband would not object if we went out to dinner one evening." He was standing very close to me. Beads of perspiration glinted in the folds of fat beneath his chin. He kissed my hand. "*A bientôt,* madame. Until—soon."

We left rather hurriedly, walked down the flights of stairs, since the elevator only carried passengers upward.

"Well," Kadmon said on the second landing, "I gather he wants his pound of flesh along with his pounds sterling. Just as I thought, a girl right away makes complications!"

"She did more than that," Arkadi announced. "For the first time he's a big man—not just in size."

On the drive back very little was said. Kadmon took out a stub of a pencil and jotted down figures in a small notebook. I stared out the window. I felt suddenly too exhausted to speak. I'd gotten up this morning at 4 A.M. But my last hour on the ship now seemed days away.

Arkadi, too, was quiet. But, as we neared the hotel, he said to Kadmon, "Did you know—I'm a Jew?"

Kadmon nodded.

"Sometimes," said Arkadi, "I forget. But this afternoon you made me remember. If I can help—you know where to find me."

"Good," Kadmon said.

When we reached the hotel and the limousine drove off Kadmon turned to me and asked abruptly, "Now. What exactly did you say to him in that great French speech? You seemed to have made the Fat Man feel he was Jesus Christ on the cross."

I didn't answer.

"As long as it's not a double cross!"

I still said nothing.

"What have they sent me here?" Kadmon exploded. "A sulky prima donna?"

"I'm—sorry," I told him. "I'm tired, that's all. And hungry. I haven't eaten for twenty-four hours."

"Come. I'll feed you." He took my arm as we crossed the street. "For the first time out, you did pretty well. God knows what you told him, but it seems to have worked."

When we reached the opposite sidewalk, he dropped my arm. Then, almost casually, he said, "Now tell me, have you any ideas about how to raise ten thousand pounds in one week's time?"

THREE

I came, as directed, at midnight to Kadmon's room. I carried an oversized box of chocolates.

Kadmon was talking to a man with bright red hair, thick lips, watery blue eyes; a man perhaps in his early twenties but with the inconclusive look of a large adolescent.

"Ruth," Kadmon said in another of his eloquent introductions, "Alexander."

Alexander pursed his lips as he looked at me. "I had bets with myself," he announced. "Either you'd be a kibbutznik with braids around your head and thick ankles. Or a scholar with spectacles. I read your dossier. But they forgot to mention a few pertinent—statistics." He gave me a fat-lipped smile. "Well, I see you've brought refreshments. Just what we need for these late-night meetings."

I turned to Kadmon. "These were in my room when I got back. The card said *Avec respect. P.P.*"

Kadmon nodded. "The Shamen."

"He also sent a bouquet of white lilacs and mimosa."

"I could wish," Kadmon said, "that he worked as quickly on other projects."

Alexander inspected the chocolate box. "Capşa. The best." He untied the ribbon. "The problem is, what will she do if he asks her out? We're supposed to remain inconspicuous, yes? Shadowy background figures. This could be a little difficult for her if she's seen around town with someone as—prominent as the Shamen."

"Let me try one of those chocolates," Kadmon said. "And I don't think any of us need go further than that in sampling the Shamen's hospitality."

I handed him the box of chocolates, relieved that he did not, evidently, expect me to charm concessions from the Shamen. Then I sat and glanced around the room.

The view from the open window held the mellow lamplights of the Calea Victoriei and a square beyond edged by the shadowy darkness of trees. The bed was in an alcove, hidden by drapes. Evidences that anyone lived in this room were also presumably behind the drapes. The section in which we sat held only a sofa, a table, several chairs, a carafe of water and hotel glasses. There was not a suitcase, a toothbrush, not even a piece of paper lying about to denote that the room was inhabited. I wondered whether this austere and meticulous tidiness was a reflection of the man, or whether it was necessitated by his mission.

Kadmon crossed to the window, pulled the drapes closed. Their wine-red color cast a diffused warmth and intimacy into the room.

"Well," he announced then, "I'll make some coffee while we wait for our calls."

Kadmon's room at midnight became, I learned, the pivotal point of Mossad operations all over Europe, for it was at that hour the calls started coming through from Mossad men in Germany, Austria, France, Poland, Yugoslavia, Greece, Italy, Switzerland. Kadmon acted as the center of information and the co-ordinator. He gave out instructions, passed on information, discussed details.

On this night it was the call from Switzerland we awaited with most anxiety; the call from a Mossad *haver*—comrade—called Zvi. He had been apprised of the meeting with the Shamen, and had, it appeared, a promising contact from whom he hoped to secure a substantial "loan" —as it was euphemistically called.

"But," Kadmon said, "I should perhaps tell you, Ruth, if Zvi *is* able to raise the down payment we need, that will merely be one impossibility overcome. Naturally, it's not only my decision about whether or not you work with us. It must also be yours. And before you decide, you must know a little of what you're in for."

He went to the sleeping alcove, pushed back the drapes and emerged with a small kerosene burner and a turkish coffeepot. "As I indicated this morning," he continued, "this work is dangerous. We operate under the shadow, you might say, of British Intelligence. Fortunately, they haven't been very efficient so far. Not concerning the Mossad, anyway. But they're trying. Trying to find out who we are. How we transfer money. How we get ships. They can have any one of us—or all of us—put in prison by coming up with proof of any small illegality. Against currency regulations. Passport regulations. Anything. We can never relax. Every move has got to be covered. Because they don't need proof that we're engaged in some big illegal operation. Any small detail will be enough to hang us."

"I was warned of the dangers," I said, "before I left Palestine."

"And what of the various difficulties of our mission? How much were you told of them?"

"Very little."

Kadmon nodded. He crossed to the sink, filled the coffeepot with water. "All right, put it this way. We have five sets of impossibilities to contend with."

He lit a flame in the kerosene burner, put the water on to boil.

"The first—to find a ship. With war obviously on its way, every ship is at a premium. So who in his right mind would lease his vessel for *illegal* purposes when he can get his price without risking his ship or his reputation? There's only one inducement that counts. We must offer the highest bid. Which brings us to our second impossibility. Where do we find the funds to offer anything at all—when every important Jewish organization in the world is against our efforts?"

"The Histadrut?" I asked.

"Yes. Of course. There is the Histadrut. And we've had some Histadrut money. We had a check six months ago. Twenty thousand pounds. I don't like to think where it came from. The workers' sick fund. Social security. Well, the money is gone. Lost. The money—and three hundred and sixty-nine illegals. Our ship was caught by the British, sent out to sea. That was in April. They haven't been heard from since."

"Did they have provisions?"

"Enough for a few days. But the ship was turned away from the port of Haifa ten weeks ago."

Carefully, with due consideration for all alternatives, he selected another chocolate from the box.

"To proceed. Impossibility number three. How do we manage—in utmost secrecy—to convert the hold of an old cargo ship into quarters which can accommodate fifteen hundred human beings? The reconversion of a ship takes time. And many workmen. Any one of whom can—talk. And if the British hear about our conversion job, we might as well stop in our tracks where we are.

"Then, of course, the matter of supplies. Cases of food. Kegs of water. Blankets. Fuel. Everything must be brought to the port and onto the ship—in secret. Supplies enough for a two-week journey. Because when we play our game of hide-and-seek on the high seas, we must figure on a minimum of fourteen days to make a trip which should take three.

"Fourth impossibility! How do we bring fifteen hundred illegal immigrants into Rumania, get them across the country and onto the ship —in silence. And if we *do* somehow get the ship, and if it does somehow manage to make the trip undetected by British patrol boats and planes, we have the final impossibility of landing our illegals in secret on the beaches of Palestine.*

These landings, of course, I knew about—as did every citizen of Palestine. For the British saw to it that the capture of every illegal vessel was well publicized in order to discourage future efforts.

Not only were His Majesty's ships—destroyers and patrol boats—on twenty-four-hour duty within Palestine's three-mile limit, but should an illegal ship manage to make it to shore, there were beach patrols of British tommies to contend with. The Arabs had also organized beach patrols; a doubly profitable business—for Jews caught by Arab patrols were invariably robbed of all their possessions. Then the Jews were turned over to the British who rewarded the Arab captors well for their efforts.

"Do you like your coffee sweet?" Kadmon asked me.
I nodded.

* *See* Appendix Six.

Carefully he measured sugar and turkish coffee into the boiling water, watched while it roiled up into a froth, then spooned the brownish foam into each of the three small cups. He let the coffee boil up once more; poured it out. "And with the *Tiger Hill*," he said, "we may well face a new impossibility." He handed a cup to me, one to Alexander. Then he sat heavily in the armchair, and sipped at his coffee.

"We can usually," he continued, "count on some co-operation from certain European officials—who are almost as anxious to get Jews out of the country as we are. Either because they hate Jews. Or because they love bribes. Or both. But here in Rumania we may suddenly find ourselves in a position where we can expect no help from officials. Quite the contrary. Rumania, you see, has approached Great Britain for a loan. Which Britain may grant—with certain conditions and stipulations. One of them being a government pledge that no more ships stocked with Jewish illegals sail from Rumanian ports."

"When you line up all the eight balls like that," Alexander commented, "you make me wonder what the hell *I'm* doing here!"

Kadmon looked at me. "No doubt you wonder the same thing, Ruth. And I quite understand. You can still be of use. Spend a few months in Europe selling land. An important job. Then return home to your husband. Your job at the Histadrut—"

"I wonder," I said, "when that call will come through from Switzerland?"

"You understand," Kadmon went on, "if you become a member of the Mossad, you'll be risking everything you have, including your life. And months of work may, in the end, achieve nothing. They can even result in the loss of the lives we're trying to save."

"I understand," I said.

Kadmon nodded. He glanced at his watch. "Perhaps Zvi is having trouble getting through. I'll try him."

He walked to the telephone, took a small maroon-colored address book from his pocket, thumbed through it, gave the number. Then he beckoned me to him.

"Why don't you talk first. I believe you used to know him. We're calling Zvi Shechter."

Zvi!

He had been a boyhood friend of my brother Poli. We went to the same Zionist Youth Farm where I'd been considered the eternal younger sister, the hanger-on. Except by Zvi. I remembered a heavy moonless night, sitting on a stone wall beside Zvi. He was leaving for Palestine in the morning. "When I eat my first orange," he had said, "I will think of you."

Present collided with past as the operator broke in. "Which language will you speak, please?"

"German?" It was half a question to Kadmon.

He nodded, and signaled me to cover the mouthpiece of the phone. "On international calls they must listen in. If one operator can't understand your language, there's usually another who does."

"Except for Hebrew," Alexander said. "They seem to be in short supply of nice Jewish girls to serve as telephone spies."

"But we don't use Hebrew," Kadmon added, "except for a few strategic words. We don't like to attract attention by puzzling our civil service friends."

The miles between the two countries were being bridged. The Rumanian operator kept repeating the number patiently to the Swiss operator. Then, suddenly, the connection came through.

"Shechter here."

"It's—Ruth."

"So! They sent you after all!"

"Well, I'm here," I said stupidly, so glad to hear his voice that I was stunned into monosyllables.

Zvi, however, exploded with questions. How was Poli? Was my brother David still in Rumania? My sister Bertha? Would I see them soon?

"Fine," I said. "Yes. I don't know. Wait, Kadmon will speak now. And—Zvi, if Poli knew I was talking to you, he'd send his regards. His love." I handed the phone to Kadmon.

Then I sat on the sofa beside Alexander and, for the first time, felt a comradeship. We both stared at the telephone as though willing it to produce the words we needed.

"We can get the house," Kadmon was saying. "But they're asking a lot. Ninety thousand. With ten thousand down payment. Within a week."

There was a long pause. "Yes, I understand. But—" His voice trailed into silence. "Yes. I see." The tautness was gone, replaced by resignation. "I spoke to Shertok yesterday. The London situation is not promising. . . . No, nothing yet from Ehud. We'll call again tonight."

We heard the shrill voice of the operator. Five minutes were up.

"Keep trying," Kadmon said. "This house we're after is the best we've ever been offered."

He hung up.

"I gather," Alexander said, "the weather in Switzerland is not very sunny."

Kadmon sat down in the armchair. He selected another chocolate. Then he turned to me. "Zvi had an appointment with the representative of the Joint. But it seems the Joint Distribution Committee is not about to do any distributing in the direction of the Mossad. Zvi spent the rest of the day seeing affluent members of the Jewish community. He collected a batch of fine excuses. And that's all."

"Other *haverim*," I said finally, "in other countries—is there hope from any of them?"

"Nothing which can mean ten thousand pounds within a week's time."

"Is there anyone *we* could try? Here in Bucharest?"

"How about Mandel?" Alexander asked. "Did you ever get that letter of introduction?"

"Introduction!" Kadmon exclaimed. "Our friend nearly laughed me out of his office. George Mandel, he informed me, did not rise to the position of bank director by distributing large sums of money backed by no collateral whatever."

"If this Mandel could help us," I said, "why don't we go directly to him? Let him say no for himself."

"There are," said Alexander, "six secretaries in the outer office. One of their functions is to interview people who wish to see Mandel. With no letter of introduction, we'd never get past the first secretary."

"Has anyone tried?"

"No," Kadmon said. "Would you like to?"

I nodded.

"Well, Berl predicts you'll have great success in reaching people in high places. They call him our Palestinian prophet. So we'll see how prophetic he is about you."

"By all means!" said Alexander. "What have we got to lose? Except everything! Mandel owes loyalty to his friends in the government. Not to us. If she comes along with her tale of our illegal operations—"

"Mandel's a Jew," Kadmon interrupted. "He may not help us. But I doubt he'd betray us."

"A Jew! Sure! A once-a-year-synagogue Jew! Look, that man knows which side of the street his bank is on. And his fine town house."

Kadmon raised his hand. "Don't upset yourself, my friend. As you point out, it's highly unlikely that Ruth gets past the first secretary. And, naturally, she won't be discussing our affairs with him."

The telephone rang.

Kadmon jumped up with surprising alacrity.

"It's Shmarya," he said to Alexander, as he waited for the connection to come through.

Alexander sat on the couch next to me. "That's our American. Shmarya Zameret. From California. And kibbutz Bet Hashita." He moved closer. His voice was low, conspiratorial. He seemed like a boy playing spy. "Shmarya's trying to organize our first ship to sail from the Atlantic coast. He's got a group of Polish Jews who were living in Germany. Pino—the Mossad man in Berlin—smuggled them over the German-Belgian frontier. Right under the noses of the Wehrmacht who were there on maneuvers."

The call came through, and Kadmon started a strange conversation. "The house can hold five hundred? Good! Well, Pino has a hundred and twenty in his family. So there's room for three hundred and eighty more tenants. For in the time of trouble he shall hide me in his pavilion."

Alexander translated the code phrases. Real estate terms were used for all matters pertaining to ships. Countries were called by the name of the haver operating there. Germany was Beit Pino, the House of Pino. Pino's family were the German Jews currently being transported to an illegal ship. Another code was based on biblical psalms, a different one was used each week.

When Kadmon hung up he seemed fairly cheerful. "Well, Shmarya's on the trail of another ship. No beauty queen, he says. But she's got a few more trips in her."

He then placed a call to Beit Ehud, Austria.

"How long has it been now?" Alexander asked.

"Thirteen days." Kadmon turned to me. "The last we heard from Ehud—he'd been summoned to the office of *Hauptsturmführer* Adolf Eichmann." Presently he said to the operator, "Please try again in fifteen minutes."

He hung up, returned to his armchair. And, as if to change the unspoken subject, he announced with forced joviality, "Well, Ruth—just in case you *do* make it past the six secretaries tomorrow, perhaps it's not unseemly that you should know a little something."

Then, in the stretches of time between the telephone calls, he told me the story of the Mossad le Aliyah Bet, why it was founded, when, how. Which ships had succeeded in their missions, which had failed. How the Mossad fitted into and was affected by the torturous events of the past few years.

And he described the small network spread over Europe; nine Mossad members, plus forty or so local men, like Alexander. However, unlike Alexander, most of the locals were given only a series of specific assignments. Bribe this official. Contact that supplier. Check the insurance records on a certain ship. Some of them did not even know that the Mossad existed. And I realized that were it not for my proposed meeting with Mandel, Kadmon would not, at this stage, have given me any more information than that supplied to the locals.

During his recital further calls came through. One was from Beit Dani: Bulgaria. There was the possibility of an apartment house. Six hundred tenants. But the cash requirement was high. And the owner was unco-operative concerning the matter of mortgages.

Other calls were less encouraging. Yulik reported that Britain now had five additional patrol boats engaged in the task of preventing illegal ships from landing on the shores of Palestine.

We put through a call to Beit Ehud at fifteen-minute intervals, for several hours.

There was no answer.

It was four in the morning by the time I got back to my room. The bed lamp cast the only light in the empty dimness, a glow made faintly green by the silk lampshade.

Then a distant church bell rang out slowly, four strokes. It seemed a magnified echo of the sound of the telephone ringing in an empty room. Kadmon had asked me to put through the last call to Ehud in Austria. For five dragging minutes I'd stood, the receiver pressed against my ear, the buzz of the telephone ringing . . . ringing . . . ringing . . . unanswered.

We had queried each haver who telephoned during the night. But no one had heard from Ehud since his summons to the office of Adolf Eichmann. Thirteen days ago.

As some sort of reaching out, blotting out, I went to the desk and started a letter to my brother Poli. Kadmon had warned me that when I wrote home I was not to mention names of people I'd met. So I described the week-long sea voyage from Haifa, the stops we'd made at Cyprus . . . Piraeus. I wrote of the train trip to Bucharest . . . my hotel room . . . and the small Jewish restaurant where I had eaten dinner.

Poli had always been the one person to whom I could talk, did talk, about everything of consequence in my life. Now I was filling up paper by writing to him of a restaurant meal—writing that I had eaten alone.

Loneliness drained through me.

I sealed the letter quickly; washed, undressed, pulled on a night-gown, and turned to the bed. It was large, very high, with a brass bed-stead. The spread had been folded back; the top sheet arranged in a careful cornered effect. Yet, the bed seemed remarkably uninviting.

There was a telephone on the bed table. I stared at it, aching to put through a call to my brother David, my sister Bertha. But Kadmon had also warned me that I was not to contact my family in Czernowitz. If they knew I was in Rumania, they would never understand why I could not come at once to visit them.

If you join the Mossad, Eliahu had said, *you must give up your personal life.*

I crawled between the chilly sheets; reached for the lamp chain, not easy to find amid the hanging beaded strands which ornamented the shade. And, in the darkness, I curled up in a far corner of the double bed.

The room seemed to echo with emptiness.

I thought of tomorrow's assignment.

Perhaps I could somehow talk my way past the six secretaries. But if I did succeed in seeing Mandel, what then? Could mere words possibly persuade a man to part with ten thousand pounds? Yet, that was all we had to offer: words, and what they might—one day—mean.

Suddenly, pressing into my head came words: the words which had sounded over and over on the Buchenwald loudspeaker: *Any Jew who wishes to hang himself is asked to first put a piece of paper in his mouth with his number on it.* . . .

I felt torn apart inside by the screaming stillness.

FOUR

THE NEXT MORNING at breakfast I smoked my first cigarette.

The hotel dining room was almost empty. Sunlight lay in the folds of the Viennese drapes; white tablecloths reflected the morning brightness. The headwaiter bowed slightly, led me to a corner table.

I asked for a newspaper, consumed a large breakfast. And when the waiter inquired as to whether mademoiselle wished anything else, I said, "Yes, cigarettes, please. Carol the First."

Kadmon appeared. Sat down. Ordered. Then he leaned back in his chair. "Well! Ready for your first mission?"

I took a deep breath. "I'm ready. But I'm afraid I'll need a new dress."

He looked at me, blinked several times. "What's wrong with what you've got on?"

"I can't go to see Mandel," I said, "in a blouse and skirt. And this is the best I have. Tel Aviv," I added, "is not exactly the fashion capital of the world."

"So we must be fashion plates," he burst out. "On our one pound a day budget."

"I don't care what I wear," I told him. "But if you want me to try to succeed in this—mission as you call it—well, I think I can do better if I look better. Yesterday the taxi driver told me I dressed like a governess."

"Are taxi drivers directing our operations now?"

"Never mind," I said. "It was stupid of me to mention it."

The waiter came back with my cigarettes on a silver tray.

Kadmon struck a match for me. "You didn't smoke yesterday," he remarked.

"I didn't feel like it." I inhaled deeply, and was promptly overcome by a fit of coughing. Kadmon poured some water into a glass, handed it to me. I was mortified. I wondered whether he would send me back to Palestine with a note attached to my dossier: vain, oversensitive, difficult to work with.

"Well," he said, "you weren't sent here as a Jewish Mata Hari. Still, I suppose we can stretch the budget to buy you a new dress."

As we walked together down the Calea Victoriei, I saw a dress in a shop window and stopped to look.

"We were on our way," Kadmon remarked, "to a less expensive store."

The dress was deep green; simply cut and elegant.

"I suppose you think it would match your eyes, or some such vanity," Kadmon said. He took out his wallet, counted out five thousand lei and placed the wad of money in my hand. "Let's hope you can make it pay off, that's all. I'll wait at the *cofetăria* down the street. The Nestor."

I entered the shop.

The saleslady came forward. She had a long, pinched face and wore a scissors on a black ribbon around her neck.

"Yes?" she said in a sour voice. "What can I do for you?" She spoke in Rumanian.

I answered in French. "I'd like to buy a dress."

She mellowed somewhat and brought out several startlingly ugly specimens for my consideration. Each had a large label attached: *On Sale*. The reason was obvious.

"That dress in the window," I said. "The green silk. Would you have it in my size?"

She brightened considerably, hurried off to the back room and emerged holding the dress against her flat figure.

"*Charmante, mademoiselle!*" she exclaimed when I tried it on. "*Ça vous va très bien!*"

I turned slowly before the mirror. The dress transformed me, not only the exterior view, but the inner being. I began to feel a faint surge of confidence.

"I'll wear it," I said.

As she wrapped my blouse and skirt in a bulky brown package she remarked, "Mademoiselle has a splendid shape. But if she can find the opportunity to buy a new brassiere . . ."

I blushed. "Yes. Thank you. I will." I also bought new silk stockings, a slip, a wide-brimmed hat, a purse, high-heeled shoes.

When I walked into the cofetăria Kadmon glanced in my direction but did not recognize me. He returned to his newspaper.

I stood before him. "Well," I announced, "I still have a thousand lei left.

"Oh," he said, half rising. "It's you." It was the first and last time he made the effort to rise in my presence. "It was money well spent," he said then. "In this dress you are fit to visit the King."

"Never mind the King. My ambitions don't go any higher than a bank director."

Kadmon smiled. He folded his newspaper. "If you do get to see him, have you any idea what you will say?"

As I sat down I glanced at the table behind us. It was empty.

"We can talk," Kadmon said. Then he added, "I'm glad to see that you're cautious about such matters."

"You put the fear of God into me last night," I told him. "God and the Rumanian police."

Kadmon ordered me a coffee. Then we worked out step by step an approach I might use, if I did somehow get in to George Mandel's office.

The Banca Comercială was an imposing place on a street lined with staid stone buildings. "I'll wait for you," Kadmon said as we climbed the steps. "If you don't see Mandel, come back to the hotel with me. But if you do see him, and tell him about our operation, then don't come to the hotel. Mandel's loyalties may very well lie with his Government friends. He may have you followed. So go to a cafe, and telephone me at the hotel for instructions."

We entered the bank.

41

Kadmon settled himself in an armchair by the wall, took out his cigar and his newspaper. I had been dismissed.

My first mission had officially begun.

In a corner behind a waist-high wooden fence there was a huge wooden desk. Behind it sat a young man with a sallow face and spectacles. He was working on some papers.

I went over to him. "Excuse me."

He paid no attention.

I tried again, louder. "I would like to see Mr. Mandel."

He raised his steel-rimmed eyes, but said nothing.

"My name is Ruth Klüger. Would you tell Mr. Mandel I'm here."

"You have an appointment?"

"I've just arrived from Palestine." I opened the wooden gate and walked to his desk. "A letter was sent. Whether it has reached Mr. Mandel as yet, I do not know."

"When Mr. Mandel has seen the letter," the young man said, "he will notify you."

I found I could be as imperious in tone as he. "I have no time to wait. And I assure you Mr. Mandel would not thank you for keeping me from him."

The young man regarded me closely, then shrugged one shoulder. "I'll fetch Mr. Mandel's personal secretary." He did not say the words, but they were quite clear: Let *him* throw you out.

The secretary was a bustling paunchy man with shiny black hair. His suit too was black, his tie and his shoes. "Mademoiselle," he said brusquely, "I understand that you wish to see Mr. Mandel. Without an appointment, this is impossible."

"Nothing is impossible when the matter is sufficiently urgent."

"Urgent to you, perhaps," the secretary said. "But Mr. Mandel's day is filled at half-hour intervals with appointments. Many of them made weeks in advance. If you'd like to discuss your problem with one of our officers—"

"It is not my problem alone," I said. "It is one which will soon affect Mr. Mandel as well."

"She says a letter was sent," the spectacled young man put in. "A letter of introduction."

"Who wrote this letter?" the secretary asked.

I hesitated. I knew the name of only one important financier. He lived in Czernowitz. "The letter was sent by Baron Max Ritter von Anhauch. You may have heard of him."

It was obvious they had.

"I will speak to Mr. Mandel's assistant," the secretary said. "Perhaps he has this letter." He walked away.

I waited by the desk. The young man returned to his papers, ignoring me completely.

I glanced at Kadmon, immersed in his newspaper.

Then, beyond him, waiting in line at a teller's window, I saw a familiar profile. When I was a child in Czernowitz I had often tried to copy it in my exercise book. I'd written the name over and over in small secret script. Often I had placed a tiny *Frau* before it. *Frau* Stefan Meta. Mrs. Stefan Meta. Me.

He was a friend of my oldest brother, David. In my eyes David's most dashing and admirable friend. When Stefan married I cut his picture from the newspaper; omitting of course the smiling face of his bride. And I'd hidden the clipping in a carefully tied box in my bottom drawer.

Before his marriage and after, I had kept up a flourishing daydream romance with Stefan Meta. But in his actual presence I invariably shrank into tongue-tied confusion.

The last thing I wanted at this moment was to meet Stefan, to speak to him. But, as though someone else had taken possession of my words, I found myself saying quite calmly, "A gentleman is standing in line over there. Stefan Meta. He too is from Czernowitz. He will tell you of my association with Baron von Anhauch."

The young man squinted through his spectacles at Stefan. "So you know Mr. Meta." He got up. Went over to Stefan. They spoke. Then they were walking toward me. I had lied and was now compounding the lie with the living witness of Stefan Meta.

He stood looking down at me.

"I'm Ruth," I said quickly, afraid he might not remember. "David's sister."

"Yes." He smiled a little. "You don't need to introduce yourself."

43

"I'm here to see Mr. Mandel. It's very important. I thought, if you knew him—"

"I'm afraid not," Stefan said. "I met him once, but only at an official dinner."

The personal secretary returned. "Mr. Mandel's assistant informs me that no letter has been received from Baron von Anhauch. If you leave your address, we will contact you when it arrives."

"Please!" I burst out. "I must see him *now!*"

"I can vouch for this young lady," Stefan said. "I know her family well. If she says the matter is urgent, I'm quite sure Mr. Mandel would not want her turned away."

The secretary hesitated. He glanced at the young man who took off his steel-rimmed spectacles and began polishing them with the tail of his tie. "I will speak to Mr. Mandel," the personal secretary said.

Stefan waited with me. He asked what I was doing in Bucharest. And when I was coming to Czernowitz. I wanted to reply in a sane and sensible manner. But the only responses I could give sounded still like the monosyllabic stammers of a schoolgirl.

When he asked where I was staying, I told him; with relief at being able to give a straight answer.

But when he asked whether he could take me to dinner that evening, I again reverted to what must have sounded like idiocy. "I don't know. I'd like to. But I—my plans aren't certain."

"I can't go back to Czernowitz," Stefan said reasonably, "without being able to tell David how you are."

I could not—in front of the spectacled young man—announce that Stefan must *not* tell my brother that I was in Bucharest. I sounded enough of an oddity as it was.

"I—I would like to see you," I stammered. "If you'll call me at the hotel, I'm sure we can arrange something."

Then I saw the personal secretary beckoning me from a doorway. "I think I'm being summoned."

"Shall I wait?" Stefan asked.

"No! Please! Thank you for your help." I glanced back at Kadmon who was watching me over the top of his newspaper. Then I hurried across the carpeted floor to the secretary. I followed him up a marble stairway and into an anteroom where several women were typing.

"Wait here," the secretary said, indicating a long wooden bench. "Mr. Mandel will see you shortly."

I sat, watching the minute hand jerk by on the wall clock. The rap-tapping of typewriters seemed an audible echo of my own nervousness.

What an insane mission! Get a banker to give you ten thousand pounds. With no collateral. And be sure not to tell him too much about who wants the money—and why.

As ammunition Kadmon had given me a single sheet of paper. However, the words written on it might serve to shake a man like George Mandel. They might conceivably make him understand the necessity for helping the Mossad.

The paper was a copy of a top-secret teletype message sent out on the eve of the *Kristallnacht*.

Kristallnacht. The Night of November Tenth. The Night of the Broken Glass.

It had started with a single bullet.

On the afternoon of November 6, 1938, a skinny, high-strung, seventeen-year-old boy named Herschel Grynszpan entered the German Embassy in Paris and asked to see the ambassador.

The boy had just received a letter from his father, a grocer who had lived in Hamburg for twenty-seven years. But the letter did not come from Hamburg. It was postmarked Zbaszyn, Poland. It described how the father, mother, sister, brother—along with some fifteen thousand other Polish Jews living in Germany—had been suddenly shipped back to Poland. Jammed into cattle cars which ordinarily held six to eight cows, and which now carried sixty to eighty human beings. When they reached the station nearest the border, they were shoved out and forced to march through the pouring rain. Some fell or lagged behind; old people, small children, pregnant women; those who were sick or lame. They were kicked and whipped by German guards. Forced to get up, move on. Herschel's father had been whipped.

When they crossed the border Herschel's family was crowded with hundreds of other Jews into the stables of a Polish military camp. They

45

had been given some bread, their first food in twenty-four hours. It was after he ate his bread that the father wrote to his son Herschel in Paris.

Impatiently, Herschel Grynszpan had waited in the German Embassy in Paris. Waited to see the ambassador.

Finally, a man came out to see what he wanted. The man was Third Secretary Ernst vom Rath.

Herschel Grynszpan pulled out a gun and shot him.

Two nights after Vom Rath's murder, pogroms of retribution erupted throughout the Reich.

The statistical results of those pogroms were carefully suppressed by Propaganda Minister Goebbels and his department. But the Mossad's man in Berlin had a contact in the Gestapo. He had obtained a report of statistics, along with the teletype message, which I carried in my purse.

During my briefing with Kadmon in the Café Nestor, I'd made notes of the statistics. I took them out now. Reviewed them. I felt for a ludicrous moment that I was back at the university, cramming for an examination.

A final exam. The results could mean life or death for fifteen hundred human beings.

During the pogroms of November Tenth, one hundred and seventy-one Jewish apartment houses had been destroyed in the cities; along with eight hundred and fifteen Jewish stores, and one hundred and ninety-one synagogues. In towns and villages no record had been made of the thousands of Jewish homes and shops which went up in flames.

During the day of November Tenth, some twenty thousand Jewish men over the age of seventeen were arrested and shipped to concentration camps; Dachau, Sachsenhausen, Buchenwald.

Nazi *Gauleiters* held competitions to see which village would be "purified" of Jews first. Men, women, even children were dragged from their homes; driven and whipped through the streets. Some were tethered to horse carts, their bodies pulled down country roads. Some were tied up, thrown into rivers and left to drown. Some were hung.

In the cities, Jews were thrown out of moving trains and apartment-house windows. Some were shot while trying to escape.

There were also cases of rape. The rapists were later expelled from the Nazi Party and turned over to the civil courts for punishment, since they had violated the most important of the Nuremberg Laws: the law which forbade sexual union between German Aryan and Jew. But those who had merely murdered Jews were not punished at all.

On November twelfth, German insurance companies had urgently requested a meeting with government ministers. They announced that they would go bankrupt if they were forced to make good the policies on the buildings which had been burned and gutted. An estimated damage of twenty-five million marks had been done. The matter of broken window glass alone came to a figure of six million marks. Naturally, if the window glass had belonged to Jews, replacement could be ignored. Unfortunately, however, most of the "Jew stores" were merely rented by Jews—in buildings owned by German Gentiles.

The Cabinet ministers settled the matter simply. Since the Jew Herschel Grynszpan had caused the pogroms, the Jews of the German Reich must pay for the damage.

Decrees were published the following day. First: All insurance moneys owed to Jews would be confiscated by the state. Second: All Jewish business enterprises and property, including jewelry and works of art, would be transferred to German Aryans. Third: Jewish subjects of the Reich would be collectively subjected to a fine of one billion marks, "as penalty for 'their abominable crimes, et cetera.'" This fine was forty times more than the amount of the loss estimated by the insurance companies.

Propaganda Minister Goebbels and his department had been kept busy for several weeks, issuing press and radio reports which stressed that the events of November Tenth were *spontaneous eruptions* of an enraged citizenry revenging the murder of Legation Secretary Ernst vom Rath."

This explanation was passed on by the foreign press. And it was accepted throughout the world. Who, indeed, could conceive of any other explanation?

However, through his contact in the Gestapo, our Mossad man in Berlin had secured a copy of the top-secret teletype message which was sent out on November ninth to all stations of the state police and the

S.D. in Germany and Austria. The message was signed by Reinhard Heydrich, head of the *Sicherheitsdienst,* the Security Service of the S.S.

This was the paper Kadmon had given me. I took it out of my purse; reread the words.

Because of the murder of Legation Secretary vom Rath in Paris, demonstrations against the Jews are to be expected tonight. November 9th–10th throughout the Reich . . . The demonstrations which are going to take place should not be hindered by the police . . . As many Jews, especially rich ones, are to be arrested as can be accommodated in the existing prisons. . . . Upon their arrest, the appropriate concentration camps should be contacted immediately, in order to confine them in these camps as soon as possible. . . .

The message went on and on, in the bland language of bureaucracy, specifying how state police and the S.D. should meet with party and S.S. leaders and the Gauleiters of every district "to discuss the organization of the demonstrations."

These detailed instructions from Reinhard Heydrich proved that there was nothing at all "spontaneous" about the Kristallnacht. They proved that the Day and the Night of November Tenth had been a government-sponsored campaign of arson, mayhem and murder aimed exclusively against Jews, and carefully organized throughout every village, town and city of Germany and the country which had been Austria.

This paper was the strongest weapon we had for our claim that the Jews who remained in Hitler's Reich were doomed.

But could this paper convince a man of the necessity of giving the Mossad ten thousand pounds?

"Mr. Mandel will see you now," the secretary said.

I started, stood up quickly.

"You will have five minutes," the secretary said. "Between appointments."

Five minutes. I felt as though he had hit me.

The carefully structured approach which Kadmon and I had worked out would take at least a half hour. And only after the dramatic climax of Heydrich's teletype message was I to mention the matter of the *Tiger Hill.*

But five minutes! What could be said—what approach could be used —in five minutes?

"This way," the secretary said.

He opened a huge leather-covered door, and I entered the inner office.

FIVE

THE MAN behind the immense mahogany desk rose to his feet and came toward me. He looked as I had imagined him; tall, imposing, his brown hair properly edged with gray at the temples. His dress was impeccable. I riveted my eyes on the edge of the folded handkerchief in his breast pocket.

He smiled at me indulgently. "So you know my friend Von Anhauch?"

I shook my head. "I—only used his name to get in here."

"I see. Do you need a loan?"

"You might put it that way."

He motioned me to a seat. "Are you in trouble?"

"We are all in trouble," I said.

"Who is—we?"

"The Jews of Europe."

I could see him withdrawing. He must think me quite mad.

"*That* is your urgent business. You have talked your way in here to discuss the Jews of Europe?"

"Please," I begged. "Don't throw me out. *Hear* me out."

He said nothing. I stared down at the carpet, a thick Rumanian rug woven with intricate designs. Five minutes! The Kristallnacht. Should I start with that? Hand him the top-secret teletype message.

You must lead up to it, Kadmon had said. *Lead into it. Then lead on from it—to the story of the Mossad.* He was right. Even with five minutes I must save this paper until the end.

I looked up at him. "Do you have a son?"

"I do."

"If his life was in danger and you could rescue him by paying fifty pounds sterling for a voyage to safety, would you pay it?"

"Now my dear young lady—"

"If you could save *another* boy—a stranger—for the price of fifty pounds?"

"Is that why you're here? You need fifty pounds?"

"I'm here to give you a historic opportunity. A chance to save not one, but fifteen hundred lives."

He laughed. "And who, if I may ask, sent you here to give me this historic opportunity?"

"My—organization."

"The name of this organization?"

I said nothing. *Don't tell him too much.* Kadmon's words pounded through my head. This man had the power, with a single phone call, to end our operations in Rumania.

"You have four more minutes," Mr. Mandel said. "If you wish to spend them in silence, that suits me very well."

"My organization is the Mossad le Aliyah Bet."

"What language is that?"

"Hebrew."

"And what is the meaning of the words?"

"The Institute of—Immigration B."

"And what is the meaning of *that?*"

I hesitated. "*Aliyah aleph*—Immigration A—is the so-called legal immigration.* Jews coming to Palestine with the proper papers. Legal certificates. *Aliyah bet*—Immigration B—well—" I shrugged. "They are—the others."

He nodded. "So you are the institute of the *illegal* immigration?"

"We're illegal," I said, "only according to British decree. To our mind, we're bringing Jews back to their homeland. A homeland promised them both by God *and* the British."

* *See* Appendix Seven.

"I take it you organize these illegal ships we read about from time to time?"

I nodded.

"Well,"—he stood up—"much as I hate to disappoint a pretty girl, I'm afraid you've come to the wrong place. I know a little about these ships; the fiasco of the *Velos*, for instance—"

"The *Velos*," I interrupted, "made *two* voyages. On the first trip three hundred young pioneers were landed in safety on a beach north of Tel Aviv. But nobody knows about that trip. Or about the hundreds of Jews who have landed safely in Palestine since that time. The secret ships—the successful ships—don't make newspaper headlines."

Mandel glanced at his watch. "I'm afraid I can't help you. I simply don't believe in your cause. In my opinion your organization is needlessly exposing people to danger, perhaps to death. I understand the old tubs you sail are often unseaworthy. They sink in mid-ocean. Death by drowning is not very pleasant."†

"Those are not Mossad ships! The vessels we use *are* seaworthy!"

"I see." He stood up. "And the Mossad ships somehow manage to sail without risk of detection by the British? The Mossad's illegals always reach their destination?"

I said nothing.

"Look"—he started walking toward the door—"if you came here representing the Jewish Agency or the Joint Distribution Committee, or if you were even sent by the Jewish Community of Bucharest, we might at least have a philosophical chat about the matter. But you come here representing some fly-by-night group I've never heard of—wanting, how much money?"

"Ten thousand pounds."

Once again he laughed, an abrupt sound with no mirth in it.

"Your collateral?"

"None."

He gave me a long look. "I can only believe that you *are* as young as you appear to be. And as innocent. And as ignorant. Otherwise, how would you have dared talk your way into my office to make such a preposterous request?"

The door opened. The personal secretary entered.

† *See* Appendix Eight.

52

"Mr. Niculescu is waiting, sir."

"Supposing," I said in a loud voice, almost a shout, "supposing you looked back in three years' time and realized that on this morning in June 1939 you had been asked to help. But you had refused. You looked back and tried to remember what your ten thousand pounds had bought. What could it have bought that was worth more than fifteen hundred Jewish lives?"

Mr. Mandel glanced at his secretary.

"Your five minutes are up, miss," the secretary said. "If you will follow me."

"Please!" I spoke only to Mandel. "I've said it all wrong. I haven't made you understand. But it's possible—isn't it just possible—that a few people can see. When thousands of others are blind. And if those who *can* see three years—five years into the future—if they can see mass murder of the Jews of Europe—are they not then committed to *do* something? To try to save lives while there still is time? You—in your position—you know better than we how soon war is coming. And when war comes the Continent will be closed. The Jews will be trapped. No one will save them. Perhaps we have only a few months left. We don't have time to wait until the Jewish Agency and the Joint Distribution Committee and the Jewish Community of Bucharest meet and discuss and investigate and pass resolutions on the matter of illegal immigration. We have a chance right now to save fifteen hundred lives. We have the ship, if we can find the money. Think of your own son. What if he were in Germany now? How much is his life worth? The life of each young man we can rescue is worth exactly that much to *his* father. We can still get Jews out of Germany, Austria, Czechoslovakia. But only if they leave all their money, all their possessions behind. The money for their passage to Palestine must be found outside. Must be found through people like you. Jews who *can* understand. Who *can* see what may happen. Who *can* help."

"Mademoiselle," Mr. Mandel said, "I'm afraid you overestimate my prescience." His tone had stiffened. My impassioned monologue had succeeded only in antagonizing him.

"Her time is up, sir!" the secretary said, looking straight at me.

If I left now I would never get in to see Mandel again. That was quite clear.

"Before I leave here," I said, "I would like to ask you just one question. How do you believe Hitler plans to make the Reich *judenrein*? By doing all he can to get Jews to leave the country?"

"My answer," said Mr. Mandel, "would be in the affirmative. And now, my dear young lady, if you don't mind, my next appointment is waiting."

"Then *why*," I said, "why doesn't the Reich encourage Jews to escape across the borders? Into Holland. France. Switzerland. Denmark. Why aren't German border guards given orders to look the other way? Instead, all border areas are off limits to Jews. And any Jew trying to escape across the border is thrown into a concentration camp. Or shot."

"Perhaps," Mr. Mandel said, "it is Hitler's way of minding his international manners."

"All right," I said, my voice rising again, "if he really wants Jews to get out, why make it impossible for them to get exit visas? Yes! Of course, the Nazis want to get rid of the Jews! *But they want to do the job themselves!*"

Once again Mr. Mandel glanced at his watch.

"Don't you understand?" I cried out at him. "We can help Jews get out. Now. While there still is time. Don't you understand—otherwise they will die!"

He looked at me steadily for a long moment. Looked straight at me. But it seemed in a chilling way that he was looking through me.

"I have a paper here," I said. "A copy of a top-secret teletype message written by Reinhard Heydrich. It will take you one minute to read it." I opened my purse. I handed it to him. "This paper proves there was nothing spontaneous about the pogroms of the Kristallnacht. This paper proves that what I say is true. The Nazis plan to do the job themselves. And they started officially on November Tenth. That was the beginning!"

He read through the typewritten paper. When he looked up he was frowning slightly. "Where did you get this?"

"The Mossad has—contacts."

"May I keep this? I'd like to make a copy."

I nodded.

"Where are you staying?"

"I'm not at liberty to say. But—" I added quickly, "I can come back to pick it up."

"At six o'clock this evening?"

Again I nodded.

"Good. I'll leave your name with the guard."

"Will you be here?"

He smiled a little. "I'll be here." He put his hand on my shoulder and I felt the pressure of his fingers. "We'll have more time then. To talk."

He removed his hand. "In the meantime, perhaps, I'll do a little investigating about your Mossad."

Investigating. It was an ominous word.

"And now, my passionate young lady, you really must go. I do have an appointment. I don't like to keep people waiting."

"Thank you, sir," I said. And I followed the personal secretary from the room.

Kadmon had left.

I went, as he had directed, to a nearby cafe.

In the meantime, perhaps, I'll do a little investigating. . . .

Had I achieved the one thing we wanted to avoid? Would Mandel's investigating mean disaster for the Mossad?

The waiter came with my turkish coffee. I lifted the spoon and watched the thick dark liquid drip slowly into the cup.

Perhaps Heydrich's teletype message had made Mandel more receptive. Perhaps I could somehow convince him to give us ten thousand pounds. The idea seemed ludicrous.

I sat like an island of gloom surrounded by waves of chattering and laughter which rose from the tables around me.

Finally, I got up, went to the telephone. Called Kadmon.

"So?" His word held doubt and disparagement.

I spoke in Hebrew, told him of the five-minute meeting. "But I'm to come back at six this evening," I said, sounding far more cheerful than I felt.

"The question is," said Kadmon, "why did he ask you back? Maybe I should be there at six o'clock instead of you."

"I don't know if you could get in. Mandel told me he'd leave my name with the guard."

"You realize there may be some unpleasantness?"

"I can take care of myself," I said.

"I was referring to the police."

"Oh," I said stupidly. "Well, if it's that—it's better they find me than you. Since I know very little."

After a moment he said, "I warned you last night there'd be risks. I suppose I can't go round absorbing them all for you."

"When I left Mandel's office—" I hesitated.

"Yes?"

"He said perhaps he'd do a little investigating about the Mossad."

The silence was eloquent as a curse. Then he said abruptly, "All right. Don't come back here until after you've seen Mandel. I'll wait outside the bank at six o'clock. But don't recognize me when you come out. Get on the same tram as I do. Get off the stop after I do. Stand looking into a shop window and wait for me. If you're being followed I'll give you instructions as I pass by." He paused for a moment. "In the event that you are arrested, you of course know nothing. Nothing more than you've already told Mandel."

"I understand." Was he dismayed, worried or reasonably pleased by the outcome of my meeting with Mandel? I could not tell.

"By the way," Kadmon said then, "that fellow you spoke to at the bank—the one waiting at the teller's window—who is he?"

"A friend of my brother's. From Czernowitz."

"Well," Kadmon said dourly, "I've just come up from the lobby. He was at the desk, asking for you. You'd better phone back and have him paged. If he keeps on asking for you, it won't help your incognito status."

"Yes. All right." My heart started thudding.

"Next time don't give out your address so freely."

"There seemed no reason I shouldn't tell *him*."

"No? I can think of a few."

"He's very influential," I said. "He helped me get to Mandel. I thought he might help us again sometime."

Kadmon merely grunted.

"What do you want me to do," I asked, "from now until six o'clock?"

"Do?" There was a long pause. "Do nothing. See a film. Go to a museum. It may be the last chance you'll have."

"Thank you," I said, and hung up abruptly.

I rang the Continental again and asked that they page Stefan Meta in the lobby.

"Well, are you psychic?" he said when he came to the phone.

I felt that all breath had been shaken from me. "When I called in they told me that a man was waiting for me. You're the only man who knows where I'm staying."

"I'm glad to hear that." Then he said, "My lunch date was canceled. I hoped you might join me."

"Yes."

He arranged to pick me up at the Café Royal in ten minutes' time.

SIX

I WENT TO THE LADIES' ROOM, combed my hair carefully, powdered my nose; tried to quell the anticipation which flared through me. Stefan was taking his friend's sister out for lunch. That was all.

He arrived punctually, paid for my coffee, and ushered me out of the crowded cafe. He had a *trăsură*, a horse-drawn carriage, waiting. "There's a restaurant I like on the Băneasa. Have you time for a leisurely lunch?"

I nodded.

He held my arm as he helped me into the carriage. Then he gave directions to the driver and we started off with a jolt.

"Well!" Stefan turned to me. "How did your interview with Mandel go?"

"All right."

"Am I permitted to ask why you were so desperate to see him?"

"I wasn't desperate. I mean—well, it's—"

"If you're in trouble, perhaps I can help."

"Trouble? Of course not!" I must control myself. Stop this idiotic stammering. If he reported back to David that something was obviously wrong, my brother would come from Czernowitz to find me. Which would, without doubt, abruptly end any career I might have with the Mossad.

I must act like a girl driving out for a casual lunch at a lakeside restaurant. And I must try until six o'clock to forget about George Mandel and my so-called mission.

I launched then into phrases I had rehearsed as I strolled the deck of the ship en route from Palestine. And I gave Stefan Meta a recital about my new career: to sell plots of Palestinian land to wealthy European Jews. "That," I concluded, "was why I wanted to see George Mandel."

"And is that why you're having lunch with me?"

"Perhaps."

He laughed. "I suppose if you can pass as a real estate agent, I can qualify as a wealthy European Jew." He asked me some technical questions, all of which I was somehow able to answer. I regained something of my composure. And, surprisingly, he became interested in buying an orange grove near Haifa.

"If you buy it," I said, "perhaps you'll come to live on it."

"Are you inviting me to move to Palestine?"

I nodded.

"If *you* invite me, I accept."

"I—invite every Jew."

"You're hospitable," he said. He put his hand over mine.

I withdrew my hand and said, to cover my confusion, "I—this morning at the bank, I wasn't even sure you'd recognize me."

"I recognized you a long time ago, Ruth."

Our eyes met and held.

"I think I first began to notice you," he said, "when I found out you were the R. Polesiuk who did the football stories for the local newspaper."

"That wasn't because I liked football so much. It was because I liked selling papers so little. When I heard there was an opening for a sports reporter, I tried for it."

"You must have been, what—fourteen at the time? You know, there's something about you that's still very much fourteen." But he was looking at me in a way which contradicted the words.

How could I carry on a conventional conversation with him for an entire lunchtime? A few minutes alone with him and all the years of fantasies seemed to have come together within me in a single urgent confusion.

To climb back again to safe territory, I asked about my family in Czernowitz.

He gave me what news he could think of. David and Sophie had

59

moved to a beautiful new apartment. Their son Gershon had turned into a teen-aged Casanova, with pimples. My sister Bertha's husband had opened a small candy factory. It was doing well. Trivial news; all reassuring. Or was it? I hoped, while in Rumania, to have the chance to visit my family; to persuade them to try to get out of Europe. But the more content they were, the more imbedded in their present lives, the more difficult it would be to convince them to leave.

Presently the carriage turned out of the Calea Victoriei, and we were on La Şosea, a broad boulevard, tree-lined, edged at intervals by large villas set back from the roadway. And then in the distance was the Băneasa; the sun sparking like diamond chips on the lake's surface.

The restaurant was nearly empty. Only the tables for two were occupied. And the two were invariably a man and woman.

"Do you prefer to eat in here?" Stefan said. "Or on the terrace?"

"Outside," I said quickly.

There were tables by the water's edge, each shaded with a bright umbrella. And there was no one else being served outside, perhaps because of the midday heat which sat heavily over the shimmering lake. I walked down to the water, picked up a handful of pebbles and tossed them out, one by one, into the reflected clouds.

I felt suffused with sunlight. He stood beside me. The sense of his nearness pulsed through me. The world was bordered by the flower boxes of the *terrasse* and the small blue lake. We were two figures in a travel poster: *Come to Romantic Rumania.* It seemed impossible to believe that within a few hours I would be keeping an appointment which could mean life or death for fifteen hundred people. Or disaster for our mission. Or, at the very least, imprisonment for me.

Stefan put his arm around me.

I looked up at him. "How—how is your wife?" I heard myself saying in the most formal manner. "And your children, how old are they now?"

He smiled a little. "Well," he said, "the girl is fourteen; the boy, eleven. Would you like to see pictures also?" He took out his wallet, showed me several photographs. The girl was lovely, with light hair which fell long over her shoulders.

"She's very beautiful," I said. "Like your wife. Except for the color of her hair."

"Yes," Stefan said. Then he added, "I may as well tell you, I love her very much. My daughter, I mean."

It seemed a strange remark for him to make.

"And your wife," I said. "She is well?"

"My wife is well. And your husband? He is well?"

I nodded.

We were standing very close. I felt mesmerized, as though I could not possibly move away from him.

After a moment Stefan said, "Our waiter waits."

We returned to the table where the white-coated man stood, staring out stiffly with proper detachment, his glance riveted somewhere in the center of the lake.

He seated us and presented elaborate menu cards.

"Will you order for me," I said. "After five years in Palestine, a menu like this seems an utter bewilderment."

I watched him as he considered the menu. *Grossfürst.* I had called him this in my childhood musings. Great Prince. The name was apt. There was something regal about him; a splendid blend of Roman and Slav. Lean and patrician, high cheekbones, long thin nose and long thin eyes which could change in a moment from remote to intense.

"I hope you like fish," Stefan said. "It's the specialty."

"I like everything. Except turnips."

He gave the order. *Ciorbă de peşte* to start. *Guvizi de Constantza* for me. "Fish from the Black Sea," he told me. "Fried. And delicious." Sturgeon for himself. And a *vin de cotnari.* "Bring us the finest vintage you have," he told the waiter. "This is a special occasion."

"Is it?" I asked when the waiter had left.

"I think it will be," Stefan said.

My hand was on the table, fiddling with the fork, pressing the prongs into the soft pads of my fingers. He put his hand over mine. "Now tell me. All about you. Since you left Czernowitz."

"It's not very interesting."

"It's you who are interesting. Which makes everything about you interesting. To me, at any rate."

I smiled a little. And I shrugged. "Well, my husband didn't take to life on the kibbutz. So we worked it out that I stayed at the kibbutz

61

during the week. And took the bus into the city every Friday afternoon. Went back at sunset Saturday night."

"Somehow that doesn't sound like the ideal arrangement for newlyweds."

"Somehow," I said, "Emmanuel and I never were newlyweds."

The waiter came with the appetizer. We ate in silence. I didn't want to speak any more about Emmanuel. I wanted this small space of afternoon for ourselves.

Then Stefan said, "Your brother once told me that you never really wanted to marry Emmanuel Klüger."

I looked up at him.

"I'm sorry," he said. "I have no right to ask such questions. Much less to know the answers."

I wanted to tell him. Why I had married Emmanuel. And I wanted to tell him about the stillborn child—the symbolic and, it seemed, fated sundering of our marriage. I wanted to tell him that I had never felt more free than I did at this moment. I had been stifled by five years of a marriage which was not made in heaven but in a private hell; a marriage made not by love, but by death.

Instead, I told him about my work at the Histadrut in Tel Aviv.

"When did you leave the kibbutz?"

"Two years ago. As you pointed out, it wasn't much of a way to be married. City mouse and country mouse."

"To tell the truth," Stefan said, "I can't quite see you as a country mouse."

"Perhaps not. Perhaps I only thought I was made for kibbutz life because it had been drummed into me since I was a child. Somehow it's not in the Zionist picture to come all the way to Palestine just to live in a one-room flat in Tel Aviv and work as a clerk in the Labor Exchange."

"That was the best you could find?"

"It wasn't easy to get work in Tel Aviv then. Emmanuel told me he was with a construction company. That sounded very grand until I found out he spent most of his time hauling bags of cement around on his back."

"And what did you do in the Labor Exchange?"

I shrugged. "Filled out forms. Filed papers. Interviewed people. None of us had just one job. We all did more or less everything. Anything.

Even our so-to-say bosses. And then one day when I was having lunch two of these—bosses sat down and asked how I'd like to make a trip back to Rumania. To sell land. And here I am."

"Five years dispensed with in two minutes," Stefan said.

"If I asked you for a summary of your last five years, would you give me any great detail?"

"I would not!"

I laughed a little. We finished the *ciorbă de peşte*, each in our separate silence.

It was not until the waiter had brought the entree, and had again retreated, that Stefan said, "The last time I saw you was at the opera. In Czernowitz. You were with your new husband. You had on a green velvet dress. I remember thinking you looked like a Renaissance painting."

Inconsequentially I said, "My sister Bertha made me that dress."

I too remembered that meeting. He had bowed as we passed and had stopped to chat. His wife was with him. Her black hair was drawn back from her face into an elaborately braided bun. She was a beautiful woman with pale skin and a classic perfection of features. She clung to Stefan's arm and she seemed always to be smiling. She had expressed great surprise when Emmanuel told her he would be leaving the next day for Palestine, and I would be following shortly. "Married a week and separated so soon. But that's dreadful!"

Emmanuel explained that he would take courses at the Technion. He must be there at the start of the semester. I, unfortunately, must remain in Czernowitz to attend to family matters.

Mrs. Meta had then commiserated with me on the death of my mother.

During the entire encounter I had been suffused with shyness. I felt dowdy and gauche next to the elegant Mrs. Stefan Meta.

"That was the first time I learned that you'd be leaving Czernowitz," Stefan said. "I realized suddenly that I would miss you."

"Miss me!" I was incredulous. "But you never even knew I was there when I *was* there."

"I knew you were there," Stefan said. "I knew. And after your marriage to Emmanuel Klüger I assumed you'd give up your wild ideas about settling in Palestine. When I learned from David the day your

63

ship would sail, I was tempted to come down to Constantza to see you off. Was anyone with you that day?"

I shook my head.

"Then I wish I had come. Although, on second thought, it's probably better that I didn't."

"Why?"

"Because," he said softly, "I might never have let you leave."

I stared at him.

Then, to change the unspoken subject, I started talking, chattering, words tumbling together, telling him about that trip to Palestine. "It was one steady storm the whole way. Our deck was filled with seasick halutzim. When the ship put in at Piraeus we staggered down the gangplank, green and pale. We decided to visit the Acropolis. But somehow I got cornered on the dock by a young man. Spewing Polish at me . . ."

And I told him then of my first encounter with illegals.

There were sixteen of them. Polish Zionists. There had been a pogrom in their town, and they'd fled; got as far as Greece. They were living by the port until they could find a ship which would take them to Palestine. But they had no certificates of entry, no legal papers, no money for tickets or bribes. Naturally, no one would take them.

Greek sailors had helped them a little, given them food. Still, they were half starved.

They knew our ship was headed for Palestine, and their skinny, sad-eyed leader begged me to talk our captain into taking them.

So I'd gone to the captain, who suggested I come into his cabin to discuss whatever it was I had on my mind. Since it was obvious what he had on his mind, I went instead to some Greek Orthodox priests on board. I talked them into giving me a little money for the starving refugees at the port. Then I went to the first-class passengers, practically shouted at them that they must give me money. If the priests had given, *they* surely could afford to give.

And they had. I'd collected fifteen thousand lei. With that I'd bribed two of the ship's officers.

That night we smuggled the sixteen Poles on board, dressed as sailors. There were four girls among them. They had to cut their hair short. We locked them in an empty first-class cabin and there the sixteen stayed for the rest of the trip.

When we got to Haifa, Poli and Emmanuel were on the pier, waving. But I pretended I didn't see them. I rushed down the gangplank, the first one off the ship.

In the Palestine Office in Czernowitz I'd been told the name of a Jewish immigration officer. Eliezer Dostrovsky. I began running all over like a mad woman, saying I had a letter for Dostrovsky.

Finally I found him, stamping papers. And I told him about the sixteen Poles. He must get them off the ship. He asked me to show him where they were. I saw my brother and my husband running toward me. And I ran—away from them. They started shouting at me. I shouted back that I'd left my purse on board. I had to return to the ship.

Then two British policemen grabbed me; wanted to know what all the commotion was about. I shouted at Dostrovsky in Hebrew, told him where he would find the Poles.

Emmanuel and Poli came up and claimed me; explained to the policemen that the excitement at reaching the Holy Land had gone to my head. So the officers released me.

But I wouldn't leave until I saw all sixteen Poles coming down the gangplank with Dostrovsky. I'd borrowed some coats and valises from a few of the first-class passengers. "So," I told Stefan, "the sixteen Polish illegals entered Palestine looking like prosperous tourists."

Stefan began to laugh. And he kept laughing.

I couldn't help it, I caught his laughter. We sat there like two fools laughing, gasping over our pastry and turkish coffee. We were laughing at more than the story of the sixteen Poles. We were laughing because we were sitting under a red-and-white striped umbrella and it was a sunny blue afternoon and we were together.

Finally I wiped at my eyes with the napkin and Stefan blew his nose and he said, "I love you."

I knew that he meant merely a passing pat on the head; avuncular approval for a crazy undertaking which had, somehow, succeeded. Even so, the words shocked through me and all the laughter went away.

I looked at him. He too had stopped laughing.

"And I want very much to make love to you," he said.

I felt weak yet strong with sudden vaulting desire. I wanted nothing more at that moment than to be with him; lying with him on a bed, on the floor, in a field, anywhere.

"Ruth—" he said. "There are rooms in this place."

I closed my eyes. Desire shriveled and disappeared. He was a middle-aged married businessman away from home. I had been fool enough to be caught up by a mesh of schoolgirl dreams. I didn't know the man at all; I had been responding to a concoction of my own fantasies.

"Is that why you picked out this charming restaurant by the lake?" My voice sounded stifled. "Because it has rooms?"

"Ruth—I've been thinking about you since I met you this morning at the bank. I feel—invaded by you. But it was a mistake to say anything. It's too soon. For you."

"Please, let's go."

"If we leave like this," Stefan said, "it will be gone. All of it. Before it has even begun."

"Before *what* has begun? What are you talking about? You're married. I'm married. You are the friend of my brother David. That's all you are."

"Is it?"

He signaled the waiter, paid the bill. We walked through the restaurant. Almost all the inside tables were empty now. I wondered whether the adjoining rooms were also empty.

The *trăsură* was waiting.

As we started back to the city, Stefan put his arm around me. I moved away, but he drew me back to him. "Darling," he said gently, "relax. I'm leaving for Czernowitz tonight. We won't see each other again if you think it should be that way."

"Yes. I do."

His arm tightened around me. His thumb moved back and forth on the bare skin of my arm. I felt almost frightened by the want and need which pounded through me.

We arrived back in the center of the city about four o'clock.

"Shall I drop you at your hotel?"

I shook my head.

"Where then?"

"I have an appointment at six."

He indicated a one-story building on the left. "Have you been in the Simu Museum? It's an excellent collection."

I said nothing.

He leaned forward and asked the driver to stop.

The Simu was a small but splendid place, built by a Rumanian millionaire to house his collection. There was a single floor of paintings, ornately framed masterpieces. A guard sat in a shadowy corner, his legs spread-eagled before him, a book resting on his pendulous belly. He was asleep. Stefan and I were, consequently, alone.

We stood before a farm scene by the Rumanian painter Grigorescu. Peasants in bright national costume, working in fields of golden wheat.

"Are you in love with Emmanuel?" Stefan said.

I stared at the painting, the detail in the hand-embroidered blouses, the brightness of the wheat.

The museum door was open, framing the picture of green lawn and city sidewalk. The next room was dim; there was no one looking at pictures; there was no guard.

I walked into the next room and Stefan followed me. I sat on a bench and he sat beside me.

Then he turned me to him; his arms went around me.

We were together, holding on to each other in the center of the museum silence. He lifted my face and kissed me. At first, frozen, I made no response; did not even draw away. Then all the pent-up desire of the past hours flared, searing us to one another.

Suddenly I broke away from him. I stood up.

He took my hand, tried to pull me back to the bench.

"No," I whispered, more to myself than to Stefan.

"Ruth—why?"

"For every reason," I said. "For every reason."

He released my hand and I walked away from him.

The guard in the next room was awake now. I wondered whether he had been watching us. I didn't care. I wanted only to escape from Stefan, into the sunshine.

I ran along the gravel path to the sidewalk.

Stefan caught up to me.

We walked down the street together, but in silence.

Presently he said, "I want to buy you something."

"Why?"

"Don't ask foolish questions."

"Well, buy me a flower," I said. "I like flowers."

We walked to the Piaţa cu Flori, the flower market; a square of small shops and open stands, alive with springtime flowers. And as colorful as the flowers they sold were the gypsy women, squatting on the sidewalk behind their huge baskets or lounging against a shop wall; long bright skirts, long black hair, gold-coin necklaces, gold loop earrings.

Stefan stopped before a slender girl, grimy and beautiful. She had plaited fresh flowers through the twisted tail of hair which hung over her half-bare breast. Her shoes were set out neatly beside her basket.

Stefan asked for twelve long-stemmed roses. She selected them carefully, named a price which was far too high, and rewarded him with a flash of smile when he paid what she had demanded. She wrapped the roses in a sheet of newspaper and handed them to Stefan. "Long live your French girl!"

"Here you are, French girl," he said, presenting me with the flowers.

We crossed to the Strada Carol where there were small shops and outdoor stalls of pots and pans, ribbons and needles, sandals and bedroom slippers.

"I'd like to get you something more substantial than flowers to remember me by," Stefan said. "Flowers fade. Unless of course I keep sending you fresh ones."

"But you won't."

"Why not?"

"Because this is the end of our afternoon."

I picked up a pair of leather sandals with slender black straps. They were my size and reasonable. I opened my purse, but Stefan paid the old woman who held out warped fingers for the money.

"I have a passion for shoes," I told him as the woman wrapped the sandals.

"In that case," he said, "I command you to think of me every time you take off these sandals and get into bed. Perhaps some of the passion will be transferred."

"Is that what you want?"

"Passion can be a lonely affair," Stefan said. "If I thought you were thinking of me, it would bring you closer."

"We'd better be getting back," I said.

"Where is your six o'clock appointment?"

"At the Banca Comercială."

"Mandel again?"

I nodded.

"I'll be damned if I'm going to turn you over to him for the evening."

"Not for the evening."

"How long then?"

"I don't know."

"They say that George Mandel is a formidable human being. That no woman can be with him long without falling under his spell. They say even his enemies can't dislike him."

"Does he have enemies?"

"I suppose no man gets to Mandel's position without collecting enemies." Then Stefan said, "May I see you afterward? For dinner?"

I shook my head.

"Ruth—my train doesn't leave until midnight."

I heard myself saying, "If you phone my hotel around nine o'clock, I'll try to be there. But if I'm not, you'll know that I wanted to be there."

"When are you coming to Czernowitz?"

"I may not be coming to Czernowitz."

"No? Why not?"

I tried to explain. "This selling of land, it's a government mission. They can recall me at any moment. Send me any place. For all I know, I may be gone from here tomorrow. Or next week. That's why I'd appreciate it if you wouldn't tell David or my aunts or anyone at all that you'd met me here in Bucharest. They would never understand if they knew I was so close and didn't come home to visit them."

"I can quite see that they wouldn't understand. *I* don't understand."

"It's—different living in Palestine. In a way, we're all under wartime regulations. Unofficial war. Unofficial regulations. Unofficial army. But everyone's in it. We must go and come, where and when we're called to duty."

He gave me a mock salute. "A fine country you've invited me to live in."

"It *is* a fine country. I wish you'd come."

He stopped on the sidewalk and turned me to him. "I think there's only one thing in the world that could make me move to Palestine."

I looked up at him. We were two feet apart from each other yet I felt that he was holding me. No other man had ever reached within me this way.

I started walking.

He took my arm as we crossed the street.

When we entered the Piata Sfăhtu Gheorghe, he said, "It is, you know."

"What is?"

"For me, anyway. It is. It."

Because I was afraid to say too much, I said nothing.

When we reached the bank he took my roses and sandals from me. "I'll deliver them to your hotel."

"Thank you."

"I won't say good-by. I'll say—until nine o'clock."

I nodded.

"Have you ever been kissed in front of a commercial bank?" He drew me to him.

"No. Don't!"

Kadmon had promised to be waiting on this street.

I ran from Stefan, up the front steps of the bank; gave my name to the uniformed guard who nodded and unlocked the massive oak door.

Then I turned.

Stefan was climbing into a taxi. He did not look back. He slammed the door and the taxi charged off.

I wondered where I would be tonight at nine o'clock.

SEVEN

THE BANK, now empty and unlit, was cavernous, heavy with stillness. The only sound was the click of my heels as I followed the guard across the stone floor. Again I mounted the carpeted stairway, walled now in shadow. We passed by rows of empty desks and entered the inner office.

Stefan was gone; that incredible sunlit world had vanished. This was reality. All that mattered was the answer which lay behind the door which the guard was now opening.

Again Mandel stood up and came from behind his desk. I noted with some relief that there was no one else in the room. He indicated the couch in the corner; asked whether I would like a turkish coffee. I nodded, and he gave a few directions to the guard. His voice was soft. I could not hear the words.

The guard retreated. The tufted red-leather inner door closed behind him. The room seemed to echo with emptiness.

Mandel sat down in the armchair. "Well, have you had a good day?"

I nodded.

"Is this your first time in Bucharest?"

I shook my head.

"So you know your way around a little?"

I nodded.

"I made several phone calls this afternoon," he said. "One was to your friend, Max von Anhauch. He never heard of you."

"I—told you," I stammered. "I just used his name—"

Another guard entered the room bearing a silver tray. He set it on the table before us and departed.

Mandel poured the coffee. "It was difficult to check your story without endangering your work. Or—you. I learned very little. So you'll have to fill me in." He took out a silver cigarette case, snapped it open, held it toward me. I shook my head. He lit a cigarette. Then he remarked, "Unfortunately, my wife has arranged a dinner party tonight. I must be home early. However—we have a little time. Supposing, as a start, you answer this question. If you can. Why should I sponsor your illegal immigration when your own leaders in Palestine have condemned it?"

Answer. If you can. But I could not. But I must. I must at least try.

"This—this morning," I started, "you mentioned the *Velos*. The first of the illegal ships."

He nodded. "Yes, I remember those newspaper pictures. The Ghost Ship, they called it. The Phantom Ship with its starving passengers. Refused entry into Palestine. And everywhere else. Trying to put in at port after port. Country after country. Yes, I remember."

"It always struck me as strange," I said. "The *Velos* had once been used by white slavers. They never had trouble landing *their* illegal cargo."

"And what finally happened to yours?"

"After two and a half months they got permission to land here in Rumania. On condition that they all leave the country at once. Go back where they came from."

"I see. After all that trouble, expense and disastrous publicity spotlighting the world's anti-Semitism—they landed right back where they started. And this fiasco should inspire me to hand over ten thousand pounds to your Mossad le Aliyah Bet?"

"The *Velos*," I said, "was not a Mossad ship. I mentioned it for one reason only. It was because of the *Velos* that our leaders put out their proclamations against illegal immigration. The Arab terrorists had started on their holy mission, murdering Jews in Palestine. We needed the British to keep peace in Palestine. Naturally, when the story of the *Velos* went into world headlines, it made the British seem like villains. Naturally, the British were furious. And naturally, there was nothing else for our leaders to do but come out with a strong statement condemning illegal immigration."

"A statement they have never rescinded."

"How can they? Be practical. If the British refuse to recognize them —to deal with them—where are we?"

"You imply that your leaders back your efforts. Off the record."

"Some of them do."

"Ben-Gurion, for example?"

"Before I left Palestine," I said, "one of our leaders told me that the Mossad had become a life-and-death operation; not only for Europe's Jews. But for the life or death of Eretz Israel. If a country of Jews is ever to come into being, he said, it will have to fight for its life. The Jews saved now will be needed later. To fight."

George Mandel nodded. "Those poor benighted people you manage to smuggle ashore will one day swell into an army strong enough to chase the British out of Palestine—wagging their Mandate behind them. Come now, young lady." He stood up.

Panic shot through me. Was I being dismissed?

"Poor benighted people." I cried out the words. "Dedicated young men and women! Pioneers! Who lived for years on training farms in Europe. Training for life in Palestine. Training to drain swamps, clear fields. And fight. Hold off the attacks of Arab terrorists. Protect the border settlements. Thousands upon thousands of halutzim. Over twenty thousand in Poland alone. With a few hundred legal certificates available to them each year. They were desperate to come. And we desperately needed them. So we started to smuggle them into Palestine. Since 1937, our ships have brought hundreds upon hundreds of them. Our secret ships. The *Atrato*. The *Assimi*. The *Artemesia*—"

My mind blanked. My words froze. I could remember only that one month ago the *Atrato* had been captured by the British. Her three hundred passengers were now in a detention camp in Palestine. Two months ago the *Assimi* had been caught by the British; sent out to sea with three hundred and sixty-nine passengers on board. The ship had not been heard from since. On the first day of June—a few weeks ago— the S.S. *Leisel* had been caught. With nine hundred and six illegals aboard. Then the *Astir*, caught. With her seven hundred and twenty-four illegals.

Mandel walked to the window. Would he turn to me now? I'm afraid young lady . . . my wife . . . the dinner party . . . guests waiting . . .

There was no time for silences. "All those ships—those early ships—gave us experience. Contacts. But the ships which came after the Kristallnacht—it's different now. It's no longer just transporting halutzim to the homeland. Now the Mossad can mean life or death to hundreds —thousands—of European Jews. Now the Mossad can—"

"Look—" he interrupted. He turned from the window. "Don't go on. I knew what I would do before you walked in here. You can have the ten thousand pounds."

The words were so unexpected that it seemed he had not spoken them.

I sat immobilized.

He smiled a little. "You say nothing. Are you so accustomed to having people hand over vast sums after a brief interview?"

"You mean—you're going to give us all that money?"

This time he laughed. "A madman, I agree. Not only the most dubious investment I've ever made. But one which could easily land me in prison. I must ask, therefore, that you keep it on a strictly anonymous basis."

"Of—of course," I stammered. "But if you ever need our help—you or your family—"

"My dear young lady," he said, "I'm not buying a life insurance policy. Or an escape hatch." Then he hesitated. "Perhaps, however, I should tell you what I am buying. I don't want you to think your arguments were all that convincing. In point of fact, they were not. But there was one sentence you said this morning which you might want to use again elsewhere. In any case, it made me decide to see you again. . . ."

He turned, stared out the window into the street. His words, when they came were flat; spoken, it seemed, by someone far away.

"Thirty-four years ago I was engaged to a girl named Rosa Grotz. She came from a small town in Poland. We went back in the summertime to meet her parents. While we were visiting her parents' home, there was a pogrom. In the morning all was peace and as usual. By afternoon, half of the Jewish Quarter was burning and nineteen people had been killed. The women were raped before they were killed. Rosa was raped before she was killed. They found out we were to be married, so they tied me to a bed. In that same room they raped her and they killed her. I closed my eyes, but I could not close my ears. I tried to drown out the sound of her screaming with my own screams. But I heard her. Sometimes, even today I still hear Rosa screaming."

I sat frozen.

Finally, he went on. "Since I was not Polish, they decided not to kill me. But for a long time afterward, I wished only one thing. That they had."

He turned to me. "You asked me this morning how I would feel in a few years' time if I looked back and knew that my ten thousand pounds could have helped to buy life for fifteen hundred people. Who now were dead. It was a well-put question. I know that the impossible can happen. Therefore, I will give you the money." He walked to the door. "And now, if you will forgive me, I must get home. My wife—"

"If you know the impossible can happen," I blurted, "why don't you get out of Europe? Now!"

He looked down at me. "Yes, I've seen it happen. Thirty-four years ago. And because of that, I can believe it might happen again. To other people. But you see, I can't believe that it can happen now—to me. My family. What would you call me? An optimist? A fool? Or—a human being?"

Then he took my chin in his hand. "After all, I suppose it was not entirely because of a girl named Rosa Grotz that I agreed to give you the money. It was also, perhaps, in some small measure because of a girl named Ruth." He took his hand from my face. Drew a paper from his breast pocket. "And it was because of this." He handed me the paper. "The message sent by Reinhard Heydrich on the night of November ninth. I copied it out in my own hand. Word by word by word."

I looked down at the paper.

Demonstrations against the Jews are to be expected tonight, November 9th–10th, throughout the Reich . . .

Mandel walked to the door. "Well," he said, "I told you this morning your people were wise in sending a young girl in to see me. I doubt that a man would have gotten past my secretaries. But now I'd like to see a man in your organization. To discuss details. Currency specifications. And so forth. Have someone phone me tomorrow at my office. Tell him to mention your name." He opened the door.

The guard was there, waiting.

My words came out stiffly. "Thank you, sir. Thank you very much indeed."

With equal formality George Mandel answered, "My dear young lady, you are very welcome."

As I followed the guard along the passageway, the full realization flooded through me. I wanted to race down the stairway, out the door, to Kadmon who had promised to be waiting. I wanted to scream the words aloud: *We have the money. We can proceed with the* Tiger Hill!

EIGHT

KADMON WAS WAITING, Alexander with him. They walked toward me as I came from the bank, passed me, proceeded down the street. I continued a few yards in the opposite direction, looked at my watch, made what I hoped appeared a sudden decision. Turned and walked back swiftly toward the tram stop.

Kadmon had instructed me in these maneuvers, which made me feel a ridiculous character in a second-rate film. But he, of course, had no way of knowing whether or not Mandel had contacted the police. Whether or not I would be followed from the bank.

There were others waiting at the tram stop. I could have given Kadmon a slight nod or smile. But, perversely, I stared at him, my face a blank.

The two connected trams pulled up; first and second class. We boarded the second-class tramway, pressed our way through the rush-hour crowd. When they descended, I waited. Got off at the next stop. And stood looking into a shop window at a display of mannequin legs encased in silk stockings, and brassieres adorning papier-mâché bosoms.

Finally, they came up to me, stopped to look in the window.

"Well," I said in my most matter-of-fact tones, "he'll give us the money for the down payment."

There was no reaction from either man.

Then Kadmon said, sounding almost indignant at the idea, "You don't mean to say he promised to give you ten thousand pounds."

"Yes I do mean to say that."

Kadmon stared at me and nodded slowly.

"I told you!" Alexander exclaimed. "That's what we need! A little sex in the pot."

I said to Kadmon, "He'd like you to phone him tomorrow. About when you want the money. And in what denominations."

Kadmon started to laugh. Alexander joined him. And I too broke into laughter.

"Incredible!" Kadmon announced. He started walking down the street. Alexander and I hurried to catch up to him.

"What magic did you use?" he wanted to know.

I recounted some of the details of our meeting. But I saw no reason to tell him the story of Rosa Grotz. I knew that the success of this, my first assignment, had little to do with me or my words. Yet, I wanted desperately to become a member of the Mossad. And I felt somehow that if given this chance I could perform with success in the future; could persuade people to give large sums of money; could be of use in other ways. I wanted at least the opportunity to try.

"We'll celebrate with a good meal," Kadmon announced. "We're meeting the head of the Palestine office in Rumania. It will be nice for once to bring him a little pleasant news."

We turned into a street which was brighter, broader. Alexander took my arm in a proprietory manner. "The Calea Văcăreşti," he informed me in the manner of a tour guide. "One of the main streets of the Jewish Quarter. As a matter of fact, I live near here. Perhaps you'll have dinner with us one night?"

I asked, releasing my arm from his grasp, "Is your wife a member of the Mossad?"

"Wife? Who said wife! I'm a bachelor. I live with my mother. I told her about you. A beautiful girl fresh from Eretz Israel. Naturally, she'd like to meet you. However, in case we stop up there after dinner I should warn you, Mother knows nothing about the Mossad or my connection with it."

I wondered again, with a stab of anguish, where I would be at nine this evening when Stefan called. And I vowed to myself that, in any event, I would not be with this thick-lipped bachelor Alexander and his mother.

I glanced at Kadmon who promptly announced, "After dinner we have work to do. Ruth did not come from Palestine to pay social calls."

It was an answer to Alexander. And to me as well.

A few minutes ago in the crowded tram, I'd envisioned myself accompanying Stefan to the station, kissing him good-by.

It was impossible. How could something which was undeniably wrong seem so right? Fortunately, fate or circumstance seemed to have a stronger will than I did. There would not be time to see Stefan again. And that was how it should be. Yet, we must see each other tonight—if even for a moment. The memories we made this afternoon must have an ending created by us. Not by the shattering inconclusiveness of a telephone ringing in an empty room.

Kadmon paused before the door of a restaurant. Even before he opened it, sound came out to meet us like a hum of bees.

We entered. The air was thick with noise, cigarette smoke and a tempting melange of smells: fresh-cut onions, dill, garlic, wine. There did not seem to be a single unoccupied seat in the room. But a waiter spied us, beckoned, and we followed him to a table against the back wall. A man was already seated; small, skinny, with a sallow complexion and dark mustache.

Kadmon made another of his eloquent introductions. "Mordechai Orekhovsky. Ruth."

Orekhovsky made an attempt to rise, but he was wedged between table and wall.

We sat, and the waiter bestowed upon us an oversized basket of rolls and a dish of pickles. Then he disappeared.

"Have you heard from Ehud?" Orekhovsky asked at once.

Kadmon shook his head.

Orekhovsky was holding a long roll. He broke it in half, a twisting motion. Then he looked down at the broken bread halves and dropped them on the table.

"I do have good news on another matter," Kadmon said. Speaking swiftly in Hebrew, he told Orekhovsky about the down-payment money for the piece of real estate in which we were interested.

Orekhovsky's eyes turned from lifeless to luminous. And the conversation turned at once into a heated discussion concerning the nationality of tenants to be accepted in the new apartment. I was surprised at this open discussion of Mossad affairs until I realized that no one could possibly overhear us. We were surrounded by a veritable wall of sound.

"I had a letter from our haver in Poland," Orekhovsky was saying. "He reports that so many requests for certificates are coming to the Palestine office in Warsaw, that the regular postman could not carry them all. The requests are now delivered in a special truck. I wrote him that here in Bucharest we not only get the letters. We get the people themselves. When I arrive at the office in the morning, they are sitting already on the doorstep, in the corridors. They even come to my house to ask for certificates. My wife has no peace. I have no peace." He turned to me. "If you want to know why Mordechai Orekhovsky, good and obedient Zionist, public servant of the Jewish Agency, if you want to know why I sit here with Josef Barpal, instigator of illegal immigration—that is why! I was against this whole business at first, I don't mind to tell you. I had many fights with your friend here, Mr. Barpal. No use to antagonize the British, I said. We must show we are law-abiding, rule-abiding people. But when the White Paper was issued last month—" He crumbled a piece of broken roll. "Thousands of men, women and children applying for legal certificates to Palestine. Thousands in Bucharest alone. And what do I have to answer them with? A *handful* of legal certificates. Literally—a handful."

"Look, my friend," Kadmon said, and he signaled the waiter. "Relax. Enjoy your meal. We can speak of these matters later."

Orekhovsky smiled a little. "Eat. That is his answer to all insurmountable problems."

The waiter appeared. With a swipe of his napkin he brushed Orekhovsky's crumbs onto the floor. And he presented me with a menu. It was handwritten and full of stains.

I studied it, without seeing the words at all. The room was warm, yet I felt suddenly chilled. I realized something of what we would be facing within the next few weeks. With the possibility of a new ship, each of our haver would be fighting for "his Jews" to be taken. And who would make the final selection? Who would take on the monstrous role of playing God? Dear sir, we select you as a survivor. Dear madame, we regret to inform you that there is no more room.

Orekhovsky put his hand over mine. "Kadmon is right. We have come here to eat. Not to agonize. When in Rumania, you must do as the Rumanians, yes? And the people here like to eat well. Like to eat a lot. And like to eat loud. So order. Order yourself a good—a memorable—Jewish meal."

The meal when it came was good, was long, was loud; with numerous dishes and side dishes. As we sat over our coffee, Kadmon remarked with some satisfaction, "A good Jewish restaurant must never have clean tablecloths when a meal is over."

Suddenly, a sharp silence descended over the restaurant. We all turned to stare at the door. Two policemen entered. Automatically, people were reaching for their documents.

"One of those men came to my office last week," Orekhovsky said to me. "They looked through our files. Of course," he added, "we have everything in code."

"That may be crime enough in itself," Kadmon said grimly.

The policemen passed from table to table, checking papers, asking questions, their voices low.

Gradually sound returned to the crowded room, but muted now. No one attempted to leave until his papers had been seen by the police. Then there was generally a hasty signaling for the check, a quick retreat.

"People start to run," Kadmon said, "even when there is no cause for them to do so."

"Do you think the police are looking for someone special?" I asked.

Kadmon shrugged. "Probably only for payoffs. In these Jewish restaurants you can always find a half dozen refugees without papers. If they don't pay up, they're shipped back where they came from."

We sat in taut silence as they approached. The taller of the two, grim and gaunt-faced, made an elaborate bow to Orekhovsky; looked through his papers and slapped them down on the tablecloth. "So, we meet once again, monsieur," he said, with menacing politeness.

He then picked up my papers, lifted my chin, turned my face right, left, comparing it to the passport photograph. He wrote my name into a small notebook.

He gave Alexander's papers a cursory glance. But Kadmon's passport received a careful perusal. "Why don't you Hebrews from Palestine stay home?" he said to Kadmon. "Don't you think we have enough Jews here to stink up the country?"

They moved on. We paid our bill and left.

Outside on the sidewalk we stood for a moment in silence.

"Well," Orekhovsky said, "I'd better get back to the office. Thanks to the news you've brought me, I suddenly have a good deal of work to do." He kissed my hand. "It was a pleasure to meet you, Ruth. Welcome to Rumania."

He walked away down the street.

"We also have work to do," Kadmon said. "Let's go back to my room."

We climbed on a tram. I found a seat next to a portly old gentleman whose hands were clasped neatly over his round and jiggling belly.

Suddenly sleep was all over me. I sat rocked by the rhythm of the tram, in a comatose state. I thought drowsily that perhaps I could have Stefan's nine o'clock call transferred to Kadmon's room when it came. But what would Stefan think, being switched to another room, hearing a man answer the phone?

It seemed impossible that a few hours ago I had been with him . . . at the lakeside restaurant . . . riding in a horse-drawn carriage through the woodlands at the edge of town . . . sitting on the bench in the private dimness of the Simu Museum, his arms around me, his mouth on mine. . . .

Then, through these mind meanderings I wondered, blurredly as if in a dream, why the policeman had written down my name in his notebook.

NINE

I JUMPED. A heavy hand lay on my shoulder.

I looked up.

"Next stop," Kadmon said.

I had fallen asleep in the tram seat. A feeling of shame swept over me. They would think me weak. They would think me unable to cope. They would think me—This phrase had begun to plague me.

As we got off the tram Alexander said, "Look, she didn't get to bed till four last night. The girl's exhausted. Why don't you let her lie down for a while?"

"No," I said hastily. "I'm all right."

But I felt a rush of gratitude when Kadmon nodded. "Have a few hours' sleep. But be in my room by midnight when the telephone calls begin."

There were two notes in my box. *Mr. Meta called. Time: 9 p.m.* And the second: *Mr. Meta called. Time: 9:30. Message: Au revoir.*

I glanced at the clock above the reception desk. Twenty of ten. Ten minutes ago and I would have been alone in my room speaking to Stefan.

Standing there in the hotel lobby his words broke over me suddenly. *It is, you know. For me, anyway. It is. It.* Words ridiculous in their simplicity. What meaning had he put behind them? A practiced step

83

forward in an attempted seduction? Or could those words match the emotions he aroused in me?

I looked again at the notes, then crumpled one in each hand. If only he had told me at which hotel he was staying.

Back in my room exhaustion again overcame me. I was afraid to lie down, afraid nothing could wake me until morning. I thought about taking a cold shower. But I found myself acting instead like one hypnotized.

I set the alarm for midnight, kicked off my shoes, pulled off my dress and crawled into bed, still clutching the two notes from Stefan.

The heavy drapes were drawn. I thought about opening the window, for the room was stifling. In a minute I would get up, let some air into the room.

Instead, I fell into a twisted nightmare. I was running through a maze. At each turning I met someone who tried to choke me. The captain of the ship I had taken from Haifa. Then the first mate who sang me a tender aria from a German opera as his hands closed around my neck . . . Eliahu Golomb appeared dressed in the uniform he rarely wore. "The commander in chief wishes to see you," an aide said. And Eliahu came toward me. His hands fastened around my neck. "I must perform this duty," he announced brusquely. "For the good of the Haganah." I screamed and ran from him, raced down a dark passageway to be caught and pinioned from behind by strong arms. Terrified, I looked up into the face of my husband. Then Emmanuel also started to choke me. I tore from him and started down a murkily lit corridor of an apartment house. A door opened suddenly and the hulking figure of the Shamen blocked the entire passageway.

There was a knock on the door. Not loud. But insistent. I scrambled out of bed, still half caught in the tangles of the nightmare.

"Yes?" I was at the door. "Who is it?"

"Police."

The dream fell away. Reality shattered around me.

I looked down. I was wearing a slip.

I ran to the wardrobe closet, pulled out the oversized man's bathrobe from the clothing supply room of my kibbutz. I put it on, tied the belt tight around my waist, clutched the robe closed at the neck.

"There must be some mistake," I said as I opened the door.

"No mistake, madame." He stepped into the room. He was not in uniform. It was one of the policemen who had examined our passports in the restaurant. He showed me his badge. I stared at it dumbly and nodded.

He closed the door behind him.

I felt no fear. I felt nothing. It was as though I must wait to see why he had come before I could react.

"May I sit down?" he said.

"If you wish."

He sat in the armchair, crossed his long legs. "Do you mind if I smoke?"

I shook my head. I even brought an ashtray and placed it on the small table beside him.

He offered me a cigarette.

"No thank you," I said.

"Sit down, Madame Klüger." He indicated the bed. "There's no need to be afraid." After a moment, he added, "Not of me, that is."

I sat on the three-legged stool by the telephone table.

He lit his cigarette and for a second the flare of the match was reflected double in his spectacle lenses. He was a bland-faced young man. His hair, slicked back, fell into strands as though he had just combed it through with hair tonic.

I realized I had barely noticed him at the restaurant. It was his companion's face which had held me, frightened me. Gaunt, faintly pock-marked, with lips which drew into a thin smile when he addressed Orekhovsky.

"How well do you know Mordechai Orekhovsky?" The same sneering sarcasm was there. It was as though his companion had spoken the words.

"I don't know him at all. We were only introduced at dinner."

"What business do you have with him?"

"None. It was a social meeting. He's interested in Palestine. And I've just arrived. My friends thought Monsieur Orekhovsky would like some up-to-date news on the country."

"And why have you come here, madame? This is no time for a woman

85

to be traveling alone in Europe. A young Jewish woman. You are Jewish, I take it?"

I nodded.

"And I presume that you did not come here as a tourist?"

"I came to sell land. In Palestine."

"You are a real estate agent?"

"Something like that."

"Please explain to me, madame, exactly what you are doing in Rumania."

"I'm not familiar with the police regulations of this country," I said. "Do you have the right to come into the room of a foreign national late at night? To ask questions? To—"

"Madame Klüger," he stood up. "You are fortunate that I was able to persuade my companion to let me make this visit. He wanted to come himself. And he has—I assure you—the right to do so. Furthermore, Madame Klüger, we have no Nuremberg Laws in Rumania which forbid Aryans to have sexual relations with Jews. My companion has a strange peculiarity. He hates Jews but he likes venting his spleen, shall we say, on attractive young Jewesses."

He was standing very close, looking down at me. I felt a first rush of fear. Was he talking for his companion or for himself?

"Did you come to warn me then?" I said. "I appreciate it." I got up hastily and went to the wardrobe closet. "If you want to see my credentials—" I pulled down the small locked case which was filled entirely with blank land-purchase forms, contracts, letters of introduction and other documents given me in Palestine to serve as proof for my cover as a representative of the Nathenya Sea-Shore Development Company, Ltd., RASSCO, and Mekoroth.

I shoved the case into his arms. "Everything is in here. The reason I have come to Rumania. My credentials."

He placed the locked case on the telephone table. His other hand yanked at the belt of my bathrobe. The robe fell open.

I made some sound, the start of a scream. His hand clamped over my mouth. I tried to pull away but he was holding me hard against him. As though he had emerged from the nightmare into my room.

"I won't hurt you," he said gently. "Relax, little Jewess." His voice was soft. He spoke in tones of suppressed passion as if uttering love words. "If you scream, I promise to arrest you."

Incredibly, my fear went away. I felt almost detached, like an observer to this scene, someone standing in safety behind a wall of impenetrable glass. I stopped struggling. One of his hands was still pressed with force against my mouth. His other hand gripped my upper arm. That was the sensation I was aware of, the pain in my upper arm. And the sweet greasy smell of his hair lotion.

"I imagine," he murmured, "that the British governor of Palestine is not going to cause an international uproar if he discovers that one of his Hebrew subjects is behind bars in a Rumanian jail. Am I correct in that assumption?"

I remained taut, motionless and without emotion.

"I have good reason to believe," he went on, "that you need a protector right now. That's why I've come. I can see to it, for instance, that if you move to another hotel your new registration form will not reach police files. Any official interested in you will assume you've left the country. And you won't be troubled. Do you understand?"

I nodded.

"Consider it, my little Madame Ruth Klüger from Tel Aviv, Palestine. I am at least more attractive than my pock-marked companion who wanted to visit you tonight. I enjoy poetry and the theatre. I attended the University of Bucharest. If I take my hand from your mouth, will you scream?"

I shook my head.

He released me.

"Sit down. On the bed."

I did so, clutching my robe closed.

"Please take off that ugly bathrobe."

I sat frozen.

"Take off the robe. I assure you, it hides your most important credentials."

"Why do you want to—protect me?" I said. "And from whom?"

"Take off the bathrobe. I want first to look at you."

Suddenly I was no longer a detached observer. I was terrified. A scream shook through me but I stared at him in silence.

"Please," I whispered.

"Or shall I remove it for you?"

Because I could think of nothing else to do, I pushed the robe from my shoulders. I still wore my slip, but I felt cringingly naked.

"Whose bathrobe is that?" he asked.

"My lover's."

He stubbed out his cigarette carefully in the ashtray. "Is that why you've come to Bucharest?"

The telephone rang. I ran to answer it.

"Darling!" I would have exclaimed this with enthusiasm to anyone at the other end of the line. Fortunately, however, it was not Kadmon or Alexander or Mordechai Orekhovsky. But even Stefan seemed a little taken aback by my tone.

"I've just finished dinner," he remarked somewhat irritably. "Alone."

"Darling," I gushed at him, "I'm terribly sorry. I just couldn't get back in time. When I see you I'll tell you all about it. When will I see you?"

"Well," he said. I could feel him withdrawing. "I have to catch the midnight train."

"Tonight," I said tenderly.

"Of course tonight. You know I'm leaving tonight."

"That will be wonderful." The tone was soft, but my words were distinct enough to be heard across the room.

"Ruth. Are you all right? You sound quite drunk."

"With love," I said. "What time will you be here?"

"In five minutes." He hung up.

"My love," I said. "I've missed you so terribly. Yes, I know. I realize how important your meeting was. But do hurry now. I have so much to tell you, my sweetheart. And it's been so long."

I replaced the receiver and turned.

He was standing now, his shoulders back. He had assumed again the stiff posture of the policeman.

I smiled at him. "Excuse me for sounding so—informal. If I hadn't said what I did, he'd have wondered. I didn't want him to suspect there was a man in my room."

I walked toward him. "I confess, I don't know anything about Rumanian police regulations. You may be entirely in your rights, coming up here like this. On the other hand, my friend is quite an important person. He may not understand that you came here only to save me from the attentions of your companion. I'm afraid he's a very jealous and possessive man. He may cause you some trouble."

"I came," he said shortly, "to offer you my protection. Since you don't need it, I'll leave."

Amazed, I watched him walk to the door. Then he turned. "Soon," he said, "the Iron Guard will return to power. If you're still around when that day arrives, you may come crying to me for protection. But then, of course, it will be too late."

Within a few minutes I was dressed and running down the corridor. The terror of my nightmare returned. I fully expected the policeman to step out of the shadows, his hands to fasten around my neck.

Reason told me that if he were waiting, it would be by the elevator so that he might follow any man who got out at the fifth floor and started off in the direction of my room. Consequently, I pulled open the heavy door which led to the stairway. And I ran down flight after flight in the semidarkness.

The hotel lobby was crowded now with elegantly dressed men and women returning from dinner or the theatre. I forced myself into some kind of composure, went out to the sidewalk and stood back in the shadows of the building, to wait.

"Taxi, mademoiselle?" the doorman said.

I shook my head.

He gave me a peculiar look, obviously wondering what I was about; a girl alone by the hotel entrance near midnight.

A taxi drove up, and Stefan started to get out. I ran forward, climbed into his cab.

"Let's go to the station," I said.

"But why? We have time." He was not only puzzled but angry. And I could scarcely blame him, after the tender promises I had given him on the telephone.

I pictured the policeman opening the cab door, demanding that we come with him. For questioning. "Please, Stefan," I begged. "Let's drive around. Through the park, or somewhere."

He shrugged. "Take us down to the Dâmbovita," he said to the driver.

"I must have sounded rather—odd on the phone," I said as the cab started off.

He looked at me. He was smiling a little. "I admit you didn't sound like the girl I took to lunch this afternoon. But I wouldn't say you sounded odd. You sounded very agreeable."

"I know you'd prefer the girl on the telephone," I said. "But—she wasn't me. There was a man I'd met. He came to my room, on business. But then he—well, suddenly—well," I blurted, "I told him I had this very jealous lover. And then, luckily, you phoned. So I pretended that you—"

"You were perfectly right," Stefan said. "I am jealous. Who the hell is this—"

I stopped his words by putting my hand over his mouth. "Nothing happened," I said. "I got rid of him. For good."

Stefan kissed my palm.

Then, suddenly, I became that girl on the telephone.

We kissed and clung together. His hand went firmly but gently over my body. An aching beauty flooded me.

"The Dâmbovita, monsieur," the driver said. "Is there anywhere special on the river you wanted to go?"

Stefan straightened up, looked out the window. The driver had diplomatically taken us to a picturesque spot, far from transversing bridges or covered areas.

"This will be fine," Stefan said. "Would you wait for us, please?"

We got out and stood by the river rail watching the lamplights like shimmering reflected moons in the dark water.

"I don't like the idea of leaving you alone here," Stefan said. "I have the feeling you're into a lot more than you've told me."

"Don't worry," I said. "I have a secret protector."

"Yes, but he's leaving on the midnight train. Now, what about all these goddamn men buzzing around you?"

"Don't worry," I said. "I've learned my lesson. No more business meetings in hotel rooms. Besides, my secret protector doesn't need to *be* here in order to protect me. Just knowing he's somewhere, that's enough. His name is Grossfürst. It suits him very well: Great Prince."

And I told him then of my schoolgirl adulation. I did not, however, tell him how I used to write his name over and over. With a Madame before it. Madame Stefan Meta.

He turned me to him, held my chin in his hand. "I'm sorry I didn't wait for you to grow up."

"No you're not. You have what you really want in life. What I mean, you have your life the way you really want it."

"I remember thinking," he said, "that girl is going to be somebody when she grows up. And some man is going to be very fortunate. It never entered my head that the man might be me. Or should have been me."

"It shouldn't have been you. I would've wanted to go to Palestine. You would've hated the idea. You told me so today."

"You never know. I might still end up there. Picking oranges."

"I hope so." The words were fervent. I meant far more by them than he thought I did.

I must try to make him understand—believe—the coming danger. I must try to make Stefan give up his town house in Czernowitz, his country villa, his several businesses. Give up everything and move himself and his family to the distant impossible land of Palestine. Impossible. To dig ditches as Emmanuel had done. To drain murky malarial swamps. To sweat in the hundred-degree heat of the desert laying lines for irrigation pipes.

For an urbane, sophisticated man like Stefan Meta—impossible. Perhaps he could resettle in one of the cities: Jerusalem, Tel Aviv, Haifa. But the cities were overcrowded with urbane, sophisticated European Jews. Which was why Emmanuel had finally taken a job digging ditches.

"Kiss me," I whispered to Stefan. "Kiss me till your train leaves."

This was not the time to dwell on the fate of European Jews. This was our time, a separate time, set apart from the rest of our lives and the rest of the world.

It was the taxi driver who finally made us draw apart. He had considerately parked some distance from us. But now he drew up and gently tapped his horn.

"Lord!" said Stefan, glancing at his watch.

We ran to the taxi.

"Excuse me, monsieur," the driver said. "But you told me you had to catch the midnight train. We'll just about make it to the station."

I was thankful for the last-minute race, the speeding drive to Gara de Nord, the hasty good-by. I stood watching as Stefan hurried away down the platform to board the train.

There had been no time for making plans to see each other again. No time for making dramatic decisions about never seeing each other again. There had been no time. And for that I was grateful.

TEN

"You're late!" Kadmon announced when I entered his room.

"So she overslept," Alexander said. "So shoot her."

"I didn't oversleep." I told them about the policeman's visit. "I wanted to wait until I was sure he'd left the hotel."

Kadmon simply nodded. "She's not here two days and already she attracts—of all people—a policeman."

"She also attracted Mandel," Alexander pointed out.

"You'll move tomorrow," Kadmon said. "I'd get you out of here to-night, except it might cause suspicion. Go back to your room now. I don't want him following you in here. Do you think by any chance he believed you? This imaginary lover business?"

"He believed me. Yes."

"Maybe," Alexander remarked, "her lover isn't as imaginary as all that."

"Well, she'll soon find," Kadmon told him, "that she hardly has time to go to the toilet, much less to have a love affair."

It was perhaps his way of informing me that I still had a future with the Mossad.

The next morning the chambermaid entered carrying a bouquet of spring flowers. She glanced at the white lilacs which had arrived two nights before from the Shamen. "Your admirer is persistent, made-moiselle."

93

Then she saw my packed suitcase open on the bed. "But you're not leaving us so soon?"

"I'm afraid so. And I'll be traveling, so I won't be able to take the flowers. Would you like them?"

"Every woman likes flowers, mademoiselle."

I tipped her and she left, carrying the bouquet.

But I kept the card. It simply said: *Good morning*.

Had it come from the Shamen? If so, the words seemed repugnant, ominous.

But if the flowers had been sent by Stefan?

The florist's name was on the card. I phoned. Yes, he would check.

"Madame? They were sent by a gentleman staying at the Ambasador Hotel. S. Meta."

"Thank you. Very much."

I hung up. I looked at the card. I kissed it.

Good morning. Suddenly the words seemed incredibly romantic.

A few minutes later Kadmon phoned. "Are you packed? I've reserved you a room at the Ambasador Hotel."

"The Ambasador?"

"If you'll be meeting people like George Mandel, you'll need a good address."

As I locked my suitcase I wondered whether S. Meta always stayed at the Ambasador when he came to Bucharest.

It was a large and luxurious hotel, perhaps the best in the city. My room was tiny; there was barely space for the bed, the dressing table and the overstuffed armchair. But I liked the room. It had none of the shadowy loneliness of my room at the Continental.

I checked in. I had a bath. I went down to the lobby. Kadmon was waiting.

And then it started.

Our days were, literally, numbered.

Kadmon and I each kept a calendar notebook, in code. The *Tiger Hill* was scheduled to sail on August first. And each day and each night were crowded with meetings to be held, contacts to be made, cables to be sent, avenues to be investigated.

Everything was a problem, for when secrecy is essential even the simplest matter presents a dangerous exposed surface. It did little for our peace of mind to know that both Orekhovsky and I had come to the attention of the police.

I'd had no visits from my would-be protector, nor had I seen him again in restaurants or on the city streets. But this fact did not eradicate the flash of fear when there was a knock at my hotel room door.

We still had heard nothing from or about Ehud Uiberall. This, too, served to heighten fear. It could happen to him; it could happen to any of us. Sudden disappearance, and no one to turn to. No one to make an official inquiry. Not the leaders of the Jewish Agency. Not the British rulers of Palestine. Not the officials of any country in which we operated.* No one to turn to except ourselves: ten Mossad members in all of Europe, and our forty locals.

"The only thing to be done about fear," Kadmon said once, "is to forget about it."

And we tried. Yet fear was always somewhere present, for we walked a perilous tightrope and when we looked down there was the yawning abyss of uncertainties and the unknown. Because we lacked experience, because there were no tested plans of operation we could follow, we had to work on the trial-and-error method. Yet, there could be no room for error. And no time.

Each separate factor concerning the organization of the *Tiger Hill* had to be correlated with the whole. This was essential. It was also impossible. For the whole picture did not exist. We were working on the matter of false passports before we knew from which countries the illegals would come. And to which country they would—ostensibly—be going. We were contacting our agents in Palestine regarding plans for landing the ship, before we had raised half the money the Shamen demanded for the *Tiger Hill*.

Yet, no single matter could wait until the preceding one had been settled, because postponement would have meant missing our August first deadline. We could not postpone the deadline because seamen were being hired, papers were being signed, insurance policies were being written. And the date on all of them was August first.

* *See* Appendix Nine.

Perhaps we were being precipitous in selecting that early date. But we acted somehow as though we had seen the secret papers of the Nazi high command. We were convinced that war was a matter of weeks away. And if war came before the *Tiger Hill* raised anchor in the port of Constantza, the ship might never sail.

Each small achievement brought further problems, further decisions. Each required careful study and correlation. Yet, there was no time for this.

The matter of water, for example.

As I sat at Kadmon's telephone one afternoon, Alexander burst into the room. He had just made contact with a distant cousin who had a friend in Brăila. This man had agreed to supply kegs of fresh water, and his price was not unreasonable.

"But I must phone my cousin tomorrow," Alexander announced. "With the order."

How many kegs of water would we need?

The decision had to be made at once—but we had not even ascertained as yet how many passengers the *Tiger Hill* would carry. The Shamen said the ship would hold fifteen hundred. Yet, Sammy Solomonides, our local in charge of the reconversion of the *Tiger Hill*, had sent back word that this was a reckless overestimation. Fifteen hundred perhaps—if we carried no supplies at all.

The more kegs of water on board, the fewer passengers we could accommodate. And there was the all-important unknown factor. The trip from Constantza to Palestine should take five days. But some of the illegal ships had been forced to go far off course to escape detection. Some of the trips had lasted ten weeks.

What use to take additional passengers if they died en route because there was no fresh water?

But how cruel to arrive—if the ship did arrive—with a surplus of filled water kegs using space which could have been allocated to five or fifty or a hundred additional human beings.

"My cousin's contact," Alexander said, "leaves in two days for Budapest. If we don't decide by tomorrow, we can forget it."

The decision, it appeared, was mine to make. Kadmon had left that morning for Greece to investigate the possibility of another ship—for even as we worked through an unbroken jumble of days and nights on the *Tiger Hill* there was always the simultaneous search for the next ship. We could not wait. We had to keep looking. For in those days when the world sat on the precipice of war, every ship that could float was at a premium.

I determined to leave on the next train for Brăila, the port on the Danube where the *Tiger Hill* was being reconverted. Before the water contract could be signed I must try to ascertain how many passengers the *Tiger Hill* could feasibly carry. Yet, I knew nothing whatever about ships.

Nor did Alexander, who volunteered with a certain eagerness to come with me.

He stood wiping the sweat from his neck with a small hotel towel. He seemed always to be leaking with perspiration. His lips were invariably wet, his eyes watery, his palms damp.

"You're needed here," I told him. "Kadmon may not get back tonight. You'd better stay to cover the telephone."

It was evening by the time the train reached Brăila. We had selected this out-of-the-way port for refurbishing and reconditioning the ship, hoping to avoid the probing of too many officials. "Buttons," I called them. There seemed to be an unending succession of them, petty officials to be bribed for permits, passes, special consideration and secrecy. Most of them wore some sort of uniform, the jacket adorned with shiny brass buttons.

Sammy Solomonides was at the station to meet me.

Kadmon had told me only that he was a Greek Jew, an agent for cargo ships. I was unprepared for this chivalrous, cultured gentleman. As we drove from the station he described in detail the countless problems he had already encountered. And the reconversion of the *Tiger Hill* had barely started.

When we reached the port, he rolled down the car window. "We won't get out to inspect the ship now. It might cause questions for a woman to be seen on the docks at this hour." He pointed. "There she is. Second from the left."

The ship had no name painted on it. Perhaps that was why I said stupidly, "Are you sure *that's* the *Tiger Hill?*"

She was small, rusted, listing to one side. She looked as though she might sink on the spot.

"You were expecting perhaps the *Queen Mary?*"

"I don't know what I was expecting. Noah's Ark, maybe. But not—that. How can we board even a hundred people on such a ship?"

It was not until that night when I climbed down the ladder into the dank and stultifying blackness that I began to understand the full realities of what we were attempting to do.

Prior to that it had all been a matter of telephone calls. Meetings. Purchasing. Bribing. Pleading for money. Making out contracts. Coded messages. Lists. Details.

Now as I stood in the trough of blackness and Solomonides played his flashlight along the stacks of boards which would serve as beds, I envisioned, with an inward shudder, human beings. Shapes bulking there on the boards; men and women entirely dependent upon us. Upon this courtly Greek Jew who stood beside me. Upon the meticulous plodding-paced Kadmon, the sweat-faced Alexander and me. We seemed a totally inadequate life-saving team.

Only one section of the hold had been fitted with boards. "That will be the women's dormitory," Solomonides said. "I figured we'd give the girls a bit more comfort. I've left three feet of space between each layer of boards. With six women lying next to each other on each side of the aisle. We can get in more men if we squeeze them together a bit more. Give each one two feet of space to lie on. Two feet of headroom. What do you think?"

"I'll lie down," I said, "in the comfort you've provided for the women."

I crawled over the boards which comprised the bottom berths. When my fingers touched the rough wall of the hold, I stretched out.

Thick, dank darkness. And through it the scurrying sound of rats.

I tried to sit up. There was only room if one ducked one's head and huddled over, round-shouldered. I made the motions of undressing. It was virtually impossible. I lay down again.

"Are you all right?" Sammy called. "Do you want the flashlight?"

"No!" I was terrified of the rats. If I held the light, I might see one. I lay in the sweltering, menacing darkness, rigid with fear, and filled with revulsion amounting almost to physical nausea.

I imagined a perspiring human body lying next to me. Someone next to her, and next to her. One would have to crawl over five women in the middle of the night, to get out. To go to the bathroom. To vomit.

The motion of the ship now was negligible as it sat, listing in the still waters of Brăila port. I imagined this hellhole tilting sharply, abruptly, back and forth, to and fro, as the small ship was tossed by the waves. I imagined myself, my bunkmates seasick. The sound. The stench.

I thought of the *Artemesia*. Kadmon had said it almost casually: "They ran into a storm. They were all seasick. Then the ship sprang a leak. The lights went out. The women—the men too, I suppose—began screaming in the hold."

I felt it now. The screaming terror. Water breaking into the seawracked darkness. The tiny berth became a coffin.

And disease! The *Katina*: hoisting the black flag. Epidemic. Two men had come down with meningitis. They died. And the Greek captain of the ship had insisted their bodies be stabbed with a dagger so their spirits could not walk.

The *Katina* was not a Mossad ship. It had been organized by a speculator. But Mossad ships were not immune from disease. I imagined my berthmate, sandwiched between me and the woman next to her, ill. Perhaps dying.

We *are* mad, I thought. To subject human beings to days, perhaps weeks of this. To organize a ship like this which could well turn into a death trap.

What right had we—the handful of us in the Mossad—to assume with such certainty that we could predict the future? Perhaps nothing worse than the Kristallnacht would ever occur. *This* was the real risk; these horrendous sea voyages. And if war came, the risks of the trip would be increased a thousandfold, for the seas would be mined.

We were wrong, those of us working so hard to dislodge people from their homes. Yes, the paperless, penniless refugees who had already fled Germany, Austria—if they had nothing, nowhere to go—let them crowd aboard our ships. If you have nothing, you can take risks, you

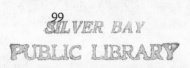

can endure such a voyage. But to try to persuade men like Mandel and Stefan to leave what they had—when they had everything—to leave it all because of a wild nightmare vision in our minds. It was insanity. Naturally, they had not listened.

I screamed and half sat up, cracking my head on the boards above me.

"What is it, for God's sake?" Sammy called out.

I tried to regain some kind of composure. "A rat just ran over my legs."

"Get out of there! What are you doing in there!"

I crawled across the boards. Sammy helped me to my feet. I was trembling.

"I hope you're planning to get rid of the rats," I said. "Before the ship sails."

"Of course." His flashlight picked out the ladder. As I started climbing up, he said, "At least, we'll try our best about the rats. It's not always so easy to get rid of them all."

We came onto the deck and I breathed in heavily of the fresh, salted night air.

I was glad I had lain there in the stifling dark. It enabled me now to give determined decisions.

Yes, space should be set aside for a small infirmary and an isolation ward.

Yes, we should take several cows on board. For fresh meat.

"Look," Sammy protested mildly. "This isn't a Mediterranean cruise. They won't be expecting filet mignon."

"The cows can act as a cover. We'll keep them on deck till we need them. If the *Tiger Hill* is spotted by a British plane they may take it for a cargo ship, carrying livestock."

Sammy shrugged.

"And I don't think," I said, "that the men's quarters should be any more crowded than the women's berths you've built already."

"Of course," Sammy said. "They shouldn't be. But, remember, the more comfort you give each passenger, the fewer you'll be able to take."

We were standing in shadow by the rail of the ship. The full moon seemed incongruous somehow casting its silver sheen across the water.

I thought of Stefan. Standing with him by the Dâmbovita. There had been no moonlight that night by the river. We had made our own. Had it been only a few weeks ago? It seemed no more real at this moment than all my adolescent daydreams.

I leaned on the ship's rail and looked directly down into the dark water. The oil floating on the softly undulating surface seemed to take the shape of corpses.

Solomonides was right, of course. The more comfort we provided, the fewer passengers we could take. Which was more important?

I remembered the card file in Orekhovsky's office. Names, neatly typed, alphabetically ordered. Names of Jews who had fled to Bucharest from Hitler's Reich. Hundreds upon hundreds of them with one hope, like a lifeline. The hope that they would somehow be able to get to Palestine.

The more comfort, the fewer passengers. Yet, the equation was not that simple.

"Look," I said, "the Mossad has, after all, won backing from a few important people. They back us—not the Revisionists, not the speculators. They back us because we've won a reputation. Our ships are always seaworthy. The living conditions are at least—bearable. But the other organizers—Kadmon told me that the hold of the *Katina* was so crowded there wasn't room to lie down. 'The hold was like one big body,' he said."

Sammy Solomonides nodded. "I know all that. I also know you're a young girl. This is the first ship you've worked on. You've probably never been down in a hold before. It's not pleasant. Having a rat run over your body, *that's* not pleasant. Don't let it distort your judgments. People can put up with a lot more than you think they can. Than *they* think they can. Especially if it's a short-term thing. And the goal is a good one."

I stared down into the water. Of course, he was right. All in the same boat.

Sammy took my arm. "Look, I'll show you around. The engine room, supply room, kitchen, toilets, washroom. You'll get an over-all picture. Then we'll go back to my place and we'll work things out. Yes?"

I nodded, grateful for the experience and wisdom of this gentle man.

We sat until dawn at the Solomonides' large dining-room table. And by the light of an elegant cut-glass chandelier we went over figures, charts, drawings of the ship's reconditioned interior.

We settled on seven hundred and sixty as the number of illegals the *Tiger Hill* could safely carry. The Shamen had claimed the ship was fifteen years old. Solomonides put her age closer to fifty. The Shamen had claimed she could carry fifteen hundred illegals. She could, if we ran another *Katina* where the passengers did not have room enough to lie down. And since a growing number of our ships were being forced to stop mid-trip to take on illegals from other ships which had met disaster, the figure seven hundred and sixty did leave some leeway of space in the face of such dire emergency.

The passenger list would also include three cows.

ELEVEN

I LEFT FOR BUCHAREST on the early-morning train.

Sammy and his wife came to the station to see me off. He stood with his arm around her. She looked up at him, said something. He laughed, kissed the top of her head.

I watched from behind a wall of glass.

The train started to move. We waved. But that picture remained long after: the couple standing close in love.

When I got back to Bucharest things started to run even faster. Time can sometimes be a friend. Now it became an enemy. And the closer it came to the August first deadline, the more implacably did the days and nights speed by.

Having actually seen the *Tiger Hill*, the bare wooden slats in the hold, I suddenly found myself able to talk myself into the offices and homes of wealthy Jews in Bucharest. Other entrees were supplied by George Mandel.

There was a strange atmosphere in these homes. People it seemed were gayer than ever, more spendthrift than ever. It was as if there were a dread epidemic rampant in the city. You did not know whether it would strike you. When it would strike you. Whether it would kill you. No use to move away. Where to move? Anyway, it might not come. So best to have parties. Dress in your finest. Go to the theatre, the opera, the ballet. Eat better than ever. Drink the great wines. Laugh louder than ever. What else could one do?

There was a sad joke going around. A Zionist is a Jew who visits another Jew to get money to send a third Jew to Palestine.

And it was that way.

More often than not I emerged from such meetings with a bank draft, a check, even cash. Not large amounts. Penance money. There but for the grace of God. Or money might serve as a propitiation to the fates. A check made out to RASSCO or the Nathenya Sea-Shore Development Co., Ltd., seemed somehow an assurance that all would remain right with the world of the wealthy Bucharest Jews.

The arrangements were extremely businesslike; contracts were signed, papers were stamped, everything officially executed.

Mr. Rabinowitz, for example, would purchase a plot of land in Palestine for one thousand pounds. However, since Jews were not allowed to send money out of the country, Rabinowitz would pay in Rumanian lei. This money was promptly turned over to Kadmon. And Rabinowitz would receive an impressively printed contract stating the specifics of the land he had purchased in Palestine.

However, if I mentioned moving to Palestine to live on this land, I invariably heard the same astounded reaction, in different words.

"I'm a Jew. But not a wild-eyed Zionist."

"Palestine! Take a look at the size of my stomach. Can you imagine me ploughing fields in the day, fighting off Arabs in the nighttime. Even the Jews would throw me out of Palestine!"

"All right," I would say, "not Palestine. Surely a wealthy, influential person like yourself must have friends, relatives, contacts in other countries who can vouch for you. Help you get a visa. It's not impossible for wealthy Rumanian Jews to get out of Europe. Not yet."

And I would quote firsthand reports about what was happening and what had happened to the Jews of Germany, Austria, Czechoslovakia. I tried to picture what might happen here. Sometimes I quoted Hitler's word: Vernichtung. Annihilation.

And sometimes, when I spoke like this, I was rent with guilt and uncertainty. What right had I to persist in my attempts at persuasion? Perhaps war would come and Hitler would immediately be defeated.

Perhaps war would not come and Hitler would make no attempt to spread his evil and his empire. To suggest that a man give up his security, his luxury, his language, his way of life—because of a nightmare vision; this *was* madness.

But day by day I became more convinced that horrendous as our vision seemed we in the Mossad were right. Every Jew in Europe *was* in danger. Vernichtung would become the word which dominated the months ahead.

So I kept on with my urging, pleading. Leave. Now. While there still is time. Make a new life while you still have the chance. Don't wait until it is too late to run.

So far as I know, I did not succeed in persuading a single Jew in Bucharest to leave the country. I was, however, surprisingly successful in raising money.

We were still far short of the ninety thousand pound total the Shamen had set. But we were at least raising enough to cover payments to suppliers, insurance companies and for the incessant bribes.

Money raising became my special province. Which did not mean, however, that I could forget about any other area. There were only two of us, Kadmon and myself, in charge of the total operation. Alexander and Solomonides carried out specific assignments.

My head often felt like a pin cushion stuck full of sharp but essential details. Remember. Do this. Don't forget that. Phone here. Run there.

Because we had no time to look things up and because it was not safe to write things down, we were always memorizing; names, addresses, telephones, streets, figures, codes.

Days and nights became a mad kaleidoscope of time and action. We forgot that sleep existed or a pillow or a bed. We ate while we sat at the telephone. Or during meetings in Orekhovsky's office. Or in Kadmon's room. Or at the Shamen's.

Through it all I had a toothache. But there was no time to visit the dentist.

Through it all the Shamen kept reminding me of our dinner engagement. "After the *Tiger Hill* sails," I would tell him, uncertain as to what exactly he expected of me after that time.

And through it all there was Stefan, miles away, but too close. Sometimes, alone in my room, I found myself talking to him, whispering *darling* to the empty air, like an idiot.

My first night at the Ambassador I had written him a brief formal note on stationery headed Rural and Suburban Settlement Co., Ltd. I had moved my office. Consequently, if he wished to pursue the matter of the purchase of land in Palestine, would he kindly contact me at the Ambassador Hotel. I had signed the letter in an illegible scrawl.

His return note was typewritten and almost as formal. It started *Dearest Ruth* and concluded *Love, Stefan*. But the words in between said nothing. His chief motivation for writing seemed to be a request that I write him no more letters. If I wished to contact him, he suggested I telephone his office.

The letter chilled me. *For me, anyway. It is. It.* What had he meant by such words? A ploy to get a girl into bed? What did he mean by this letter? Forget me. Forget that afternoon we spent together? Forget that hour by the Dâmbovita River.

I tore up the letter. I would do as he wished. But had he meant any of it? *For me, anyway. It is. It.* I wanted desperately to know whether those six simple words had been used before on other passing afternoons away from home. Or had they been—as indeed they had seemed at the time—words wrenched almost unwillingly from deep inside him?

The next evening, as if in answer, flowers came. This time the card merely said *Stefan*. When I got into bed I left the bed-table lamp on, and in the faint light the long-stemmed yellow roses glowed with beauty.

He sent flowers two or three times a week. And there were messages in my box: *Mr. Meta called*. However, the calls always came in the daytime when I was rarely in my room. In the evenings the phone rang often. But it was never Stefan. I assumed it was difficult for him to call once office hours were over.

There were also several letters. They were always short and said little. Perhaps, I reflected, he had been burned once by writing passionate love letters to a woman. What warmth there was in his formal little notes seemed almost coded. *I want you—to be happy.*

I want you. I read such phrases over and over; the rest of the world fell away. There was only my consuming need to be with him.

There was no feeling of shame or guilt. Why should there be? It was hurting no one, threatening no one, this love affair so private that we were never even together; so impossible that we communicated, it seemed, by a kind of intense telepathy. And through flowers.

I tried several times to telephone him.

I did not call from my room, for Kadmon paid the hotel bills. He went over each item like a niggardly accountant, and I wanted to avoid any questions as to whom I had telephoned in Czernowitz. He had made it clear that I was not to contact my family who lived there.

Nor did I call from the telephone booth in the Ambasador lobby. I did not wish to draw attention to a special number; one which I requested not be charged to my hotel bill.

But I did go several times into the lobbies of other hotels to put through a call to Stefan. It was an impossible business. The phone booths, though often plush lined and elegant, were like boiler rooms in this midsummer weather. I would lift the receiver, heavy as a brick, crank the handle. And eventually someone from the post office would shrill "Hello."

Getting a long-distance call through generally turned into a shouting session. Repeating the number again and again. Connections breaking off. Lines emitting strange mechanical sounds. And the long-distance operator at the post office seemed invariably to be a sour snappy woman dedicated to sabotaging one's call.

The process always took so long that I could not wait. Each time I entered the phone booth in a state of high suspense. In a few moments I might actually be speaking to him. And each time I left the booth frustrated, exasperated, feeling stupidly close to tears.

Once, however, early in the morning, the lines miraculously were clear.

I was stunned into silence when I heard his voice.

"Hello." He jiggled the receiver. "Hel-*lo!*" He sounded annoyed.

"It's Ruth."

"Oh." There was a long pause. "How are you?" Obviously there was someone with him.

"I'm calling about the orange grove. I wondered whether you were seriously interested."

After a moment he said, "I am. I'm very seriously interested."

"Well—that's good. Because I—am too."

"I'd like to come to Bucharest. To discuss the matter further."

"When?" The word burst out. I was embarrassed at the eagerness in my voice.

"When would be convenient for you?" Stefan said.

"I don't know. I'll try to be free whenever you can come."

"All right. I'll be at the Ambasador Hotel on Monday night. Can you call me there after nine o'clock?"

"Yes. And Stefan. It won't be like the last nine o'clock."

"Fine," he said formally. "I think we'll be able to do some business. Until Monday then." And he hung up.

To do some business. If any other man had said these words I would have found them gross, repugnant. The words, said by Stefan, sent an urgency pulsing through me.

In the sweltering phone booth I closed my eyes. I was in his room at the Ambasador Hotel. I emerged from the bath fresh and powdered and he was waiting. .

"I've been waiting like this," he said. "All of me, ever since I left you."

I went out of the phone booth, through the hotel lobby, into the street.

The morning sun was bright in my eyes. I walked along, filled with the sound of his voice. *Until Monday then. Until Monday then* . . .

A car horn blasted.

As I jumped back I felt the wind of the speeding automobile brush against me. I saw the angry shouting face of the driver.

I stood on the sidewalk, trembling inside.

I had not even realized that I had stepped off the curb, into the traffic. Mooning along about Stefan, I had almost been killed.

The shock brought chill reality.

You must give up your personal life. I remembered the words, the warning spoken by Eliahu Golomb in the Café Storch on that morning which now seemed so far away. It had been easy then, to agree. My husband and I had so little personal life.

Give up your personal life. I had accepted. And now I must obey.

The words had been a warning. Now they were a command. One I fully understood. This mission demanded everything that was in me. All my time. All my strength. All my wits. A single mistake could mean disaster for the entire *Tiger Hill* operation. And it was obvious that mistakes could be made all too easily if one were hung over with last night's love. If one were embroiled in a personal turmoil.

An affair woven of fantasies, long-distance love-making, lonely reveries; yes, with this I could cope. But to take it any further . . .

I was afraid. He was coming to the Ambasador Hotel on Monday night. And I was afraid.

Why had I made that telephone call? It had been some sort of reflex action; a stupidity left over from a love affair which might have been, in another life.

Should I phone him again, tell him that I might be out of town? Should I write him, trying to explain? But he had made it very clear that he did not want personal letters. Furthermore, there was nothing about the Mossad that I could put onto paper. And only an explanation of this mission could make him understand.

Perhaps it was best that he was coming. I could explain then why I was in Bucharest; what I was involved in. And why I could not allow myself the full luxury of being a woman in love.

For the first time in weeks I tried to reserve a few hours which would belong to me rather than the Mossad. I asked Kadmon whether I might attend to some personal business on Monday night.

Kadmon said abruptly, "Is he coming here?"

I looked at him, startled. "Is who coming?"

"Who? Who knows who? The man who sends you flowers."

We were close, Kadmon and I. Not only because we were together for hours each day. But because we complemented each other, worked well together. Yet, never in all the days and nights we spent in each other's company had we discussed anything of a deeply personal nature. He had never been in my room; had never seen the vases of flowers.

"Of course I know," Kadmon said. "You're my assistant. And you're still, I may tell you, on trial here. It's my duty to know what you're up to."

Up to! Anger shot through me. Did he think he owned me body and soul?

"Look," I managed to say quite calmly, "I am not—up to anything at all. The man happens to be an excellent contact. He's wealthy, influential. He may turn out to be another George Mandel."

"I forbid you," Kadmon announced ponderously, "to tell him anything about our operation. I decide who our contacts are to be. And how much they are to be told."

"I'm aware of that," I said.

Kadmon lit a cigar. "All right," he said. "I will meet him with you on Monday night. We'll invite the gentleman to dinner. I will judge how helpful he may be."

TWELVE

As IT TURNED OUT, however, neither Kadmon nor I met Stefan Meta
for dinner on Monday night.

There was, instead, another meeting.

A coded cable had arrived late Monday afternoon from Palestine.

YULIK INSISTING HIS FAMILY ALONE FILL ENTIRE WEDDING
SUPPER TABLE STOP ESSENTIAL YOU DECIDE GUEST LIST
IMMEDIATELY STOP PLEASE ADVISE HOW FAR CONSTRUC-
TION ON NEW HOUSE HAS PROGRESSED STOP WHAT IS SIT-
UATION RE MEMBERS OF EHUD'S AND PINO'S FAMILY AND
YOUR OWN.

It was urgent that we determine the passenger list of the *Tiger Hill*,
a list composed not of names but of nationalities. From which countries
would our illegals come?

Zvi Shechter was scheduled to arrive from Geneva that evening.
Kadmon left a message at his hotel asking that Zvi join us immediately
for the meeting at Orekhovsky's office.

It was a meeting which might have taken place in some subchamber
of hell. The setting instead was a spacious room in the Zionist Building on Strada Anton Pan. The building had once been a luxurious
mansion. But now the bedrooms, the salons, drawing rooms, ballroom,
even the oversized bathrooms had been converted into offices; local
headquarters of Zionist groups and political parties in Palestine. Their

names were on plaques, in Hebrew and Rumanian, by the huge front door. The only impressive plaque, brass and highly polished, was that which read "Jewish Agency and Palestine Office." The others were wooden or tin. Some had been turned upside down or scribbled over by children of the street. The Zionist Organization of Rumania. The Zionist Women's Organization, WIZO. The General Zionist Party. And others, their names rain washed and now scarcely legible.

Kadmon and I climbed to the mezzanine floor in silence. It was after hours.

Usually this stairway was crowded with sound and motion. Young men and women rushing up and down, shouting out to each other in Rumanian, Hebrew, Yiddish, German, Polish, Russian. On the streets outside they were silent, were strangers. But this building was theirs. They had written their names on the once-white walls in crayon and pencil and pen; had carved their initials on the banisters. They wanted to leave their mark. Here they would be remembered.

As Kadmon and I walked down the dimly lit corridor, I felt wracked and ashamed to find myself thinking of Stefan.

I was entering a meeting where a few men would sit for a few hours, playing God. These we will rescue. This number. This nationality. Those must wait for another ship, another chance. Or perhaps for death.

I was walking down a corridor to such a meeting and part of my mind was concerned with Stefan's reaction to the letter I had left in his box at the Ambasador Hotel. A letter written in haste; some words about an important meeting. Unavoidable. I would phone when it was over.

It was unforgivable, degrading to be caught in an emotional morass when I was on a mission like this one.

Palestine Office. The name had been freshly painted in defiant black letters.

Kadmon shoved open the door, strode in before me.

Orekhovsky was alone, watering his plants. He looked up, nodded, said nothing. And kept on with his watering. Small innocuous-looking plants set out on a shelf by the french windows and along his desk.

The desk was the only impressive piece of furniture in the room.

There were also many chairs, of all denominations: straw-seated, leather-covered, straight-backed kitchen chairs.

Kadmon and I sat down.

"They're doing nicely," Kadmon remarked after a moment.

"The plants, yes," Orekhovsky said. "They grow well. Especially when they're by the window for the afternoon sunlight. I rotate them. Each plant gets a week by the window."

He took his seat behind his writing desk. "Have you heard yet from Ehud?"

Kadmon shook his head.

The door opened. Zvi Shechter entered the room and the oppressive silence fled.

Zvi seemed always to bring a crowd with him, even when he came alone. There was much clapping of backs, shaking of hands. And he embraced me in a hard bear hug. "Well, how is the little sister?"

He was the same effusive young pioneer who had, at seventeen, sat at our kitchen table with my brother Poli as they made plans for the new Zionist youth camp they had organized for the district. *Hashomer Hatzair* they called it. The Young Watchmen.

He was as handsome and impeccably dressed as always. He had just come from the station, he announced, as he settled in the only armchair, his legs stretched long before him. Anyone else, after a twelve-hour train ride from Switzerland, would have looked rumpled, grimy. But Zvi Shechter seemed to shine. His white shirt, open at the throat, had surely come straight from the laundry. His well-polished shoes fairly gleamed. His hair was combed into neat waves. Poli had told me once that every morning after his shower Zvi combed in his waves carefully with Brilliantine, and then wore a hair net for a half hour while the waves set and dried.

This self-centered young dandy, son of an affluent textile manufacturer, had always seemed a strange candidate for a Zionist youth leader. Yet, he had a magnetism, a dynamism about him and a sincerity which drew forth respect and followers. He and Poli had left for Palestine, with legal certificates, in the late 1920s. And each had helped to establish a new kibbutz.

Zvi was an opposite of my quiet and modest brother. Yet, being with him now filled me with the presence of Poli and I felt a wrenching homesickness for my brother and for the closeness we had known until I came on this mission to Bucharest.

"How's Poli?" Zvi Shechter demanded.

And I had to confess that I did not know. We had not written, not after the first few letters. There was so little that I could say. And Poli seemed to understand.

"And how's Emmanuel?"

Again I shrugged one shoulder.

Kadmon cut in. "She's been a little too busy for keeping up on her correspondence."

"Am I late? Apologies." Meir Cotic had entered, the lawyer of the Palestine Office. And the unofficial legal adviser of the Mossad. His particular speciality was an essential one: bribing authorities.

Cotic was a suave and elegant bon vivant. He knew his way around women. And with the same natural ease he could turn a phrase in a manner which suggested that a sum of money might be forthcoming if Monsieur would only sign the proper paper or look the other way. If, however, Monsieur was not about to comply, Cotic was adept at covering up any imagined implications.

Abruptly the meeting began.

In a garish twist of conversation we turned from local gossip to a discussion of cyphers and doom.

Which Jews from which countries should be rescued on the *Tiger Hill?*

Orekhovsky, sitting behind his fine mahogany writing desk, suddenly became an imperious figure, speaking with flame in his words.

The passengers must come from Rumania. There were many reasons. There would be no borders to cross, no risks of capture. The Rumanian Jews could be easily organized; taken by bus, car, train in groups of twos, threes and tens to the port of Constantza, from which the ship would sail. There would be far less expense involved; far fewer people to bribe. And secrecy would be almost assured, for we could appeal to an inverted patriotism. Railroad and port officials would be helping to cleanse their country of "Jewish scum."

"Fine," Zvi Shechter said. "Very neat. Very practical. But suppose you were a Jew in Berlin now?"

"Unfortunately," Cotic cut in, "we *must* be practical. Not emotional.

Naturally, if we could rescue a thousand German Jews for the same risks. And the same price—"

"Price!" Zvi exploded. "Are we in the meat business? Save so much per pound?"

"It's fine to talk," Cotic said, "when you have money to back your words. We have no money! My friend, we have *no money* to lay a pathway of bribes from border to border."

"We've found money before," I said. "When we had none. We contracted for the *Tiger Hill* when we had nothing even for the down payment."

Zvi turned to Kadmon. "How many Czechs have we carried on our ships? Any at all? I suggest we turn our efforts to organizing a transport of Czech Jews to sail on the *Tiger Hill*. They're in as much danger now as Jews in Germany or Austria. Eichmann arrived in Prague last week. He's already set up his Central Office for Jewish Emigration in Prague. He's sitting there in a fine big suite in the Jewish Community Council Building. Seventy thousand Jews, he announces, must emigrate this year. And to encourage the process he'll take three hundred Jews a day, street by street, and send them to Dachau, where, he says, they will soon become very keen on emigration.

"But, one small problem. How are they to emigrate? They must pay their way out of the country. With what? Jewish bank accounts have been frozen. Jewish businesses have been seized. Jewish workers have been fired. And now, with the new flood of refugees from Austria and the Sudetenland, the Jewish population of the Bohemia-Moravia area alone is well over one hundred and twenty thousand. Well, maybe we can save a thousand of them on the *Tiger Hill*. It's easier, after all, than trying to get Jews out of Austria or Germany. The Czech border is closer to Rumania. And since the country has only been part of the Reich for four months, perhaps the borders are not that well patrolled as yet and—"

Kadmon broke in. "Perhaps! Perhaps! Our ship sails on the first of August. We have no time for perhaps. Yulik has already organized a contingent from Poland. You speak of numbers. Czechoslovakia may now have a Jewish population of three hundred thousand. Poland has a Jewish population of three million three hundred thousand. The largest and the most concentrated population of Jews in Western Europe. This one statistic may be reason enough for Hitler to turn next on Poland. Think of all the Jews he could eradicate from the earth by the bombing of Warsaw alone. No bother about setting up Central Offices of Emigration. No need to trouble *Untersturmführer* Eichmann. Or Heydrich. Or the Gestapo. Let the handsome young boys of the air force do it. Quickly. Legally. Acceptably. With bombs."

"If you talk of statistics," Cotic said, "I remind you that there are more Jews right here in Rumania than in any other country except Poland. Seven hundred and fifty thousand Jews. And Hitler doesn't need to risk a world war. And Eichmann or Heydrich don't need to cross any borders. Our Jews don't need to wait for invasion. We've got our own home-grown Gestapo. There's a lot of dangerous feeling right now in the towns and villages of Bessarabia and Bucovina."

"I second that," said Orekhovsky grimly. "And I would like to make a further point. It can come any time. And it can come overnight. Remember, Hitler himself wrote in *Mein Kampf:* 'In 1918 there was no such thing as systematic anti-Semitism in Germany.' But, my friends, as we all well know, there has always been such a thing as systematic anti-Semitism in Rumania. When I was a boy of six I learned about it. There was a pogrom in our town. A small one. I was in school. I didn't even know it was going on. They hung my mother from a tree in our back yard. When I came home and saw her I thought she had invented a new kind of game, a new kind of swing. I ran to her, laughing. Then I saw that she was dead." He nodded. "As I say, here in Rumania it can come so very quickly."

Kadmon relit his cigar. Orekhovsky broke a yellow leaf from the geranium plant on the desk before him.

After a long moment I said, "Perhaps we can in some way—compromise. Take refugees who have already made their way to Rumania. From Germany, Austria, Czechoslovakia. Yes, the danger here can come overnight. But for these refugees caught here without papers, without visas—for them the danger would be doubled. And if we took people already in Rumania we wouldn't run the risk of border crossings. And we'd still be—"

"We'd be what?" Zvi turned on me. He was like a stranger. His eyes burned. His words burned. "We'd be safe. We wouldn't run risk. Is that what we're here for? To stay clear of risks? *The degree of danger!*" His fist hammered against the arm of his chair. "The degree of danger." His words hammered against the walls of the room. "That's the prime principle they go by when they distribute *legal* certificates. The degree of danger the Jews of each community face. I suggest we accept that principle too.

"Jews who've already escaped to Rumania, they're months away and miles away from the camps. The Jews in Germany, Austria, Czechoslovakia are a knock on the door away. A pistol butt away. These are the Jews we must get onto the *Tiger Hill.*"

Kadmon raised a hand, placating. "My friend, we all agree with you. But if we save space for, let us say, five hundred of those in the greatest danger, and we can't get them out—what happens to that empty space?"

"*Then,*" Zvi burst out, "then we take refugees already here in Rumania."

"But it requires time," Kadmon said, "to get false papers, photographs. Every illegal on our ship must have a visa. With his photograph on it. This can't be arranged in the last few minutes. Remember, the ship sails in twenty-one days."

Zvi sat down. "The hell with it," he said. "You know all the answers. You decide."

We stayed in that room until close to midnight. Case histories were spread out like corpses on the table. New accounts were given of new horrors being perpetrated on Jews in the Greater German Reich. New prognostications were made about the fate of Jews in Rumania and Poland.

Finally, Kadmon looked at his watch. It was time for the telephone calls from the haverim. He shoved himself to his feet. "We must go."

"I would like to make an official motion," Zvi said quickly. "I move that *habchira*—the choosing—should be determined by a single principle: the degree of danger. I move that we reserve all space on the ship for seven days. Reserve it for Jews from the Reich. After that time if we have no success, we will meet again—for further decisions."

I nodded. Kadmon shrugged. Orekhovsky stared at a potted plant on his desk. Cotic wiped his hand over his mouth and chin. And in this manner Zvi Shechter's motion was carried.

I followed Kadmon down the dimly lit stairway.

Pino's family. Ehud's family. They would be the honored guests at the wedding supper. If they were able to attend.

Ehud's family. We had placed a call to Ehud Uiberall every night for a month. The only response had been the buzzing sound of the telephone ringing over and over into an empty room.

THIRTEEN

WE WALKED BACK to the Continental. Or, to be more accurate, Kadmon strode, I half ran. It was the way we held many conferences, on the city streets, hurrying between one meeting and another.

On a tram, in a taxi we could not talk. But in the streets our conversations went unheard, and the minutes between meetings went unwasted. Or so Kadmon chose to believe.

He had no sense of time or distance. "Come," he would say. "It's a few blocks from here. It's quicker to walk." The few blocks would turn out to be a good mile. And I generally had to break into an awkward lope to keep up with him.

"It's incredible!" he said now as we hurried along the street. "The few of us there in that room, and the handful of others, our so-called network—of ten! Ten of us, covering eight countries. We are the largest single rescue operation in the world today. Working to save Jews. Where are the others?" He stopped suddenly, turned to me, and he almost shouted the words. *"Where are the others?"*

An elderly gentleman passing on the street gave us a strange look.

"He's drunk, monsieur," I said swiftly in French. "Pay no attention." We walked on then in silence.

Kadmon was the calm, the contained one among us. *Hacham* I often called him. It meant, in Hebrew, the elder statesman, the wise one. His way was careful, plodding; he gave meticulous consideration to every detail. He had a streak of cautiousness which often seemed to me uncalled for. That this man should stop in the street and shout words indicated only how enraged he had become during the meeting in Orekhovsky's office.

I understood this anger, for I felt it often enough myself. A flailing, all-encompassing, impotent fury directed helplessly against the entire world.

When we returned to Kadmon's room we found Alexander ensconced in the armchair, his feet on the velvet-covered settee, reading *The Times* of London.

Kadmon locked the door. "Any calls yet?"

Alexander shook his head. He held up the paper. "Here's an interesting item. Dated June eighth. Two patrol boats are being built at a cost to the British taxpayer of fifteen thousand pounds each. For use off the coast of Palestine. Two fine new high-powered patrol boats. To track down our ancient illegal tubs."

The telephone rang.

"That should be Yulik," Kadmon said. "He knew we were meeting tonight."

He sat down by the phone, lifted the receiver. There was the shrill voice of the long-distance operator. Even from where I stood across the room I could hear the single word: "Vienna."

Kadmon closed his eyes briefly.

Vienna. Ehud Uiberall. The call for which we had waited all these weeks.

Or was it one of Ehud's locals finally getting through to inform us that our haver was in a concentration camp? Or was dead.

I prayed often these days. Prayed in the same fleeting way that we held conferences while rushing along a city street. Please God, let this negotiation go through. Please God, grant that this man may be charitable.

Now it seemed that my whole being turned into one mighty prayer. Let it be Ehud on the line. Well and safe.

All of the other haverim I knew at least from telephone conversations, from coded letters and cables. And an unshatterable unity had grown up among us. Indeed, these men seemed closer to me now than my own family. In this strange, perilous limbo world in which we lived they *were* my family.

But of Ehud I knew very little.

Once, while we were waiting for a call to be put through to Vienna, Alexander had remarked, almost wistfully, "He is, I suppose, the most charming fellow I've ever met."

I had built for myself from such random remarks a vivid picture of Ehud. And as we waited now for the line from Vienna to be cleared, I had the agonizing sense that I waited to hear the fate of my brother.

Suddenly Kadmon sat up straight. His face went pale. He said in Hebrew, "It is you, then."

I stood where I was, frozen. Alexander leaned forward in the armchair. Ehud was alive. We could tell little more from the few Hebrew sentences Kadmon spoke. The man at the other end seemed to be talking nonstop as though afraid he might at any minute be interrupted.

Kadmon said some brief coded sentences about the *Tiger Hill* and the meeting we had just held. "We'll reserve seats for your family at the wedding supper. But can you let us know within a week how many will attend? After all, the wedding takes place on August first. We won't have much time if we're going to send out other invitations."

This time Ehud's answer was brief. And within moments Kadmon hung up.

He sat there. He stared at the opposite wall.

Then he began to laugh. "Do you know where he—" the words were caught up in laughter. "Do you know whose phone he was speaking from? The phone of his friend—the anti-Semitic ambassador from Slovakia!"

This did not seem so uproariously funny. Alexander and I waited while the bursts of laughter—an explosion of relief—lessened, then came under control.

"Well," Kadmon said finally, "he's managed to stay out of prison. He and his few local boys have been organizing a transport to go through Yugoslavia to the Adriatic. He hasn't contacted us or anyone on the outside since early June. For the simple reason that whoever controls foreign calls from Vienna has made it impossible. Whenever he tried to get through—no matter what number he asked for—no matter whom he said he was calling—no matter what name he gave for himself—the answer was always the same. The line was out of order.

"He tried every trick he could think of. Every contact he had. Then, last week he met, of all people, the ambassador from Slovakia.* The Slovak ambassador is new, inexperienced, and, says Ehud, the embassy in Vienna is rather hungry. So he gave the ambassador an—inducement. And as a result he was phoning from the privacy of His Excellency's office. Probably," Kadmon added, "the most expensive telephone call Ehud has ever made. The ambassador has no love for Jews. He required quite a substantial sum for the use of his phone."

Silence spread through the room. The silence of relief.

Other calls came through then. One from Yulik, in Warsaw. His family, he insisted, was a large one. Everything had been arranged. They were very eager to attend the wedding supper. When would the invitations be sent out?

"In a week," Kadmon told him.

Pino, in Berlin, had managed to get a call through to Geneva. Zvi Shechter's local was covering the phone there. It was he who reported that Pino wished to reserve eighteen places at the banquet table. How would Pino's family be traveling to the wedding? Through which route would they come? The local in Geneva could answer no questions. He had been told only one simple sentence. Eighteen places. The lives of eighteen German Jews might be saved.

There were calls from Sofia, from Greece, from Istanbul, from Paris. Then there were the inevitable lists, records, details concerning the *Tiger Hill* to be gone over with Kadmon. It was three in the morning by the time I got back to the Ambasador Hotel, exhausted. I craved only one thing: sleep.

The lobby was empty, except for the concierge at the desk and a man who sat in an armchair by the elevator, reading the paper.

As I approached he stood up and came toward me. It was Stefan.

I felt, inexplicably, angry. I had wanted to be prepared for this meeting. Even though it would end what had never truly begun, I wanted

* When Germany overran Czechoslovakia, the new nation of Slovakia was created as a so-called "independent" state.

at least to look presentable. And here I was bedraggled, weary, hair uncombed. I had not even washed my face for hours.

He seemed as withdrawn as I felt. He merely nodded at me, waited while I got my mail from the box, followed me into the elevator. And got out with me at my floor.

"I'm sorry," I said, as we walked down the carpeted hallway.

"I echo your sentiments."

"Were you waiting in the lobby very long?"

"Since midnight."

"You shouldn't have."

"I wanted to see what time you came in. And who you came in with."

I said nothing.

"This is a strange assignment you're on. Were you out selling land in Palestine until three o'clock in the morning?"

"That often happens," I said. "There are dinner parties. In wealthy homes."

"You went to a dinner party in a skirt and blouse?"

I opened my pocketbook, found the room key. He took it from me and unlocked the door. We entered, and for a long moment stood in the dark room, saying nothing.

Stefan closed the door.

I switched on the bed-table lamp.

"Well," he said, "what have they given you here? A broom closet with a bed?"

"It's big enough for my purposes."

"Not for mine."

I went to the sink, wet one of the stiffly starched towels, wiped it over my face.

He sat on the bed. "I gather your organization is strapped for funds. Otherwise they'd do better by you."

I didn't answer.

"Perhaps they could do with a donation?"

"Yes. They could."

"I don't suppose I could specify as to how I would want my funds allocated?"

"No."

He stood up, came over to me. "What *are* you involved in? Why don't you tell me what you're really doing here?"

"I have told you."

"That may be part of it. Is it all of it?"

"Maybe you'll meet the man I work with. He'll answer your questions."

Suddenly he said, "If you knew how I've missed you." He took my hands and drew me to him. "Oh, my God," he whispered. He held me hard against him.

My weariness evaporated. My arms went around his neck. I said something. Where did the words come from? "Why did you wait so long? Why didn't you come here before?"

"Because I wanted to so much." He started walking me backward toward the bed.

"No." I broke away from him. "We can't. Don't you know that?"

"We must. Don't you know that?"

"I can't."

After a long moment he said, "Because of my wife?"

I nodded. "And because of—me. Don't you understand? I would love you too much. I would need you too much. I couldn't—function."

"If I said I would leave my wife?"

I came to him. I put my hand over his mouth. "Don't ever say that. Don't ever say that again."

He kissed my fingers as they pressed against his lips. Then his arms went around me again.

I began to tremble. He held me tighter. "Hush, little one," he whispered. "Hush."

And then, for no reason, or for every reason, I started to cry.

He sat on the bed, pulled me onto his knees. "Look," he said, and he kissed me gently on the cheeks, on my nose, on my lips. "I didn't come all this way to make you cry. Look, my little love, I'll be in Bucharest for a few days. What you need now, from the looks of you, is some sleep. We don't have to settle all our problems at three o'clock in the morning." He wiped tears from my cheeks with his fingertips. And he held me, rocking me a little, murmuring love words, until I almost fell asleep in his arms.

He reached down and took off my shoes. Then he slid me off his lap onto the bed and he covered me with the sheet. "I order you to go straight to sleep," he said. "Don't even get up to undress. Or wash. I want you to be fresh for tomorrow."

I looked up at him as he leaned above me. I felt about three years old. "What's happening tomorrow?"

"I'm taking you to dinner and the theatre."

He leaned over and kissed me gently. The three-year-old within me fled. I wanted to slide my arms again around his neck, to draw him down to the bed with me. But I managed somehow to lie still.

"I'd invite you for breakfast tomorrow," he said. "But I prefer that you sleep late. Tomorrow night you just might not sleep at all."

He went to the door. "I'll call for you at seven tomorrow evening. Good night, little one."

I heard the door close behind him.

Presently I got up and turned the key in the lock. "Doors have locks," Kadmon had told me once. "Get into the habit of using them. Always."

I changed into a nightgown, brushed my teeth, got back into bed, and yearned for Stefan as I had during the dark hours of many lonely nights.

The phone was on a small table by the bed. It would be so simple.

Connect me with Stefan Meta, please. . . . Hello. I was wondering whether you have a nice room. Whether you'd like me to come and say good night, properly. . . .

In the midst of my imaginings I fell asleep.

The next day was as frantic and crowded as all the other days and nights we had spent on the *Tiger Hill*. Kadmon told me at four o'clock that he had set up a date for me to have dinner with an official at the Panamanian Embassy. Subject: the purchase of Panamanian visas for our *Tiger Hill* illegals. Such meetings, he informed me with a rare display of his clumsy humor, were best held at mealtimes, since the most crucial part of the transactions would be under the table.

"Sometimes," he added, "such negotiations take time. Try to show up for the telephone calls at midnight. On the other hand, if you're not there, I'll understand."

As I started to leave the room he said suddenly, "By the way, whatever happened to your friend? Did he come to town on Monday?"

"Oh," I said a bit blankly. "I believe he'll be here tomorrow, if you'd like to meet him."

Kadmon consulted his small diary which he kept in an undecipherable code consisting mainly of illegibility and Hebrew letters. "Tomorrow at three-thirty. We can meet downstairs in the lobby."

I nodded. "I'll ask him when he gets in. He also is busy. I'll let you know if he can make it."

I phoned Stefan at the Ambasador.

Yes, he would be delighted to meet my superior the following day. If Kadmon accepted him! If he became a member of the Mossad! If Stefan and I were working together! I interrupted my own flood of fantasies by informing Stefan that I would not be able to see him for dinner. But I would, I added hastily, meet him at the theatre.

"I refuse," he said, "to accept your apologies. I have reservations at the Luzana. A table for two in the garden. Flowers. Lanterns. Gypsy violinists. What could be more important than that?"

"Please, Stefan," I said softly. "I can't. So don't go on about it."

At length he said, "All right. Meet me in front of the Baraseum Theatre. At eight-thirty. Sidy Tal is playing."

"Till eight-thirty," I said. And I hung up quickly.

The dinner meeting with the Panamanian went well. But I wondered uneasily whether he would retract his promises when I announced that I must leave early.

At eight o'clock I glanced casually at my watch, and gasped. "I'm terribly sorry! I had no idea the time was going so fast. I have an appointment. I must leave this minute."

My escort seemed distinctly vexed. It was obvious he expected payments other than those specified in our verbal contracts. But almost at once he assumed a gracious veneer. "Perhaps you will allow me to invite you again? When you have more time."

"I would be delighted."

"And perhaps at that meeting we need not confine ourselves to details of business."

Business. It was as good a word as any for *baksheesh*. Bribes.

He finished his cognac, paid the bill, escorted me to a cab. "My driver is off tonight," he apologized. "Otherwise I'd drop you in my car."

I imagined that his driver was off every night. An official of his rank would not have a chauffeur and car.

I thanked him profusely, climbed into the cab, waved to him. He had promised me one thousand Panamanian visas. On the strict understanding that they would never be used for attempted entry to Panama. And at a cost of one hundred pounds sterling per visa.

I got out of the taxi at the Calea Văcăreşti, several blocks from the theatre. It was another of Kadmon's directives. When traveling in a public conveyance, never go straight to your destination.

I hurried down the street to the theatre. As I turned the corner the name "Sidy Tal" blazoned out in colored lights from the marquee. Huge likenesses of the actress smiled from placards as I reached the entrance.

Stefan was waiting in the empty lobby.

"You're late," he said, taking my arm. "I'll have to train you better than this." He opened the door to the theatre darkness. An usher protested in loud whispers that we could not be seated until the act was over. Stefan reached into his pocket. And within moments we were escorted to our places, second row center.

It was strange, sitting next to him in the dark. I could barely concentrate on the musical, though it was dramatic enough—about a girl who wanted to escape from her bourgeois Jewish upbringing. She ran off with a South American dandy, who sold her as a white slave. The setting was the early twenties, and it was reputed to be a true story. But it seemed a lugubrious fairy tale. And more insistent than any impassioned words sung by the destitute girl on the stage was the simple sentence which Stefan had spoken last night. *Sleep well. Tomorrow night you may not sleep at all.* This was the chorus, the refrain, the motif which echoed through me as I tried dutifully to concentrate on the famous Yiddish operetta.

At intermission, Stefan said, "Look, I can tell you the rest of the story when we're back in the room. Shall we go?"

"Is the ending happy?"

"Always," he said.

"That's all I really need to know."

There was a *trăsură* waiting. We climbed in. And as the driver clucked to his horse, Stefan put both arms around me. I leaned forward. "You're very indiscreet," I told him. "Suppose some friend of your wife should be walking down the street."

"I have no wife," Stefan said. "Didn't you know that? I'm in love with a girl who has green eyes which are wise and sad. Because she comes from an old rabbinical family. *Two* old rabbinical families."

"She sounds dreadful. Like someone out of an old Yiddish operetta."

"She's not quite real," he said. "That's true. But I may succeed in changing all that."

I tried to bring the conversation back to a realm of sanity. "My superior has given me permission to write my brother David that I've been sent to Bucharest. To sell land."

"Your superior is most generous."

"He said this in case someone from Czernowitz should happen to see me here. And report back home—"

"So what am *I* to report to David? That his sister and I shared a hotel room on Tuesday night? That I am insanely in love with her? That I made a valiant effort to stay away from her? But I have ceased being valiant. Life is too short and too hard and too unpredictable for such amenities."

"Tell David that you happened to run into me in a bank in Bucharest. That I'm well and working hard. That I'll be seeing them soon. And that you took me to see a performance of *The Drunkard* on Tuesday night."

I wanted this carriage ride to go on and on. This lovely limbo time with the clacking of horses' hoofs . . . the soft light of the street lamps . . . snatches of lives framed behind the bright oblongs of open windows . . . people strolling on the sidewalks, sometimes laughing. The summer nighttime of the city. And Stefan holding my hand.

When we reached the hotel, it would end. Then, somehow and somewhere I would have to make him understand.

Where would we go to talk? In the hotel restaurant? Or his room?

Not in his room. If I went there I would be defeated before I started. All my sound arguments silenced by the waiting bed.

"Stefan," I said, "could we stop somewhere?"

"For what?" Stefan said.

"An after-theatre supper. Something of that sort."

"I've ordered an after-theatre supper," Stefan said. "The champagne should be cooling right now in my room."

Stefan, if you love me you must not make love to me. How could I convince him of the logic in this? There was no logic. A man and a woman in love must make love. That was the simple human logic. Could we be together and then in the morning walk away from each other? He could, perhaps. Could I?

We reached the Ambasador. Stefan paid the driver. We walked together into the hotel.

. . . Separate rooms and separate lives . . .

It would not be a casual affair. For me, anyway, it would be consuming. I don't belong to myself right now. So I can't belong to you . . .

Stefan, in the world as it is today you too must be free—without divided loyalties. Free to go where is best, free to do what is best for your family. For your children.

I had said these words over so often, to myself. Now I must say them aloud. To Stefan.

We crossed the lobby and I stopped at the desk; asked for my key and messages. Solomonides had called and Kadmon.

There were four messages in Stefan's box. "From your wife, sir," the concierge said. "She telephoned four times. And this just came, sir. A telegram."

Stefan opened it. His face went pale.

He handed the telegram to me. "Viorica," he said, "is my daughter."

I looked down at the paper with the strips of words pasted on it. *Viorica seriously injured in automobile accident.*

Stefan glanced at the clock behind the desk. "I can still get the midnight train," he said.

He turned away from me and walked to the elevator.

I waited in the lobby. I wanted to be with him. To help him pack. To help him. But he had turned away from me.

When he came down with his suitcase, I went to him.

"Stefan—may I come to the station?"

"Yes," he said. "Please." But he spoke in a distant, formal manner. In the taxi we sat without speaking, like two strangers.

I wanted to reach him, to share his agony. But I did not know how.

When we reached the station Stefan said to me, "Why don't you keep the taxi? Then I won't have to worry about how you got home."

"No," I said, "I want to see you off."

But he shook his head. Then he paid the driver. "Take her back to the Ambasador Hotel," he said. He got out of the cab, closed the door.

As the taxi started off I saw Stefan walking quickly with his suitcase toward the entrance to the station.

FOURTEEN

I DID NOT HEAR from Stefan for almost a week.

I wanted to call, to cable, to write. But I did not dare. Was his daughter dead? I had visions of the girl lying under the wheels of an automobile. I remembered her face from the photograph Stefan had shown me as we stood by the lake. The beautiful girl with light hair which fell long over her shoulders. I remembered the words Stefan had said then. *I may as well tell you, I love her very much.*

Why didn't he contact me? Was it guilt? Did he feel in some suppressed way, as I did, that his daughter's accident might be some form of retribution?

Then, late on Tuesday night, six days after he had left Bucharest, his call came.

I was working at the small vanity table which served as my desk; a table covered now with papers, lists, charts, notes, names. For tomorrow we were to make the final decision. Who was to sail on the *Tiger Hill.* From which countries our new immigrants would come.

When the telephone rang I picked it up, expecting to hear Kadmon's voice. He had promised to notify me as to the time and place of the meeting.

The operator said, "A call, mademoiselle, from Czernowitz. Hold on."

I felt suddenly empty. When he spoke I could not answer for a moment.

"Hello," he said again. "Ruth? Can you hear me?"

"How is she?"

"She'll recover."

"Thank God," I said, so softly that my words could never have carried across the wires.

"She may be able to walk again," he said.

What was there to answer to that?

Words filled me. But I could only speak with silence.

At last he said, "I'm sorry I haven't called before. Forgive me."

"Of course," I whispered.

"I won't be able to get to Bucharest for a while. I go to the hospital every day."

"Yes. I understand."

Then he said, "Perhaps you'll be coming to Czernowitz one of these days to see your family."

"Perhaps."

The line went dead.

I said, "Hello, hello," several times. But I knew he was gone. Then I said, "Good-by, my love." And I hung up.

Several minutes later the phone rang again.

He had been cut off! He was calling again.

It was Kadmon.

"The meeting," he said, "will be in your room. At three o'clock tomorrow afternoon."

It was an incongruous setting for such a meeting.

Orekhovsky's pale face was reflected in the gold-framed mirror which hung above my vanity table. Kadmon sat on the narrow bed with its elegant dark blue velvet spread; sat smoking his cigar like a business-man at a board meeting.

Cotic perched on my bulky brown suitcase. Behind him was a framed watercolor of a boy by a stream, fishing.

The room was wallpapered in pink. The decor was gilt trimmed. Sunlight flickered against the hanging crystal drops of the chandelier. And we sat in this small confine of elegance, making the final decision about which lives to save.

"All right," said Kadmon heavily, "we have abided by the motion passed and carried at our last meeting. We have waited for seven days. Naturally, we all hoped we could fill our ship with Jews from the Reich. Pino had a plan. But it's fallen through. As for Ehud—" he shrugged. "We haven't been able to contact him again. However—" he exhaled the cigar smoke slowly. "We have heard twice a day from Yulik Braginski. He has his five hundred and one halutzim packed and ready to go. They're waiting right now in hotels in the suburbs of Warsaw. He's even leased a special train to take them from Warsaw to Constantza."

"On whose authority did he do this?" Cotic burst out.

"Look," said Kadmon, "if each of us waited for someone else's authority, nothing would get done. As Shmarya once put it: The Mossad is an orchestra in which each of us is a soloist."

"Look here," Orekhovsky said abruptly. "We can still stick to the motion we made: choose our passengers by the degree of danger they're in. The Poles at least have papers. They belong somewhere. In my files I have hundreds of refugees from Germany, Austria, Czechoslovakia. They've managed to make their way here. But they have no papers. Every day they live in fear of being sent back. We must take these refugees from the Reich. The ones who belong nowhere. Who belong to nothing. Except the human race. Which doesn't seem to count for much these days."

"You forget one small factor, my friend." Kadmon tapped his cigar ash into the ashtray. "We have no time to round up eight hundred individual refugees. To get each one a transit visa. A false passport. A Panamanian visa. The hard fact is that the bulk of our passengers must come from one large organized group. For a while there it looked as though Pino could get a few hundred out. But instead the figure turned to eighteen." He leaned forward. The stolid businessman mien disappeared. "Look, if we take the Poles, the *Tiger Hill* can sail on schedule. And if she doesn't sail on schedule, she may not sail at all."

He glanced at me. For my vote? I nodded agreement. I was convinced that the Polish Jews were in greater peril than the Jews who had escaped across the borders of the Reich. True, these halutzim had papers. But papers would mean little once the Germans had marched into Poland. And this I was certain would happen in a matter of months.

Kadmon turned to Cotic, who also nodded. Then he wiped a handkerchief over his forehead and under his eyes. "Why did we meet here?" he demanded suddenly. "In this stifling little room."

"Because," said Kadmon, "the police were at the Continental this morning. Asking questions about Josef Barpal. I'm moving out when our conference here is over. In the meantime, this seemed the most likely place."

"All right," Orekhovsky announced loudly. "I agree. Take the five hundred and one Poles. But there's plenty of room left over. Who else do we take?"

"Well," said Kadmon, "it seems there are fifty-four Bulgarians. Ruth can report on the Bulgarians."

"So-called Bulgarians," I said. "They're from Russia. They're all halutzim. They were living in Bulgaria without papers. Without money. The first repairs on the *Tiger Hill* were made in Varna, and they got wind of the ship. They followed her when she was brought to Brăila. And they boarded the ship."

Orekhovsky exploded. "On whose authority?"

"On no one's authority," I said. "But they're living right now in the hold of the ship. Along with thirteen pioneers from Latvia. And fourteen from Lithuania. They've settled in. They have their committees going full blast."

"If I had informed *my* people!" Orekhovsky shouted, "they too would be settled in. If I had—"

"No one informed them," Kadmon said sharply. "They found out. Would you like the job of dislodging them? Eighty-one young Zionists. Idealistic. Well trained. They're needed in Palestine."

"Fine!" Orekhovsky jumped to his feet. "If this were a year ago. But times have changed, my friend. And the Mossad has got to change along with the times. Yulik's people are haverim too. All right. I can understand your logic there. A large group, already organized. But *these* people—to take up space which could be allotted to desperate refugees—"

"Look," Kadmon cut in. "If we take the Poles, plus the eighteen from Berlin, plus the youngsters already aboard, that still leaves one hundred and sixty places to be filled. I submit, my friend, that with the little time we've got left, and with all the work to be done, you'd be hard put to cope with more than that number in any case. How about it? You can choose the remaining one hundred sixty from your files."

Orekhovsky sat down. He said nothing.

"So." Kadmon tapped out the glow of his cigar. "I take it we're all in agreement." He returned the cigar to his breast pocket, where several more were lined up like small sentinels. "By the way," he extracted a clipping from the cigar pocket, "I thought this might interest you." He unfolded the paper carefully. "It's dated July twentieth. Excerpts from a speech made by the Colonial Secretary. His report before the House of Commons on illegal immigration into Palestine. I quote. 'Mr. MacDonald announced that in the past two months British patrol forces on land and sea had captured three thousand five hundred and seven illegal immigrants. Between five hundred and one thousand were thought to have entered the country undetected. And some four thousand intending illegal immigration were at this very time converging on Palestine in ships attempting to force their way into the country.'"

Cotic laughed bitterly. "Four thousand! I wish we could oblige by fulfilling his estimates."

Kadmon refolded the clipping, returned it to his pocket. "Unfortunately, the Colonial Secretary has every possibility of obtaining accurate reports for one of those figures. Three thousand five hundred and seven illegals have been captured by British patrol forces within the last two months."

The sailing date was only days away.

The *Tiger Hill*, fully provisioned, had been moved from Brăila to Constantza. A string of port authorities had been handsomely bribed to overlook her presence there. The refugees Orekhovsky had chosen were packed and ready to leave Bucharest. Others were already living in boarding houses in Constantza. And Yulik's five hundred and one haverim were about to board the transport he had leased to take them from Warsaw to the Rumanian port.

Then, suddenly, Kadmon received a call from Istanbul. He must come at once. Owners of a ship called the *Dora* had agreed to meet with him.

"Everything's in order here," I assured him. "The only commodity we need is what we always need, more money. And I certainly know the drill about that."

Kadmon nodded. "Well, whatever comes up, I expect you'll be able to cope." His tone of voice, however, directly contradicted his words.

The morning after his departure for Turkey, I entered my room elated. I had just returned from an interview with a textile industrialist, Lieberman. He had given the Mossad a check for eight hundred pounds.

The telephone rang.

It was Mandel. "Ruth, I've been calling your room for two hours. I must see you at once."

"I'll come right away."

"No. Stay where you are. Get Kadmon there too."

"He's on his way to Istanbul."

"Good God," Mandel said. He hung up.

Ten minutes later I opened the door to his knock.

His face was grim. He closed the door behind him. There were no preliminaries. "Ruth—when the transport arrives at the Rumanian border, it will be stopped. Sent back to Warsaw. And the *Tiger Hill* will not sail. It will be impounded by Rumanian authorities. An investigation of the entire matter has been ordered by Premier Calinescu."

I stared at him.

Calinescu! He had been in power only four months and already they called him *Dictatorul*. The man with the sardonic smile and the black patch over one eye. It was said that he ruled Rumania with one eye and an iron fist.

"It can't be true," I said to Mandel. "It must be just rumor that you heard."

Mandel shook his head. "You may be sure that it is true. A British delegation is here in Bucharest. To discuss the loan Rumania wants. Oil is the chief collateral. But there are other stipulations. Among them, no more illegal ships are to sail from Rumanian ports."

"Our transport will not be sent back to Poland. The *Tiger Hill* will sail." I spoke the words slowly and firmly, as though they were an order. An order to whom?

"My dear child . . ." Mandel said. He looked at me. He shook his head. Then he sat down in the armchair.

"You must *do* something," I cried out at him. "You must know *some-one* who can help us."

"Why should anyone help?" Mandel said. "The Premier's orders are based not only on national policy. But on national need. Why should the government jeopardize the loan this country needs for the sake of a shipload of foreign Jews?"

I refused to hear him. "You know Tatarescu! He *must* be important. He was Premier once."

"Once," Mandel said, "is a long time ago. Now he sits at a big desk in the Government Building. Pushing papers."

"And you know Gafencu, don't you? Surely *he* could help!"

"The Foreign Minister," Mandel said, "is the last person who'd want to become involved in such a matter."

"Please! We must see *some*one! The orders must be reversed!"

"There is no one," Mandel said, "who can rescind the orders of Calinescu."

"Please!" The word was a scream. "We must at least try!"

"Ruth!" He stood up. "Get hold of yourself."

He had never spoken sharply to me before. His tone served as a slap across the face.

"Look," he said then, "if you like, I'll call Tatarescu. It won't do any good. But at least the man can be trusted. He won't get you into deeper trouble than you're in already."

As he made the call I stood staring at him. Not seeing him. Seeing the refugees, over one hundred of them now, living in the hold of the *Tiger Hill*. Seeing the halutzim on the train from Warsaw. The sealed transport. They might be singing. Songs in Hebrew. Songs vibrant with hope. Because they were on their way at last to the homeland.

"Well," said Mandel as he hung up. "He'll see you in his office at eleven o'clock, day after tomorrow."

"Day after tomorrow!" I cried. "But the transport will be sent back to Warsaw by then."

"It was the best I could do. He has a crowded week. He leaves for vacation on Friday."

"There must be someone we can see right away. Someone with more power."

Mandel stood up, took both my hands in his. "Don't you know, my dear," he said gently, "if there were anything at all I could do to help, I would do it? But there is nothing. There is no one."

I nodded.

"It seems so impossible," he said. "After you've worked so incredibly hard. Accomplished so much. Now that the ship is ready to sail—"

Tears pressed behind my eyes. I turned away.

"Keep in touch with me," Mandel said.

Again I nodded.

"My dear . . ." he said. Then, abruptly he opened the door and left the room.

I stood watching him as he hurried down the hallway. He did not look back.

I closed the door.

The room filled with an exploding silence.

I had never felt so totally alone. Kadmon was on his way to Istanbul. Orekhovsky and Alexander were on the morning train to Constantza where, so the plan went, they would make final arrangements for the secret boarding of our passengers.

But, perhaps, for some reason, they had not yet left.

I phoned Alexander's home.

His mother answered. "Who's that? Who's speaking?"

"A business associate. Is he in?"

"In? He's never in. He never stays home any more!"

"Do you know where I might reach him?"

"He went out of town. He never tells me where he's going! Who is this?"

"If he calls, would you ask him to contact Ruth. Right away."

"Ruth who?" Her voice was filled with suspicion.

"Just Ruth." I hung up.

I phoned the Palestine Office. Orekhovsky had also left.

I asked to speak to Cotic. "The *rodan* has impounded our house!" I told him. "He won't let Yulik's family in!"

After a moment Cotic said, "How do you know this? Are you sure?"

"I'm sure. Can you come over? I'm at the hotel."

"Right away," Cotic said. "Have you any plans?"

I hung up.

Plans.

There is no one who can rescind the orders of Calinescu.

Any plans!

Should I phone Yulik? Perhaps he would want to cancel the transport? But would he? Even if he knew, might he not insist that his halutzim try to get through? At least across the border. They would be better off in Rumania where there were seaports and ships, and some hope of escape. Better off than in land-locked Poland where they were trapped.

If somehow they could make it across the border. And then disperse into the countryside. To hide until we could . . . Could what?

No more illegal ships are to sail from Rumanian ports.

I put through a call to Yulik Braginski.

The lines to Warsaw were tied up. "Try late tonight," the operator said.

Late tonight. The transport would be on its way.

By tomorrow afternoon it would reach the Rumanian border town of Grigore Gica Vodă.

There it would be turned back by the stationmaster.

The stationmaster at Grigore Gica Vodă!

I took Lieberman's check from my purse. A check made out to Nathenya Sea-Shore Development Co., Ltd. Eight hundred pounds.

I telephoned Gara de Nord.

"There are no through trains, madame, to Grigore Gica Vodă. You can get a train to Rădăuți. Then take a bus or taxi to the border. The train to Rădăuți leaves in forty-five minutes."

I phoned Mandel's office. Lieberman's check would be meaningless to a local stationmaster. Mandel must have his bank change it into Rumanian lei.

But he had not returned; nor did his secretary know when he was expected.

Lieberman! His bank would cash the check for him. I put through a call to his office. Monsieur Lieberman was out to lunch. He was not expected back until three o'clock.

There was no time for further calls.

I took a small suitcase from the closet; threw in some documents, a towel, perfume, a fresh blouse. These, plus a check made out to a land development company in Palestine, did not seem very potent weapons against the orders of the dictator of Rumania. Still, at the moment I had nothing else.

FIFTEEN

I WAITED in front of the hotel for Cotic; waited as long as I could. Where *was* the man? How long did it *take* to get from the Palestine Office?

If I missed the train to Rădăuți—

A taxi drew up before the hotel, and I jumped in.

"Please! Gara de Nord! Hurry!"

As we were halfway down the block, I saw Cotic entering the Ambasador Hotel.

"Wait!" I opened the cab door. "Please wait for me!" I scrambled out, almost fell to my knees, ran to the hotel.

Cotic was by the elevator.

"Come with me. Quickly!" I said.

In the taxi, as we hurtled down the boulevard, I told Cotic what had happened. We spoke Hebrew; our emergency code for conversations which could be overheard. Few Jews knew the language, and certainly no one else did.

Then I opened my purse, took out Lieberman's check, signed it over to the Palestine Office, and gave it to Cotic. "You must get to your bank right away. Deposit this in the Palestine Office account and draw out sixty thousand lei. Then bring it to me at Gara de Nord. My train for Rădăuți leaves in a half hour."

Cotic nodded.

"After that," I said, "go back to the bank. Draw out all the money in the Palestine Office account. And bring it to Constantza."

Cotic protested. "I can't just clean out the account. I've got to have Orekhovsky's permission for such a thing."

"I give you permission. I take full responsibility."

"Look," said Cotic, "to bribe one small town stationmaster—that at least may be worth a try. But to approach a whole slew of port officials—you may as well throw the money into the Black Sea. They're not going to risk their jobs or their necks by ignoring the orders of the most powerful man in Rumania."

"I don't suggest you start dispensing funds," I said. "But you can investigate the situation down there. Tomorrow afternoon, wait in the stationmaster's office in Constantza. I'll phone you there. By that time maybe one of us will have a plan. If we do, one thing is certain. It's going to cost money."

Cotic nodded.

"Driver," I said, "stop. This gentleman is getting off."

The cab pulled over to the sidewalk. "Please." I begged Cotic. "Hurry. I'll be waiting for you by the train to Rădăuţi. I'll be outside the first carriage."

As we drove off I saw him standing on the sidewalk looking for another taxi. Was it possible that he could get to his bank, draw out sixty thousand lei and reach Gara de Nord in a half hour's time?

The station platform was a mass of shoving, waving, shouting people. I stood on tiptoes, trying to see through the crowd.

A mother beside me held up her infant, flapped its tiny arm. "Goodby, Papa," she shrilled in a high falsetto voice, as though she were speaking for the child. The baby began to cry.

People banged against me as they hurried past with heavy suitcases. A loud blast came from the engine. The conductor strode by. "Boooard. All aboard."

I climbed onto the first step. Should I leave without the money?

The train started to move slowly.

Then I saw Cotic, far down the platform, running.

I shrieked; started waving frantically.

He came charging through the crowd, racing along the platform.

I kept screaming at him. Or for him.

He reached me, handed up a paper bag. "Your lunch," he yelled.

The engine emitted a shrill whistle.

I climbed the iron steps and entered the corridor, clutching the paper bag.

It was early morning when the train pulled into Rădăuţi. My eyes felt grainy from lack of sleep, my bones heavy with exhaustion.

The station was deserted.

The man behind the ticket window lay on a bench at the back of the small room. His mouth was open and he was snoring. A sign at the grill window read *Please Ring Bell*. I did, loudly.

He awoke, grumbling, and came toward me.

I shoved one hundred lei across the counter. "I need a taxi at once to drive me to Grigore Gica Vodă. And back. I must be here tonight. To make the next train to Bucharest. Do you know a driver? I will pay well."

The man regarded me closely. His face was bristly with stubble. "*How* well will you pay?"

"Double the regular fare."

"I'll phone my brother. The phone call," he added, "will cost you a hundred lei."

I handed it to him.

He went to a phone at the back, cranked the handle. Then he spoke in a dialect I did not understand.

He returned, smiling. Several teeth were missing. Those which remained in his mouth were yellow. "My brother says it's too hot to drive. But he agrees to lend me his car. Since I'm off duty soon, I myself will take you."

"That's very kind of you."

"I didn't tell my brother," he said, "that my passenger would be a young woman, traveling alone." He awarded me another of his yellow-toothed smiles.

The car was like an oven inside. We opened the windows wide, but the early morning sun slanted in and the breeze was a blast of hot air.

After fifteen minutes the driver suggested pulling into a roadside restaurant for breakfast. The place he indicated had a large sign above the door: *Rooms*. I told him I had no time to spare for anything. Furthermore, if he could get me to Grigore Gica Vodă by three o'clock, I would increase the fare I had promised by fifty per cent.

I then curled up on the lumpy back seat and pretended to fall asleep. Pretense turned into reality. I slept as though in a coma.

I awakened to the smell of the driver's sweat and garlic as he shook my shoulder. "We made it," he informed me when I opened my eyes. "Fifteen minutes to spare!" He pointed to the station clock.

I sat up, blinking, yawning. Then I reached for my small suitcase. Had he discovered the money Cotic had given me?

"May I sit in here a moment, to freshen up?"

He made an expansive gesture. "Be my guest! In fact, I had hoped, that you might be more than that. Perhaps you'd have a drink with me?"

"I'm sorry," I said. "But I can't. I'm here on business. I won't have time for pleasure."

He gave me a sour look. "What about the fare?"

"I'll bring it to you in the pub."

He shrugged and walked off.

Immediately I opened the suitcase. The packet of money was still there where I had hidden it. I counted out three separate piles, placed them in three envelopes, which Cotic had thoughtfully provided. One for the driver. One, containing five hundred lei, in the event that the stationmaster proved unco-operative. Into the third envelope I placed fifty thousand lei.

Then I squatted down in the back seat, changed my blouse. As I combed my hair and wiped the travel grime from my face, I looked out the car window at the crowded station platform.

Grigore Gica Vodă was only a small country town. But it was a town with a swollen station. Trains crossed here from central Poland and Galicia. Smuggling was the local industry. And the stationmaster, as chief recipient of bribes, was, I suspected, a far more influential figure than the mayor.

Had he ever been offered a bribe concerning a shipment of human beings?

I got out of the car, hurried along the platform, knocked at the door of the stationmaster's office. There was no answer. I shoved at the door and it opened. An old man sat there, his legs on the desk. He was picking his teeth with a twig.

"Excuse me. Are you the stationmaster?"

He spat unconcernedly on the floor.

I repeated my question, somewhat louder. Perhaps he was deaf.

"Stationmaster's gone home."

It had somehow never entered my head that I might be unable to locate the stationmaster. Did the fact that he had gone off duty mean that no more trains were expected today? Had the transport already arrived; had it been sent back to Warsaw?

"Excuse me," I said to the old man. "Has a train passed through here today, from Warsaw?"

"Couldn't tell you that, fraulein." Again he spat.

I took several crumpled bills from my pocketbook. "Could you telephone the stationmaster for me?"

"He has no phone."

"Well—" I took out several more bills, handed them to him. "If you could find him for me. It's terribly important. Tell him—I have a message for him. From Generalrat Max Ritter von Anhauch."

The old man held the money up to the light; smelled it. "All right. I'll try to find him, fraulein. But I make no promises." He got to his feet. "I have to lock up if I leave here. You wait in the pub." He looked at me. "No, not in the pub. You had better wait in the restaurant in back of the pub."

"Thank you," I said. "And please, if you find him—don't forget. Tell him I have a very special message for him. From Max Ritter von Anhauch."

The station pub was dim and exploding with noise; voices quarreling, laughing, calling for drinks in a melee of languages: Ukrainian, German, Rumanian, Polish. The place smelled of vodka, tuică and beer. There was also the penetrating odor of hide, for even in the heat of summer peasants wore sheepskin vests, handsomely embroidered but badly cured and reeking.

My driver saw me and came over.

I gave him the envelope I had prepared. "This covers the fare. I wonder if I could ask you one small favor?"

"At your service, mademoiselle."

"I'd like to know whether any trains have come through today from Warsaw. If so, what was the destination of each of them."

"That's simple enough to find out," he said. "For someone in my profession."

He left the pub, and I headed for the restaurant in the back room. Then I sat, staring at the door, as if willing the stationmaster to enter.

I was suddenly filled with the certainty that I had made a disastrous mistake; had rushed down a dead-end road. I should have remained in Bucharest instead of cutting myself off from all possible contacts. Even if the stationmaster did show up, why should I imagine he would risk his lush lifetime job for fifty thousand lei?

These thoughts had been with me since I left Bucharest. But now they congealed from worrying doubts into conviction.

A waitress stopped by my table. I ordered *cascaval*, black bread and lemonade.

When she had gone, my worries mounted.

Without thinking, I had drawn Von Anhauch's name into our conspiracy. I had used it as a way of telegraphing a message to the stationmaster. I wanted him to know that it would be worth his while to meet me. Otherwise, he might not trouble to come.

However, if he did show up, he might merely agree to let the transport through; then pocket the money I gave him. And contact the police. I was attempting to subvert the direct orders of the dictator of Rumania. Von Anhauch was a Jew. I had mentioned his name. Who would believe that Von Anhauch knew nothing of this matter? I would be arrested. He might be arrested.

He was a Jew. Did that give me the right to enlist his aid without his knowledge in order to help save five hundred of his fellow Jews? Should every Jew automatically become his brother's keeper?

The driver returned with the news that no trains had come today from Warsaw.

I thanked him with relief and with another hundred lei.

"When will you want to go back to Rădăuţi?" he asked.

"Within the hour."

He smiled. "Perhaps then you won't be in such a hurry."

"I told you," I said, "on *this* trip, unfortunately, I am in a hurry. I must be back in Bucharest tomorrow morning."

"In that case," he said, "the fare to Rădăuţi will be the same as the fare to come here."

I nodded.

"Next time," he said in a dour voice, "I won't trouble myself driving so far on such a hot day!" And he went back to the pub.

The waitress came and set down my order. The plate was greasy, the glass grimy. But I was hungry and thirsty, and the cheese and bread looked fresh and delicious.

As I lifted the glass of lemonade, a dead fly dropped in it. Then another fell onto my hand. I glanced at the ceiling which was decorated with sticky strands of flypaper. Obviously, the one above my head was old, dried out; for as I sat there several other flies dropped onto the table; tiny corpses, their legs sticking into the air.

I took the bread and cheese, moved to another table, finished eating. Would the stationmaster come? Had I made this long trip for nothing?

Then I saw him standing in the doorway, a tall, heavy-set man in a blue uniform.

He came over to my table.

"Fraulein, you have been asking for me?"

"*Ja, Herr Station Meister.*"

He sat down, removed his cap, wiped a band of sweat from his forehead. "Hot," he said. "A terrible heat. Even for July."

I agreed, and as he ordered himself a beer and rolled a cigarette we went through the preliminaries which always preface a business conversation.

He was the first to come to the matter at hand. Yes, indeed, he informed me in heavily accented German, he had often seen Generalrat von Anhauch when that fine gentleman changed trains at this very station.

I mentioned that the generalrat evidently remembered the stationmaster with cordiality, for he had given me an envelope, a gift, to present with his felicitations.

The stationmaster nodded and remarked that God should bless the good generalrat.

Then I mentioned the matter of the special transport which was, even now, en route from Poland. I paused. He said nothing, but his lips thinned to a straight line.

"It appears," I said carefully, "that there was some mixup. Certain government officials were under the impression that the five hundred young Jews arriving on the train would remain in this country. Quite naturally, official orders went out to return the train to Warsaw."

He was frowning now.

"What the government people did not know, however, is that a ship is waiting to transport these five hundred Jews to a country of safety. Panama."

"So you say, fraulein. But why should I believe you?"

"Because I have proof." I took from my case a packet of receipts, insurance documents. All bore the name S.S. *Tiger Hill*. Some read *Destination: Panama*. Most were quite meaningless. Carbon copies of bills paid for food supplies, engine repairs. However, the very profusion of the papers seemed to impress him.

"Well!"—he placed his heavy hand on the pile of papers—"if what you say is true, then I shall wait for confirmation of the fact from the transport ministry."

I tried to smile. "You know as well as I do, Herr Station Meister, that government red tape may take weeks to unravel. By the time you receive an official order, the five hundred young Jews will be back in Poland. This is a serious matter, sir. If, as we expect, Hitler invades Poland—these same five hundred Jews may well be dead in a matter of months, instead of living in safety in South America. This is why Von Anhauch is so concerned. This is why he has sent you a gift in recognition of your efficiency. And your humanity." I took out the envelope containing fifty thousand lei.

He slipped it into his pocket, nodded, and stood up. "I shall have to see, fraulein, whether any further communications have come in about the transport. Excuse me, please."

"Wait!" I said hastily. "There is something else! If the transport goes through and the passengers reach Constantza in safety, there will be another gift forthcoming. Twice the size of the one the generalrat has already sent."

The stationmaster nodded. "Wait here, please."

He strode across the restaurant and his figure was lost in the crowded dimness of the pub.

Had he gone to phone Von Anhauch? Or the police? Or the government officials from whom he had received orders about the transport? Fifty thousand lei seemed to me a substantial sum of money. The hundred thousand I had promised seemed exorbitant. But what would it mean to a man who made a career of accepting bribes?

Presently the stationmaster returned. "I would like to ask you a few questions, fraulein." He sat down. "This additional gift you mentioned from Generalrat von Anhauch, when exactly would it be forthcoming?"

It appeared that he *had* been sufficiently impressed by the fifty thousand lei.

"An emissary will be sent to you," I said, "as soon as the transport reaches Constantza."

"What if I fulfill my part of the operation, but the train is stopped within Rumania and ordered back to Warsaw?"

"The—appreciation for your co-operation will be forthcoming in any case."

"What assurance do I have of this?"

"You have my word, Herr Station Meister."

Abruptly he broke into loud laughter. Several people at the restaurant tables glanced at us. "Your word! What is that? The word of a university student. Or are you Von Anhauch's secretary? Who are you? You've haven't even told me your name."

"Because my name is of no matter." Was he merely playing with me, keeping me here at the restaurant table until the police arrived? "If you don't feel that you can co-operate"—I got to my feet—"I'm afraid we must work through other channels. Perhaps you would therefore be so kind as to return—"

His hand was on my arm. His laughter had ceased. "Don't be so impetuous, fraulein. I'm interested in your proposal. Particularly because I'm a humanitarian at heart. But you must realize I risk a good deal by doing what you ask."

I sat down again. "I know that, sir."

"I have a request to make of you." His hand was still on my arm. I made no move to draw away. "Would you care for a beer, fraulein?"

I shook my head.

"I have a good position here, fraulein. I've no desire to lose my job. Or to land in jail, for that matter. However, there is a way out. If you will agree."

I nodded slightly.

"You and I, fraulein, are the only ones who know that I have received any orders regarding the Polish transport. A little tampering with the telegraph apparatus will mean I must call in the repairman. He can serve as my witness. The orders? What orders? I received no orders about this transport. Ah, yes. Well, perhaps because my machine has not been functioning properly for the past few days!"

"Herr Station Meister," I said softly, "God will bless you till the end of your days for your goodness."

"I'm afraid, fraulein, that depends on which God one prays to. Your Jewish God seems to be turning his back on his own people these days. I think I can forget any blessings I might receive from those quarters."

I had no answer to that. I could only smile.

It was hard to believe that he had agreed to help us; that he would not simply pocket the money and then send the transport back to Warsaw. Yet, somehow I felt that he was what we called "a good *goy*": a Gentile who accepted our baksheesh—and then fulfilled his part of the bargain.

"I would like to ask two small favors of you, Herr Station Meister." He nodded.

"You will certainly be boarding the transport when it arrives," I said. "Would you deliver a letter from me? You can hand it to anyone on the train."

"That should not be impossible, fraulein. The second request?"

"I would like to make a telephone call from your office to Constantza."

He shrugged. "If you can get through. As you know, the long-distance lines are usually tied up in the daytime."

I signaled for the waitress.

"Please," the stationmaster said. "Let me take care of the bill. After all, I am wealthier than I expected to be this week."

As I waited in the stationmaster's office for my call to go through, I wrote a letter in Hebrew to Levi Schwartz.

Whenever possible, a Palestinian went along on every Mossad ship. He acted as captain, leader, organizer of our illegal passengers. Levi was the Mossad member accompanying the *Tiger Hill* transport from Warsaw to Palestine. I told him of Calinescu's orders; advised him of our arrangement with the stationmaster. And I promised that approaches were being made to important Rumanian officials. His train should proceed through Rumania as slowly as possible. Our hope was that by the time it finally reached Constantza, all difficulties regarding the sailing would be dispensed with.

The connection to Constantza came through suddenly. Furthermore, Cotic was there, waiting for my call. And I could hear his voice very clearly.

Perhaps all this was a good omen.

I described what had transpired. And I suggested that Cotic use the money he had brought to Constantza to bribe a few of the top port and railway officials.

"I told you already," he announced in vehement Hebrew, "that's not going to work. Not down here!"

"Wait." I said. "What you don't know is that I have an appointment tomorrow at eleven with Tatarescu himself!"

"Tatarescu? So? The Minister of the Interior—what does that mean?"

"He was Premier once," I pointed out. "He has far more power than you may realize. He can get to Calinescu."

"Perhaps. But he certainly can't—"

"Look." I interrupted sharply. "All I'm asking is that you somehow get the officials down there to stall things for three days."

"*All* you're asking! All you're asking is the impossible!"

"You can try, can't you?" I shouted at him. "The fact that the transport will be arriving in Constantza should give them some reason to believe you."

"Believe me when I tell them—*what?*"

"When you tell them that in seventy-two hours, Calinescu's orders will be rescinded."

"You're an optimist," Cotic said bitterly. "And in these times being an optimist is synonymous with being a bloody fool."

"Will you at least try?"

There was a long silence. Then Cotic said, "So—all right. I'll try."

SIXTEEN

THERE WERE TWO LETTERS waiting when I got back to the Ambasador Hotel the following morning.

The first envelope, addressed in Stefan's small, precise handwriting, sent a shock of excitement through me. I felt ashamed, and opened the other letter.

It was signed "G"; a few lines bidding me to contact him after my eleven o'clock appointment. The note was written in pencil on lined, schoolboy stationery. Mandel, I reflected, quite enjoyed the business of playing secret agent.

The letter from Stefan was the warmest I had ever received from him. "My love," it began. "I never knew that I could miss one small-sized redheaded girl so much."

A single sentence, and I felt his presence as intensely as if he were standing beside me.

His daughter, he wrote, was doing better. He was therefore able to come to Bucharest. At any time that suited my plans. I must send him a telegram at once. He would, in fact, dictate it for me. "Come immediately. I love you. I can't wait."

I asked at the front desk for a telegram form. I wrote: *Business requires I leave Bucharest. Will contact you upon return.*

The Government Building on Boulevard Brătianu was a splendid edifice; gray stone with ornate carvings, a cobbled courtyard, ornamental wrought-iron gates. And a sentry's booth with a sign requesting all visitors to stop there.

I did so, gave my name.

The officer checked his list and directed me to the ornate doorway across the courtyard. There a uniformed page led me up a red-carpeted stairway; then down a long corridor lined with leather-covered doors. I began to feel like an overage Alice in Wonderland.

He stopped at last, opened a door, made a half bow and departed. There was a second wooden door. I opened it. A young man came toward me. "Madame Klüger," he said. "The Minister will be with you shortly. This way, please."

I followed him into a small anteroom. Louis XIV chairs lined the walls. A colorful hand-woven Rumanian carpet covered the floor. Velvet drapes had been drawn to keep out the hot morning sun. The room proved a luxurious torture chamber. For fifty interminable minutes I sat there, thinking of all the excellent reasons I should run away.

I'd phoned Kadmon's hotel in Athens, hoping to get his consent for this interview with Tatarescu. But Kadmon could not be reached.

I remembered his words, his and Alexander's, when I'd first suggested seeing George Mandel. They had been worried I might reveal too much; endanger the entire Mossad operation by some careless comment. Mandel, they took care to point out, knew top officials in the government. He might well show more loyalty to them than to the Mossad.

Now I was sitting in the anteroom of one of Mandel's "government contacts." The most important one. The government already knew about the *Tiger Hill*. However, they did not, presumably, know the individuals behind the operation.

What right had I to come, with no authority at all, expose myself, expose the others to arrest? Rumanian prisons were not noted for their considerate treatment of inmates; particularly those of the political variety. Would I be one of those who succumbed under torture; who gave names which brought about an entire chain of arrests? Could anyone be sure how he would behave before he was tested?

It was insane. I was sitting here in this splendid room, working myself into a frenzy of fear. Of course I was right to come here. How else could the *Tiger Hill* be saved? The bribing of "buttons" could do just so much. It could get the transport of five hundred across the border; as far as Constantza. It could get their train sidetracked for several days, while negotiations went on. But no amount of bribery could move a ship out to sea when the Premier himself had ordered the vessel impounded.

The only way to rescind that order was through high government contacts. A man like Tatarescu could at least get to Premier Calinescu.

The door opened. The secretary entered. "The Minister will see you now."

I followed him into Tatarescu's office.

It was a huge room. At the far end was a huge desk. Tatarescu sat behind it; not a man, but a Power. His face was lean; his eyes tartaric, piercing. He did not stand. He did not smile. He said nothing at all.

And I simply stood there. I felt there was an abyss between us, impossible to cross. I was quite unable to walk forward to his desk. Nor could I bridge the gulf by words.

Suddenly I remembered a sentence I had read somewhere. *Every great man sits on his behind.*

I walked to the desk. *"Bonjour,* Excellency."

He nodded, indicated a chair.

"Thank you for seeing me," I said.

He glanced at his wrist watch. "Unfortunately, we don't have much time. I have a luncheon appointment in ten minutes."

I started to speak. One of the speeches I had rehearsed on the train.

He listened carefully, but his face was impassive.

When I came to the climax of my plea, he interrupted. "I'm afraid, Madame Klüger, I can't quite agree that this is any life and death matter."

"We have good reason to believe, Excellency, that Hitler plans to exterminate the Jews of every country he conquers. We also have good reason to believe that the Germans will be in Warsaw within a few months."

"And I, Madame Klüger, have good reason to believe that the second coming of Christ is scheduled for one-thirty this afternoon."

I looked at him in raging despair. "Don't you see, the ship is waiting! We've taken every precaution to protect your country from—contamination! Even if the Polish Jews wanted to jump out of the train, to stay in Rumania, they couldn't! It's a sealed train. They can't get out. Not till they board the ship. They can be escorted there by armed guard, if you want it that way!"

"What's the name of this ship?"

I hesitated.

"How can I help you if I don't know the facts?"

The question was reasonable enough; but the voice was scarcely sympathetic.

"You say, Madame Klüger, that you are from the Jewish Agency. I thought this organization was connected with Palestine. Not Panama."

"Palestine has quotas, as you know, Excellency. When the quotas are filled we must look elsewhere for ports of—safety."

"And this ship of yours, madame, this nameless vessel, is it one of those tubs which will founder and sink two miles out of the port of Constantza?"

"It has passed every test, sir."

"You can assure me that your ship is not one of those illegal enterprises which are making the British so unhappy?"

"I cannot pretend, Excellency, to know *all* the enterprises which make the British unhappy. I must confess that we are concerned with one matter only: the saving of human lives. We haven't made any great study of the pleasures and prejudices of politicians."

"And that, Madame Klüger, if I may say so, is a failure on your part. You tell me the orders concerning your ship were issued through some misunderstanding. I submit, Madame Klüger, that this is not the case at all. Your ship is the *Tiger Hill*, am I right?"

I said nothing.

"I happen to know," Tatarescu went on, "that the orders concerning that ship were not issued accidentally. They were not issued by some underling, in the Premier's name, as you would so blithely have me believe. The orders were issued by the Premier himself. For very good and sound reasons."

The telephone rang. He picked it up. "I'm ready," he said. Then he stood up. "Well, Madame Klüger, you have presented your case. I'll have it investigated further. If anything happens, I'll let George Mandel know."

"George Mandel," I said hastily. "Please don't involve him. He knows nothing of this matter."

"I'm sure of that," the Minister said with what might pass for a smile. "Nevertheless, since you've declined to tell me where I can contact you—"

"I'm in transit," I said. "I have no address."

"Then—" he shrugged. "I have no alternative but to contact Mandel." He was walking me to the door.

I looked up at him. "Thank you for seeing me. Thank you for anything you may be able to do for us."

"You are most welcome, Madame Klüger," he said.

I walked back across the cobbled courtyard, half blinded by tears. Rage and bitterness seethed within me. This anti-Semitic world, so busy making walls, barriers. All this great united effort put forth. For what? To protect the world against men and women like the five hundred young Polish Jews who wanted only to find some place where they could live in safety and raise their children, like other human beings.

And those of us who tried to help—those few of us—were made to feel like beggars. Or like hunted criminals, fearing arrest.

I took a cab to Mandel's office.

I needed to tell him nothing. Tatarescu had already telephoned.

"I was terrible!" I exclaimed. "I said all the wrong things! I should never have gone there at all!"

Mandel smiled a little. "It seems he found you impetuous, impatient, impertinent. He also mentioned that you had good legs."

"Do you think he'll investigate the Mossad? Do you think we need fear him?"

"He can't help us," Mandel said. "On the other hand, I believe he's rather sorry he can't. Whether that's because of his good heart or your good legs, I don't know. In any case, I'm sure he won't make things any more difficult than they already are."

"Don't you know anyone else?" I begged. *"Anyone* who could help us?"

"Well . . ."

The word held some faint hope.

"What?" I demanded.

"I'm going to a dinner party tonight. Brătianu will be there. Malaxa. Other important industrialists. I could bring you along. Maybe somehow you'd find some help."

"Do you think there really might be a chance?"

"I don't. But—" he shrugged. "Have you any other plans?"

I shook my head. At least the names—Brătianu, Malaxa—sounded imposing. I would have to call Kadmon and Orekhovsky when I left here. It would give me, in any case, something to say. Something which sounded like a plan. It was better than admitting that the road seemed irrevocably closed.

"I would like to go with you. And," I added, "I look forward to meeting your wife."

"My wife," said Mandel, "will not be there. She's indisposed."

"I'm sorry."

"I wonder—" He hesitated. "It will be a rather formal gathering. You have a suitable dress." It was a statement and a question.

"I have the green silk. You've seen that often enough to know it. Will it qualify?"

"You'll need a long dress," Mandel said. "Look, give me the pleasure of dressing you for the occasion." I started to protest, but he cut me off. "After all, I've already contributed a substantial sum to this effort. Surely, you won't object if I add another few thousand lei?"

It seemed a strange and inappropriate way to proceed. Mandel buying me a dress to go to a dinner party. Surely there must be something more dramatic, more constructive I could do. But what?

"I'll have the dress delivered to your hotel this afternoon," Mandel said. "In the meantime, you go back and sleep." Again, he raised a hand to stop my protests. "It's obvious that a fresh-looking vibrant young woman will have far more success tonight than one who is gray with exhaustion. But first, before you go—" He placed a pad and paper in front of me. "Write down your dimensions. If that's not classified information."

I did so.

"I'll pick you up at the Ambasador at eight," Mandel said. "And perhaps something will actually come of this party. Who knows?"

Back in my room I put through a call to Kadmon in Greece, and to Cotic in Constantza. Then I looked at the bed and decided to follow Mandel's orders, while I waited for the calls to come through. I doubt at that point that I could have done anything else.

The shrill of the telephone awakened me.

It was the front desk. "There's a messenger here, madame. With a package for you."

"Please," I said sleepily, "send him up."

The dress was black velvet, floor length. It came from one of the finest shops on the Calea Victoriei.

I tried it on and turned slowly in front of the mirror. It was a beautifully made gown; it clung without seeming to. And it was cut very low in front. It was certainly not a dress I would have chosen myself.

I'd brought a jewel-encrusted necklace from Palestine. It belonged to my Russian great-grandmother; had been passed on from daughter to daughter as a kind of portable savings account. But the heavy pendant set with chips of semiprecious stones was now regarded as old-fashioned, ornate and ugly. I'd tried to sell it several times, but was offered so little I decided to keep it.

I put it on now, hoping the pendant would cover some of the bare cleft. Worn with the simple black velvet gown, the necklace took on a new elegance.

I brushed my hair loose around my shoulders and went back to the mirror. I looked like someone else entirely. However, maybe she would have more luck than I'd had.

The telephone rang.

"Your call to Constantza, mademoiselle."

This time Orekhovsky was on the other end of the wire. There was a tremor in his voice as he told me that the transport had arrived. "It was something incredible," he exclaimed. "We had been trying to convince a certain gentleman, Cotic and I. A very expensive gentleman. We told him that the Premier's orders would be rescinded in forty-eight hours. He laughed at us. We told him we had inside information. If he turned down our offer, he would end up with nothing. In two days he would be kicking himself black and blue in remorse. Then suddenly—like a vision—there came the transport chugging down the track! The transport which, he had been told, had been sent back to Warsaw. So—the long and short—he began to believe us. He accepted our offer. Or, should I say, our offering. He had the transport shunted to a sidetrack. It may remain there, he says, for forty-eight hours. But if he receives no counter orders by that time, the transport goes back to Poland. And the *Tiger Hill* will be impounded."

Orekhovsky had said all this in a swift rush of Hebrew.

Now, suddenly, his voice grew hesitant. "Things did go well, didn't they, with the Minister of Interior?"

"Not just *well!*" I exclaimed. "I'm on my way now to meet Malaxa, one of the wealthiest men in Europe! We couldn't do better than *that!* And one of the Brătianus. And—" I broke off. "I shouldn't mention names which can't be translated into Hebrew or code."

"Of course," said Orekhovsky, "I understand. Well, keep in touch. Good luck. And—God bless you."

I hung up and sat by the telephone, tears running down my face. What was I doing? Why was I misleading him? There was no hope. There was no plan. There was no reason at all to expect that the Premier's orders would be rescinded in forty-eight hours.

But perhaps if Orekhovsky knew this his own dismay would be seen at once by his important gentleman. Orekhovsky had no poker face; he was no play actor. Perhaps, instinctively, I had done the right thing.

Once again the telephone rang.

"Madame Klüger, Monsieur Mandel is waiting for you in the lobby."

The dinner party was one of those tortured dreams where you try to run but cannot move; you try to scream but cannot utter a sound. All the people surrounding you, hemming you in, have no idea of the terrible urgency. They laugh, jest, chatter away. And pay no attention. Pay you no attention at all.

Mandel understood of course.

He knew that we had no time. He knew that we had no other chance. He kept trying.

He approached one guest after another; tried to explain without saying too much. Then brought each gentleman over, introduced him to me. But each seemed so fearful that I might ask for money or favors that he retreated hastily, after a smatter of small talk.

Then Mandel introduced our host, a man reputed to have much influence in government circles. He was remarkably ugly; squat, red-haired, with the unapproachable look of a sullen bulldog.

"Well, now," he said abruptly, "George was telling me some story about Jews and trains and ships."

A maid came by carrying a silver platter of caviar. She was followed by a butler with a trayful of drinks. "What are you drinking?" our host said. "Have you tried whiskey? An English drink. Very fine. I recommend it." He handed me a glass; took one himself. Then he bowed slightly. "Very pleased to meet you, Miss—Uh—" And he returned to his wife who was, Mandel had told me, the daughter of a professor at the University of Iasi.

Mandel informed me that Malaxa, the millionaire industrialist, was not coming to the party after all. He was home in bed with a cold. And Brătianu had not as yet arrived. He then went off to corral a Monsieur Manolescu, who, he assured me, would be highly sympathetic, and who might be influential enough to help.

Monsieur Manolescu was a distinguished-looking man with a sun-tanned face, graying sideburns and a charming smile. Diplomatically George Mandel withdrew, muttering something about bringing us hors d'oeuvres.

"Let's sit down," Monsieur Manolescu said.

I sat beside him on a small settee in the corner.

"Now," he said with genuine interest, "what's all this about?"

I tried to keep my voice low and warm; none of the urgent, shrill intensity I had shown with Tatarescu. I tried to capture some of the drama of the story. "Right now—as we sit here surrounded by luxury—at this same moment that train crowded with young men and women is on its way. For two days they've been literally imprisoned. Not allowed out of the cars. But I've been told their spirit is wonderful. Because they're confident the orders will be rescinded. How could it be any other way? It would be too inhuman. Too unjust. Too unnecessary. That's why I wanted to meet you tonight. I knew if you were told the story—if you understood—" I left the sentence hanging. He had not said a word thus far. I needed to have some reaction from him before I could judge how much it might be safe to reveal. Would he want to know the name of the ship? Would he mention illegal immigration?

"Do you know," he said, "you're the most refreshing girl I've met in months."

I stared at him.

"I'd like to hear more about your endeavors," he said. "But it's rather difficult talking here. In this chattering mob. What if we meet later tonight, when our respective dinner partners have been dispensed with?"

"Monsieur Manolescu," I said, "I ask only one thing of you. That you be honest with me. Because there's so little time. And wasting it tonight—in a restaurant, a nightclub or in bed—can mean that eight hundred human beings may die."

After a moment he said, "Well, that sobering thought might take some of the fun out of the proceedings at that." He reached for the pendant hanging around my neck, and examined it. "Russian?"

I nodded. "It belonged to my great-grandmother."

He set the pendant back in place, his fingers resting briefly in the cleft between my breasts. "All right," he said. "I'll give you what you ask for. Honesty. I can tell you right now that I can't help you. Calinescu is a new dictator. Old contacts, old influences, even old money mean very little. Not to this man. I suppose he's one of the few people in the entire country who can't be bought."

"But he *is* being bought. By the British!"

"Ah, yes. But his cause is the country. Not his own pocketbook." He stubbed out his cigarette. "Frankly, I don't think there's a man in this room who would even try to help you. Calinescu is talking now of nationalizing a number of industries. Most of the men here are industrialists. They stand to lose millions if his plans go through. Yet, so far as I know, no one has dared to approach Calinescu on the matter. If they won't speak out on their own behalf, you can hardly expect them to approach the Premier on behalf of a shipload of strangers."

"So I'm wasting my time here tonight?"

"I would certainly say so. And," he added, "you might have wasted a good deal more of it, if I hadn't been so gallant as to tell you the truth."

"I appreciate your gallantry."

"Well," he said, "I too had a great-grandmother. A very proper old lady. Once in a while I take perverse pleasure in acting in a way which will not send her spinning about in her grave."

The butler announced that dinner was served.

Manolescu stood up. He kissed my hand. "Perhaps," he said, "we'll meet again at a more leisurely time in our lives. And perhaps then we'll give my great-grandmother a proper whirl in her grave."

"Perhaps," I said.

I watched him as he walked away, to join an exquisite dark-haired woman wearing a diamond tiara. I felt suddenly, unaccountably, jealous of her. What must it be like to be wealthy and secure?

Mandel returned and I told him what Manolescu had said. "There's no point in staying here any longer," I burst out. "There's no one here who will help me."

Mandel nodded. "I must say, the best I've been able to arouse is a polite lack of interest. A few so-called gentlemen got quite indignant. What lack of good manners on my part to bring such a matter to their attention! Especially at a dinner party!"

"Then I must leave at once. Can you call me a cab?"

"Now wait just a moment," said Mandel. "When did you last have a meal?"

I could not remember. Perhaps it was the black bread, cașcaval and lemonade at the station restaurant in Grigore Gica Vodă.

"I advised you to sleep, for the good of the cause," said Mandel. "I now advise you to eat. For the same reason. The engine, after all, must occasionally be refueled." He took my arm. "You said there was no one in this room who could help you. Well, there is one person. Your hostess. She's famous for her dinners."

As it turned out it was fortunate that I stayed, for our hostess did help—in a most unexpected way.

SEVENTEEN

THE DINING ROOM was the most splendid I had ever seen. The cut-glass chandeliers were festooned with flowers. There was a raised gallery at the far end of the vast hall, and it was here that we ate, at a half-moon table set with golden dishes and crystal goblets.

The cuisine was French and, as Mandel had predicted, each dish was a masterpiece. But the meal seemed to go on interminably. And so did the conversation. I felt trapped in this company, mired in the chit-chat and gossip which arose from the table. The chief conversation piece was the King and Lupescu; the courtiers and those who courted royal favor. The stories, whether true or apocryphal, pushed the political realities of present-day Europe far away.

Rumania was a bright and beautiful land, and people like those gathered here tonight seemed to believe the country could cut herself off from the rest of Europe by stringing up colored party lights along her borders.

They took their cue quite obviously from King Carol and his *camarilla*, the courtiers who lived under the twin flags of *dolce vita* and *joie de vivre*. Hunting. Gambling. Balls. And orgies.

Carol had won quite some notoriety for the highly democratic manner in which he distributed his royal favors to females of his realm. From whore to noblewoman he went, sometimes in the same night. With no respect for any of them. Except one. Madame Lupescu, the beautiful, slender redhead with creamy skin and green eyes. A woman with strength and intelligence. He had met her years ago in Sinaia, the daughter of a Jewish druggist. She was the undisputed and, it seemed, the irreplaceable chief concubine.

There had been one other love in Carol's life, an officer's daughter, named Zizi. One of the dinner guests had recently seen her in Paris. And the conversation bubbled around the tale of the two young lovers. Carol had married Zizi when he was nineteen. But the marriage was promptly annulled. It had, however, been well consummated, for Zizi gave birth to a son. He too was living in Paris.

Carol, of course, had a properly royal son, Prince Michael, the handsome product of his properly royal marriage to Queen Helena of Greece. He had, however, divorced Helena. It was Lupescu who ruled as unofficial Queen.

Alive with wit, the gossip skipped on, detailing new illicit love affairs brewing among the *camarilla*, and new women who had caught the King's ever-roving eye. Even Crown Prince Michael, age seventeen, qualified as a frothy dinnertime subject, though his tastes thus far ran more to fast cars and fast driving than to fast women.

Then from out of the bubble and babble of conversation I heard the single word "Hebrew?" It was a surprised exclamation.

I turned to listen.

"Yes," said our hostess. "You should have seen me! Serving the *dulcaeţă*, the coffee and *cozonac*—all in ancient Hebrew!" Her laughter broke like champagne over the table.

"Oh, *do* say something, darling!" a plump, bejeweled lady exclaimed. "Can you actually gabble away in the language?"

"Hardly!" said our hostess. "Papa just taught me a few simple sentences. And, I assure you, I promptly forgot every word as soon as Father Galaction had gone out the door."

Father Gala Galaction! The name seemed to explode in my head. He was the priest who had translated the Bible from Hebrew and Greek into Rumanian. King Carol's Bible, it was called.

"I wonder," I said suddenly, "did Father Galaction call it King Carol's Bible because of his close connections with the court?"

Our hostess looked at me in some surprise, as if wondering what this uninvited guest was doing at her table.

"Or," I pressed on, "did he call it that merely because it was done during Carol's reign? Like—the King James version."

"I suppose a bit of both," said our hostess.

"Then he does know the King?"

"I really have no idea," said our hostess. She turned to the gentleman on her left. And I turned to Mandel.

"We must get to the King!" I said, my words covered now by the laughter and conversation which had resumed all around us.

"My dear girl," said Mandel. He put down his knife and fork and he looked at me. "Have you any idea how long it takes to arrange an audience with a king? I've tried it on several occasions. On matters which I believed affected the finances of the country. The most I could manage was a brief meeting with His Majesty at an official reception. And it took me five months to achieve that."

"But," I persisted, "*you* didn't produce the King Carol Bible. I'm sure Gala Galaction will help us. Why wouldn't he? It's what we should have tried at the beginning! King Carol is the only one in the country with the power to reverse Calinescu's orders. Perhaps if we left right now we could see the priest tonight."

"It's past midnight," Mandel pointed out. "Do you want to wake the old fellow out of his sleep?"

"Yes!" I laughed, with relief.

Looking at it rationally, it was impossible that I could ever reach the King of Rumania within the next forty-eight hours. And if the impossible did somehow occur there was no reason whatever to expect that the King would rescind his Prime Minister's orders. But I was not very rational at that moment because at least, and at last, I had a plan.

I managed to follow Mandel's sensible advice. We did not march off at once to awaken Father Galaction. Instead, I behaved like a gracious guest for the rest of the evening. I had good reason now to enter the conversation. Indeed, I found myself leading talk around by the tail.

I had, of course, heard of Gala Galaction. He was a highly respected Rumanian writer before he became a priest. I had not, however, known until this evening that Galaction taught Hebrew at the University of

Iasi. Most Greek Orthodox priests learned to read and write some Hebrew as part of their biblical studies. Some could even speak it in a halting manner. But Father Galaction, according to our hostess, could speak Hebrew as fluently as he spoke French.

The priest, I assured myself, obviously had an intense interest in the ancient Hebrews. Why would he cut off such interest when it came to the Hebrews of today? He would of course do what he could to get me to the King.

The King—who had a Jewish mistress. A mistress—who had much influence upon the King.

But the more I inquired, the more it seemed that this part of the cycle was merely wishful thinking. The fact that Lupesca was Jewish had produced countless difficulties for the King. It certainly had not created any soft spot in his heart for the Jewish people.

I knew something about Calinescu's relationship with the King. But there were men at this dinner table who knew both the outer aspects and the inside truths. And none of those inside truths seemed to bode well for the success of our mission.

Calinescu had been put into power because Carol needed a strong man; a premier who was able to accomplish what then seemed impossible—the suppression of the Iron Guard.

In December 1937, King Carol had tried what proved to be a disastrous experiment. He had appointed one of Rumania's most noted anti-Semites to head a new government: Octavian Goga.

Some said that Carol had taken this step in order to propitiate his people for his indiscreet choice of concubine. Most believed, however, that the reasons went deeper. If Carol could convince Adolf Hitler that Rumania had her own flourishing brand of fascism, the Germans might not trouble to cross Rumanian borders. A political alliance would prove less expensive and more expedient for the Nazis than a military take-over.

Predictably and promptly Goga passed a law depriving one third of Rumania's Jews of their citizenship, and with it their right to earn a living.

Goga, however, lasted only forty-four days. The Premier was not dismissed because of his anti-Semitic decrees. But because of the men who carried them out: The Iron Guard. In a single month under Premier Goga the power of the Iron Guard had swelled to monarchy-shaking proportions.

The Guardists' leader was Captain Corneliu Codreanu, who had founded his movement in 1924. And the Guardists' program number one was, and had always been, persecution of Rumania's Jews.

Goga himself fostered a purely *national* form of anti-Semitism. Looting Rumanian-Jewish shops. Beating up Rumanian Jews on the streets. Burning Rumanian synagogues. Even an occasional murder. Rumania for the Rumanian fascists. And all this was fine with the King.

However, it soon became evident that Goga's henchmen—the Guardists—were goose-stepping right along with Hitler's Wehrmacht. They were nurtured by Nazi propaganda and funds. They were out to turn Rumania into a German satellite. The King into a puppet. His mistress into a corpse.

So Premier Goga had been dismissed.

It proved far less simple, however, to quell the now rampaging power of the Iron Guard. The King had tried the job himself, with a scholarly Premier whom he could control. To no avail. He had therefore fired the stately old patriarch Miron Christea. And he had appointed as Premier the one-eyed lawyer Armand Calinescu; a man of dynamic will, a man who could be ruthless in action. Perhaps the only man in the country who could put down the Iron Guard.

Carol—undoubtedly on Calinescu's insistence—had also wiped out all of Rumania's political parties. He formed a new party; a quasi-military party. The National Renaissance Party. Its members wore handsome blue uniforms. Its undisputed head was Calinescu.

And Rumania's new dictator had done an amazing job of suppressing the Guardists. Suddenly the prisons were filled with members of the Iron Guard. Furthermore, leaders of the movement had been shuttled from one prison to another. And, en route, many of them had been "shot while trying to escape." One of those shot was Captain Corneliu Codreanu, who was killed in a forest near Bucharest.

King Carol was out of the country at the time, visiting—as it happened—Adolf Hitler. Rumor had it that Calinescu had decided to kill the Iron Guard founder, leader and idolized hero before the King returned. He was afraid that Hitler might have persuaded King Carol to stop his suppression of the Iron Guard. Better take the irrevocable step before the King returned.

A new violent uprising of the Guardists was feared after the murder of Codreanu. But Premier Calinescu had once again proved his strength. The swaggering green-uniformed Guardists seemed to disappear from the scene. All through Rumania's seventy-two precincts more and more Guardists were rounded up, imprisoned. And unofficial orders went out that two Iron Guardists in each precinct should be shot—as a warning.

But from everything said at the dinner table that evening, one fact became amply clear to me. Neither Calinescu nor Carol had any particular interest in suppressing anti-Semitism. The Guardists had been suppressed for one reason only: They seriously threatened the power of the King.

The present lessening of anti-Semitic tensions in the country had been the accidental by-product of the outlawing of the Iron Guard. Nothing more.

And there was no reason whatever to expect that Calinescu or the King would jeopardize the possibility of a British loan, which the nation badly needed, for the sake of a shipload of "illegal" Jews.

Nevertheless, I left that dinner party with more hope than I'd come with. And I left with something more concrete than hope: a letter of introduction from our hostess addressed to Father Gala Galaction.

At seven-thirty the next morning I got into a taxi and gave the address. "Ten Strada Cornea." Priests, I assured myself, start the day early. Better to be told that Father Galaction had not yet arisen than that I had arrived too late; he had already left.

It would be another sweltering day. Already a misty heat was rising from the sidewalks. I rolled down the taxi window and held the hair up from my neck to catch some of the faint breeze.

We turned off the Boulevard Brătianu, drove through still-sleeping side streets and then past the Piaţa Philanthropia, the open-air market alive with color and commotion. Peasants squatted on the sidewalk beside their mounds of tomatoes, eggs, melons, eggplants. Vendors stood by their stalls chatting, calling to customers; early housewives out with their shopping baskets making their selections.

Had it been only six weeks ago that Stefan and I strolled through the market at Piaţa cu Flori?

I was plagued by such memories. They came constantly; a comfort and a torment. Anything, everything reminded me of him. How many times had I seen him walking down how many streets, only to hurry after the man who, it turned out, looked nothing like Stefan at all.

The Boulevard Philanthropia was crowded with cars and bicycles. The trams and buses were already jammed. We drew to a sudden halt as a group of gypsy whitewashers crossed in front of us, their long-handled brushes held high, marching in gay parade. Then they turned, waved at us tauntingly, as though delighted to have stopped traffic on the boulevard.

"Can't you honk, do something?" I said to the driver.

He shrugged. "Honking won't help."

It was true. In this city of lassitude, it seemed that nobody hurried. And nobody cared about time passing. It often took a letter four days to reach its destination on the other side of town. And no one complained.

"Please!" I exclaimed to the driver. "I've got to get there!"

Obligingly, he pressed on his horn. Whereupon, a few of the gypsies came over to inquire as to whether we would like our car whitewashed. Then they laughed with high good humor.

A horse and buggy had drawn up beside us, and I noticed the fat face of the driver, who was staring at me. His eyes were small and beady, his skin, the color of yellow parchment. He smiled, and I looked away.

The man was a Scopiti. Kadmon had, on occasion, pointed them out to me. They belonged to a strange sect. The men were permitted to marry. But after the birth of his first child every male was castrated. The sect was now almost extinct. All the men seemed to work as carriage drivers. And they all seemed to have the same fat yellow face.

Somehow the Scopiti's strange smile filled me with dread.

It was past eight o'clock by the time we finally turned down the narrow, tree-lined and cobbled Strada Cornea.

Number Ten was a small, whitewashed brick house with a bay window and a front porch. I rang the bell, and after some minutes the door was opened by a woman in a scarlet dressing gown. I thought for a moment I must have the wrong address. She seemed an unlikely person to be staying in the house of a priest. She was sensuously attractive, with large dark eyes and a mass of red hair which fell loose over his shoulders.

I handed her my letter of introduction. She glanced at the envelope addressed to Father Gala Galaction, and indicated that I should enter.

I waited in a dimly lit hallway while she ascended the stairs. I had never been in a priest's home before. I'd expected somehow a monastic-type dwelling with a crucifix hanging on a bare wall.

This was a home like any other in Bucharest. A lushly colored Rumanian carpet hung on the wall. The chandelier was cut glass, the stairway, wood paneled.

"Come up, please." The woman spoke from the top landing.

I climbed the stairway, and there at the top waiting to greet me, was a figure who might have stepped from the Old Testament. A stately patriarch with a long white beard and a long gray robe. As he turned to lead me down the hallway I noticed that his hair too was long, tied in the back with a piece of black string.

He opened the door to his study, ushered me in. I had seen only one other room like this one. The library of Berl Katznelson, a room overtaken by books, manuscripts and papers. Piled on the desk, on chairs, on the floors; walls lined solid with jammed bookshelves.

Father Galaction motioned me to a chair. He sat behind his desk, pushed some papers to one side. "Well, my child," he said in Rumanian, "this letter tells me only that you wish to see me. It gives no hint of the subject matter."

I spoke in Hebrew. "I am from Palestine, Father."

He smiled and answered me in Hebrew. "It's not often I have the chance to practice the language. Sometimes I speak to myself in the mirror. And talk back to myself. But a dialogue like that is somehow not quite the same thing."

The door opened and the redheaded woman entered carrying a silver tray with the traditional *dulceață*: two small plates containing preserves, two small spoons, two small glasses of water.

"You've met my daughter, Leanța," said Gala Galaction.

The woman had pinned up her hair now. And suddenly she looked familiar. A sharp stab of memory went through me. Sitting with Stefan at the theatre. Sitting in an agony of closeness, our legs touching lightly, our fingers touching beneath the seat. Trying to concentrate on the play, but aware only of the flooding desire to be with him alone.

"Excuse me," I said to the daughter of the priest. "You are not, by any chance, an actress?"

She smiled. "I am, by any chance."

"And a good one," said Gala Galaction. "She's with the National Theatre."

"It's not possible that you could have played one night in something called *The Drunkard*. With Sidy Tal."

She laughed. "It is possible. Was my Yiddish so bad that I stood out like a very sore thumb?"

"Your Yiddish was very good." She had played a small part, but Stefan and I had noticed her because her accent was strange.

"I've learned some Hebrew," Leanța said. "From Papa. But, of course, no Yiddish at all. Sidy Tal taught me the part. She thought it would be great fun to see if I could—pass."

I asked whether she had known a singer and actress named Ernestina Pola.

"I knew of her, of course," said Leanța. "A beautiful girl. And brilliantly talented. What a tragedy that she died so young. But why do you ask about Ernestina Pola?"

"She was my sister."

We spoke on for some moments about Ernestina Pola, the famous sister I had never known. We spoke about the National Theatre. The Yiddish theatre. The Sidy Tal Theatre. I began to wish fervently that this effusive Leanța would leave us. And, as if sensing my edginess, the priest held up one hand. "Madame Klüger has informed me she came here on an urgent matter," he said to his daughter. "Perhaps you two can discuss play acting some other time."

We had finished our honey and water. Leanța took up the tray and departed.

The priest winked at me. "My daughter, at the age of thirty-nine, is still stagestruck. Once she gets started on the theatre, it's hard to stop her."

Yet, the conversation had served a purpose. I felt relaxed now. I felt that I knew the priest and his daughter. I felt that Father Galaction would understand; that I could tell him the full story of the ship which was called illegal.

The priest smiled at me. "Now, how can I help you?"

I told him about the *Tiger Hill*. He listened intently, made no interruptions.

When I had finished, he nodded. Silence stretched between us.

Then the priest sighed. "You think, my child, that I have some power to help you in this matter. But I cannot help you. I have nothing to do with politics."

"Forgive me, Father. This is not a matter of politics. It is a matter of humanity."

Again he nodded. "Yes. True. A matter of humanity. And therefore a matter for God. Trust in Him, my child. He will guide you. He will see that His people are returned to their promised homeland." Whereupon he proceeded to quote Scripture. "And I will give to thee, and to thy seed after thee . . . all the land of Canaan, for an everlasting possession."

"Father," I said, "we have less than forty-eight hours left. God does not always work that quickly."

He smiled, the removed, beatific smile of an aged angel. "You ask for an introduction to the King of Rumania. I don't know the King. I've met His Majesty only once for a private audience. When I presented my Bible to him and wrote an inscription."

"But a man like you, Father, surely you know someone close to the King, someone who could get me an audience."

Again the long silence. Then he shrugged. "Perhaps Colonel Sidorovici. The King's aide-de-camp. But whether the colonel is in Bucharest now, I have no idea. And the King is undoubtedly at his summer palace. No one but fools like you and me remain in this city in July."

"I'd have time to travel to the summer palace. If I could get an audience tonight. Or tomorrow."

The old man laughed. "My child, remember, a king is a king. To see him at all is an impossibility. You talk as though he sits with an open appointment book, ready to receive you the moment you arrive in Sinaia."

There was a knock on the door.

"*Oui?*" the priest called, switching from Hebrew for the first time. "*Entrez.*"

It was Leanța. "Father Galdau is waiting, Papa."

"Ah, yes," said Gala Galaction. "Ask him to come up." He turned to me. "You'll forgive me, my dear. I'm afraid I have an appointment."

"Of course, Father." But I made no move to leave.

Gala Galaction went to his bookshelf, selected a black leather-bound volume. He returned to his desk, took up a pen, opened the volume. It was the King Carol Bible. The pen scratched, but did not write. He took another, carefully inscribed some words on the flyleaf.

I watched him, choked with impatience. Would he not telephone Colonel Sidorovici—now! Before his visitor came up the stairs.

Father Galaction handed me the Bible. "With compliments of the translator."

He had written: *For Ruth Klüger, eloquent spokesman for her People. Respectfully, Father Gala Galaction.*

"Thank you, Father," I said, still sitting. "Do you think—" I ventured then, "perhaps you could phone Sidorovici before your visitor arrives?"

Gala Galaction smiled. "My impatient young lady, it is not yet nine o'clock. I doubt that the colonel starts his day before ten."

"Shall I wait here then or—"

"My visitor is counselor to the Patriarch on Foreign Relations of the Church. We have, in fact, an appointment with a high church official. We must leave very shortly. I can only suggest that you give me a number where you can be reached. And sit by the telephone until you hear from me again. I will certainly call you today." Then he added, "One way or the other."

"Thank you, Father. I am staying at the Ambasador Hotel."

"Quite an elegant place."

I smiled a little. "When you deal with elegant people, Father—kings and such—it helps to have an elegant address."

"Quite so, my child."

There was a knock on the door. Father Galdau entered. I had expected an aged, bearded, black-robed replica of Father Galaction. But this counselor to the Patriarch was young and handsome. He wore no beard.

We were introduced. Leanța was waiting to see me out.

"Thank you, Father," I said to Gala Galaction, as though I were some penitent who had been relieved of the burden of sin. "You have helped me greatly."

I took a cab back, for I wanted to detour down the Calea Victoriei and past the Royal Palace. It was as I had expected and feared. The royal standard was not flying above the Palace. The King was not in residence.

As I entered my hotel room the telephone started ringing. I slammed the door behind me; ran to answer.

It was Cotic. "I'm at Gara de Nord," he said. "I just got in. I have bad news."

"What's happened?"

"Our friend has changed his mind. He threatens to impound the *Tiger Hill* at once."

"No!" I cried out. "He can't."

"He can. And he will. Unless we fatten his bank account with an additional nine hundred thousand lei. He wants the money by tonight."

"Have you got more money here?"

"You instructed me," said Cotic, "to clean out the Palestine Office account. And I followed orders. Now, can *you* get up nine hundred thousand lei? The train leaves for Constantza at eleven this morning. Can you be on that train—with the money?"

"No."

"What do you mean, no?" he exploded. "Do you want the ship impounded?"

I told him about Galaction; about the King. "I'm certain the priest can arrange an audience. I *must* wait here for the telephone call."

"Once the ship is impounded," Cotic said, "even the King can do nothing. That you may be sure of."

"Then you must go back to Constantza. You must buy time."

"With what?"

"Perhaps—Mandel," I said.

175

"Look, when he gave us the down payment, we promised the fellow we wouldn't be dunning him any more."

"I'm well aware of that," I said. "But if we need the money so fast— I don't know anyone else."

"Tell him it's a loan," Cotic said. "With seven hundred and sixty men, women and children as collateral."

"Call me back in five minutes."

It was not yet nine o'clock. I tried Mandel at home. He had left for the office. I tried the office. He had not arrived.

When Cotic phoned again I said, "You must go to Mandel."

"I can't do that. Look, getting money is your specialty. And Mandel's your specialty too."

"I'll keep phoning him," I said. "But you must go to the bank and wait there for him. If I have to leave here before I speak to him—"

"All right," Cotic said. "I'll go to the bank. If we can get the money I'll bring it down to Constantza." He hung up.

I sat staring at the telephone, hope colliding with despair.

I tried Mandel's office again. He was not there. Nor did his personal secretary know when he was expected. "Mr. Mandel's first appointment is eleven o'clock," the secretary said in chill tones. "I'm afraid that's all I can tell you."

"Will he be in before eleven?"

"I have no idea, miss."

"Please. Ask him to call Ruth as soon as you see him. Or hear from him. It's urgent."

"I will give him your message," the secretary said. And hung up.

Eleven. The train left for Constantza at eleven. If Cotic were not on that train with the money, the ship would be impounded. If that happened, the King would never interfere. Nor would we want him to, for the story would then become front-page news—which would mean the end of our operation in Rumania.

When would Mandel call? Or the priest?

The telephone stood on the bed table, black, silent.

There was something else on the bed table. The Bible which Gala Galaction had presented to me. The King Carol Bible.

I picked it up, turned through the pages looking for words which might somehow help. I paused at the page headed Jeremiah. The Lord had said to his prophet:

Arise ye, and let us go up to Zion . . . behold, I will bring them from the north country and gather them from the coasts of the earth, and with them the blind and the lame, the woman with child and her that traveleth with child together; a great company shall return thither. They shall come with weeping, and with supplications will I lead them; I will cause them to walk by the rivers of waters in a straight way, wherein they shall not stumble. . . .

I turned a single page and my eye caught upon another set of words.

For tomorrow we shall die.

EIGHTEEN

THE TELEPHONE RANG.

I grabbed the receiver in such haste that I knocked the phone to the floor.

"Oh, God!" I exclaimed, pulling it up. Had I broken the thing?

"You call on God, I hear," said the priest. "And he seems to be listening." His voice was jubilant. "You have an appointment with Colonel Sidorovici. You must be at the Royal Palace in twenty minutes."

"Will I see the King?" I blurted.

"My dear child, to see Sidorovici without waiting a month is, in itself, an impossibility. But," he added, "the colonel is aware of the fact that you wish an audience."

"How can I thank you, Father!"

He hesitated a moment. "Perhaps you won't. When one asks for an audience with the King, one is required to give all the particulars. I'm afraid I told Sidorovici everything you told me. I hope I had your permission to do so."

"Of course, Father," I said, rather weakly. We had been so cautious at every step about giving out facts. Mandel and Gala Galaction were the only two outsiders who knew the full story of the *Tiger Hill*. I'd revealed so much to the priest only because he seemed completely sympathetic, and I hoped to win him as an ally for the future. But I'd stressed secrecy throughout. I had therefore never imagined that he would do anything more than try to arrange an appointment.

"There was no other way," the priest said. "Sidorovici had only a few minutes for me. I had no time to contact you. He kept asking questions. If I hadn't answered, we'd have lost any slight chance there might be for an audience."

"I understand, Father."

"Besides," Galaction said, "the colonel was interested. Especially when he learned your refugees were all young people. It seems he already knows a good deal about your Zionist Youth Movement."

A man in high position who already knew a good deal. And who might now know far too much. Nevertheless, I did not wish to say anything that could sound ungrateful. So I changed the subject. I asked the stupidest imaginable question. "If I do see the King, what shall I wear?"

The priest laughed. "My field, I'm afraid, is ancient languages. Not high fashion. But I believe when visiting the Royal Palace, it is customary for ladies to wear some sort of hat."

I took out the only hat I owned, the white cartwheel I'd bought on my first morning in Bucharest. Then I put on the green silk dress I'd bought that same morning, six weeks and another lifetime ago. The dress had become a veritable uniform. I'd worn it when visiting government officials, suppliers, wealthy Jews from whom we hoped to raise funds. It still, however, held its shape, and somehow produced an aura of style.

I dressed swiftly; then waited in the hotel hallway. It seemed that the more I wished to hurry the more lethargic the elevator became.

The Ambasador Hotel was not far from the Palace. I crossed the Boulevard Brătianu; half ran down several sidestreets till I reached the Calea Victoriei. The street was almost deserted. Few people strolled the sidewalks in the broiling noonday sun of late July. Certainly, I was the only one rushing to get anywhere.

"Si-do-ro-vi-ci." I whispered the syllables aloud, like an incantation. Let him be sympathetic. Not merely interested, as the priest had put it. Too much interest could lead to disaster. Was I hurrying to an audience with the King? Or to arrest? "They have no need to kill you in Rumanian prisons," Kadmon had told me. "While you wait in your cell for the day of your trial, you rot away and die."

The narrow street broadened into the Palace Square. The royal standard had not been raised. The King had not returned.

I hurried past the high wrought-iron fence and entered the West Gate to the Palace. Two guards stood at stiff attention in bright blue uniforms, with black jack boots and silver helmets topped with white horsehair plumes.

"Ruth Klüger," I said. "I have an appointment with Colonel Sidorovici."

One of the guards gave an imperceptible nod, and I entered the cobbled courtyard. Like every resident of Bucharest I had passed by the Royal Palace often, for it is situated in the busiest center of the city. And I had, on occasion, lingered with a cluster of passers-by outside the fence when it was rumored that His Majesty or Prince Michael was about to arrive or depart. From the other side of the fence the Palace seemed a suitable setting for the operetta version of a monarchy. A four-story building of white stone and marble with tall arched windows, fluted columns and a long second-floor balcony which stretched in front of the throne room.

Now, however, as it loomed directly before me, the Royal Palace was suddenly a frightening place. Sentries marched in rigid rhythm, each with a gun over his shoulder. A huge man with a long black beard stood by the west door. His long blue coat was embroidered with the royal crest which glittered gold in the morning sunlight.

Again, I gave my name. He opened the heavy door, directed me to the reception room to the left of the entrance. As I sat waiting, a torment of questions beset me. Had Cotic succeeded in reaching Mandel? If so, had Mandel supplied the exorbitant amount of money we needed? If so, had Cotic made the train to Constantza?

The success of our *Tiger Hill* operation rested on timetables and tenuous shreds of hope. I was here in the Royal Palace to beg for the freedom of a ship and its passengers, without even knowing whether or not my efforts were already in vain.

A tall slender man entered the reception hall. He wore a white uniform with gold epaulets, gold buttons. He stopped before me. "Madame Ruth Klüger?"

I nodded and stood up quickly.

"I am Colonel Sidorovici."

I hurried along beside him, amazed that he would come himself to fetch me. We went down a long hallway, wood paneled, hung with tapestries, studded with bronzes on high marble pedestals.

The colonel's outer office was a place of great activity, more than I had seen before in this city. Several male secretaries sat at desks typing swiftly. Everyone else was hurrying about with sheafs of paper or talking intently on one of the many telephones.

Sidorovici's private office was, however, almost oppressively quiet. The heavy drapes, thick carpets, stolid furnishings seemed to absorb all sound. And it was stifling. Even the Royal Palace was not immune to the intense heat which blanketed Bucharest in the summertime.

"Please." He indicated a chair.

I sat, trying to look more relaxed than I felt.

"I understand you're from Czernowitz."

"Yes, sir." I managed.

"I'm a Bucoviner myself." He smiled, then leaned back in his chair. "Father Galaction has told me your story. I want you to know that I sympathize. I've had a good deal to do with the Rumanian youth movement, and over the years I've met a number of your Zionist pioneers. I have great respect for them."

He sounded sincere, not as though he were trying to lead me into a trap.

"Well," he said, "it seems the good Father has put God on your side. For the moment, anyway. The King hasn't been in Bucharest a single day this month. But he returned from Sinaia this morning. He has several important meetings today. However, he's free until lunchtime. You can see him right now."

I sat up straight. "The *King?*"

"I must advise you, however, that His Majesty knows about the *Tiger Hill*. And he wants to hear no more about it. He agreed to see you only out of—curiosity. Now, if you want to freshen up a bit before the audience, you may use my accommodations." He indicated one of the doors which led from his office.

I rose and went toward it, feeling as though I were sleepwalking. I was to see the King!

The washroom was replete with marble basin, gold-plated spiggots, and a full-length mirror. I looked as warm as I felt. As I patted powder on my shiny nose I noted that my hands were shaking.

When I emerged Sidorovici said, "Let's see you without the hat."

I took it off.

He nodded. "Leave it here."

"But I thought a hat was—"

"In this instance, you can forget about protocol. However, let's see your curtsy."

He put out his hand. I held his fingertips, bent my knee.

"Lower," said the colonel. "All right. At ease. Now, I suppose you know all the ground rules. Of course, you will stand when the King enters. Use the third person. His Majesty knows . . . His Majesty may have heard . . . Don't ask questions of the King. Don't speak until you're spoken to. Stud your sentences with Your Majesty. Or, sir. The King is a stickler for formality. At first meetings in any case. Now, any questions?"

"Yes. Why does the King want to hear no more about the *Tiger Hill?*"

"Come," Sidorovici said, "we don't want to keep His Majesty waiting."

He opened the door, strode through the outer office. I hurried after him.

As we went down a long and empty hallway, his manner changed, his voice dropped. He spoke so softly I could barely hear him. "You've heard that walls have ears. In this palace they certainly do. The whole place is wired with dictaphones. Some installed by the King. Some by his enemies. But in the hallway we can't be recorded if we walk quickly and speak softly. I'll tell you briefly what you're up against. I shouldn't, of course. And please never reveal what I've told you. Or that I've told you anything."

"You have my word."

I had said this sentence yesterday afternoon to the stationmaster at Grigore Gica Vodă. He had laughed. Colonel Sidorovici did not laugh. He nodded.

"Some months ago," he said, "the King visited Great Britain. The visit was deemed a great success. But not by King Carol or his Cabinet. Because, unfortunately, the financiers of the City of London refused to back up the welcome of Buckingham Palace. The King had traveled to England to seek a loan. He returned home without it. However, we're again in negotiations for a loan. And today we're in a better bargaining position. With war so obviously coming, Britain needs our oil. But she still calls the tune. And one of the most important notes of that tune concerns the illegal ships which have sailed from Rumania's ports. We are to cease closing our eyes to such ships. We are instead to close our ports. Which is, of course, why Calinescu gave the orders he did concerning the *Tiger Hill*."

"Is there any approach—?"

"None that will achieve what you want."

"Then why did you arrange the audience?"

"To oblige Father Galaction. And to oblige the King. You live up to the Father's billing, which is fortunate. I assure you, if you were not a beautiful female you would wait months for an audience. And then, if you saw the King at all, it would be in the throne room, with hundreds of others." He looked down at me. "You have one very special qualification. Which is why I suggested you leave your hat in my office. You may have heard that the King is partial to redheads."

Lupescu, of course, was famous for her flaming red hair. I wondered for a moment whether Sidorovici also served as one of the King's scouts.

We went down several steps and entered a chandelier-lit, carpeted passage. "The King is in the *Casa Noua*," Sidorovici said. "He does not wish it known, as yet, that he is in residence. Therefore, we take the corridor."

I had heard about this Casa Noua—the New House; the small villa built for King Carol in the tree-filled gardens behind the Royal Palace. The King had announced that he wanted the villa because he disliked living in the formal vastness of the Royal Palace. "Food," he said, "always tastes better in small houses."

But Rumanians surmised he had other reasons for the construction of the Casa Noua.

I wondered when Magda Lupescu had last come down this corridor.

Then I wondered how many other ladies had come through this convenient passage which connected the Palace to the King's private quarters. Lupescu, they said, was the ideal mistress. Secure in his affections, she understood his need for constant extracurricular affairs.

Was I being speeded into the royal presence because of my red hair?

We walked out into a room done in red velvet and gold. An officer at the door saluted. "His Majesty will be down in a few minutes, sir. He asks that you wait in the library."

We entered a room to the left. The door clicked closed.

It was a surprisingly small room, comfortably furnished, like the book-lined library of any well-read and well-to-do citizen of Bucharest. Except for the paintings. Behind the desk hung a large oil painting of Elizabeth, Rumania's first Queen. There was a painting of King Carol's mother, the beautiful Queen Marie, granddaughter of Queen Victoria and of the Czar of Russia. And there were several El Grecos. I had read somewhere that King Carol owned the finest private collection of Grecos in the world.

The only imposing piece of furniture was the huge mahogany desk which held three telephones, a vase of flowers, a golden clock and a thick stamp album.

"Does His Majesty collect stamps?" I said, surprised that I could manage this calm conversational tone.

"The King," said Sidorovici, "has been told by several dealers that his collection is the third most valuable in the world. He began saving stamps at the age of seven."

"May I hope he proves as dedicated in the matter of saving lives."

The colonel accorded me a polite smile. Then glanced at his watch. "His Majesty should be here any minute. Punctuality is one of the courtesies of kings. Another is that your audience won't be interrupted. No telephones will ring. No secretaries will enter."

"How long will we have?"

"If His Majesty is not in uniform, he must leave at quarter of one to dress for the luncheon reception. That will give you about twelve minutes."

A door opened. King Carol entered. He was wearing a gray suit. Twelve minutes.

He walked toward us. This man, the center of so much gossip, of so many legends. This man who was, despite all, loved by the people of his land. This King. I felt completely awed by his presence. He held out his hand. I touched his fingertips, made a deep curtsy, looked into his face. He was a far more handsome man than he appeared in the many likenesses which hung in cafes, shops, public buildings and homes throughout the country. His hair was blonder than I had imagined; his eyes, a brighter blue.

"Please be seated," the King said in French.

There were two chairs before his desk. Sidorovici and I sat. The King remained standing. "Would you care for a coffee, Madame Klüger? An aperitif?"

Twelve minutes. I did not want to waste them sipping coffee. "No thank you, Your Majesty."

"I understand you are living in Bucharest, Madame Klüger."

"Yes, Your Majesty."

"And how long do you plan to remain in our city?"

"I don't know, Your Majesty. That depends." Would the precious twelve minutes be swallowed up in small talk? Could I launch into the subject of this audience before it had been broached by the King?

Colonel Sidorovici cleared his throat. The King glanced at him, then he turned back to me. "Well, Madame Klüger, I'm told that you wish to enlist me in your illegal enterprises."

"I wish to offer Your Majesty the opportunity to play a unique role. One which will be remembered and respected by history."

He smiled rather indulgently. "Come now, Madame Klüger."

"One day, Your Majesty, humanity will look back. And make its reckoning. And on that day Your Majesty will be remembered—perhaps as the first national leader to stand on the side of compassion and justice. At a time when all the rest of the world stood idly by. Or looked the other way."

He glanced at Sidorovici. The smile had gone. Had I displeased him already?

"Your Majesty is known and loved as a man who cares about people."

He interrupted, a slight edge to his voice. "Indeed, Madame Klüger, I do care about people. My people. Just as you care about yours. It so happens that Premier Calinescu's orders are in the best interests of my people. Therefore, Madame Klüger, I really have no wish to discuss this matter further."

Your wish is my command. The royal command. Was I being ordered to cease and desist?

"Perhaps," said the King, "it was unfair of me to grant you an audience. But, I confess, I was curious. Most organizations send pompous old men to represent them." Again he smiled. Then he sat behind the desk. "How long have you been involved in this work, Madame Klüger?"

"I arrived here in June, Your Majesty."

"Your activities keep you very busy?"

"Yes, sir."

"No summer vacations, I assume. Nothing of that sort."

"I'm afraid not, Your Majesty. When one is involved in the saving of human lives, one must forget one's own life. One's own pleasures."

"That seems a pity, Madame Klüger. Since one has so few years in which to be young."

"It is because of Your Majesty's interest in youth—in the young people—that I hoped you might help. Your Majesty, the five hundred and one Poles aboard the sealed transport are all young. In their early twenties or less. Think of your own young men and women in the Straja Tarii. Our young men and women waiting on the transport are the same. They're the same age. They have the same hopes for a full life. They've had the same kind of intensive training."

"Training?" said the King.

I felt I was amusing him mightily. But not knowing what else to do or say, I plunged on. "Training for the life they will lead in Palestine, Your Majesty. Life on farms. In the border settlements. That brilliant plan which Your Majesty conceived and put into action last summer, sending university students among the peasants. To teach. To help. Our pioneers—as we call them—are exactly *like* those idealistic young men and women. They've committed no crime, Your Majesty. They harbor no evil plots. They're guilty of one thing only. They were not born into the Catholic faith. Or the Greek Orthodox . . . Protestant . . . Buddhist. Because they were born as Jews, they may die. Be murdered. The *Tiger Hill* may be their last road to safety. Their last road to life."

"Come now, Madame Klüger," the King said. "Don't you exaggerate just a little? I can understand, these well-trained youngsters don't want to waste what they've learned. They are determined to reach Palestine. One way or another. But to imply that if they are sent back to Poland they will be put to death! You do your cause no service, Madame Klüger, by indulging in such dramatic overstatements."

He was playing with me. He had no interest whatever in what I was saying.

But silence would gain me nothing. How many more minutes did I have. Five? Nine? I plunged on.

"Your Majesty recently visited Germany. You must have seen the street parades, heard the crowds shouting, 'Jews must perish!' Your Majesty has heard the words of the 'Horst Wessel,' the song which has practically become the German national anthem. *'Wenn das Judenblut vom Messer spritzt, dann geht's nochmal so gut.* When Jewish blood flows from the knife, things will go much better!' Your Majesty has heard the fervor with which those words are sung. By everyone. Everywhere in the country."

"Yes," the King said. "I admit the position of Jews in Germany is— unenviable. But as I understand it, your passengers are Polish Jews."

I opened my purse, took out the packet of newspaper clippings which I carried with me always. They had proved my best weapon in the constant fight to raise funds. Editorials from *Volkisher Beobachter,* Hitler's official newspaper. And from *Das Schwarze Korps,* the publication of the Gestapo. "With Your Majesty's permission, I quote from an editorial in *Das Schwarze Korps.* 'Because it is necessary, and because, after all, no power on earth can hinder us, we will now bring the Jewish question to its totalitarian solution.'"

I glanced at him. He had picked up a large magnifying glass which lay on his stamp album. He was staring through it, abstractedly. Had he stopped listening altogether?

"And what, Your Majesty, *is* this totalitarian solution to—the Jewish question? The article makes it quite clear. I quote, 'The actual and definite end of Jewry in Germany and *its complete extermination.*'"

I folded the clipping, put it back in my purse. "That particular article was published last year, in November. Today, of course, the complete extermination of Jews in Germany also means extermination of Jews in Austria. And in Czechoslovakia. Tomorrow, extermination may very well include the Jews of Poland. May very well include the five hundred and one young Poles who are waiting to board a ship which will bring them to safety."

The King stood up. To dismiss me? I kept on talking, trying to quell the terrible trembling within me. This was our last chance. I kept on talking in the frantic hope that the courtesy of kings would prevent his interrupting me.

"Your Majesty referred to the *Tiger Hill* as illegal. Is it illegal to try to save innocent lives? Is it illegal to bring young men and women to the homeland they've been longing for and training for since childhood?"

"Madame Klüger." There was for the first time an edge of impatience in his voice. "Britain makes the laws for Palestine. May I point out that the ruler of one country does not circumvent or sabotage the laws of another. May I further point out that you, with all your commendable sincerity and dedication, may in fact be working against the better interests of your own people."

He came from behind the desk. He stood directly above me. He seemed about ten feet tall.

"I recently met with a British delegation on another matter. I am sure I divulge no state secrets, Madame Klüger, when I tell you that as a form of reprisals against illegal immigration, the British may cut off the allotment of legal certificates for six months. Or more. I put it to you, Madame Klüger, may you not lose more than you gain by persisting with these illegal endeavors?"

I was stunned. None of us had ever thought that the British would use this severing weapon. To cut off the paltry trickle of legal immigration. It was unthinkable.

But I tried to answer with a shrug. "Your Majesty, the British grant us only three hundred and fifteen legal certificates each week. The *Tiger Hill* alone holds three times that number. If she is not impounded, she can make many trips. And the *Tiger Hill* is just one of our ships."

"All right," the King said. "Sail away. But not from Rumanian ports."

"Find other ports. Your Majesty, that is what the whole world is saying today. Find other countries to cross. Not ours. Find other countries to sail from. Not ours. Other countries to land in. Oh, some nations have been most generous—with their suggestions! Why recently Britain announced that she would be willing to transfer some of her unused U.S. immigration quota to German refugees. Unfortunately, the United States rejected the offer. *They* suggested that the Jews be sent to the Venezuelan plateau north and south of the Orinoco River. But Venezuela declined—despite the fact that this region is virtually uninhabited.

"In fact, Your Majesty, commissions have been set up to study the matter of resettling the Jewish refugees in many places which desperately need people to work the land, to create industries. Vast sections of Australia, Canada, Colombia, Uruguay. Big nations and little. Northern Rhodesia, British Guiana, Kenya, Tanganyika, Alaska, Mindaneo. All have been suggested. All have refused. But each time the commissions make a new proposal, rumors of hope go out. Rumors which enable civil servants to sell false visas at high prices. And Jews who've been stripped of all their money somehow manage to scrape together enough to buy a visa. And to pay for passage. Only to be told when they reach their new promised land that the visas are worthless. Only to be sent back where they came from."

He was frowning a little. Had I bored or annoyed him, going on like this? But what else could I do?

"Your Majesty, for over a year the Intergovernmental Committee on Refugees has been trying to find some place to resettle Jews fleeing from Hitler. So far, the only concrete thing they've been able to accomplish was the settlement of a few hundred refugees in the Dominican Republic.

"This is not because the Intergovernmental Committee does not try. They try very hard. But the barriers are up. The world is closed. The Jews are doomed. Unless some ruler, a man of courage and compassion, a man like Your Majesty, sets an example. Takes a stand. Others then may have the courage to follow. Your Majesty has only to lift the telephone, put through a call to Calinescu. And by that single effort, Your Majesty will have saved more Jewish lives in one minute than the Intergovernmental Committee has done during the past twelve months."

The King walked to his desk, resumed his seat. I glanced at Sidorovici, who nodded slightly.

"Madame Klüger," the King said, "you ask me to look at this matter from your point of view. I would ask you now to look at it from mine. As you know, Rumania is in a highly vulnerable position. We're trying to preserve a precarious balance. To control the Green Shirts within our borders. And to keep the Black Shirts out. But to lift the telephone, as you suggest, is not so simple a matter. To do what you ask would not only infuriate the British, but the Germans as well. Picture the headlines in *Das Schwarze Korps*: 'KING CAROL, THE JEW LOVER, AIDS ILLEGAL JEWISH AGENTS'."

"Your Majesty," I exclaimed, "we are certainly no more anxious to make headlines than you are. Our vessels have been called the Secret Ships. The Gray Fleet. The world knows very little about them. Where they sail from. Who is on them. Where they land. There is no reason that the story of the *Tiger Hill* should be any different. One day, when it all is over, the world will know. And then the name of King Carol of Rumania will be remembered and revered as a truly great ruler who showed the way. But not today, Your Majesty. Today, secrecy is the very foundation of our operation."

He gave me a wry smile. "Somehow, Madame Klüger, once a king is involved, the story seems inevitably to reach the press. Even if that story is a completely apocryphal one." He glanced at the golden clock on his desk. How many more minutes? When would he dismiss me? Panic chilled me.

"Your Majesty, I give you my word, only Father Galaction and Colonel Sidorovici know of this audience. No one else will ever know. I promise you that."

"You have nothing to hide, my dear young lady. For I shall not become involved."

I plunged on, as though his last pronouncement had not been made. I grasped frantically at a puzzling note which had entered my mind when Sidorovici told me about the British loan. "Your Majesty—it is said—I have heard—though it may not be true, that Rumania hopes for a British loan. That this is the reason Calinescu issued his orders concerning our ship. But, Your Majesty, is it not a fact that the loan would be obtained—if at all—from private bankers. Not from the British Government itself. If the loan seems a wise and profitable one, why should the bankers not proceed? Why should they be affected by the quite extraneous factor of a small ship sailing from the harbor of Constantza? A ship which is, according to its papers, sailing for Panama. Not Palestine."

Once again he glanced at the colonel. Should I have mentioned the British loan? Had I revealed too much? Would he know that Sidorovici had given me some brief background before this meeting? Our last chance and I was antagonizing both the colonel and the King. And at any moment the audience would end.

I rushed on. "As for the Germans, should the matter of the *Tiger Hill* ever come into the open, Your Majesty need only say that you were, after all, abiding by the Reich's own policies. Cleansing Rumania of Jews. Your own Jews and foreign Jews. For not only the Poles will be aboard, Your Majesty. There will also be Rumanian Jews. As well as Jews who have fled from Germany, Russia, Latvia. If the ship *were* impounded, how would you get them all *out* of Rumania? Escort each to his respective borders? They might well remain *here*, Your Majesty. More Jewish scum to add to the six hundred and fifty thousand Jews already contaminating your country. Those and the unrecorded numbers of paperless Jewish refugees who've already made their way here from the Greater German Reich. Naturally, Hitler would understand why Your Majesty wanted to get rid of the *Tiger Hill* and its stinking cargo as soon as possible!"

King Carol laughed. "I could use you on my staff, Madame Klüger. You understand our need to speak out of both sides of our mouth in different words at the same time." He made an expansive gesture to the colonel. "She is not only an attractive young woman, Colonel. She comes with an attractive offer. The chance to become a future hero of humanity. And a fashionable anti-Semite of today. All for the price of a single telephone call."

"Your Majesty," I said, very softly, "will you make the call?"

"No, Madame Klüger."

The word seemed to explode in my head. *No.*

The King looked again at the golden clock. Then he glanced at Sidorovici. There was no mistaking his meaning. My time was up. The audience was ended.

But he had not yet officially dismissed me. "Your Majesty." I cried out the words. "If you were not a king—if you were not a king and you loved a woman who happened to be a Jew—"

He looked at me. His blue eyes were cold as bullets.

"If she were one of the Rumanian Jews waiting, hidden in the hold of our ship. If you could save this woman you loved. And seven hundred more young men and women. If you had it in your power to save them. But you turned away—"

My words shrank into silence. Silence which seemed then to shatter the room.

The King turned away abruptly, strode to the window.

I had done the unforgivable. All Europe gossiped about King Carol and his mistress. But no outsider ever made the slightest illusion to Lupescu before the King. This was the one forbidden subject. And I was well aware of the fact.

Yet, I did not wish my words back. He loved this woman. As Crown Prince he had given up his right to the throne, because of Lupescu. He had gone into exile, because of Lupescu. He had allowed his little son, Michael, to become King so that he could continue living abroad with Lupescu. He had finally returned in 1930 to dethrone his son and proclaim himself King, promising his followers that he had cut himself off from Madame Lupescu forever. But he was unable to live without her. Two months later he sent for her. He loved this woman, the red-haired daughter of a Jewish druggist.

I knew he had once issued an edict, in an attempt to keep her return to Rumania a secret. Anyone mentioning her name in public was subject to arrest.

He could summon his guards. He could have me arrested. He could have us all arrested. He could end the activities of the Mossad.

I looked at Sidorovici. He frowned and shook his head.

I had lost. The *Tiger Hill* was lost. And perhaps much more than the *Tiger Hill*. The *Hilda*. The other ships which we hoped to sail from Rumanian ports.

The King moved from the window. He seemed to be studying a small painting on the wall. Then he turned to Sidorovici and said in an off-hand way, "Do you like this Greco here? I had it moved from the throne room. I thought it might be displayed more effectively in a small room like this one."

"I agree, sir," Sidorovici said.

The King nodded. He started toward the door. "I'm afraid I'm rather late," he said, speaking, it seemed, to himself. Then he turned again to Sidorovici. "And this other matter? What is your opinion on that?"

"I think that Your Majesty should comply with the request."

"Yes? For what reason?"

"Your Majesty," Sidorovici said, "Madame Klüger does not ask that Rumania become a haven for Jews. Merely that a ship which has already been organized now be allowed to sail. I believe that what she says is true. By a simple phone call, which no one need know about, Your Majesty may well be saving over seven hundred lives. To save even one life, sir, is a privilege not granted to every man."

"Your Majesty," I said, "there is a line in the Talmud: 'He who saves a single life, it is as though he has saved the entire world.'"

The King looked at me for a long moment. Then he said, "You may have heard, Madame Klüger, that baksheesh rules in Rumania. Unfortunately, this often seems to be true. They make up little jokes about us. Mania means madness. Kleptomania means madness to steal. Rumania means madness to steal, applied to a nation. Incredible as it seems, it is sometimes possible that large sums of money paid to small officials can even override the orders of a prime minister. Would you believe that, Madame Klüger? But I want to make one thing quite clear. I know nothing about the sailing of the *Tiger Hill*. Nor does my Prime Minister. Calinescu gave orders. Firm orders. Somehow there was a slip-up." He shrugged. "Baksheesh, perhaps." Suddenly his tone grew angry, his voice loud. "However, it will never happen again. Do you understand that? In the future a far closer watch will be kept on all our ports. Anyone who disobeys Premier Calinescu's orders for any reason whatsoever will be prosecuted. Do you understand? Do I make myself quite clear, Madame Klüger? No more illegal ships will leave from Rumanian ports."

Stunned, I stared at him. "But the *Tiger Hill* may sail?" My words were almost a whisper.

"I don't want to hear the name of that ship mentioned again in my presence," said the King. He nodded at me curtly. His hand was on the door knob. Then, once again, he turned. "But Colonel Sidorovici seems to be interested in this ship. I imagine he would like to be informed as to whether or not she succeeds in landing her passengers safely in Palestine."

NINETEEN

THE TRAIN TO CONSTANTZA was oven hot, yet I sat shivering. I had managed to see the King; he had promised our ship would sail. Yet, I felt no elation. Instead, a vast darkness seemed to stretch before me.

"Excuse me, mademoiselle. Are you all right?" The elderly man opposite was leaning toward me. His eyes were large behind the heavy spectacle lenses. "You look ill. Would you like my jacket?"

I had kicked off my shoes, was sitting on my legs, had crossed my arms over my chest for warmth. I could not control the shivering which shook through me.

"Thank you," I said. "If it's not too much trouble."

I watched gratefully as he took his jacket from the rack. I had rushed straight from the Palace to the station to catch the train to Constantza. Consequently, I had nothing with me except my pocketbook. I had even left my hat in Sidorovici's office.

"Lie down," the man said. "Try to sleep. You look as though you need it."

I lay, my knees drawn up tight against my body, and he spread the coat over me. It smelled of tobacco and sweat; did nothing to warm me. And my shivering did not stop.

He watched me anxiously, a pale-eyed protector. When anyone opened the door to our compartment he signaled them away.

Presently I fell into a heavy sleep.

"Young lady, we're coming into Constantza."

I opened my eyes. Outside the grimy window the sun was sinking behind the town. A minaret flashed by, silhouetted against a scarlet cloud.

I sat up. "Thank you for your coat. I feel much better now."

"Are you sure? Shall I find you a taxi? I have time to spare. I've come down to meet a ship, but she's not due in for a few hours. I could take you where you're going."

I had a fever; my eyes burned. I wanted the help of this kind stranger. I wanted him to take charge; find me a taxi, get me to a hotel or to a doctor. "It was just exhaustion," I told him. "I'm quite well now."

I had to visit the transport. I had to find Cotic, Alexander. Orekhovsky. I could not come accompanied by a stranger.

He did, however, see me to a taxi. As he bent over to close the door, he said, "Wherever you may be going—please, stop and see a doctor first."

"Yes. Thank you for helping me." I waved good-by to him out the open window. Then I said to the driver, "The office of the stationmaster, please."

He turned to give me a puzzled look. "You could get there quicker by walking."

"I want to lose my companion."

He winked. And we took off with a lurch, hurtled around corners, down side streets. And pulled up fifteen minutes later some hundred yards from the spot in which we had started.

The stationmaster was an older replica of the man who had taken charge of me when I first landed at this port six weeks ago. Fat, greasy-skinned, smelling of garlic. He looked at me blankly when I asked whether our passengers had boarded the *Tiger Hill.*

"Is the ship still here?" I asked.

"She's here."

Cotic had arrived in time with the nine hundred thousand lei!

"But," the stationmaster said, "she won't be here long."

"She's moving out," I said, "as soon as our passengers board her."

"No one's boarding that ship, young lady. We've had our orders."

"But the new orders!" I cried.

"We've had no new orders. The ship's to be impounded, that's all I know. And at one minute past midnight, your stinking transport heads back to Poland."

"You *will* be receiving official word," I told him firmly. "In the meantime, I'd like to see the transport. Where can I find it?"

"Just turn to your left, miss. Cross the tracks. And follow your nose."

The train had been relegated to the sidetrack farthest from the station. When I neared it the smell was so overpowering that I started to gag.

For three days and nights the transport had been standing here. For three days and nights five hundred and one men and women had been locked into six sealed cars. For three days and nights human feces and urine had dropped through toilets onto the tracks. Flies swarmed low like a moving black net.

I even felt pity for the Rumanian police assigned to patrol outside the train.

As I reached the transport, I saw faces staring from the windows. They were muted by evening into a sameness. Men with stubble beards. Girls with unkempt hair. Halutzim. Pioneers. Trained to combat malarial swamps and Arab marauders. Trained for the rigors of life on a border settlement. But trained for this? To be locked up for days in a sweltering, stinking, crowded railway carriage.

I approached one of the policemen, informed him that a message was coming through from the highest authority. The passengers would shortly be taken to the ship. In the meantime, I wished to speak to Levi Schwartz who was on the train. Then I opened my pocketbook, handed him five hundred lei.

He took a gun from its holster, a key from his pocket and entered the first car.

As I waited, I felt suddenly faint. But whether it was the overwhelming stench, the flies, the heat, or some illness which was invading me I did not know. I leaned against the train and prayed for strength.

I had never met Levi Schwartz, nor had he ever been described to me. But as he came toward me now, accompanied by the Rumanian policeman, I felt that I recognized him; that I had known him all my life.

He was a short man, stocky, with black hair and a ragged growth of black beard. His features were irregular, his smile rather crooked. He grasped my hand. "Ruth. We've been waiting for you."

We walked away from the transport and the police who patrolled up and down by the track. There was a stubble of grass and open space, and we headed toward it.

"You've already become a legend on our train," Levi said.

I looked at him in surprise. He was the legend; this man who had sailed as guide on the *Velos*, the first illegal ship. And who had, since then, practically made it his profession, sailing with the Mossad's illegals: destination, Palestine.

Quickly, I told him of my audience with the King. "I was sure when I left him that Carol meant to help us. But, after all, I suppose he was just playing games."

"Maybe not," said Levi. "You say he was off to some luncheon. Then important meetings in the afternoon. The man's been busy. For all we know he might be talking to Calinescu right now."

"And if he's not, your transport will be sent back at midnight. We have no more money. No way to buy more time."

"All right," said Levi. "Since you managed the impossible once, try it again. Call up the King on the telephone."

A policeman was coming toward us. "Back to the train, you!" he shouted at Levi. He stood watching us, gun at the ready, as we returned.

Levi took a deep, lung-filling breath.

"Is it unbearable inside?" I asked.

"The heat is, yes. In the afternoons we feel we're being fried alive."

"Do you get enough food? Water?"

"No complaints about food. Thanks to Alexander. The Good Provider, we call him. But no matter how much water he gets us, it can never be enough. We've all got a nonstop thirst. And, of course, no one's had a wash for a week."

I asked where Alexander was now. Cotic. Orekhovsky.

"Cotic showed up this morning just in time, with a fat wallet. That's what bought us our new reprieve, until midnight. Then he and Ore-

197

khovsky had to go back to Bucharest. Alexander's out scrounging us up some food for tonight."

Sudden faintness washed through me again. I stumbled and Levi caught me. Then his hand went over my arm. Up to my face. "You've got a flaming fever!"

"I'll go now," I said, drawing away from him. "I'll try to get through to the King."

But Levi held onto my arm. "There are three doctors on the transport. Maybe you can bribe your way on board. Let one of them have a look at you."

"There's no time. I'll be all right."

Many faces were crowded now at each of the windows. Young faces, but haggard, hollow-eyed. It was like looking at a line-up in hell.

"Do they know why they're stranded here?"

"They know everything," Levi said. "I've learned that, at least. The best way to help people endure is to let them participate."

I told him that King Carol had demanded secrecy. "If by some miracle he does help us, no one must know about it."

"Right!" said Levi. "Let His Majesty just give us the chance to oblige."

The policeman slid back the bolts on the train door. And Levi grasped my hand hard. Then he climbed the narrow iron steps. The door clanged shut behind him.

As I walked away I heard the sound of stones on glass. I turned. Children had gathered outside the transport. They were pelting the train windows with rocks. The policemen seemed not to notice.

Then one of the children started shouting. The rest took it up in a chant. "Jewish pigs, go home. Get out of here. Go home."

Go home. What else were we trying to do but to get them out of here? Get them home. To Eretz Israel. A land they had never seen. But the only true homeland they knew.

Six hundred lei bought me the privacy of the stationmaster's back room and the right to use his telephone. The number of the Royal Palace was in the Bucharest telephone directory. But could a stranger call up and ask to speak to the King? Sidorovici's home number was not listed. Perhaps the priest knew it. I ran my finger down the list of G's: Galaction. I gave the number to the operator. As I waited, faintness swept through me again. I started counting aloud as a way of clutching on to consciousness.

"No answer," the operator said curtly. And cut the connection.

I came to in a cold sweat, slumped in the chair. If I could only hang on for a few more hours. I picked up the receiver, gave the number of the Royal Palace. I was put through at once: this line perhaps had priority over all others in the realm. I asked for Colonel Sidorovici, was told that he had left his office at six. It was forbidden to give out the colonel's home number.

I took a deep breath then, and asked to speak to the King. "His Majesty," I said quickly, "requested that I meet him this evening at the Casa Noua. It is essential that I talk to him at once."

"One moment," the operator said.

The loud ticking of the clock sounded like a grotesquely magnified heartbeat.

Presently, another voice spoke. A man, this time. "I'm sorry, madame. His Majesty left for Sinaia several hours ago."

"Is he going to Peles Castle?"

"Yes, madame."

"Will he reach there before midnight?"

"I'm afraid I cannot tell you, madame. His Majesty may stop somewhere overnight."

Carol, I had heard, liked to travel at night. It was a convenient and conducive time for a king to turn adventurer.

"If you wish to leave a message, madame, it will be relayed to His Majesty's secretary in the morning."

"Thank you," I said, "but the morning will be too late."

I hung up and sat staring at the phone. It seemed to swell and recede before my eyes. I touched the cord of the telephone; lifeline of hope, noose of despair. How many thousands of times during the past weeks had I sat by a phone, waiting; willing it to bring me the words we needed. Words concerning money. Provisions. Fuel. Visas. Insurance. Sailors. Words weaving into a fabric, a reality. A ship which sat in the port of Constantza, waiting to sail. A ship converted, provisioned and paid for. A life-saving ship with several hundred refugees already hiding in the hold. A ship which would now be scuttled because the promised words had not been forthcoming. The final words. I fastened my hands around the long, skinny neck of the telephone. And suddenly started to cry.

Presently, automatically almost, I put through another call; to George Mandel.

Despite the King's request for secrecy, I had phoned Mandel from the station just before my train left for Constantza. And I had told him of Carol's promise. It was essential that someone have all the information, someone at the hub. Cotic, Alexander, Orekhovsky and I were all operating in different orbits. Since it was difficult for us to contact each other, Mandel had become the focal point for messages, instructions, new developments. And now, I prayed, he might know someone who could help.

This time the waiting was riddled with the querulous voices of operators. The lines to Bucharest were tied up. *What* number did I want? I heard other conversations broken into. Snippets of ordinary lifetime talk. A woman was giving a recipe. A man was recounting details of a vacation in Dubrovnik. Suddenly, I heard Mandel's voice.

"The message did not come through," I said.

He answered with silence.

"At midnight," I said, "our time is up. The transport goes back. Shall I try to phone Sinaia?"

"You'd never get through," Mandel said. "Nor would I. But Gafencu is staying at a villa in Mamaia. He can, at least, reach the person you want to contact. Take a taxi to the villa. Hold on. I'll get you the address."

Within minutes I was on my way. I had promised the driver double fare if he got me there quickly. We hurtled along the coast road through the darkness.

"Please," I said. "Can you close your window?"

"Close it?" the driver exclaimed. "It's a sweating hot night."

"I'm ill. I'm freezing." My voice broke. I must keep control. Gafencu. I clung to the sound of his name. The Foreign Minister would help us. He had long been known as a liberal. And I was not coming to him now to ask the impossible. Merely to request that he make a telephone call.

Of course, he would not put the call through unless he knew the whole story. And if I revealed the King's role, Carol would know I had broken my promise. This fact alone might well enflame the King's anger: might make him retract the tenuous offer he had made to help us. He had, I'd heard, a swift and violent temper.

Still, it seemed a chance we must take. We were caught in a vice-like trap of time.

"Hold on," I found myself whispering aloud. "Please. Hold on."

Perhaps I fainted then. Or simply slept. I was on the floor of the cab. The driver was shaking my shoulder. "Miss, let me take you to a doctor!"

I tried to climb out of the car, lurched forward. He caught me.

"I've got to get inside," I insisted. I leaned against him heavily as we started up the gravel entranceway to the villa. The walk to the front door seemed interminable. The driver lifted the heavy knocker, banged imperiously.

The door opened. A butler stood there.

"I must see Monsieur Gafencu," I said.

The butler merely stared at me.

"The matter is most urgent. I must see him at once."

"Very good, miss. Will you wait?"

There was a bench by the entranceway. Thankfully, I sat. "I'm quite all right, now," I said to the driver. "But please wait for me."

He nodded and did not move.

"Outside," I added gently.

"If you need me, miss, send the butler to call me," he said. And he left.

Gafencu was wearing wet bathing trunks and a towel slung over his shoulders. He was barefoot. As he walked toward me I thought in a fuzzy, removed manner that this was the most handsome man I had ever seen.

The film-star Foreign Minister, they called him sometimes. He was also the most popular politician in the country. Aside from his charm, his brilliance, his contacts, Grigore Gafencu had another weapon at his disposal: *Timpul,* the daily newspaper, which he had founded and which he edited for many years.

"Mademoiselle." He stood before me. "You asked for me?"

"Forgive me, sir." I got to my feet. "I would never have troubled you at this hour were it not—" Abruptly I sat down again.

"Are you all right?" He sat beside me. The concern in his voice was genuine.

Dance music was playing somewhere. Laughter came from the garden. The butler walked toward us, carrying glasses of champagne.

"Would you like some?" Gafencu asked.

I shook my head, and he waved the butler away.

Then, speaking quickly, I told him the story of the ship which sat waiting in the harbor some twenty miles away. I told him of Calinescu's orders. My visit to the King. And His Majesty's promise which had not yet been transmitted to the port authorities.

Gafencu frowned. But he said nothing.

"I know His Majesty meant to help us," I burst out. "Perhaps, somehow, he could not reach Calinescu. But we have no time to wait. Please. They're returning the transport at midnight."

Gafencu got to his feet. "I'll get dressed. We'll see the stationmaster together. And we'll sit in his office until we get a telephone call through to the King."

I opened my eyes. The young taxi driver was kneeling beside me. I was lying on a bench in a shed of some sort. I smelled the salt air of the sea. "What's happened?" I asked. "What time is it?"

"Almost midnight, miss. You passed out in the taxi."

"The transport—?" A spear of pain went through me. I gasped for air.

"Miss! What is it?" He helped me to sit up. Gradually, the pain receded. And, as we sat there, he told me.

Orders had come through. From Calinescu himself. The passengers on the transport were to board the *Tiger Hill.* The ship must be outside the three-mile limit by dawn.

I seemed to hear the young man's voice from a distance. Was he speaking in a dream of my own making? Was it true? The *Tiger Hill* would sail?

He reached into his pocket. "I'm returning this to you." He opened my purse. "Two thousand lei. Some fellow with red hair gave it to me. Said I should look after you till he could come for you."

Alexander.

I moved out of his protecting arms. "Who are you?"

"A student. I work nights driving a cab."

"What's your name?"

"Juliu Muresanu." Then he added, "My mother's maiden name was Friedberg." He got up, went to the door of the shed. "Can you make it a little farther? There's something you might want to see."

Before I could answer, he had lifted me into his arms and was carrying me out of the shed.

We were at the far end of the harbor. It was a moonless night and it was raining. There was a black hole in the darkness: our ship.

I heard it then, the clacking sound of a train moving slowly along the track to the pier, where it drew to a halt.

As we came closer we saw the guards; heard the sound of heavy bolts sliding back.

The first figure to emerge stumbled on the narrow iron steps, fell to the ground. It was a woman. She did not speak, but she raised her arms and her face to the night rain. Several men clambered down after her, helped her to her feet. And silently hurried off.

The train doors seemed to disgorge them then. Hump-backed figures; halutzim wearing knapsacks. A few also carried a mandolin, an accordion or a violin.

They had obviously been ordered to absolute silence. But, upon emerging, most of them raised their faces to the rain and breathed in deeply.

We sat on the ground near the transport, watching until the six cars were empty; watching the young men and women hurrying along the pier.

The rain stopped and a damp misty moonlight pressed through the clouds. We could see them now quite clearly as they moved in a solid line up the narrow gangplank.

"Were any more passengers boarded?" I asked. "Before these from the train?"

Juliu Muresanu nodded. "About a hundred."

The refugees who had been secreted in boardinghouses and small hotels in Constantza, they too were now in the hold of the *Tiger Hill*.

We saw the gangplank raised. We saw the ship slide through the harbor toward the open sea.

"This is something to watch," Juliu said softly. "The moon came out just in time."

"We may not be the only ones watching," I told him. "There may be others who'll find it worth their while to inform the British authorities. Still—what can you do? One can't bribe the moon."

I started to laugh. It seemed I had made an incomparably funny joke. I laughed till I wept; huge, gasping, shuddering sobs.

His arms went around me again. "Don't," he kept whispering. "Hush. Don't. I've got to get you out of here."

But I refused to move. And we sat there by the empty transport until clouds again shut off the moonlight. And the *Tiger Hill* disappeared into the endless dark.

PART TWO

August 1939 to February 1940

TWENTY

THERE WAS A KNOCK on the door of my hotel room.

I lay in bed, staring up at the ceiling. Perhaps it was the chambermaid. Or Alexander returning with a doctor.

But I did not move. I had expended my last traces of energy on the train trip from Constantza to Bucharest.

The knocking was repeated, louder.

"Who is it?" I called out.

"Bernhard Sternberg."

Sternberg. I had met the man only once. He was head of the Revisionist Party in Rumania. The Revisionists, too, were Zionists. They too were involved in illegal immigration. Often Kadmon had said of them: If they'd only work with us. As it is, they often seem to be working against us.

I got up, put on my robe, unlocked the door.

Three men strode into the room. All of them tall, handsome, well-dressed. They looked like bankers, corporation executives. Sternberg introduced them curtly. One man I had heard of: Aron Propos, head of the Revisionist Youth Movement in Poland. The second man was with the Revisionist Party in London. I did not catch his name.

"Forgive us," Sternberg said, "for interrupting your siesta. But this is a matter which can't wait." He closed the door, sat in the armchair. The other two men sat down on the bed. Since I did not wish to be sandwiched between them, I remained standing, leaning against the door.

"We have a transport of twelve hundred people arriving from Poland," Propos announced. "They're due at Grigore Gica Vodă in a few hours. We want you to get them through."

I said nothing.

"We know how you managed things for your people," Sternberg said. "We want you to do the same for ours."

I began to feel dizzy and closed my eyes briefly.

"Never mind the pained look," the man from London said. "We don't have time for dramatics. Look, we have the money. Our ship is waiting in Sulina. But police are patrolling the Polish border. They've got orders to let no more illegals through."

Propos said, "You're not well, are you?" He took my arm, led me over to the bed. "Sit down."

I did so. And they started to talk then, all at once. Dizziness spun through me. I barely heard what they were saying. Phrases they spoke shot through my consciousness. "Jabotinsky orders it. Stavsky commands . . ." Their excitement mounted. Their voices rose. Then the man from London spoke. His words came slow and heavy. "We are not asking you. We are ordering you to get our transport across the border."

I stared up at him. "I don't take orders from you."

"They are Stavsky's orders."

"I don't take orders from Stavsky." I picked up the telephone, asked for the reception desk. "There are three gentlemen in my room. They were not announced. I am asking them to leave. You will see them come down in the elevator. Please do not allow them upstairs again unless they are announced."

"What the hell!" the man from London exploded. "Are you busy teaching us etiquette lessons when we're trying to rescue twelve hundred people?"

I went to the door and opened it, holding onto the knob to hold me up.

The man from London stood over me. "If you don't help us, you will have to take the consequences. We will know where to find you. Do you understand that?"

"Listen," Sternberg said, "forgive him. He's a little crazy now. We all are. But you've got to help us."

"I'll try," I said. "Tell me where I can reach you."

"Can we wait here?" Propos asked.

I shook my head.

"For Christ sake!" said the man from London, "talk about prima donnas!"

"Shut up," Propos told him. He wrote out a telephone number, handed it to me. "When can we expect to hear from you?"

"In half an hour."

They left, and I locked the door behind them. Then I went back to bed.

Sickness swept over me again, nausea, chills. What should I do? Whom should I call? Kadmon was still in Turkey. I had no address, no contact for him.

Twelve hundred people headed toward Grigore Gica Vodă. A nightmare repeating.

I picked up the telephone, asked the operator to put me through to the Royal Palace.

"Colonel Sidorovici, please."

A secretary answered. I gave my name. Another secretary came on the line. Finally, I heard the colonel's voice. "Well! Congratulations!"

"I would like to thank you," I said.

"Perhaps you will thank me in person? Look, you left your hat in my office. Why don't you meet me at the Café Nestor at six o'clock. I can return it to you."

"I would like very much to see you," I said. "But right now I'm sick in bed."

"Nothing serious, I hope?"

"I'm sure not."

"Have you seen the doctor?"

"He's coming." Then I blurted, "I'm phoning because—I've just found out that twelve hundred more are coming from Poland."

The line seemed to go dead.

"Colonel . . . ?" I said softly.

When he answered at last the words were curt; the voice hard. "I understood that we had your promise. There would be no more."

"Colonel, our group had nothing to do with this—effort. But I've just been approached by those who organized it. Somehow they heard—"

"I understood we had your promise on that matter too," Sidorovici said. "No one would know of the channels you took."

"No one does know."

"Then why have they come directly to you?"

"My chief is not in Rumania now. As his assistant—I am the one they must come to. For help."

"Well, tell them," Sidorovici said, "that nothing can be done. The borders are closed. A special contingent of police has been sent. I saw the orders myself. I strongly advise you not to persist in any way with this matter." The words sounded menacing.

"I understand," I said.

"Do you? I hope so. For your own sake."

Perhaps he was speaking in this manner because his phone was tapped. Perhaps if we met again—in person—the sympathy which he had shown would return?

"When—I'm better," I said, "may I come to pick up my hat? Or, maybe—at the Café Nestor?"

"I'll send a messenger with your hat. Are you still at the Ambasador Hotel?"

"Yes."

"Very good," the colonel said. "I hope you make a quick recovery." He hung up.

I felt shattered.

An open door—a golden door—had been slammed in my face.

It was *their* fault. *They* had made me make this telephone call. Revisionists! Kadmon had often spoken the name in scorn. In despair. And I echoed it now, magnified into hatred.

We should have been close. They were more our brothers than anyone else in the world. The Revisionists and the Mossad were the only two organizations fighting to smuggle Jews out of Europe and into Palestine. Yet, we were often at odds. Our ends concerning illegal immigration were the same. But our methods were very different.

If we were an illegal organization, the Revisionists were even more illegal. We had, at least, the approval of some of the Jewish Agency leaders. But few of these leaders condoned the activities of the Revisionists.

Perhaps with good reason.

The Revisionists were led by a militant, middle-aged Russian-born Jew named Ze'ev Jabotinsky.* He scorned what he considered the mealy-mouthed beliefs of the Jewish Agency. You'll never win Palestine, he insisted, by buying the land from Arab landlords; then painstakingly draining swamps, irrigating deserts. And, finally, laying legal claim to the land you've reclaimed. We must, he said, regard Palestine as our land right now. We must comport ourselves as a free people, whose country is being subjugated by the British. We Jews must win back our Promised Land by force.

The British had exiled the fiery Jabotinsky from Palestine, for life. Consequently, he now traveled throughout Europe and America expounding his views, collecting funds and followers. He was a slender, distinguished-looking gentleman who wore a pince-nez; a man with genuine charm and charisma, a magnificent orator. He had built up a militaristic organization of several thousand young men and women, all of whom lived outside of Palestine. They wore uniforms of a sort. And what they lacked in munitions they made up for in zeal, which often approached fanaticism.

The Revisionists had numerous programs and platforms; one of them being illegal immigration. Their chief of illegal immigration was Abrasha Stavsky, a bull-like young man who had once—erroneously as it turned out—been convicted of murder.

Between the press publicity Jabotinsky engendered and the combative, heavy-handed manner of Stavsky, which was emulated by some of his men, the Revisionists were regarded by many as an overbearing, irresponsible lot. And because our endeavors concerning illegal immigration overlapped, the Mossad often found itself condemned by association.

When it came to illegal immigration, the Revisionists knew even less about ships and the sea than we did. Furthermore, they seemed to make little effort to learn. I'd often heard it said that they used fireworks rather than hard work to achieve their ends. It frequently happened, therefore, that at the last critical moment they came to us for help. Not asking, but demanding we bail them out of trouble.

* *See* Appendix Ten.

Many of their ships had, however, gotten through. They'd succeeded in landing many hundreds of illegals in Palestine. And whenever we could, however we could, we helped them.

Their transport of twelve hundred was heading now toward Grigore Gica Vodă. Twelve hundred young men and women. I suddenly saw again the first girl who had stumbled off our train at the port of Constantza. I saw her raise her face and her arms to the night rain.

All my anger fled. The Revisionists—whatever their methods—were trying to save twelve hundred human beings.

I put through a call to Mandel; explained the situation in the terse kind of telephone code he had learned to use. He told me what I already knew: There was nothing whatever he could do about the matter. "And," he added, "there's nothing you will do about it either. If you have any sense."

I lifted the receiver to call Orekhovsky, but the operator interrupted to say that the hotel doctor was on his way up to my room.

Orekhovsky was out. I asked his secretary to try and trace him, have him call me at once. The matter was urgent.

The doctor was a callow young man who tried to adopt the brusque bedside manner of a septuagenarian. Yet, when he examined me, all his embarrassed youth returned. He kept averting his eyes and frowning.

As he put away his stethoscope his medical assurance returned, but the frown remained. He asked me several questions; then made his pronouncement. "You have a high temperature. You're a very sick young woman. You must follow my directions to the letter. Otherwise, I cannot be responsible."

The telephone rang.

I reached for it, but the doctor was there first. "I'm sorry," he said. "Madame Klüger is too ill to speak to anyone."

I could hear Orekhovsky's voice at the other end. His expression of surprise.

"Please!" I told the doctor. "I must speak. It's terribly important."

His frown deepened.

"I know who it is," I said. "I've been hoping for this call. Also, it's—confidential."

He sighed. "You women! Even with double pneumonia and pleurisy!" He handed me the telephone. "I will wait outside."

When he had gone, I told Orekhovsky about the visit of the Revisionists. About my call to Sidorovici. About the doctor's pronouncement. I told him that I could do nothing at all.

"Then nothing can be done," Orekhovsky said flatly.

"Don't say that," I flared at him. "It's always possible at least to try."

"So—" I heard the shrug in his voice. "All right. I will try."

I gave him the telephone number Propos had handed me. "Be sure to call. Right now. They'll be waiting."

The doctor returned to my room, and I hung up quickly.

He had secured a linen sheet and a pile of bath towels from the chambermaid. He proceeded to soak the sheet in cold water. Then he directed me to strip naked. He lay towels on the bed, bound up my body in the chilly wet sheets, and encased me then in dry towels.

I felt that I was being mummified. A sodden weariness overcame me. I could not even protest about the imprisoning sheets and towels.

I heard him giving me stern directions. He was writing out prescriptions. And he mentioned some miraculous new medicine which he would try to procure from Switzerland. In the midst of his directions and prescriptions I fell asleep.

In the days that followed, I could not distinguish reality from delirium and tortured dreams. The flowers which appeared on the dressing table: Were they from Stefan? Or a mirage? The stifling heat of the small room; did my own burning body create it? Was I in prison, in chains; or merely wrapped again in the accursed wet sheets?

I was swimming through black icy waters. I kept shouting, "Let them go!" But there was no one to hear me. Was I swimming toward shore? Or, out to the ocean?

I saw visions of that first young girl who had stepped off the transport in Constantza. She tripped, fell to her knees. Then raised her arms soundlessly to the night sky. Sometimes in my dreams the girl screamed out; a shriek which rent the darkness. She screamed for help. She screamed, and no one heard. Sometimes the girl was me.

Coughing wracked me. Stabbing pains speared through my chest.

The doctor came and went. The chambermaid. Alexander. Orekhovsky. Cotic.

And one day Stefan was there.

He sat on my bed, holding my hand in the hot darkened room. He bathed my face with a cool washrag. Sometimes he kissed my forehead. I had longed for him. Yet, as he sat beside me, I wished him away. I did not want him to see me like this.

On the seventh day of my illness, the crisis came. I shivered and sweated for hours. Then my temperature plummeted. I lay spent, unable even to move my head from the pillow. But when the young doctor arrived he smiled as though he had engineered the entire course of events. "I *knew*," he exclaimed, "that the crisis would come on the seventh day! I told you so. Sometimes it comes on the ninth day. But in your case I knew it would be the seventh. I was really quite certain," he declared, "that you wouldn't die." Then he extracted an envelope from his pocket. He shook out several pills. "Finally!" he said. "I thought they would get here too late. I had to have them sent from England."

He brought me a glass of water; held out two white tablets on his hand.

"Sulfa. Take two every four hours."

"Sulphur?" I managed a feeble attempt at humor. "With a fire and brimstone chaser?"

"It's spelled s-u-l-f-a. Sulfanilamide. The wonder drug, they call it."

Something, in any case, worked wonders.

Perhaps it was the pills. But, more probably, Stefan's four-page letter. The style, as always, was formal and precise. But it was the first long letter he had ever written me. He had telephoned the doctor, who said that after five days of complete bed rest I might be able to venture out at progressively increasing intervals each day.

I know you, little one, Stefan wrote. *If I am not there to oversee your convalescence, you will do far too much too quickly!*

He then detailed an itinerary of my recovery. On my first day out we would go to Cişmigiu Park. The few blocks' walk from my hotel would be all I should attempt for a start. We would sit at the cafe by the lake. He would order me yogurt and *kafir* (buttermilk) which, in fact, I detested.

The next day we would venture farther; to the Terasa Cercului Militar. This was a splendid open-air cafe at the crossing of the Calea Victoriei. The umbrella-topped tables were set on a raised terrace overlooking the street. It was a romantic place, especially at dusk when the haunting music of gypsy violinists colored the summer evening.

But Stefan made no mention of gypsy violins. *This time,* he wrote, *I may allow you to graduate from kafir to Azuga* (his favorite beer). *And covrig* (a kind of pretzel; filling and fattening). *Then back to the hotel for a rest. Dinner in my room. After dinner, to bed.*

"Darling," I whispered, "so terribly circumspect!" *After dinner, to bed.*

The letter went on in this manner; everything practical and to the point. He closed, however, with the most tender words he had ever written to me: *Good night, my little love. My own love. Please dream of me. Your Stefan.*

I followed orders. I dreamed of him.

In fact, I had little else to do. The doctor had decreed "No visitors." He had removed the radio from my room. He had banned the daily newspapers.

The doctor did not, however, disconnect my telephone. Orekhovsky kept in daily contact, to report on the *Tiger Hill*. But the report was always the same. Nothing had been heard yet from the ship. And his comment was always the same: "No news is good news." At first he spoke the words with genuine cheeriness. But after several days the same sentence began to sound ominous.

As for the Revisionists' transport from Poland: There was nothing, Orekhovsky said, that could have been done. He himself had journeyed to Grigore Gica Vodă. The police were thick at the borders. Their commandant had orders to report direct to Calinescu himself. The train had been allowed across the border for the time it took to be shunted onto a sidetrack and turned around. The twelve hundred young Jews were back now in Poland.

At times I felt wracked with torment. Our people on the *Tiger Hill* —what would happen to them? And to the twelve hundred young Jews who had been returned to Poland? To the three million three hundred thousand Jews in Poland? And the hundreds of thousands trapped now in Germany, Austria, Czechoslovakia . . . ?

My mind blanked at the statistics. They lost reality. I wanted to forget the world and its horrors. I wanted to create my private place and time, with Stefan. I needed to.

Since there was nothing I could do in any case but lie in bed, I tried to force the torturing thoughts from my consciousness. I existed in a virtual vacuum, sleeping most of the time, with days drifting lazily into nights. And I played with the pleasantest of dreams; dreams which centered entirely around the week of convalescence which Stefan had planned.

For this brief interlude, he said, he wanted me to become one of the pampered ladies of Bucharest society. And dutifully—delightedly—my imaginings went along with this.

Like the ladies who lived in elegant idleness, I would sleep every day till eleven; have breakfast in bed. Perhaps in bed with Stefan. I might then visit a beauty parlor. Or an exclusive dress shop on the Calea Victoriei. Then luncheon at some charming secluded restaurant; a place with long, snowy tablecloths—for we would hold hands beneath the table. Or perhaps we would stop at the Consumul Dragomir, the gourmet grocery close to the Royal Palace. We would buy caviar, wine, fruit, cheese, bread. Then back in Stefan's room we would have a picnic. And we would spend the long lunchtime in the manner adopted by so many in Bucharest's sparkling social set where the husband visited his current mistress for afternoon hours of love. (Never would he be so gauche as to return unannounced to his own home for lunch and a nap, in the manner of more prosaic Bucharest businessmen. For it was understood that his wife might spend her lunchtime entertaining her lover, perhaps at home.)

I had often been rather appalled at the carefully regulated code of dishonor which accompanied this system. But when it came to my own visions of the forthcoming week with Stefan, I found myself intensely aware of the special attractions of these private hours set aside for love.

My imagination roamed the city and its environs. We had box seats at the opera. Then we drove in a horse and carriage down the Şoseaua

Kisilef, and when we reached the Arc de Triomphe we kissed in the moonlight.

Or we were strolling through the woods by Snagov Lake. Stefan spread his coat in a grassy glade where afternoon sunlight laced through the trees. I lay back watching the blue filigreed sky as he read me poetry. After a bit he leaned over and kissed me. We did not get too far with the poetry. "Let's go," he murmured. "Let's get back to the room."

All of my daydreams seemed, in fact, to lead back to the same place: the double bed in Stefan's room at the Ambasador Hotel.

I did not ask to see the newspapers; I did not want to read of the war which was coming. I did not plead with the young doctor to have my radio returned to me. I wanted nothing to do with the world. I had come too close to death, and my dreams of Stefan, my longings for Stefan were wondrous affirmations of the full glories of life. I tortured myself with exquisitely detailed visions, but it was the sweetest type of torture there is.

Gradually I began to recover. And Stefan began to write every day. He also phoned more often.

"I'm in touch with your doctor," he told me one night. "We've decided that the best thing for you is to get right away from Bucharest. A week's holiday in the country. That's what you need. And that's what we're having."

I said nothing.

"Ruth? Is that all the enthusiasm you can muster? Silence."

"That will be—wonderful," I said.

"I'll send you some travel folders, my darling. You can pick the place."

I lay awake a long time that night, reveries clashing with realities. In a way I preferred the reveries. They presented no problems.

In any case, I went into training. Not for a week picked from a travel brochure. But because, with the slow return of strength, came the full realization of the vast amount of work to be done.

I dutifully followed doctor's orders; drank milk, ate as much as I could and took regular walks down the hotel corridor to bring strength to my rubbery weak legs.

One morning, after one of these workouts, Kadmon entered my room. He had just returned from Istanbul. Negotiations for the *Dora*, which at one point looked so hopeful, now had fallen through. The owners had upped their down-payment demands. And we could not raise the money to meet them.

"Well," Kadmon announced, settling himself in the armchair, "your doctor tells me that for someone who was nearly a basket case, you're making a good recovery. Now, what I'd like to know, do you think you'll be able to stagger to the airport next week? I'd like you to come to the Zionist Congress."

I stared at him.

He smiled and took out his cigar. "Not as a voting delegate, you understand." He lit up his cigar. "As my assistant. And," he added magnanimously, "as a full-fledged member of the Mossad."

I felt as though I had been sanctified. The Twenty-first Zionist Congress! Chaim Weizmann would be there. Ben-Gurion. Ben-Zvi. Moshe Shertok. Eliahu Golomb. Berl Katznelson. The most important Zionist leaders in the world. From all over the world.

"I had a terrible time getting plane reservations to Geneva," Kadmon said. "You can imagine, these days, everyone wanting to get somewhere else. With Switzerland a top choice destination. But—" he blew out cigar smoke in a contented ring—"I finally managed. Of course a plane costs twice as much as a train. But never mind the expense. A train trip would knock you out too much."

I had never known him to be this considerate.

He promptly explained. "We need you there. Berl will make an important speech. He'll try to get the Congress to back illegal immigration to Palestine as a new official policy. Naturally, he wants every member of the Mossad on hand to act as lobbyists. What goes on in the hallways, the cafes, the hotel rooms before his speech may be just as important to the outcome as what Katznelson says on the chamber floor."

"When do we leave for Geneva?"

"The Congress opens August sixteenth."

I nodded.

"Do you think you'll be able to make it?"

"Of course I will." I then asked the question I had put every day to Orekhovsky. "Has there been any news yet about the *Tiger Hill?*"

Kadmon hesitated.

"Please," I said. "What?"

"We finally had word this morning. The ship has been sighted by the British. She's being followed."

After a long moment I asked, "Does that mean she won't be able to land?"

"It means a secret landing will be just about impossible."

"The *Tiger Hill* people will be sent back to Europe?"

"Look," said Kadmon, "she may be a ship with a charmed life. After all, it was impossible that the Polish transport got through. It was impossible that the ship sailed from Constantza. Perhaps she's still riding high on the impossible. In any case"—he stood up—"there's nothing any of us can do from here. Except, maybe—you should excuse the expression—to pray."

He left shortly after that. There seemed suddenly nothing to say.

After going through so much, after coming so close, would the *Tiger Hill* passengers be sent back to Europe? Or sent out to sea? Was this ship of hope to be a voyage to death?

I sat staring blindly at the print on the wall: the boy by a stream fishing on a summer afternoon.

There was a knock on the door.

The bellhop, with my mail. It contained a thick packet, postmarked Czernowitz.

It seemed that Stefan too had Switzerland in mind. Enticing brightly colored brochures of Gstaad, Locarno, Interlaken, Lugano. Pictures of vacationers swimming, sailing, sunning, dining outdoors in the shade of striped umbrellas.

I threw the brochures into the wastepaper basket. And I wrote to Stefan, a brief businesslike note. I would be attending the World Zionist Congress in Geneva. All other plans must therefore be canceled.

TWENTY-ONE

IT WAS QUARTER PAST EIGHT in the evening. The evening of August sixteenth. In fifteen minutes the Twenty-first Zionist Congress would be called to order. It could well be the most important Congress in our history.

Since we had no official homeland, the International Zionist Congress—held every two years—became the one time when Jews of the world had a focal point. This year the Grand Theatre was our capital city. The laws were made here. The elections were held here. It was a democratic government of the highest order; including all the factions and frictions, all the discussions and debates.

From my seat in the gallery I tried to single out faces.

There! Coming through the doorway: Ben-Gurion! Almost at once his short, stocky figure was swallowed from view by the men who surged around him.

Making his way down a crowded aisle, Joseph Baratz, one of the founders of Deganyah, Palestine's first kibbutz. And there, the man across the hall from me at the hotel; handsome, affable, always smiling; Levi Skolnik, member of the Jewish Agency Executive.* And Moshe Shertok, short, slender, with a small black mustache; the man who held the second most important position in the Jewish Agency.† As

* See Appendix Eleven.
† See Appendix Eleven.

head of the Political Department he was, in effect, the Yishuv's Foreign Minister. He was a man accepted, admired and, above all, well liked in the international diplomatic community. He was a man with a natural warmth, an intense and genuine interest in the other person —a quality which at once turned a stranger into a friend. He was a brilliant man, sophisticated, a great wit, a great storyteller. He spoke nine languages perfectly. I had met him several times; each separate time remained incandescent in my memory.

And there—that tall, imposing gentleman with the short goatee: Weizmann! The great scientist who had led the complex negotiations which resulted in the Balfour Declaration. The man who had helped turn a hope into the promise of a national homeland. Tonight he would give the keynote speech.

Our heroes and our history, milling about on the floor below. There seemed to be two separate species of men. Those like B.G., Baratz, Skolnik had weather-tanned faces, baggy suits, shirts open at the neck. Some were already in shirtsleeves, for heat hung like a pall over the Grand Theatre.

And there were the others: the well-dressed, pale-faced gentlemen from England, South America, the United States.

This Congress, we knew, would bring forth a bitter struggle. Between the Activists: those who would fight against the White Paper and for illegal immigration. And the Legalists: who insisted we risked whatever we had gained if we broke laws; we must try, by the time-honored methods of co-operation and verbal and written persuasion, to change the crippling strictures set down by the White Paper.

The side that a man stood on could be determined in most cases by whether or not he wore a necktie, and by the country from which he came. Kadmon had reported to us last night that the Yishuv, almost to a man, were now ardent Activists. But the farther one lived from danger, the more Legalistic he became.

A sudden thunder of applause broke out. Dr. Chaim Weizmann was walking to the podium.

Youth group representatives came parading down the aisles carrying the Zionist flag, singing "Hatikvah."

Like a single body, the audience rose to join in. Voices swelled, seemed to press back the very walls.

"We have not yet lost our hope . . .
To return to the home of our forefathers . . ."

It was a mass vow taken by delegates from every land. We will not let you down. We will help you return to the homeland.

The anthem ended.

We took our seats.

Silence stretched over the hall; the same awesome silence that falls in the synagogue on Yom Kippur eve, the moment before the *shofar* is blown.

Dr. Chaim Weizmann, president of the World Zionist Congress, took up the gavel. The gavel used by Theodor Herzl at the First Zionist Congress, and used at every Congress which had followed.

I thought of Herzl's words spoken at that first Congress in 1897: "If you will it, it need not be a dream."

The entire world was against us. Yet, if we at this Congress willed it, we could save hundreds of thousands of Jewish lives.

This Zionist Congress was the Mossad's only hope. If the five hundred and twenty-nine delegates at the Congress—representing Jewish organizations all over the world—if they, as a body, backed illegal immigration, proclaiming it our last road, our only remaining chance for rescue—then our organization could spread and grow. Money would be forthcoming from powerful Jewish groups and individuals who were now afraid to help us. And money was the crucial ingredient. Money, which we now lacked completely.

Money to buy ships, to convert them, to supply them. Money to purchase exit visas, transit visas, entry visas, passports; all the rest of the assorted documents essential to the escape of each illegal. Money for bribes: the path of every convoy; every ship was paved like a road of gold with baksheesh.

Money. To buy lives.

Dr. Weizmann raised the gavel; struck it three times.

Quiet spread quickly.

He started to speak.

"It is fitting that our Twenty-first Congress—our coming-of-age gathering, so to say—should take place in this great international center, for it was here in Switzerland that our Zionist flag was first raised forty-two years ago."

There were more preliminaries. And then—"We meet at a grave juncture in the history of our movement and of Jewish life."

It would come now. Weizmann was a powerful speaker, who could tear the heart out of an audience. His words would arouse the world; let them know that we desperately needed their help.

For now they did not know. Did not believe. Newpaper accounts of the horrors were dismissed as propaganda.

But Weizmann, the statesman, the man of stature, would make them believe. When *he* related the stark facts, they would listen. They would understand. They might even—act.

And this was the best platform he could have. Over two hundred journalists were waiting to report his speech; journalists representing the most important publications in the world.

" 'The avowed adversary hath spread out his hand' and has openly proclaimed his determination to exterminate the Jews."

Yes! Extermination! You, Dr. Weizmann, will make the world understand what it is impossible to understand. That this is not just another wave of pogroms. The goal is extermination of Jews. All Jews. This is why we must rescue every Jew we can. Get them out legally or illegally. But get them out!

He went on; his voice deep, sonorous. The voice of a prophet.

"Great Jewish centers of learning and culture have been swept away. Historic communities which but yesterday were playing a noble part in the rescue of their fellow-Jews have themselves become the victims of ruthless oppression. . . . Hundreds of thousands of Jews are faced with cold pogroms, physical torture, destitution. Many have been driven to seek release by their own hand from the horrors of their existence. . . .

"It needs the eloquence of a Jeremiah to picture the horrors, the human anguish of this new dispersion; a new Book of Lamentations to depict the present plight of Israel among the nations."

You, Dr. Weizmann, are our own Jeremiah! They are listening! Look at them! The delegates, the journalists, the distinguished visitors crowding this hall. They sit forward in their seats. There is not a sound. When you recite the horrors . . . when you state the statistics . . . when you speak in specifics of the immigration barriers set up in every country, your words will be heard. They will be taken up by other men, in other lands.

The introduction was perfect. Calm, controlled. Now would come the soul-shaking oratory for which he was famed. Now would come the words to blaze open the heart of the world.

But—incredibly—he proceeded to another subject entirely. He started *thanking* everybody!

"There are nations which have nobly demonstrated their active sympathy."

I sat back—unbelieving. *Which noble nations? Which ones? Shanghai, do you mean? The only spot on earth which has put up no immigration barriers to keep out Jews!*

"There are countries," he continued, "which have received and today shelter many of the fugitives from the fires of persecution. England has done important and human work, especially for Jewish children."

England! Noble mother of the White Paper! England! Of course! A Jewish male can still get into England—if he has legal proof that he is bound for someplace else. A Jewish female can get in—if she has legal proof of a job waiting for her, as a maid. A Jewish child? He too can get into England—if a British family agrees to adopt him legally, until age eighteen.

And what of the United States, Dr. Weizmann? I hope you will not forget to mention their noble quota statistics!

"Smaller nations, including the country whose hospitality we now enjoy, have generously received many of the wanderers."

Switzerland, Dr. Weizmann? What of those official Swiss complaints to the German Government—about the masses of Jewish refugees crossing her border? What about those "measures she will take to protect herself from being—swamped by Jews"?

And still he went on!

"They have not asked for gratitude for their humanity. Indeed, it would be an offense to offer them gratitude, for they regard it as ordinary human decency to lend a helping hand to men, women and children fleeing from fire and flood. But, though these nations did not expect it, the Jewish people are deeply grateful."

Grateful! How many times, Dr. Weizmann, have you pleaded with officials for a handful of visas? Not permanent visas! Not even visitors' visas. Merely transit visas! Permission to travel across their hallowed soil in order to escape to—some place. How many times, Dr. Weizmann, have you begged for these visas only to be refused! Dismissed! Unless, of course, there was enough money for bribes too large to be refused. Money! Don't you understand, we need money! And you—with your words—are closing the purse strings. Locking the vaults.

"I have always tried to avoid overstating my case. But in this solemn hour I am reluctantly compelled to say that the British Government has gone back on its promise."

This was his overstatement! This reproving tap on the wrist!

He went on, in tepid tones, about the British White Paper. And finally referred to "the crowning evil of the suspension of Jewish immigration for the next six months."

Now, at last, it would come! The famous fiery oratory. He had purposely kept the tenor low so that the climax of his speech would shatter his audience with sudden dramatic force. Now he would throw into the blazing spotlight the hushed secret subject of illegal immigration! For it was in retaliation against illegal immigration that the British had canceled all entry certificates to Palestine for the next six months.

This was *why* we must organize our own immigration on a massive scale. We could not risk being caught like this on the twisted hooks of British politics.

But Dr. Chaim Weizmann said nothing whatever about illegal immigration. He had opened the door a crack—only to quickly close it.

"Our policy has not failed," he announced. "It is others who have failed us. . . . Ours is the sorrow, but not the shame."

He mentioned—almost in passing—like a phrase of poetry: "Hundreds of thousands of our people are homeless, driven from coast to coast, scattered like chaff before the wind." And he ended, at last, with the conclusion that "We have a formidable task, but united in firm determination, and in the spirit of brotherly co-operation, we shall surmount all difficulties. I greet you all, and hope and pray that we may be brought nearer to our ultimate goal by the Twenty-first Zionist Congress, which I now declare open."

I sat frozen, stunned, sick at the thought of the words not spoken, the facts not given, the crucial opportunity thrown away.

How many of the two hundred journalists would consider their job done when they had covered the opening address by the leader of world Zionism? How many would even trouble to return to later sessions? Berl Katznelson—the only spokesman we could be sure of—was not scheduled until the end of the week. How many reporters would be left to hear him?

And, Kadmon had told me, there was already much dissension. Powerful factions were fighting to see to it that Berl would not be put on the agenda.

The applause which followed Weizmann's speech pattered off; applause far less tumultuous than that which had greeted his arrival on the stage.

"Ruth."

I turned.

Kadmon was at the end of the aisle. I got up, excused myself past a line of knees, followed him out into the corridor.

"Well," he said, "what did you think of it?"

I was so filled with anger, disappointment that I could not speak at all.

"The less said the better, eh?" Kadmon gave me a wry smile. "Maybe that was his motto when he wrote the speech."

The corridor was crowded. Clutches of people carrying on intense conversations in a babel of languages. The rat-tat-tatting of typewriters from adjoining rooms. Messengers—youth group representatives—darting in and out, rushing up and down the hallway.

"Shmarya sent me a note on the floor," Kadmon said. "He's waiting for us."

Shmarya. We had spoken so often on the phone that I felt I knew him like a brother. I knew his rich laugh; his every inflection, his wry humor, his habit of interjecting "you see" throughout his sentences.

And, of course, I knew much about him. He had come to Palestine from Los Angeles at the age of fourteen to fulfill the deathbed wish of his father: Let the boy be educated in Palestine. Shmarya had never gone back to the States. But he had kept his American passport. That one factor alone made him invaluable to the Mossad. Shmarya Zameret, the American tourist, could travel around Europe free of fear.

"There he is!" Kadmon said.

Leaning against the wall, smoking a cigarette. He looked much as I had imagined him. Tall, young, husky, handsome.

"He's just come from Greece," Kadmon said. "He has news for us about the *Tiger Hill*."

With huge enthusiasm the two men shook hands. Then Shmarya turned to me. "So, this is our Ruth."

"Well!" said Kadmon, "what of the *Tiger Hill*?"

Shmarya exhaled the cigarette smoke slowly. "She's on her way to save hundreds of illegals on board the *Prosola*. Which is sinking."

"The *Prosola*?" Kadmon exclaimed. "For God's sake, what ship is *that*?"

"She was organized privately."

"How did you learn this?" Kadmon demanded.

"I was in Piraeus, you see, when the *Tiger Hill* tried to put in at Rhodes. For water."

"They've run out of water?"

He looked at me. "Well—almost. They're down to a half cup a day per person."

"What happened at Rhodes?" Kadmon asked.

"Levi Schwartz sent a message to the port authorities, you see. Requesting water. He was answered by shots. But he managed to get word to me. Since then, I've been in touch with him by wireless. They've almost run out of food and medical supplies. They tried to put in at Antalya. The Turkish police were magnanimous. Sold them moldy bread. But no other food. No medicine. No water. Then the ship was ordered away—by a patrol boat with a machine gun on board."

"Like a plague ship," Kadmon said grimly.

"Perhaps by this time she is."

We stared at Shmarya. It was this we dreaded most of all. Sickness on board.

"Well," he said, "half the passengers are sick. And, aside from that, most of them have dysentery."

I remembered the night I had visited the *Tiger Hill*. Lying alone on a wooden shelf in the hold I had tried to imagine what it would be like in this dark and airless hell with a woman on each side of me, a woman who might be sick. The thought alone had caused revulsion to rise within me.

Now it was happening. Right now, during these steaming nights when it was too hot to sleep—even in a comfortable bed. Right now, during these unbearably blazing days. Over seven hundred human beings—half of them ill—crowded into the hold. And they were on their way to pick up hundreds more on the sinking *Prosola*.

"On August ninth," Shmarya said, "one of the girls died."

"From dysentery?" Kadmon asked.

"No. She'd had scarlet fever, you see, just before the trip. But she insisted she was well enough to go." He stubbed out his half-smoked cigarette, tucked it into his pocket. "They were afraid the sailors would panic—maybe mutiny—if they learned there was a dead body on board. So at one in the morning Levi Schwartz said the kaddish in a secret ceremony. Then they tied the girl to a plank and dropped her overboard. The girl's name," he added, "was Zipora Levits."

I remembered the tortured hours we had spent trying to work out the impossible equations: how much space for food, fuel, water. How much for human beings. I had suggested that a small cubicle be built as an isolation ward.

Sammy Solomonides had protested. "You could sleep eight people in that space."

"But if someone gets a contagious disease," I'd insisted, "we must have an isolation ward. What good carrying more passengers—if they die?"

I was grateful now that I had been adamant. The ship at least had its isolation ward.

"A few days later," Shmarya said, "another girl died."

"From scarlet fever?"

He looked at me. "I don't know. That was the last message I had from Levi, you see. It simply gave the date of the death. And the girl's name. Yonah Shimshelevitz."

"We must say nothing about the *Tiger Hill* to anyone at the Congress," Kadmon announced. "They'll use it as a weapon against us." Then he looked at his watch. "I have an appointment. Come to my room at midnight both of you. I'll have someone there you might want to meet.

He shook hands again with Shmarya and hurried off down the corridor.

TWENTY-TWO

A YOUNG MAN TURNED from the window as I entered Kadmon's hotel room at midnight. He was strikingly handsome with dark hair, gray-blue eyes.

"Well," Kadmon was grinning. "Maybe I don't need to make introductions."

"Ruth," the young man said.

"Ehud."

We shook hands, though I felt like embracing him. For how many days had we waited in dread to hear whether Ehud Uiberall was alive or dead? Then the explosion of relief when his call came through from the office of the Slovak ambassador. But our worry about Ehud was always there, an undercurrent. He was the only local who had been made a full-fledged member of the Mossad. He was, therefore, the only Mossad member who lacked even the flimsy protection of a foreign passport. Furthermore, while virtually every Jew in Austria went far out of his way to keep out of the way of the Gestapo, Ehud—because of his mission—often walked straight into Gestapo headquarters.

It was a strange and dangerous situation.

There were some factions in the Gestapo who wanted to make the Reich *judenrein* by letting Jews out and getting Jews out. These men saw the Mossad activities as an aid to their own ends.

There were other factions who felt that every Jew in sight was a fit subject for arrest and imprisonment.

At times the Gestapo had actually helped the Mossad. At other times

Mossad members had been threatened with expulsion, imprisonment or death. This changeable attitude had nothing to do with Mossad activities. It was based entirely upon factions and jealousies within the Gestapo itself. Consequently, when a Mossad man was summoned to Gestapo headquarters, it was uncertain as to whether or not he would ever be seen again.

Ehud's predecessor in Vienna, a kibbutznik named Moshe Auerbach, had been ordered to get out of the country within twenty-four hours. The order was signed by Adolf Eichmann, head of the Central Office for Jewish Emigration in Vienna.* When Auerbach left Austria, his twenty-one-year-old local, Ehud Uiberall, was appointed by the Mossad as their man in Vienna.

"Well," Kadmon announced, "Ehud was telling me about his last encounter with Eichmann. Sit down, Ruth. Relax. Have a drink."

Kadmon's joviality came, I was certain, from the same feeling as I had; a sense of amazement and thanksgiving. Ehud Uiberall was here with us in the safe city of Geneva.

Ehud refilled his glass. "As I was saying, this time Eichmann had an extra piece of office equipment. A bullwhip. He slashed it at me. Shouted out, '*Sau Jud! Drei Schritte vom Leibe!*' So—" Ehud shrugged —"I obliged. Stood exactly three feet from him. And listened to his harangue. About how lazy we were. How little we were doing. He began to shriek. 'This pack of lice is imbedded here. You'd better start getting more Jews out. Otherwise, I'll show you how *I* get rid of them!'

"When he finally stopped ranting at me, I said, 'The trouble is, *Hauptsturmführer*, you frighten people so much they're afraid to come to the Palestine Office. If you'd call off your police—if you'd let people line up in peace—if you'd let other countries know that you want them to take in Jews—if you'd make your policies clear—then things would be much simpler. We could help you get more Jews out of the country.' At which point," Ehud smiled a little, "we actually had quite a reasonable conversation as to how all this could be accomplished. I ended up by promising to try to win the backing of this International Zionist Congress to help him get every *Sau Jud* out of the Greater German Reich."

"Too bad he can't speak at the Congress," Kadmon said. "Between

* *See* Appendix Twelve.

231

Adolf Eichmann and Berl Katznelson we might just win our case."

Ehud nodded. "I must say, from what we heard at the opening session, we need that kind of headline team."

There was a knock on the door.

Shmarya came in with another haver whom I knew well, but had never set eyes on. Yulik Braginski. Code name Shimon. Or Yehuda Ragin. Or Alexander. Or, because he had a penchant for diagnosing maladies, the Doctor.

Yulik who—with Dani Shind—had founded the Mossad le Aliyah Bet in the Polish town of Kazimierz in the summer of 1937.†

Kadmon had told me that Yulik was in his early forties. He had not, however, mentioned that Yulik was handsome, blue-eyed and blond.

After a new round of introductions, Kadmon announced, "Well, it seems that our young man in Vienna has worked out two new rescue methods." He then turned the meeting over to Ehud, who described his plans.

The first centered around an Austrian engineer named Karthaus, who had contracts to build roads in Yugoslavia.

"He's a Nazi," Ehud said. "But it's only uniform deep. He joined the Party because he believed that Austria would benefit by becoming part of the Reich. But when he saw with his own eyes Nazis beating and kicking Jewish children . . . old women forced down on their knees to scrub the gutter, with acid poured into the scrub water . . . such everyday sights—well, Karthaus got a little sick. First he was going to quit the party. That's when I met him. We had a few talks. And Karthaus decided he should keep his party position and use it to try to help Jews get out of the country."

Ehud leaned forward. He spoke with eagerness and assurance. "We worked out this plan. Karthaus has a contract to build roads in Yugoslavia. He'll send to the Yugoslav authorities the names of experienced Austrian road builders he needs on the job. About three hundred at a time. As you know, the Yugoslavs aren't rushing to grant transit visas to Jews. But they need laborers for building roads. So they'll give Karthaus temporary working permits for his crew. With these visas, he can get his crew out of Austria. They'll travel across the border in

† *See* Appendix Thirteen.

overalls and working caps. On the other side, they'll become tourists, in sunglasses and summer suits. They'll cross the country to a port. And take a pleasure cruise to some island in the Bosporus. Then they'll be dropped off—to be picked up by a Mossad ship heading for Palestine."

"I take it," said Yulik, "these pleasure cruises are also to be sponsored by the Mossad?"

Ehud nodded. "They seem a good way of getting our people off the Continent. Since passengers for day cruises need no visas or passports. But naturally we can't leave three hundred people stranded on an island. The whole thing hinges on the Mossad ship coming that same night to take them to Palestine."

"It's a good plan," Yulik said.

Kadmon nodded. Was he thinking, as I was, of the impossibilities involved in trying to co-ordinate the two operations? "Let's hear your other scheme," he said.

"This one," said Ehud, "starts after the tourist season ends. I've been in touch with the Donau Dampschiffahrts Gesellschaft. A state-owned company which runs pleasure cruises up and down the Danube. I pointed out to the directors that since they don't have much use for their cruise ships once the cold weather sets in, they may as well lease them to us. They agreed to try it. For a high price. But I had to convince them that their ships would return before they get frozen in. The company's insured against damage from ice. But there's no insurance against loss of use of their ships. If they're frozen in, the company loses all use of their ships for months. And we lose all use of their ships forever. Not to mention the fact that *these* tourists will have no visas of any sort. So, if a Mossad ship isn't waiting at Sulina to take them away—" He ended his sentence with an eloquent shrug.

"We might be able to work out something," Kadmon said slowly. "Our friend the Shamen has a tub he's promised to lease to us. An old lady called *Hilda*. A cargo ship. But if the deal goes through we could have her reconverted by November."

"Is it sure, this ship?" Ehud asked.

Kadmon shrugged. "What's sure these days? But if we can get up the down payment, the Shamen says he'll hold the ship for us till September fifteenth."

"Would that we had a few such fat friends in other countries," Yulik said.

"Look," said Kadmon, "he's a businessman. Like all the rest."

"Correction. Not quite like all the rest." Shmarya stood up. He refilled his glass. "During the last three months I suppose I've met with just about every shipowner who set foot in Athens or Piraeus. Naturally, I tell them I've got all kinds of backing. And they believe it. After all," he grinned, "don't I look like a rich American? But as soon as they get the first glimmer of the kind of cargo we'll be carrying—that's it. Thanks. Good-by. And who can blame them? Why should they risk having their ship impounded, maybe a jail sentence to boot, when they can get their price with a finger snap for legal cargo?" He looked at Kadmon. "My friend, if you were on the waterfront dealing with shipowners every day, you'd offer up prayers by the hour for the continued good health of your fat man."

Kadmon nodded. "We'll take up that proposal at our next meeting. Right now we've got a few more immediate projects to discuss."

The meeting lasted until three in the morning. We all received specific assignments, in three separate areas.

We must visit consulates, embassies, legations to collect—or to buy —as many permits and visas as possible. Visitors' visas. Transit visas. Work permits. Papers with official signatures, stamps and seals; essential ingredients for each separate rescue.

We must meet with the presidents and treasurers of all the organizations at the Congress; try to extract promises of funds.

And we must act as a lobby: to prepare the way for Berl Katznelson's speech. And to press for a vote after it. A vote in which the Twenty-first Zionist Congress sanctioned illegal immigration.

Early the following morning Ehud and I had breakfast on the terrasse of a cafe on the Quai de Mont Blanc. A bright white excursion boat plied its way down Lac Leman. Beyond, the imperious mountains rose, framing the scene in majesty. To the left a haze of light green vineyards climbed up the hillsides. And, in the far distance, the peaks of Mont Blanc jutted through soft clouds. The sunlight cast a glinting sheen over the glacial slopes.

I thought of the travel brochures Stefan had sent. One day perhaps we would come here. We would sit in the early morning sunlight, having breakfast overlooking the lake. One day we would have our time. Our place. Together.

The waiter stopped by, handed us an elaborate breakfast menu. I glanced at the prices, and ordered. *"Un petit déjeuner."* Kadmon had trained me well. If I asked for a second glass of juice at a meal, a slightly pained look would cross his face. He seemed to have our one-pound-per-person-per-day allowance branded on his brain.

"Deux petits déjeuners," Ehud said to the waiter.

Perhaps his thoughts lay along the same lines, for he said with something of a laugh, "I hope none of our brethren see us in this posh place. I feel as though I'm sitting in a synagogue in my swimming suit."

I laughed too. Then I said, "Speaking of money, I've been wondering how you raise the money you need. It's impossible enough in Bucharest, where Jews are still allowed to be rich. But in Austria!"

Ehud nodded. "You're right. It's one of the worst problems we have. Naturally, Eichmann thinks all the Mossad funds come from Palestine. If he knew we had to raise our money from Austrian Jews! And then, of course, to make matters worse the Nazis only allow small denominations to be circulated. So, what I do manage to collect is all in five-mark . . . ten-mark notes. You need a whole suitcase to carry enough for one transaction. I never hear 'Hello, how are you?' any more. It's just, 'Give me the suitcase.'"

"When this Congress is over," I said fervently, "things will be different. Money *will* come from the outside. You won't have to risk your life trying to raise funds and trotting around with a suitcase."

"Well, let's bloody well hope someone loosens up a little," Ehud said. He lit a cigarette, exhaled the smoke slowly. "I had a rich uncle in Vienna. When I was really stuck I could go to him. He kept his money hidden under the floor boards. Last week my aunt came home. She found the floor boards ripped up. They had taken my uncle. Nothing's been heard of him since. I tried to use my connections to trace him. But, so far—" he shrugged, and pressed out the cigarette.

Around us the world went on in gaiety and summer beauty. Women in summer dresses walking along the Quai. Sprays of music from the excursion boat carried in by a soft breeze. People chatting and laughing at nearby tables.

"I have a brother in Vienna," I said. "He's married. They have a little girl. They sent me her photograph just before I left Palestine. She's a beautiful child with blue eyes and long blond hair."

"Give me your brother's address," Ehud said. "I'll try."

I looked at him. Tears pressed behind my eyes. "His name is Arthur." I wrote down the address, handed it to Ehud.

"Why didn't you let me know before?" he asked.

I didn't answer. Deep within me was the feeling that those of us chosen for the Mossad should not ask for preferred treatment for our own families. When we spoke to each other on the telephone Ehud's family referred to the Jews of Austria. Pino's family were the Jews of Germany. How could I interject a plea, a request for the special safety of Ruth's family: Arthur and Rachel and the little girl, Erika?

But now, sitting with Ehud at this lakeside cafe, the request could be made.

"In his last letter," I said, "Arthur talked about going to Czechoslovakia. He thought he might get a job there. He's a brilliant scientist. Then he'd send for Rachel and the child."

"Why Czechoslovakia?" Ehud asked.

"For the same reason that thousands of other Jews fled there from Germany and Austria. The Czechs don't know about anti-Semitism. And they refuse to be taught."

"Which was why Eichmann was sent there. Have you heard about his Central Office in Prague?"

I shook my head.

"Well," said Ehud, "it's like the one in Vienna. With a few embellishments. For instance, when the applicant appears at the door of the Emigration office he's beaten up by a uniformed S.S. man. Then he must announce his former profession in a specified way. Your brother for instance would say: 'I was a Jewish scientist, thief and criminal.' After this he enters the assembly line; goes from room to room, official to official. By the time he emerges all of his savings and property have been signed over to the authorities. And then, though he's penniless, he must pay a personal duty, ranging from twenty to a hundred thousand crowns."

"But if all his money has already been taken?"

"According to Eichmann, a few months' treatment in a concentra-

236

tion camp makes them realize quickly enough just how and where they can find the money."

"*Mademoiselle. Monsieur. S'il vous plaît.*"

The waiter had returned. With elaborate ceremony he set out a silver coffee service and cups, a wicker basket of croissants, a dish with dainty curls of butter, covered pots of *confiture*.

We watched him in silence.

When he had departed, Ehud said, "If your brother and his family are still in Vienna, perhaps I can get them signed on as part of a Karthaus work crew. Your sister-in-law could be listed as a secretary."

I tried to thank him, but he stopped me. "The first job is to find them."

A boy passed by our table selling newspapers. Ehud bought the Swiss journal *Neue Zuricher Zeitung*. I watched him as he turned quickly through the pages.

I had come to dread opening up the paper every morning, switching on the radio news.

Hitler had begun a war of nerves. Its weapons were rumors which exploded like bombs, and kept on resounding. Never-ceasing barrages of rumors, slander and lies. The Reich's biggest propaganda guns were now trained on Danzig and the Polish Corridor, where Germans were "being oppressed." All Germans must be reunited in a Greater Germany. Danzig and the Corridor must be returned to the Fatherland.

It was the Sudetenland all over again. But this time with a difference. This time there would be no Munich. This time if German armies invaded, there would be war.

Ehud showed me a newspaper picture of a handsome smiling family on a beach. "Seems hard to believe," he said. "Right this minute people —thousands of them—are vacationing on the French Riviera. Lying on beach towels, sunning themselves without a care in the world."

I looked at the caption. *Joseph P. Kennedy, Ambassador to the Court of St. James's, vacationing with his wife and nine children on the French Riviera.*

"Well," said Ehud suddenly, "I had you to myself for half an hour. Looks like I'll have to settle for that."

Dani Shind was hurrying toward us across the terrasse.

I knew Dani from Palestine; a young man with blazing red hair and a pockmarked face. He had been a shepherd before he became a member of the Mossad. At first glance he seemed like an innocent boy. But he was a man of steel. His eyes pierced. He rarely smiled.

"I've been looking all the hell over for you," Dani exclaimed. "There's a meeting in Kadmon's room. Now."

"What's wrong?" said Ehud.

Dani lowered his voice. "The British have announced that not only will all legal immigration to Palestine be stopped for six months. But—" his lips tightened—"the *resumption* of legal immigration will depend upon whether or not *illegal* immigration stops."

After a long moment Ehud said, "It's unbelievable. At a time like this."

"Now the Congress *must* see it our way!" I exclaimed. "What on earth does legal immigration amount to anyway? Five thousand certificates every six months. That's less than a thousand a month. If the Congress backs us, we can save that many people a *week!*"

"Unfortunately," said Dani Shind, "the—Elders don't see it that way. The word has just gone out. No mention whatever is to be made about illegal immigration."

Ehud asked the question quietly. "What about Berl's speech?"

And quietly Dani answered, "Berl Katznelson's speech has been canceled."

TWENTY-THREE

"You're late," Kadmon said brusquely, as we entered his room. "The meeting's over."

"We just learned about it," Ehud told him.

Kadmon went to the window, stood staring out. His voice was low, the words expressionless. "We have got to see to it that Berl is given his chance to speak. That was the message of the meeting."

He turned to us then, turned on us. "We have four days. All matters to be acted on by the Congress must be presented within that time. You must live in the corridors of the Grand Theatre. More is decided there than in the official sessions. Corner everyone you can. Anyone of importance. Anyone with a vote. You must make them understand that this Congress will be committing an international crime if we are not heard. Berl Katznelson must be given his chance to speak."

Days sank into nights. Nights faded back to daylight. We followed instructions. We lived in the halls and meeting rooms of the Grand Theatre.

I went from one delegate to the next. "Listen . . . please . . . may I talk to you for just a moment . . . excuse me, my name is Ruth. I'd like to speak to you before the session begins . . ."

Some listened in silence. Some promised to give consideration to my arguments. Some listened only long enough for me to pause for breath. Then they invited me to cocktails, to dinner, for a walk along the lake when the nighttime sessions were over.

Such invitations appalled me. I found it incredible that people—our people—could eat, could laugh, could carry on as though all was right with the world: God's in His Heaven. Was He? Why have You forsaken us?

Yet, in the Bible I found arguments which certain delegates seemed embarrassed to cut short. Palestine, the Promised Land. Promised to Jews by the Lord God. A promise repeated in almost every book of the Old Testament.

And I will plant them upon their land, and they shall no more be pulled up out of their land which I have given them, saith the Lord thy God.

And I will give to thee, and to thy seed after thee . . . all the land of Canaan, for an everlasting possession.

And they shall dwell in the land that I have given unto Jacob, my servant, wherein your fathers have dwelt, and they shall dwell in it even then, and their children, and their children's children forever.

I quoted such passages to various rabbis I managed to corner in the corridors. One of them told me, "So, young lady, you think illegal immigration is fulfilling some sort of biblical destiny? Unfortunately, those words are a bit anachronistic. Today, Britannia rules the waves. Not the Lord God."

Most of the rabbis, however, would listen, nod and look contemplative. I felt hope that I had won allies among some of them.

Then, at the Friday afternoon session, the American rabbi Solomon Goldman, spoke. In ringing tones he proclaimed that the scholar and teacher Johanan Ben Zakkai was regarded as a greater Jewish hero than Bar-Kochbah. Indeed, the fighters Bar-Kochbah and Judah Maccabee had been *excluded* from the Jewish canon. The Jews had always been law-abiding. We must not break this tradition.

Rabbi Goldman also used the Bible—to condemn illegal immigration. And his long and passionate speech drew long and passionate applause.

We listened in ever-mounting despair to each of the speeches made by the distinguished delegates.

The words "illegal immigration" were never mentioned. Yet—though unspoken—the words were there in many of the speeches. And the words were condemned.

Though not, of course, by all.

Ben-Gurion made a stirring address before a meeting of the Labor Faction. A meeting held in closed session.

"Jews," he declared, "*should* act as though we were the State in Palestine; should act so until there is a Jewish State there. Should act as Englishmen would in their land if their land was in danger."

This small, stubborn man, our political leader in Palestine, cried out for "a daring patriotism which expresses itself in an insistence on continued immigration under all circumstances,—whether it leads to clashes with the authorities or not."

But even he did not speak the forbidden words.

Then, on Saturday night, another famous delegate spoke. The hall was packed to hear him; the press section filled. The American rabbi Dr. Abba Hillel Silver was one of the most influential men at the Congress; a tall, imposing gentleman, known for his stirring oratory.

In sonorous tones he proclaimed: "We must not yield to emotion or passion. . . . We must not act as though we are the State, when we are not. This will expose us to disaster. In our desperation, we must not put weapons into the hands of our enemies. We must not make a strategic blunder."

I sat listening to him, trying to fight back tears of rage. *Would you speak this way, Rabbi Abba Hillel Silver, if you lived in Berlin—instead of Cleveland, Ohio?**

On Sunday morning I woke up to the somber clanging of church bells.

I lay, staring at the ceiling, afraid perhaps to get up.

Dr. Silver had spoken last night until midnight. It had then been announced that Berl Katznelson would speak at the Sunday-morning session.

Sunday, the day of rest for most of the journalists covering our Congress. They had stayed late last night to hear the famous, brilliant and

* *See* Appendix Fourteen.

eloquent Dr. Silver. How many would trouble to get up early this Sunday morning to hear Berl?

He had been allotted a speaking time which should, by rights, have been devoted to inconsequential matters such as procedural regulations. But soporific subjects such as these had been discussed, endlessly, at the second session of the Congress—as though this were some placid period in Jewish history when there was nothing more urgent to speak about than reports of local Zionist elections which had taken place in the forty-three constituencies, and regulations concerning the abuses in the sale of *shekalim*.

The sound of the church bells shivered out into silence.

I got up, went to the open window. It was early; there was little traffic. The streets were almost deserted. A few men were having breakfast at the sidewalk cafe across from the hotel. Sunlight poured its brightness onto the street, heightening its colors. Everything looked as though it had been freshly painted the day before.

Then I closed my eyes, for sudden dizziness swept through me.

If you must go to Geneva, you have got to take care of yourself, the doctor had said. *Eat properly. Get plenty of rest. You came close to dying. You don't want to push your luck.*

I had not even troubled to remember his words until this moment. Somehow I'd managed to keep on; sleeping two or three hours a night, never sitting down to a meal. For every hour away from the corridors and hotel lobbies might mean missing a contact who could prove vital when it came to a final vote.

At the twelfth session, the political resolutions of the Twenty-first Zionist Congress would be read.

If one of these resolutions condemned illegal immigration, Jews would be helping to seal the fate of their brothers.

If no mention was made of illegal immigration, the Mossad could only continue to struggle along; a small operation, constantly desperate for funds.

But if the Congress sponsored illegal immigration—then we could start to operate in a manner which matched our elaborate plans. Then nothing could stop us. Except war.

I breathed in deeply, hoping the dizziness would leave me.

I could not afford to be sick again.

It was very early; perhaps if I slept for a few more hours. I got back to bed; rang the hotel operator, asked that she call me at nine o'clock. Then I settled down into the softness of the feather pillows.

I startled awake as a chambermaid unlocked my door and entered the room, broom and bucket in hand.

"Oh, mademoiselle, pardon!" she exclaimed, starting to back out.

"Wait!" I called. "What time is it?"

"Eleven o'clock, mademoiselle. All the others left long ago. So I thought—"

The others! The delegates! For this hotel was crowded with them. Eleven o'clock. The session had started!

I was out of my room in minutes, running down the stairway, through the lobby, to the doorman.

"A taxi! I'm terribly late!"

He shrilled at his whistle. Again and again. Were all the cab drivers sleeping this Sunday morning?

Finally, an ancient vehicle wheeled around the corner, sidled up to the hotel.

I jumped in. "The Grand Theatre. Hurry, please."

We hurtled noisily through the empty streets; sped across the Pont du Mont-Blanc, charged down the tree-shaded Grand Quai, along the Rue de Rhone, through the Rue de Strand, to the Grand Theatre. I paid the driver double, showed my pass to the doorman. Ran up the marble stairway. Entered the balcony. And heard his voice, resounding through the microphone, filling the great hall.

Berl.

His voice was calm, controlled. It held no anger.

"From this place some words were spoken by Rabbi Silver that I can't ignore. For the words were like stones; stones thrown at the refugees who are already on the seas. The words were like a knife in the back of Zionist policy."

A wave of mutterings, protestations arose from the floor below.

I saw Uri, Kadmon's teen-age son. There was an empty seat next to him.

"Did I miss much?" I said, sitting beside him.

Uri's hands were fisted in anger. "They wanted to adjourn the session. They marched through the aisles protesting. They didn't want to let him speak. And now that he's up there—" His voice broke.

"Please," Berl was saying in Yiddish. "Please . . ."

The hall was crowded with opponents, the so-called Legalists.

Telescoped by perspective, Berl Katznelson seemed so small a figure as he stood alone on the podium. Gray-creased suit, blue workman's shirt, the bush of graying hair. He took a sip of water. Then he raised both hands for silence. But there was no silence.

"They finally allow him to speak," Uri burst out. "And they won't listen to the man!"

Finally, the hall quieted. But the indignation could still be felt. The silence crackled with it.

Then Berl continued—speaking Yiddish, the common language of the common Jew—"I remind Rabbi Abba Hillel Silver of the higher law, which must violate temporary restrictions—*lawless* restrictions—if Zionism is to survive."

He stopped for a moment, sipped more water. Then he went on, speaking rapidly now, pausing occasionally to look at his notes.

"There is an aliyah that is called the illegal aliyah. Everything in this lawful world is very lawful. Lawful governments. Lawful conquests. Lawful documents. Even lawful breaking of promises.

"Only the aliyah of the Jews—based on the ancient biblical mandate that we reach the Holy Land—only this is not lawful.

"And here we witness a very strange thing. With what understanding this aliyah is looked upon by the British Parliament. And with what lack of understanding it is looked upon here at the Zionist Congress . . .†

"Even the sea shows understanding and pity for our refugees. A few weeks ago a small boat of twelve elderly Jews from Germany approached the shores of Palestine. It was a boat without a motor. Without professional sailors. The smallest storm could sink this small boat. How many miracles must have happened to those twelve people at sea?"

Applause started at the back of the hall.

† *See* Appendix Fifteen.

Uri and I picked it up, clapping furiously. But the sound petered out, like pebbles thrown into the resisting waves of silence.

And Berl went on. "In our newspaper *Davar* we ran a story recently. Five boats arrived. Only one had a motor. These small boats held a total of one hundred and forty refugees, many of them pregnant women. And thirty children. The captain had put his passengers on these small boats forty miles from shore. And left them. But the sea was kind to them and brought them safely to shore."

He paused. "If the sea," he said, "would listen to some 'important' Jews, it probably would act differently."

Laughter rose from the audience. Bitter laughter. And more applause.

"We are told," said Berl, "that this aliyah bet—this so-called illegal immigration—is a nonselective aliyah. That it may contain 'bad elements.' And I listen. And I think, since when are *you* so—selective?

"Year after year we said and said again that Eretz Israel cannot take just anyone, because she needs young people. People who have courage and know how to work. People who will go into the army. People who are fit for every emergency.

"Then *you* were the ones who were angry at *us!* You said that we held this policy out of party interest. That we were discriminating between one Jew and another. You asked us not to prefer a young Jew to an old one; a pioneer to an old storekeeper.

"Now—" his voice rose for the first time—"when the great holocaust comes—and the Jewish refugee is running from hell, from Germany, Austria and Czechoslovakia—and wants to come to Eretz Israel, now *you* start talking about 'selectivity.' . . .

"*Why*"—he cried out—"why do the institutions of help and immigration stand so far away? Are they afraid that they'll dirty their hands? Instead of helping they come—and *criticize the quality of the immigrant.*"

Silence.

Silence could speak, I realized suddenly, with many voices. Was this the silence of shame?

He sipped some more water. Then quietly he continued. "I think that every Zionist should be happy that—with all the misfortunes which have come upon our settlers in Eretz Israel—*we* are still able to help Jews out of this great catastrophe.

"If the American Jews are not allowed to take in the Jews running away from hell—they should at least help in another way. They should help the ones that *dare* to help!"

He paused for a long moment. "I believe that the day is not far away when songs will be sung and even special prayers will be written for the well-being of our illegal seamen. And—who knows—maybe even prayers will be said in the temples of America."

Again, laughter rose from the hall. Again, applause.

He had them now; their attention caught on the hooks of sarcasm.

"This aliyah bet," Berl went on, "is in my eyes a huge human problem. A moral problem. And a problem of Jewish brotherhood. Which immigration in the world is more lawful, if this aliyah is *not* lawful?

"And which laws in the world are lawful, if saving a Jewish life is *not* lawful?"

He stared out at his audience. And they, as a body, it seemed, stared back at him. In silence.

"I, myself," Berl went on, "am also an illegal immigrant. And, although we like to worship our past, I dare say that the illegal aliyah of BILU and of the Second Aliyah was not more important than the aliyah of today.

"*This* illegal aliyah has a very important mission in our struggle.

"There were the days when the small Jewish shopkeeper dreamed about Eretz Israel, and started coming. Then—after Herzl—came the days of the doctors, lawyers, students. The Second Aliyah. To many these seemed the days of glory. Then came the boys without diplomas who worked in the orange groves of Petah-Tikvah and Galilee.

"And when I ask myself who is now the natural bearer of the struggle for our existence, my answer is—the scattered refugees on the seas. They will not allow the gates of Eretz Israel‡ to close before them. They will not let the conscience of the world rest in peace. They will not permit Sir Malcolm MacDonald to implement the White Paper. The Jewish refugees will be at the head of the struggle. *And we must all join their army.*"

‡ *See* Appendix Sixteen.

The applause started slowly. It swelled. It rose through the hall in waves. Thundering waves, which turned the tide.

Men were standing. Men were cheering.

Uri and I were on our feet; we too were shouting.

Those who still remained seated were suddenly small, shamed; the enemy defeated.

Berl Katznelson stood alone on the stage. But we were alone no longer.

His figure wavered, was blurred out by my tears.

TWENTY-FOUR

IT WAS SUDDENLY EASY.

Smiles. Handshakes. Welcomes. Promissory notes. On Sunday after Berl's speech, and on the day which followed, I ran from the temporary office of this Jewish organization and that; seeing presidents, chairmen, treasurers. Suddenly Mossad was no longer a word to be spoken in secret, in shame. Suddenly we were no longer outcasts.

But was it now too late?

The following evening, headlines seared the front pages. Berlin announced that Foreign Minister Joachim von Ribbentrop was flying to Moscow to conclude a nonaggression treaty between Germany and the Soviet Union. Though the treaty had not yet been signed, we knew that the all-important secret agreements must have been reached. Though the treaty had not yet been published, we knew that every word of it could be translated into a single word: war.

As the French ambassador to Berlin had written two months ago: *Hitler will risk war if he does not have to fight Russia.* For two months the French ambassador had pleaded that France and Britain negotiate a treaty with Moscow. But nothing had been done.

Now Hitler was lifting the last roadblock to his war machine.

I returned to my hotel late that night, switched on the bedside radio. Swiss country music flooded the room; bright-colored, redolent of high mountains and yodeling goatherds. It was interrupted by a terse announcement: Monsieur Coulondre, the French ambassador in Berlin, had reported to his foreign office the start of German troop concentration.

At nine-forty on Thursday evening, August twenty-fourth, the twelfth session of the Twenty-first Zionist Congress was called to order. The closing session.

Eight political resolutions were read and adopted by an overwhelming majority. The first resolution did not mention the words "illegal immigration." But the words were there all the same; the words were there for all who wished to read them:

"The sacred bond between the Jewish people and their historic homeland cannot be severed, and nothing will prevent the Jews from returning to their country and rebuilding their national home."

The session went on until 1:40 A.M. Chaim Weizmann gave the closing address. He ended by saying: "I have no prayer but this: that we will all meet again alive."

The next morning was the time of good-bys.

Our hotel, the Cornavin, was near the railroad station; therefore, many delegates made appointments to meet in the lobby for final instructions, for final farewells, before their train took off.

We tried to approach every American delegate we saw. Our words were different, but our cry was always the same: Don't forget us. You must try to open the gates. You must tell them what's going on with the Jews in Europe. You must make them understand what will happen if we do not have help.

Everyone seemed in a desperate hurry to leave. Some were headed back to safety. Some to uncertainty. Some to virtual suicide.

Pino Ginsberg was one of these; the Mossad man in Berlin.

It was he who had inaugurated the astounding concept of marching into Gestapo headquarters to insist that they help his organization in their efforts to get Jews out of the Reich. He had endured the shouting, the screaming, the curses of the Gestapo chiefs; had then merely shrugged and announced that if the Nazis did not accede to his demands, his organization would take their funds and their efforts to another country. After all, he pointed out, the Reich was not the only nation which wanted to get rid of its Jews.

In the end, to everyone's amazement, the Gestapo had provided the training farms for pioneers, the exit visas and the promises of non-interference which Pino Ginsberg requested.

That, however, was last summer.

Now, a year later, the situation was such that the Mossad ordered Pino not to return to Germany. He was to remain in Geneva, to await further instructions. His initiative, daring and experience would be used elsewhere.

But Pino had other thoughts on the matter. "There is too much to do in Germany," he told us. "I must go back while there still is time."

I watched him as he walked out the door of the Cornavin hotel; a tall and lanky, balding man with a deep voice and an imposing manner. He was thirty-two years old.

I have no prayer but this: that we will all meet again alive.

Ehud Uiberall was also ordered not to return. He was instructed to go to Palestine. His fiancee was already there. He had done enough. He had risked his life too often. To go back to Vienna now would be taking a train ride to almost certain death. He did not even have the paper protection of a foreign passport.

But Ehud merely repeated the words Pino had spoken. "There is too much to do. I must go back." Then he had added with something of a smile, "If I don't make it, maybe they'll name a kibbutz after me one day."

Shmarya left for Greece, Dani for Turkey. And, since Kadmon had been ordered back to Palestine for further consultations with Mossad leaders there, I was to handle the Rumanian operation alone. "From now on," Kadmon told me, "you'll have to be the soldier and the general."

Kadmon, Uri and I boarded a train for Genoa. From there we had been promised space on an Italian ship which would stop first at Istanbul, then at Constantza.

The train trip to the Italian port took two nights and a day. It was baking hot. The aisles were jammed. We stood most of the way. Everyone, it seemed, was either rushing home or running away from home in these deadline hours before war split the Continent.

When we reached Genoa it was raining drearily, a suitable background for the crowds of passengers disgorged from the station doors into the streets. Gray people in the gray wet summer twilight. No one spoke. No one smiled.

We took a bus to the port; then sat in a cafe for three hours while Kadmon tried to get a call through to Alexander in Bucharest.

Finally, he emerged from the phone booth looking grim.

"Well," he announced, "it seems that now, with war about to break out any day, the Shamen has received a number of very interesting offers for the *Hilda*. The fat one has therefore decided he can't afford to risk such a valuable ship on an illegal enterprise. This ancient leaking old lady has suddenly become a beauty queen in his eyes."

Kadmon sat down heavily. "I instructed Alexander to try to stall the Shamen till you get there." He looked at me dubiously. "I trust," he said, "that you will be able to cope."

We sailed that night. Kadmon, Uri and I had been allotted a single berth in a cabin with three Greek Orthodox priests. We slept in rotating shifts; four hours each.

In Istanbul we said good-by. As I stood on deck, watching Kadmon and Uri plod down the gangplank I felt a deep rush of affection for this stolid sometimes exasperating man who had been my chief and my mentor and perhaps a father figure for the past three months. When he reached the pier Kadmon turned, waved. I waved back. I felt suddenly desperately alone.

The ship sailed into the port of Constantza on Friday, September first. It was early morning. As I stood in the jostling crowd of the customs shed, frustration and impatience mounted. I *had* to make the next train to Bucharest. Yet, no one here seemed to be moving. There was only one customs man to handle the hordes of jostling passengers.

Suddenly, like a tidal wave, a word swept through the crowd. I heard it first in Rumanian. *Razboi.*

It surged up then in other tongues. *La guerre! Rat! Krieg!*

War!

Then the baggagemaster was standing upon a pile of suitcases stacked on the counter. He crossed one arm over his chest; raised the other arm high in the air. In his peaked cap and his brass-buttoned uniform he looked like some ludicrous little general.

"Quiet!" he shouted out, over and over, until the assembled mass of passengers all turned toward him. He made his announcement three times: in Rumanian, French and German.

"Several hours ago, at dawn—at 5:40 A.M. to be precise—the German radio announced that German troops were marching across the Polish borders. At this moment German planes were bombing Polish railways, bridges and cities."

Then the baggagemaster raised both hands for silence. A smile spread across his face. "Ladies and gentlemen, I am happy to announce that, because of the emergency, we have scheduled an extra train to Bucharest. It will leave the station at ten-fifteen."

I managed to get onto that extra train. It was a strange ride. Passengers spoke to each other in subdued voices. What will happen? Will France and England declare war? Will the Poles fight? When the Germans take Poland, what will happen to Rumania? No one had any answers to offer. Each question was met with a shrug, a shake of the head. But that sampling of humanity, jammed close in the train corridor, was united in fear, in foreboding. Each had his own problems brought on by the baggagemaster's announcement. But each knew that the other's life was likely to be rent apart somehow in the months ahead. This sudden closeness in spirit brought on an unfamiliar courtesy and consideration. When the train lurched and we jarred against each other there were smiles, apologies. We were all, I felt, like refugees in a hurtling train bound we knew not where.

Once I was pressed against the glass of a compartment. I stared at one of the passengers fortunate enough to find a seat; an inordinately fat woman, with rosy cheeks and plump little hands. She was eating a piece of cake, chewing rapidly as though in a race, and when she finished her fat fingers plucked each cake crumb from her dress and from her sweaty chest half-bared by the peasant blouse. With jerky motions she brought each crumb swiftly to her mouth. She seemed a ludicrous yet pathetic figure searching desperately for every last morsel of the placid, normal life which she might never find again.

Yet, once we reached Bucharest it was as though the baggagemaster's announcement had never been made. The streets were filled with strolling shoppers; the sidewalk cafes were busy. The traffic on the Calea Griviței and Boulevarde Elisabeta was heavy; the air punctuated by the honking of horns. As my cab neared the Ambasador Hotel I saw a newsboy on the corner shouting, "*Editie Speciala.*" He held up the newspaper and the headlines were so large I could read them from half a block away. GERMANY INVADES POLAND. Yet, no one seemed to be rushing to buy the paper. Perhaps Bucharestians felt if they did not read the news it would somehow go away.

As I stood at the front desk of the Ambasador's lobby filling out my registration form, the concierge snapped his fingers, obviously to summon a boy who would take my bag and escort me to the room. Nevertheless, I glanced behind me—and saw a policeman put down his newspaper and rise from the armchair. It was the officer who had come to my room; ripped open my robe.

He was striding toward me, smiling a little.

I picked up my suitcase, dashed out. A taxi was pulling away from the curb. I yanked open the door, jumped in. "Quick. Hurry."

"Where to, mademoiselle?" he inquired.

The policeman came charging out.

"The Banca Comercială," I said.

The policeman ran toward us shouting, "Halt! Stop!"

But, incredibly, the taxi lurched off down the street.

I looked back, saw him signaling another cab.

We sped round the corner with a screech of brakes. "I've noticed," the driver remarked placidly, "that passengers running from the police are generally more generous than most."

"Yes," I blurted, "that must certainly be true."

I looked back. The street seemed filled with taxis.

What did he want of me? Had he learned of my Mossad activities? Or had orders gone out to round up all foreign nationals? Was he coming to arrest me? Or to offer himself again as my "protector?"

As we swerved around another corner I realized I had made a stupid blunder. I had blurted out Mandel's address as my first thought of safety. But we had always been careful to keep our connections with Mandel buried in secrecy.

"Look," I said to the driver, "instead of that other address, will you take me to the post office. As quickly as possible."

"*Entendu, mademoiselle!*" We sped down the next block; in and out such a labyrinth of side streets that I felt certain we had lost my pursuer.

When we reached the General Post Office I gave the driver a tip which was, I hoped, large enough to make him forget the first address I had given, should he be called in by the police for questioning.

I hurried into the post office, one of the few places in the city where public telephones were available. Here, however, news of the war had obviously taken hold. There was a long queue before each phone booth.

I stood in the line farthest from the door, and as I waited I kept glancing toward the entrance, certain that he would enter any moment. All my dreads and fears of the future seemed to have centered suddenly in the sallow-faced person of the police officer.

Finally my turn at the phone booth came and I was able to reach Mandel at his office. I told him I could not return to the Ambasador. Could he work his magic to get me a reservation anywhere else? He took my number, promised to call me back as soon as possible.

In view of the long line of people impatiently waiting I knew the phone would remain incessantly busy once I left the booth, so I hung up but pretended to go on speaking, hoping that those outside would not observe me too closely. They did, however. An imperious gentleman with a monocle and cigarette holder was next in line. He began rapping on the door of the booth. I paid no attention whatever; kept on chattering into the dead phone. "Please, dear George," I intoned softly in Hebrew, "I know hotel rooms will be an impossibility now. But do try, dear George. You must understand that I can't go from hotel to hotel asking for a room. I would certainly be caught if I did so. Please hurry, dear George. The gentleman outside knows very well I am talking to no one."

I began to feel faint in the stifling heat and stench of the public phone booth.

Finally, the telephone rang.

"I've found you a place," Mandel said. "A two-room flat in a house owned by a friend of mine."

"Wonderful," I exclaimed. "Where is it?"

He told me the address. A street called C. A. Rosetti; a beautiful residential block, ten minutes from the center of town.

"Is it very expensive?"

"Don't worry about that," Mandel said. "Just get there right away. They're expecting you."

"Bless you, dear George." I had never called him by his first name before.

I hung up quickly, rushed out to the street, signaled a cab, and climbed in, praying I was not being followed.

Then, down a side street, I saw a flash of the Dâmbovita River. Suddenly the memory of Stefan was all over me. We were there by the river, his arms around me; we were saying good-by.

The taxi moved on; the river view disappeared. But in that brief moment I determined that I must get back to Czernowitz, if only for a day. I must do my utmost to persuade Stefan to leave. And my brother, my sister, my aunts. Czernowitz was close to the Polish border. How long would it take the German Army to overrun Poland? Then, perhaps to enter Rumania? They must get out now. While there still was time.

The taxi turned into C. A. Rosetti Square; a placid tree-shaded place where nursemaids sat rocking their charges in perambulators, and children played at the base of C. A. Rosetti's statue, a staid-looking gentleman seated for his iron-cast immortality in an armchair.

We drove slowly through the quiet street which was lined with stately elms and oaks and splendid stone villas replete with wrought-iron balconies, french windows shuttered against the afternoon sunlight, and splashes of color—the street-side view of the rear flower gardens. An oasis of quiet only a block from the traffic-busy Boulevard Pache; a splendid hideaway for the illegal operations of the Mossad.

My new landlady was waiting; a gracious smiling woman who greeted me as though I had just returned home after a long absence. "I hope you like the apartment," she said. "We had it done over for our married daughter. But as soon as it was finished, her husband got a job in Paris, and they moved away. I was keeping the room for them, hoping they'd come home soon. But now, with the war—" she shrugged. "I suppose it's better they stay away. If he came home he'd only have to go in the army. So when George Mandel phoned—" she smiled at me. "Well, come see the flat. I hope you like it."

I did.

There was an anteroom with hangers for coats, a small kitchen, a bathroom with a huge tub. The main room was large, with a window overlooking leafy treetops. It was furnished with a table, sofa, chairs, a bookshelf. There were red curtains to the back; behind them a high double bed, a bed table—and on it that most cherished of all objects—a telephone.

"The phone is an extension of yours?" I asked.

"Not at all. My daughter insisted she would not live with us unless she had her own private line. We had to wait for months. But we finally got the phone—just as she left for Paris."

"How much do you want for the flat?" I asked, afraid to hear the answer.

"Would five thousand lei a month be too much?"

I hesitated. Kadmon would have left at once. But the flat was perfect for our purposes. "I'll take it," I said. And for some reason I embraced this lovely smiling woman.

Then I asked for news of the war. I had heard nothing since the early morning announcement in the customs shed. But my landlady, whose name, she informed me, was Mrs. Schecter, knew little more. "My radio's been on all day. But the newscasts give no details. German troops are moving toward Warsaw. The Luftwaffe is bombing bridges, railroads, cities. Including Warsaw. There are many Polish casualties."

"What about England? France? Their treaty agreements with Poland?"

Mrs. Schecter shook her head. "No word at all."

When she left, I took a bath, then pulled back the drapes and lay down on the bed. In a moment I would start making phone calls. And I would ask Alexander to bring me my radio which was in storage at the Ambasador Hotel. But for a small luxurious space of time I shut the world away while I lay in a half dream looking out at the room. And my thoughts centered again upon Stefan. It was another life. This was our room. I lay waiting for him to come home. He would lie beside me on the bed.

Afterward, we would remain side by side talking softly as evening gray crept through the rectangle of sky and muted the green of the treetops which we could see out the open window. Then, a long while later, I would get up and start preparing dinner. . . .

I picked up the telephone; called Alexander. As usual, his querulous mother answered. No, she did not know where her son was, or when he would be back. Who wanted him anyway?

When I left my name and my new number her voice turned brittle. She seemed to think I was relentlessly pursuing her son. I wanted to assure her she had nothing to worry about.

I managed to contact Orekhovsky, Cotic and the Shamen, whom I saw later that evening at his apartment. I brought Orekhovsky along.

"Why is it," the Shamen inquired, "that you always seem to travel about with a chaperon?"

He was in high good humor as he sat in his armchair pouring out brandy; lord of the manor. The war obviously boded well for his shipping business. For a time working with the Mossad seemed to have engendered some small flame of humanity in his deep-buried soul. But this had obviously been quenched by the lures of war profiteering. He now wanted sixty-five pounds sterling per passenger; more than twice as much as he had demanded in the case of the *Tiger Hill*. Plus an additional guarantee of ten thousand pounds to be delivered in four days' time.

I tried, but this time there was no bargaining. The Shamen remained smiling, gracious and adamant.

Orekhovsky was no help at all. He sat somberly, nodding sometimes, but saying little. News of the war seemed to have stunned him into immobility. He had relatives and many friends in Warsaw.

Finally, sustained by the promises of funds we had received at the Zionist Congress, I agreed to the Shamen's terms. And we departed.

"You were right," Orekhovsky assured me as we walked together down the dark street. "We must get ships now, whatever they cost. Only ships can save us from destruction."

Alexander and I spent the following day in the city, approaching contacts for funds. I also sent cables and, when possible, got calls through to some of the presidents, chairmen, treasurers of the numerous organizations who had given us promises in Geneva. But in each case news of the war provided ample reasons why funds would not now be forthcoming. Perhaps if I went myself to plead . . . But by afternoon the radio announced that the French Parliament was meeting to discuss an ultimatum to be sent to Germany. If the French declared war, Rumania would undoubtedly close her borders. If I left the country, I might not be able to get back in.

Our fund-raising efforts in Bucharest were virtually fruitless. Although Jews of the city still seemed to wrap themselves in the comforting reassurances that Rumania would remain neutral, the war would not touch them, still—when it came to signing checks for the Mossad—their fingers grew suddenly paralyzed. Deep in every man's heart was the realization that he might, after all, need all his assets to save his own family. Besides, most of the men we went to that day had already given money for the *Tiger Hill*.

I determined to leave for Czernowitz the following night. The city had a large and wealthy Jewish community. We had never approached anyone there for funds. Max Ritter von Anhauch lived in Czernowitz. His name alone had twice proved an open sesame for me; gaining me entrance into Mandel's office, and then gaining me the ear of the stationmaster at Grigore Gica Vodă. Perhaps now, Von Anhauch, one of the wealthiest Jews in Rumania, would provide the down payment we needed to secure the *Hilda*.

Acting as though the hope had already been changed into pounds sterling, I phoned the Shamen to inform him that I would be out of town for a few days. When I returned I would have the money he wanted.

"Since your last visit," he said, "I have had four other very interesting offers for the ship."

Early the next morning I was awakened by an imperious knocking at the door of my room. I slipped into a dressing gown and hurried to open it. A grinning Alexander stepped inside.

"I have brought you three items," he announced. "First, a *wagon-lit* reservation for Czernowitz tonight."

"A berth!" I exclaimed. "However did you manage *that?*"

Alexander shrugged. "I have a few contacts of my own, you know." Then he added, "The other two items I mentioned are waiting downstairs. They've just flown in from Palestine. Shall I bring them up?"

I nodded, and he left. I took my clothes into the bathroom; washed and dressed quickly.

When I emerged, Alexander was sitting, legs spread wide, arms stretched along the back of the couch as though he owned the apartment and all within it. There were two young men standing in the doorway. One strode forward. He was husky, tall and handsome. I liked his smile. "Forgive us for getting you up so early." We shook hands. "I'm David Arnon."

The other man was equally young, but seemed somewhat more diffident. He remained standing in the open doorway.

"Yitzhak Hecker," he said in a soft voice. He was short, thin, with dark blond hair and gray, sad eyes.

"Come in," I said. "Shut the door. Sit down. Will you have some coffee?"

Alexander then completed the introductions. The two young men had been sent from Palestine for two purposes. The first, to buy arms; some of which they would bury here in the forests, for use—if necessary—by the Jews of Bucharest. The rest would be smuggled back to Palestine. The boys' second mission: to train Jews in Bucharest in methods and skills of self-defense.

"These two fellows were sent to you by Yehuda Arazi," Alexander concluded. "With orders that you help them in any way possible."

The Mossad was illegal enough, without involving itself in a second —even more suspect—branch of activities.

"Well," I said, *"my* orders don't come from Yehuda Arazi!"

David dismissed this difficulty with a smile. "We come with more than orders. We come with news. About the *Tiger Hill.*"

Though I'd thought about the ship constantly, even dreamed about her in torn nightmares from which I woke sobbing, I had heard no news about her since Shmarya's dismal report at the Zionist Congress two weeks ago. A ship which had run out of food, water, medical supplies. A ship overcrowded with sick passengers, on her way to take on hundreds more illegals from the *Prosula,* which was sinking.

"What was the last thing you heard about her?" David asked.

I told him.

"Well," he said, "the captain and crew of the *Tiger Hill* threatened to mutiny if the *Prosula* people were taken aboard. Nor were the passengers on the *Tiger Hill* any too enthusiastic. They claimed the ship couldn't hold one extra body. But the Mossad men, Levi Schwartz and a few others who had boarded the *Tiger Hill*, sent the captain and crew onto the *Prosula* while they directed the boarding operations. Then, the *Tiger Hill*—with one thousand one hundred and fifty-nine passengers aboard—set off again for Palestine."

David sat down. He lit a cigarette. I wanted to cry out: But what happened? Are they safe? For God's sake, give me the details later. Just tell me—are they safe?

But the man seemed intent on telling the story in his own excruciating way, and I held back my words.

"The Mossad," he went on, "decided to try for a landing on the deserted coast of Ashdod. They hoped to avoid the British patrols. Of course, this meant that hundreds of very sick passengers might have to march five miles or more to the nearest Jewish settlement in the desert. But—" he shrugged—"the first priority was getting them to shore at all. Especially since they'd already been sighted by the British in the Mediterranean."

Again David paused; blew out the cigarette smoke slowly. Yitzhak, perhaps sensing my frenzy of impatience, broke in: "To make a long story very short," he said, "they tried to land at night. They thought they would make it. But suddenly they were spotted by a British patrol boat. Caught in the beams of two searchlights. The British opened fire. Two passengers were killed."

Fury, despair rose like nausea within me. *Killed*. Killed for what? For the inhuman crime of trying to save their own lives?

"Who were they?"

David answered. "One was a doctor. Dr. Robert Schneider. From Czechoslovakia. One of the *Prosula* passengers. The other was Zvi Binder. Very young. A pioneer. From Poland."

"And the ship?" I asked. "Was it captured?" No wonder they fed me the story slowly, preparing me for disaster.

But David said, "Somehow that hulking old lady of yours managed to

260

get away, outside the three-mile limit before the patrol boat could catch her. But," he added quickly, "that was only the start of her troubles. The *Prosula* people were no stalwart halutzim. They'd had no training; no preparation for such emergencies. They were terrified by the shooting. They demanded that no more illegal landings be attempted. They wanted the ship to give itself up. The captain and the crew, quite naturally, agreed with them. Why should *they* risk their lives for the sake of a thousand Jews? On the other hand, the *Tiger Hill* people, after all they'd been through, were not prepared to give up at this late date. So a civil war broke out on board.

"The Mossad men, however, remained in control. And they decided on the impossible. On the night of September first, they rammed the ship as close to shore as they could get. Off the coast of Tel Aviv."

I gasped. Tel Aviv! The most populated beach front in Palestine.

David laughed suddenly, a sound of pure joy. "I was there. If I hadn't been, I'd never have believed it. The Mossad had organized men with fishing boats, row boats, ropes. Meanwhile, the beach started swarming with people. They were carrying towels, blankets, extra clothing. The refugees came off the *Tiger Hill*. Those who still had any strength at all swam for shore. They came walking in from the waves; crawling onto the beach. But most of them had to be brought to shore in boats. Then, as they landed, the Tel Avivians took over. Wrapped them in blankets, towels; helped them change clothes. And hustled them off to their own homes."

I, too, started to laugh. It was incredible!

"And the British police?"

"Naturally," David said, "it didn't take them long to realize what was going on. But when the police got there the people on the beach turned on them, throwing rocks, shoes, sand. There were about a hundred police. But they were outnumbered ten to one. The police were armed of course. But the people on the beach were armed too. With fury. They'd seen. They'd seen the two dead bodies carried along the beach. They'd seen the refugees struggling to get to shore. Being dragged out of the waves by their rescuers. They'd heard, of course, about the conditions. The stinking, crowded ships. The suffering of the passengers. But most of them had never seen. Till this moment. And they managed to get about half of the *Tiger Hill* passengers off the ship.

And hidden. The British searched house after house. They found no one."

"And the others—those who were not hidden?"

"Yes," David said. "Well, they were arrested. Sent to the Sarafand camp. But I doubt they'll be returned to Europe. Their numbers will probably be deducted from the legal certificate allotment."

Laughter and tears welled within me.

Our ship—which had started as an argument with the Shamen . . . our ship aided by the directives of a king and a foreign minister . . . our ship which had outmaneuvered the minefields of the Mediterranean, British patrol planes and boats . . . our ship which had sailed on despite the sickness, hunger, thirst of its passengers and the near mutiny of its crew . . . our ship had reached the shore. With the exception of the two who had died at sea and the two killed by the British, all the passengers were now in Eretz Israel. One thousand one hundred and fifty-nine men, women and children. The legal allotment for the month of August had been eight hundred and thirty-four.

"Look," Alexander said, "these two boys have been on the plane all night. How about fixing them some breakfast?"

I stood up, glad to be able to cover my emotions by the routine acts of putting on coffee and scrambling eggs.

Alexander then suggested that the boys, having nowhere to stay, might be allowed to use my apartment until I returned from Czernowitz.

"Of course," I said.

"We may have to store some supplies here," David remarked. "Would you mind that?"

"Munitions?"

He nodded. "It would just be temporary. We've been given a lead on some pistols and Sten guns. If we can get them, they'll all fit into a few suitcases."

"All right," I said. "But I expect to be back in a few days. I'm afraid by then you'll have to find some other place for your hardware. I doubt my landlady would be too thrilled if she discovered a stack of guns stashed in the closet."

"*Entendu!*" David said.

Yitzhak stood up. "That radio Alexander brought with him—could we try it?"

Alexander plugged it in. After some raucous static we heard the sound of clanging church bells, not unexpected on a Sunday morning. In which country were they ringing? My radio was an excellent one. It often picked up stations in France, Poland, England.

I was in the kitchen when David called sharply, "Come here!"

I ran into the next room.

The three men were standing close to the radio, which now was silent.

"The BBC," David said tersely. "Chamberlain will speak in a few minutes." He turned up the volume dial.

Suddenly the room was filled with the slow deliberate words of the British Prime Minister. "I am speaking to you from the Cabinet room at Number Ten Downing Street. This country is at war with Germany."

TWENTY-FIVE

I LEFT THAT NIGHT on the train for Czernowitz. The train which would take me to Stefan. The train which would take me home. The two seemed synonymous.

As we rolled from the station a blast of chill dusty air swept in through the open window of my tiny roomette. There was a knock on the door, and the porter entered; a young, fair-faced man with a small mustache. He promptly shut the window and pointed to a bell by the bed. "Anything you desire, mademoiselle, push here, and I am at your service." He did not bow, but his voice did. He seemed an anachronism already. How long would such amenities continue; gracious porters, comfortable quarters in a wagon-lit?

I asked that he awaken me at six-thirty the next morning and as he departed he remarked, "Mademoiselle, the compartments to the left and the right of you also have ladies in them."

The world exploding into war and he imagined that I might be concerned about the advances of some Lothario to the left or to the right.

Presently I climbed into the narrow berth. The sheets were damp and the bed rattled in steady rhythm.

Tomorrow—would I see Stefan?

I had not phoned to tell him that I was coming. Nor had we been in contact since my return from Geneva.

Perhaps with the outbreak of war he had taken his wife and children to his villa in the mountains. He had described it to me: a sanctuary, a retreat guarded by ancient trees and backed by a towering cliff. The storeroom, he'd told me, was stocked with enough canned goods and provisions to last for weeks.

If Stefan was still in Czernowitz I would do my best to persuade him that his mountain sanctuary could become a death trap. He must get his family out of Europe, now.

If Stefan was in Czernowitz . . .

I had always allowed myself the luxury of daydreams. But now that I was on the train to Czernowitz, fantasies were transmuted into conflicts. I wanted to see Stefan. I had to see him. I was afraid to see him.

I tried to force all thoughts of him from my mind.

After a while, encased by weariness, I fell asleep.

I awoke hours later, and turned to look out the window. It framed a distant inferno. Orange flames licked upward against the darkness; fire silhouetted gaunt tower skeletons which prodded the low night sky. Dark smoke trailed against the moon-streaked clouds. We were passing oil fields. It seemed that the flames would set the sky afire. Flames of war which could sweep like wildfire over the continent. I had come to Czernowitz for the first time at the end of such a war. Now I was returning at the start of another.

The train sped on into the dark night. I closed my eyes and tried to sleep. The sound of the wheels was transmuted into the distant sound of cannon. The train was speeding back into my childhood.

I was bundled into a blanket against the winter night, held close in my aunt Bertha's arms as the carriage creaked and jolted along the night road.

I had been roused from the warmth of my bed, deposited in a carriage along with my two aunts and my grandmother. In the far distance the sky was lit by fire, shaken with a strange thunder. The only explanation I had been given was: "It's the war."

"Can't you hurry?" Aunt Bertha called out to the driver. "For the sake of the child?"

He turned to look at us. "I too have children. I must leave you here and go back for my own."

"Not here!" Aunt Sophie cried. "We will perish!"

"I'll take you to the next human place we come to. Then you must get out and manage for yourselves."

The next human place proved to be a barn surrounded by snow-frozen fields. The driver shoved open the barn door. Aunt Bertha carried me inside. I heard the whinny of a horse and was certain I had been brought back to my father's house and for a treat was permitted to sleep in the stable. The hay which my aunt piled about me for warmth had a friendly familiar smell. Tomorrow, I thought, Papa will take me onto his horse and we'll ride through the fields together. Then I fell asleep.

My father had an estate in Russia, near Kiev, where I was born. He also held a concession on a border estate near Kuczurnicz, between the Ukraine and Austria—in one of the sections where Russian and Austro-Hungarian armies clashed back and forth in a constant seesawing battle. No matter who won in each day's battle, the Jews in these territories lost. The Russian Army slaughtered Jews for being enemy sympathizers. The Austro-Hungarian Army murdered Jews for being Russian spies. The two armies seemed to have only one battle cry in common: Death to the Jews. And they had many opportunities for carrying out their objective. Of the ten million Jews in Europe, eight million lived in the Russian and Austro-Hungarian empires. Ours was just one of the Jewish families fleeing in fear from town to town. Just one of the families which had been split by the war.

I had been sent off with my aunts and my grandmother. We were trying to reach my aunt Shaindl's farm, where it was hoped, we might be out of the way of the war.

As the train sped on toward Czernowitz I lay in my berth staring out the window. Dawn fingered through the night sky, and farm houses were faintly silhouetted. Because of the soft darkness they were houses of dreams or memories. And, for the first time in many years, other long-forgotten moments appeared complete and vivid from the haze of childhood.

We had remained in that barn through the winter, for my aunts and I came down with a fever and could not be moved. The barn was a cold and drafty place with wind slitting like knives of ice through cracks in the wooden walls. But at least we were reasonably safe, for the peasant family who owned the barn worked out an agreement with my grandmother. She became their housemaid, in return for which they provided us with food and kept our existence a secret.

By spring we were strong enough to travel, and made our way—chiefly by trudging along muddy roads—to the home of Aunt Shaindl. Like other refugees on the road, we lived mainly on potatoes and sugar beets which we dug up from the frozen fields at night.

My aunts and grandmother kept urging me on with descriptions of the warm bed and the fine meals we would have at Aunt Shaindl's.

We rode the final lap of our journey in a farmer's cart, and I was asleep when we reached our destination.

I awoke the next morning in a huge bed, half buried by a feather comforter. The walls of the room were painted white. Outside the window, framed by white curtains, were blossoming trees and the sun was shining.

I started to climb out of bed, but I was dressed in a long nightgown and I stumbled over it. I was sprawled on the floor when the door opened. A woman came in. Her blue-black hair hung to her knees. She held a comb in one hand.

"Did you sleep well, little one?" She picked me up. "I am Tante Shaindl."

She was beautiful. But that is not what struck me about her.

"Where is my mother?" I said softly. Then I started to shout. "Where is my *mother*?"

It was the first time I had mentioned my mother for many weeks. But Tante Shaindl looked like my mother, and I could not keep the memory shoved away.

She took me into her arms and I sobbed against her breast for my mother. When I stopped crying Tante Shaindl brought me into the kitchen. I was there having a huge breakfast when a blond-haired boy strode in. He looked me over. Then he announced, "I'm your cousin Menachem. I'm seven. And I can hit you whenever I want."

He was as good as his word. When we were alone together his chief delight seemed to be pulling my hair and hitting me. Circumstances, however, soon brought us close.

One morning we awakened to find the doors of the house locked, the shutters closed. There was a clatter of hoofs outside. Menachem and I ran to peer through the slatted shutters. We watched in fascinated horror as a group of dark-skinned, slant-eyed men brandishing sabers galloped by, yelling strange-sounding words into the early morning street.

"They are Cossacks," my grandmother said. "The Russians have taken the town."

My three aunts had disappeared. Aunt Shaindl's husband, Samuel, brought us to the kitchen window and pointed to a hillock on a distant field.

"Your aunts are hiding there. In the potato storeroom."

"Why can't we hide too?" I demanded.

"The Cossacks," my uncle said, "do not harm small children. They look for young women. You and Menachem are needed to bring food and water to the aunts."

My uncle and his older son, Solomon, left at daybreak every morning to work in the fields. And Menachem and I, dressed like peasant children, went out at noon with a heavy bundle wrapped in a black shawl. "We are carrying lunch for our father," we were instructed to say, should anyone stop us.

No one did. For a week we made our way to the underground shelter without advent. It was a dank, damp place with a floor of mud. The only furnishings were piles of potatoes and blankets spread over dried cornhusks. My aunts played out the game with us, made us feel we were heroes in a huge adventure.

Then one afternoon we saw a group of Cossacks galloping toward us across the field. Behind their horses, tied and dragging on ropes were women, screaming. Menachem and I hid behind a tree. As they came close the horses were suddenly brought up short. The men slid from their backs, lowered their trousers, fell upon the shrieking, struggling women.

I cried out. My cousin covered my mouth with his hand.

There were many men for each woman. It lasted a long time.

When we arrived home we found that the house had been broken into, the furniture smashed. My grandmother was locked in the closet, sobbing, moaning. She had been beaten. Menachem found a scribbled note from his father. The Cossacks were taking him and Solomon to serve in the Russian Army. The note ended with a short command:

Leave Zylona at once. Zylona was the name of his estate. It was a beautiful name. It meant green.

We left that night; not knowing where we were going, knowing only that we could not stay. My aunts smeared their faces with mud and coal dust, wore ragged clothes.

"I want my face dirty too," I said. "I am grown up now and I too am afraid of the Cossacks."

My grandmother agreed. "You are grown up now. You are, after all, three years old."

So I had stove black streaked on my face and was proud to be ugly along with my aunts.

Since the Cossacks had stolen our horses, we set out again on foot.

After several weeks of walking we reached a town called Nielnitza near the Dniester River, and we decided to remain there. We had, by that time, no need to make special efforts to look ugly. We were skinny, filthy, ragged, barefoot. The possessions we carried with us from Zylona had been taken from us by soldiers or peasants. Yet, we were no worse off than the thousands of other fleeing refugees who clogged the roads.

We fled from war: from raping, pillaging soldiers, from the sound of cannon fire, from towns where disease was rampant, from angry peasants or barking dogs sent to drive us from a field where we had settled for the night. But we did not flee from the enemy. Who *was* the enemy? The Russians? Or Austrians? My father was Russian, my mother Austrian. Most of her children had been born in Russia. We spoke both languages at home. My mother's mother and my aunts, Bertha, Sophie and Shaindl, had been born in Austria. But both sides of the family had lived most of their lives near border towns which, even in peacetime, often switched from Austrian to Russian control and back.

Consequently, when we arrived in Nielnitza and found it had now been taken by the Russians, we did not flee as did some of our Austrian roadway companions. A military hospital was being set up. This could mean work for the aunts. And, perhaps, if we settled in a Russian military town we might hear some word of Uncle Samuel and Solomon.

We found a room, lit only by one window. But it was a large room, and there was a loft. Menachem and I were delighted at the thought of climbing a ladder to sleep in the hay. The loft, however, was turned over to a more vital occupant: the chamber pot. I slept on the table which was upended every night to make a crude sort of crib. The aunts, Grandmother and Menachem slept on piles of sawdust spread on the dirt floor.

When the military hospital was organized the aunts stood in line throughout the night to apply for a position. All three were chosen. Aunt Bertha was put in charge of the children's crèche. Aunt Sophie became a nurse at the hospital. Aunt Shaindl worked in the hospital kitchen. My contribution was to come down with a virulent case of the measles, which Menachem caught. This was followed by a month-long bout with scarlet fever.

One day when I was alone in the house, still weak but recovering, there was a knock on the door. My grandmother had gone to the market and Menachem to the village well for our daily supply of water. I was afraid to open the door. Then a voice called out, "Shaindl." I recognized the voice. But when I opened the door I did not recognize the man. He was gaunt. His face had a strange, waxy cast. He wore the tattered uniform of a Russian soldier.

"Rutichka," he said softly. "Don't you know me?"

He turned and beckoned to another man who stood in the shadows. He also was thin, tall, ragged. They entered the house and bolted the door. Uncle Samuel and Cousin Solomon had come home. A doctor at the Russian hospital, a man named Colonel Gregori Nikoliev, had told them where to find us.

Uncle Samuel coughed all night and slept in spasms. By morning he seemed to be sleeping soundly. Then Aunt Shaindl screamed out, "He is dead."

After that night Aunt Shaindl remained the same serene woman she had always been. But she did not laugh any more. And she never again caressed Menachem or me.

Solomon had been wounded. Colonel Nikoliev removed a bullet from his shoulder. But infection set in, and his fever mounted.

I had found an old vodka bottle on the road which I washed carefully and treasured as a toy. I brought it now every day to the children's crèche, secretly poured my cupful of milk into it and took the bottle home to Solomon, explaining that these were extra rations. But he did not improve.

Then, late one afternoon, my aunt Bertha brought home the Russian doctor, Colonel Nikoliev. He lifted me high in his arms and said that he knew a girl just my age.

"Who is she?" I demanded. But he did not answer.

I liked him at once. He was a huge man with a shock of blond-gray hair and eyes alive with tiny flecks of brightness.

He tended to Solomon. Afterward he turned to me. "Will you go for a walk with me?"

"Yes," I said. "And then you will take me for an airplane ride."

He laughed. "All right. Agreed."

My aunts did not know what had possessed me. Nor did I. But I insisted on the plane ride.

There were two pilots. The colonel and I were the passengers. He removed his leather belt, fastened it around me, held it tightly throughout the ride. And we laughed and sang, soundless songs for our voices were carried away by the rushing wind.

When we returned to earth I informed the colonel that I loved him very much, and suggested that he marry Aunt Bertha so that he could come to live with us.

When he took me home, however, he discussed a far different matter. He told my aunts that we must leave Nielnitza as soon as Solomon was well enough to travel. This town, he said, would be a slaughterhouse before the war had ended. We must escape while we could. "Go to Czernowitz," he advised. "It has been retaken by the Austrians. The city is now in flames. But I don't think it will become a battlefield again. It was, after all, the capital of the province; the people will start to rebuild. You will be safer there. It may be a place where you can settle."

None of us wanted to leave. But the colonel insisted.

A few weeks later he commandeered a truck and drove us many miles to the Prut River. We could see smoke clouding up from the city on the other side. We could even smell it.

"That's Czernowitz," the colonel said. "Don't cross by the bridge. It may not be safe. Find someone with a rowboat to take you over. Stay as long as you can on the outskirts. It will be easier to get food at the beginning if you're near the countryside."

He helped us down from the truck. "I must leave you now. Although I would like to go with you." He was speaking to all of us, but somehow only to Bertha. He gave her a packet of Austrian marks and a large parcel of food.

Then he picked me up in his arms and kissed me. When he set me on my feet again I held tight to his coat. Gently he straightened my fingers. "Go now," he said to all of us. "I won't see you again. But I won't forget you."

We did, however, see him again, Aunt Bertha and I. We saw him in Springbrunnenplatz in Czernowitz. We saw him shot to death.

There was a soft knock on the door of my roomette. "It is six-thirty, mademoiselle."

"Yes," I said, startled back to the present. "I'm awake. Thank you."

I washed and dressed quickly. Then I sat staring out the window as daylight spread over the hilly countryside of Bukovina. Fields of wheat shimmered under the early sun. Men in sleeveless belted tunics were already at work. And by each cluster of white-washed, thatched-roofed cottages stood children waving at the train.

We came to the river Prut which reflected the bright cloudless blue of the sky. The river Prut, which my aunts, my cousins, my grandmother and I had crossed in a rowboat twenty-one years ago.

Within minutes we would reach Czernowitz.

Suddenly, memories were blocked. I felt stifled by a pounding excitement.

The sun sparked on the glass roof of the station.

Then, incredibly, I saw him. Stefan. He was standing on the platform. He was holding a suitcase. He was with his wife.

TWENTY-SIX

I DESCENDED from the train at the front of the long platform, far from Stefan. And I hurried through the station.

Where was he off to, with his wife? Their home in the mountains? Where were the children? Was he perhaps leaving Rumania—getting out of Europe, as I had so often begged him to do? Had he tried to contact me in Bucharest last night?

Perhaps they were merely going visiting. His wife had relatives in Rădăuţi.

Were Stefan and I pawns in some strange game of fate, move one figure in, move the other away? Should I feel relieved—my turmoil of conflicts concerning our reunion settled in one swift stroke? I felt instead pervaded by intense and bitter disappointment.

I climbed into a taxi.

"Hotel Schwarzer Adler," I said to the driver.

I stared out the window at the passing streets, and I tried to wrench my mind free from Stefan.

Czernowitz had changed. Buildings had been painted, streets newly paved; the city looked cleaner, brighter, more prosperous. Every sidewalk was edged solid with parked cars. Most of them had Polish license plates, with suitcases and cartons tied to the roof. Many had people sitting inside; children waving out the windows. The war was one day old, and already there were refugees. How many thousands . . . hundreds of thousands more would there be before the war ended?

We drove past the mansion which had once housed the Austro-Hungarian military government. Suddenly the two wars merged into one. Time kaleidoscoped backward. It was on the sidewalk outside this building that Colonel Gregori Nikoliev had been shot.

He had escaped from the Russian Army; had come to Czernowitz and to Bertha. He arrived late one night, ladened with provisions: bread, salamis, cheeses, hams. He had carried me from my bed, wrapped me in a blanket, held me in his lap while I joined the midnight feast.

As we ate and drank hot tea the colonel and the aunts discussed his next move. He had come dressed like a ragged refugee. It was decided that he should remain with us, as a member of our family until the war was over. Then he and Bertha would marry. And he would send for his little girl. His wife, he told us, had been killed in the war.

I went back to bed filled with a deep feeling of security. The colonel had come. He would take care of us.

The next morning we were awakened by a heavy pounding on the door. Three soldiers strode into the house; the security police. They had received reports, they said, that a stranger had entered our house late last night.

They took the colonel away for questioning. Bertha followed them, crying out that they were mistaken; this man was her uncle from Kiev.

I ran after them.

They took the colonel into the mansion which housed the Austro-Hungarian military government. My aunt and I waited outside in the street.

A short time later the colonel came from the building, followed by two soldiers with guns. They motioned him to stand against the wall. A few people had gathered on the sidewalk. One of the soldiers announced that they were about to shoot a Russian spy.

Shots split the air. The colonel fell to the ground.

I started screaming.

One of the soldiers carried me home. I kept screaming.

The Emperor and Empress of Austro-Hungary were scheduled to arrive in Czernowitz that afternoon. I had been the schoolchild selected by the headmaster to make the floral presentation. I wept and screamed for hours, and said that I would not present flowers to an emperor whose soldiers had killed the colonel. But my grandmother told

274

me firmly that I must go. If I did not, the security police might arrest all of us as Russian spies. She washed my face and hooked me into the new red dress which my aunt Bertha had fashioned from a bedspread. I made the presentation as scheduled.

Bertha, however, did not emerge from the house for weeks.

It was, strangely, a newspaper picture taken of that floral presentation which had enabled my mother to find me.

One night Aunt Shaindl woke me to say, "Someone is here to see you."

A lady was leaning over me. She was dressed in black, with a black shawl over her hair.

"It's your mother," Aunt Shaindl said.

I turned away and pretended to be asleep. Or, perhaps, I was asleep. It was a dream.

But Aunt Shaindl was shaking my shoulder. "Rutichka, wake up."

"That is not my mother," I said loudly. "I don't want to see her. I don't know her."

The war had been over for several years. I was now almost eight. I had a firm picture of my mother's face in my mind; a made-up face. This was not my mother.

"She came all the way from Czechoslovakia to find you," my aunt Shaindl said.

Czechoslovakia, the sausage-shaped country. In school we were studying the new map of Europe, made after the World War. Czechoslovakia was a place easy to draw and hard to spell. It was not a place in which my mother lived. That I knew.

"She brought you nice things," Aunt Shaindl said. "A new coat you can wear to school tomorrow." I could hear by my aunt's voice that she was crying.

"I'll wait outside," the lady said softly.

My aunt washed my face. She brushed my hair carefully. She dressed me. And as she did so she told me the story of this woman, my mother, living in Czechoslovakia, coming across a picture of a child in an old issue of a weekly journal. The child was presenting flowers to the Emperor and Empress of Austro-Hungary, standing on the steps of the Municipal Building in Czernowitz. The caption below the picture had given the name of the child.

"Your mother left at once for Czernowitz," Aunt Shaindl said. "She even brought you presents. A doll, and a beautiful blue coat. How did your mother know that you badly needed a coat?"

She took me into the room where my aunts and grandmother were waiting. Three candles were burning and the petroleum lamp. The lady held out her arms to me.

I shied away, clung to my aunt Shaindl. "Are you going to take me away from here?" I said in a loud, rude voice.

The lady came over to me. "Don't you want to see your brothers and your sister?"

"I have only one brother," I said. It was surely a trick. There was my brother Poli; that was all.

The woman looked at Aunt Shaindl. "We have not spoken of her brothers or sister or of you," my aunt said. "We thought it was better."

"You remember Poli," the woman said, "because he is nearest you in age. But there are two other brothers. The oldest is David. He was fighting in the army. We still hope to find him. And there is Arthur. He is at the university in Vienna. There is also your sister Bertha. Your sister and your aunt are both named after your great-grandmother."

The woman squatted down before me, not touching me. "And you had another sister, Ernestina. She was an actress and a singer. You look the way she did when she was a child."

"Where is she?" I asked.

"Ernestina died when she was nineteen."

I knew she was not my mother, but perhaps she felt sad because her daughter had died and she was looking now for someone to fill this daughter's place. I came into her arms and stood stiffly, obligingly, as she embraced me.

After that she gave me the blue coat. It was too long, but I liked it. She had also brought me a doll with yellow braids and eyes which opened and closed.

The next morning she took me to school. She stood for a long time talking to my teacher.

"That's my mother," I said to the girl at the next desk. And the word buzzed around through the classroom. One child, Antonia, said loudly, "She's making it up. She has no mother. She's a liar."

I did not feel offended. Probably Antonia spoke the truth.

I hoped so.

I didn't pay much attention to my mother and the teacher talking. I kept on doing my sums. We always had arithmetic during the first hour of school. But after a while the teacher came over to me. She put her arms around me and kissed me and said that I was excused.

"Children," she announced, "say good-by to Ruth."

Outside I said, "Are you planning to take me away with you?" I felt sorry for this lady. She was pretty, with large green eyes and black hair which came into soft curls around her forehead. I liked the way she looked. And I had to admit that she looked very much like my aunt Shaindl. Also, I liked the doll she had brought me. I had never before seen a doll with eyes that opened and closed. But despite all this, I certainly did not plan to go away from Czernowitz, to leave my aunts and my grandmother and my school.

"It is very hard to get a place on the train," the lady said. "I was able to get a reservation for tonight. Without a reservation we would have to stand all night in the corridor of the train."

I turned to stone.

The day passed in a haze. My aunts took me here and there to say good-by. I didn't feel like saying anything to anybody.

My cousin Menachem told me not to feel bad. When he was big he would come and rescue me. I said I did not feel bad. I told him I had two brothers besides Poli, and two sisters, only one was dead. And I was going to live with them in Czechoslovakia and have a mother, as he did.

My grandmother did not come to the station to see us off. When I went in to say good-by, her head was shaking on her thin neck, shaking and nodding. Her head shook like that whenever she was troubled.

"I hope by the next time I need a haircut, you will be back," my grandmother said. She had, one week ago, allowed me to cut the ends of her long gray hair. "No one cuts it as nicely as you," my grandmother said.

It was night when we went outside. We took a fiacre to the station. My aunts were with us, but they seemed to have receded somehow. It was as if they were afraid to talk to me. They spoke only to my mother, in low voices. I felt sudden hatred for them, allowing me to go off like this without any protest. For the woman whom I now called Mother, I felt no hatred. I felt nothing. That was the best way. To continue like a stone.

At the end, before the train came, they all were crying. Except me.

The huge train stormed into the station.

"You'll come back," each of my aunts said as she kissed me good-by. "You'll come back to visit us, I know."

"Maybe I will," I said. "And maybe I won't." Mother took my hand and I went with her up the high steps and into the train.

The corridor was jammed tight with people. We had only one place in our compartment, so Mother held me on her lap.

Surprisingly, I fell sound asleep.

I woke with a start as the train lurched. It was morning. We were at a large station. People in our compartment were moving about, standing up, sitting down, rearranging luggage. The window was open. A man outside had a little cart. He was selling sandwiches and hot tea.

"I'm thirsty," I said to my mother. "I wish I could have some tea."

The soldier sitting next to us told my mother that we would be at this stop, Lemberg, for half an hour while the train changed engines. So my mother got up and said she would fetch me some tea. "You stay here," she told me. "Don't move from the seat or someone else may take it. I'll be right back."

I watched her through the window. The man with the tea and sandwich cart had moved on and she followed him quickly.

Suddenly the train started to move. I could not see my mother any more from the window. I started to cry. I cried terribly, not with tears but with shouts. I kept shouting, "Mother, Mother." For the first time I knew that this woman was really my mother. She had found me and now I was being taken away from her.

The people in the compartment tried to hush me, to comfort me. The soldier tried to take me on his lap. I hit out at him. "I want my mother," I screamed.

After what seemed a long while, the train stopped somewhere. The station had gone, there were only tracks outside, and a large wooden shed. I started for the door.

"Stay here," the soldier said. "Your mother will find you." He stood up and held onto my arm.

I kicked and hit at him again.

"Let her go," one of the women said. "Maybe she is right. Who knows what's happening?"

He released my arm and I shoved my way through the crowded corridor and got off the train. The shed was locked but there was a long bench outside it and I sat there.

At first I thought that my mother would come, but she did not come. A man drove by in a cart loaded with cases. He noticed me and climbed out of his cart. He asked my name, but I would not tell him.

"Are you lost?" He was a kind man, but he frightened me because he wanted to take me away. "Let me take you back to the main station," he kept saying. "To the stationmaster. You don't want to sit here all alone in the cold."

But I did want to sit there. If I moved from this spot I was certain my mother would never find me again.

"I'm waiting here for my mother," I told him. "She'll be right back!"

The man went away and I sat there through the morning and into the long gray afternoon. I was shivering in my blue coat, which was not very warm after all.

Any time I saw a man approaching, I hid behind a large wooden crate until he had passed. I did not want anyone coming to take me away from this place.

After a while hunger was replaced by terrible pains in my stomach. I finally stopped believing that my mother would find me. But as the winter afternoon darkened into night, she came.

She looked so little, and her eyes were so swollen.

She said, "Why do I always lose you?"

She was holding me, and I said, "Don't shake, Mama. I wasn't afraid. I knew you would come."

I tried to walk but I couldn't because my feet had started to freeze. So my mother had to leave me alone again. But this time although I screamed and wailed, I did not really feel afraid. She came back presently with a man who carried me all the way to the main station. We went into the room of the stationmaster, which was warm. Mother gave me hot tea and held the cup while I drank it in small sips. Many men came in, men who had been looking for me. They had suggestions as how to make me more comfortable. But my mother would not let anyone do anything for me, except herself.

She explained what had happened. The train we were on had been sidetracked while engines were being changed. It had made several stops on various sidetracks before being returned to its original place in the station. No one in our carriage remembered just where I had decided to get off.

People were sent looking for me, but by hiding behind the crates I had, it seemed, managed to escape their detection.

"Your mother must have run ten miles, back and forth, hunting for you," the stationmaster said. After a moment he gave a little laugh. But nobody else joined him in laughing, so he patted my head and went away.

Later, however, he came back to tell us that we could not get another train to Reichenberg until late the following afternoon. Until that time, he would be pleased if we accepted his invitation to stay at his home as guests.

My brother Poli was waiting at the station when we arrived at Reichenberg. He too was a stranger as my mother had been. But when he took my hand as we walked from the station, I felt that I somehow remembered him.

"You're pretty," Poli said. "I'm glad," he added, "to have someone in this family littler than me."

It was snowing when we came outside. I was frightened by the strangeness. There were large buildings and cars.

We climbed into a tram and I sat by the window. The frost on the pane made flower patterns. Mother was telling me about the fine times I would have in Reichenberg. "Poli will take you to the zoo," she said. "And to the circus."

"I don't want to go without you," I said to my mother.

A huge mountain loomed into the distance. "That's near where we live," Poli said.

"On the top of the mountain?"

My brother laughed; it was a wonderful sound. "No," he said, "at the foot of the mountain. But there is a little train to the top and I will take you there."

We got off the tram, walked down a snowy street and stopped before a house which was numbered eleven.

Inside the apartment Poli pulled a chain, and there was light. In Czernowitz our room had been lit only by petroleum lamps. I had never seen electric light bulbs close before, and Poli tried to explain how they worked.

"Not today," my mother said. "She is too tired to learn the principles of electricity today."

She fed us and put me to bed. And she stayed with me while I was falling asleep.

"How about my father?" I asked, almost asleep. "You found me. Will you find him?"

"No," my mother said. "He was killed in the war."

"What did he look like?" I asked.

"He was very tall with red hair and a red beard. When you were twelve months old, he used to take you riding on his horse."

I seemed to remember this. Or perhaps it was something nice to imagine as I fell asleep.

The next day my sister Bertha came from Prague where she worked. I wished she had not come, because calling her Bertha made me keep remembering my aunt Bertha in Czernowitz. I tried to block out the other life, the other world. But the name Bertha in the air all the time made this difficult to do.

It became more difficult as the months passed.

I had told my mother that I was grown up; that I knew how to cook, how to wash clothes, how to do many things.

"You are not going to cook here," my mother said. "Or to wash clothes. Here you are not going to be anything but a child."

My brother Poli took me to the zoo and the circus. We went up to the top of the mountain. And my sister Bertha made me a fine wardrobe of clothes, even a very impractical white velvet coat.

But I became more and more lonesome for everything that I had been used to. I did not understand the new language, and I sat in the classroom as though I were deaf and dumb.

One day I left school early without waiting for Poli to call for me. I took the little train up to the top of the mountain, and I did not come down again.

It was Poli who found me. "Why did you run away?" he said.

I told him I didn't know.

That night my mother sat by my bed and stroked my hair. "If we all went to Czernowitz," she said, "would you be happy?"

I sat up in bed and hugged her so hard that she laughed. "Stop!" she said. "You will break my bones."

The return, however, proved something of a disaster.

My brother Arthur did not come with us. He remained in Vienna, at the university. We'd still had no word about my brother David. My sister Bertha was the chief breadwinner of the family. She had made a good living in Prague as a costume designer. But there was no place for her in Czernowitz. In addition, she had left a lover in Prague to come with us. Without ever saying so, she blamed me for disrupting her life. And I did not blame her for blaming me. She also blamed my mother for giving in to me. And in Czernowitz there were frequent arguments between them.

My mother gave Hebrew lessons. She earned very little and was out of the house much of the day and many evenings.

Poli sold newspapers after school, and I worked in a bakery scrubbing floors and washing pots. For this I was paid each evening with a loaf of bread.

We lived in two small rooms, which had once been a store. I kept comparing this damp, squalid place with the spacious, comfortable flat in Reichenberg.

Every morning when I wakened I felt guilt upon me like a sickness. I was certain my family wished I had never been found.

Even as I grew older I found myself always trying to atone; especially to my mother.

Perhaps this was why I had agreed to marry Emmanuel Klüger.

I was in Vienna, at the university, when word came that I should return home. My mother was very ill.

I left for Czernowitz at once, but by the time I reached my mother's bedside an invisible gauze of death seemed to be stretched over her.

Her dark luminous eyes were now glazed, her skin was sallow, her hair had gone white. Her voice was whisper thin.

I sat by her bed, trying to talk about everyday matters, trying to pretend that she was not dying. I told her about the university, my courses, my professors. I told her about my plans to go to Palestine when I graduated. My mother was a dedicated Zionist. She had instilled the fever in me. To help rebuild the ancient homeland of the Jews. To help create a new Jewish nation.

Since I was small we had talked about our plans to go to Palestine together. Now I said, "I will go there, Mama. Get a job. Set up a home for you. Then I will send for you."

Quite calmly my mother told me, "In a few days I will be dead. You are too young to be left alone. I want you to promise me that you will marry."

Horrified, chilled by her talk of death, I could not speak.

"Promise me," my mother repeated, her words taut.

"I promise," I whispered.

She seemed to relax against the pillows. "Emmanuel Klüger has asked for your hand. I gave my permission. He is a fine young man. He comes from a fine family. I can die knowing that you will be well taken care of."

"Yes, Mama," I said.

She smiled a little. "I told Emmanuel that if you agree I would like the wedding to take place one month after the period of mourning ends."

"There will be no period of mourning, Mama. You're not going to die. You're not." Tears clogged my throat. I did not want her to see me cry. I left her bedside.

She died that night.

After my mother's funeral I had realized in my more rational moments that I must break the promise; stop the forthcoming wedding. But I did nothing. I was immobilized by an aching sense of loss and by a stunned inertia. Emmanuel and his sister Rosa made all the wedding arrangements. My brothers and sister were pleased that I was marrying into such a respected and well-to-do family. And Emmanuel seemed to love me. He even promised to move to Palestine after our marriage.

283

This, I reassured myself, was of utmost importance. After all, I would have been married, in all likelihood, to Gidon Katz, the medical student I was going with in Vienna. Except that Gidon was horrified at the idea of living in Palestine. And I was an ardent Zionist.

One month after the period of mourning ended, I married Emmanuel Klüger. I admired him. I liked him. Perhaps one day I would come to love him. I was fulfilling my mother's deathbed wish: that was my thought on my wedding day. I felt closer to my mother on that day than I did to my new husband.

Emmanuel was kind, tender, understanding on our wedding night and I was grateful. We sat by the window sipping champagne, saying very little to each other.

We were in the bridal suite of the Hotel Schwarzer Adler. The chambermaid had turned back the top sheet over the blankets on the huge double bed. The purpose, I supposed, was to make the bed look more inviting. To me it looked brazen, frightening.

After a time Emmanuel said, "I will wait till you're ready." That night he slept in an armchair by the window.

We were driving up to the hotel now. The past meshed into the present.

The facade of the Schwarzer Adler had been cleaned. Horse-drawn carriages were lined before the entrance. A uniformed doorman came to take my small valise. As he did so he inquired, formally, as to whether I had a confirmed reservation. I told him I had made the reservation from Bucharest. He nodded dubiously. "I hope we still have the room, mademoiselle. With the war, you know, we have had many unexpected guests—from Poland."

As we entered I was startled to see that the elegant lobby had become a crowded dormitory. Armchairs and potted palms had been moved back against the walls to make way for lines of cots. Some of the unexpected guests were still asleep in cots and chairs.

Fortunately, the Schwarzer Adler clung onto its prewar rules and regulations. I had told them when my train was due in. The concierge informed me that they planned to keep my reservation for one hour after that time. If I did not appear by then a family of Poles would be given my room.

I had not been inside the hotel since my wedding night. The room I had now was the size of the dressing room I'd had then. I opened the french windows and leaned out. A grotesque figure from the past came up the street. Shmoiger, he was called. Nitwit. No one knew his real name; where he lived; where he came from. He was a bulky man who wore a woolen scarf around his neck summer and winter. His head was always covered by a dirty cap. His nose was fat, his eyes so small they could barely be seen in his fat face. But they could be felt; piercing eyes. His cheeks were bright red from the tiny blood vessels which seemed to be bursting at the surface of his skin. Sharp bristles stuck from his jowls. His hands were monstrous, always dirty. He dressed in rags. And he shuffled along like an elephant, but quickly.

He lived by his own special brand of begging. His territory covered the most elegant streets in the city. He would appear at the Ringplatz, the Herrengasse, the Theatergasse. And if someone refused to favor his outstretched hand, Shmoiger shouted loud insults which attracted notice because they generally turned out to be true. He somehow knew about the intimate life of the town's most prosperous citizens: which elderly judge frequented the cabarets of Bucharest with a teen-age girl, which prominent banker was sleeping with what general director's wife.

As I watched Shmoiger now coming down the street with his lumbering shuffle, I felt a strange sort of gratitude. Shmoiger remained eternally ageless and the same; a welcome home to the city of my childhood.

I turned abruptly from the window, went to the telephone. Presently, through eruptions of static, a voice inquired, *"Was wünschen Sie?"*

Czernowitz had been part of Rumania since 1919. Yet, some of the prewar generation went stanchly on as though they still were citizens of the Austro-Hungarian Empire. They considered Rumanians a dissolute people and they never troubled to learn the language. This operator sounded the staid and abrupt Austro-Hungarian type. I answered her politely in German. "I would like to be connected to the office of Max Ritter von Anhauch."

"I will call you back, *Gnädige Frau*. It may take some time. As you know the porter must put the call through the exchange in the Central Post Office."

When I'd left Czernowitz six years ago this procedure had frequently taken so much time and caused so much frustration that it was usually simpler to deliver one's message in person. Obviously, the situation had not changed. I felt, however, that I needed some sort of prior introduction before appearing at a man's office to ask for ten thousand pounds.

Perhaps I should rest while waiting for the call to come through; rest, and pray and plan.

I slipped out of my sandals, lay down on the bed. I felt taut as a spring. What if I failed; if I could not raise the money here in Czernowitz? Four days the Shamen had given me. Four days—or he would lease the *Hilda* elsewhere. Should I have taken this gamble? Should I have come so far from our base of operations in Bucharest?

The telephone rang, jangling the silence of the room.

I jumped up. They had gotten the call through quickly.

"Hello."

"Ruth—it's Stefan."

Silence exploded. I could say nothing.

"I'm in the lobby," Stefan said. "What's your room number?"

I looked at the round white disk in the center of the phone. I said, "Forty-eight."

"I'll be right up."

I stood there, staring at the telephone until the operator said, *"Ja? Was wünschen Sie?"*

I hung up. "What did I wish?" she had asked.

"I don't know what I wish," I said softly. "I—don't know."

TWENTY-SEVEN

HE KNOCKED ON THE DOOR. I opened it quickly.

He strode into the room. "For God's sake," he said, "why didn't you let me know you were coming?"

He shoved the door closed, locked it, and he took me into his arms. "You idiot. You little lovely fool. Did you mean to surprise me? It's only luck that I was in the city."

He kissed me.

I started to laugh and almost to cry. "When I saw you at the station with your wife, I thought—"

"She's gone back to our place in the mountains. The children are there." He picked me up and carried me over to the bed. Then he stood, looking down at me.

"Stefan—"

Slowly he unbuttoned my blouse. His hands went over my bare shoulders.

"I—can't," I said faintly, the words almost unspoken.

His fingers pressed into my flesh.

I knew only one thing. I was his. The essence of our beings belonged together.

"I can't."

"Why can't you?" His voice was strange; the words spaced and flat.

"I would become obsessed by the need to be with you again . . . and again. The need to belong to you."

"That's how I want it to be," he said.

"I don't even belong to myself now. That's why I can't belong to you."

"What the hell are you talking about?" he said very slowly. He stood up, went to the window. "Is this why Emmanuel wants to divorce you?"

"He doesn't want to divorce me." I cried out the words at him. "You don't understand!" How could he? *I* did not understand. But I tried, hopeless, helpless to explain. Yet, even as I spoke, I yearned to have him stop my words. Take me in his arms. *Stefan, I want to belong to you.* Those were the words I was crying out as I told him about the Mossad, the *Tiger Hill*, the *Hilda*. The eight hundred Jews we hoped our ship could save.

"Stefan, my life belongs to them now. Not to me. I'm living on energy that I don't have. There's nothing left over."

He was staring at me. He repeated my sentence. "Nothing left over."

Was this all he had heard? Were these the only words which had meaning for him? "I love you, Stefan. If we went to bed I'd be lost in my love for you. That morning, after I phoned you and you said you were coming to Bucharest . . . after that call I walked along with my head and my feet in the clouds . . . and I very nearly got run over. I didn't even know I was crossing the street. Stefan . . ." I began to cry. "Don't you understand. I love you too much. If we were together—how could I just go away again? Not knowing where I'd be sent. Or when. Our time here together in this hotel room would turn into a torment for me later. It would tear me apart. And you—" I could no longer see him because of the tears. I wiped them away. But I could not stop crying. "Would it be so simple for you? Who knows what will happen here in the next few weeks or months? You may not love your wife. But you do love your children. Remember when you got the telegram about Viorica? I became a stranger to you. And you were right. You have to be like that. Your first loyalty has to be to your family now. But if we were lovers, wouldn't you—Stefan, wouldn't you feel torn, divided—?"

He came to me. He sat on the bed. He wiped my tears with his fingertips. "I feel that already," he said. "Maybe, as you seem to think, I'm living in a world which has gone. But I still see things very simply. Yes, my first loyalty must be to my family. But they're safe in the mountains.

288

They'll be safe. No matter what happens. You're here right now. The here and now. That's what matters. There may not be any tomorrow."

The telephone rang.

"That's my here and now," I said.

Von Anhauch's secretary was on the line. I explained that I was the sister-in-law of Israel Mencher; that I was in Czernowitz for the day on a most urgent matter. A matter of life and death. Of many lives— or many deaths.

The secretary sounded rather startled. She asked me to hold the line. Presently she informed me that Herr von Anhauch had a board of directors' meeting in half an hour. If I could get to his office right away, he would be happy to see me.

"I'll be there in ten minutes," I said, and hung up.

"Saved by the bell," Stefan said.

"Oh, don't," I cried. "I don't want to be—saved. Don't you know that what I want most in this world is to be with you? But I can't let it matter what I want. Or even what you want. Not now."

He stood looking at me, saying nothing. There were only the outside sounds of traffic, and the distant singsong words of Shmoiger, the beggar. *Gib mir a pur lei.*

"Shmoiger and I have the same theme song," I said. "Give me a few pennies."

"I suppose I should say that if I can help you, I'll try."

"Thank you," I whispered.

The words of Shmoiger came clearer now. *"Gib mir a pur lei."* "All right, old fellow," Stefan said. "I'll give a few pennies. I'll give a thousand pounds. Come to my office, Ruth, after you see Von Anhauch. I'll have the money for you. And I may be able to set up a few more contacts."

"Thank you," I said again. Is that what he had meant by helping me?

Abruptly then, he left the room. There was a sound of finality in the way that he shut the door behind him. The air seemed to tremble with emptiness. Or was it I who was shaking?

I walked to the window, watched the hulking figure of Shmoiger as he shuffled off down the street. *"Gib mir a pur lei."*

His words carried back like a dirge.

I walked out of the hotel into the flaming sunshine. I had hoped that Stefan would be waiting; that he would take me to see Von Anhauch. But he was nowhere in sight. I climbed into a cab.

The office of Generalrat Max Ritter von Anhauch was an imposing place furnished in heavy Biedermeier, the walls hung with fine oil paintings. Von Anhauch himself was a courtly and elegant gentleman who fitted admirably into the setting. He was gracious. He listened politely. He told me how much he admired my brother-in-law, the lawyer Israel Mencher. He said that he had read Berl Katznelson's speech concerning the aliyah bet. He shook his head gravely when I asked about the latest news reports from Poland. And, at last, he instructed his secretary to withdraw two thousand pounds sterling from the safe in one-hundred-pound notes.

I had, I confess, hoped for a more generous response. Had the failure been mine? Had I not pleaded our case with sufficient eloquence?

In answer to my unspoken thoughts Von Anhauch said, "As you may imagine, during the past few days I've had many calls for funds from many directions."

He stood up; a dismissal. But I never departed from a fund-raising session without trying to persuade the man to leave with his family, now, at once, while there still was a chance.

"Herr von Anhauch," I said, "before I go, may I ask one question? When you switched on your radio this morning you heard the whine of bombs being dropped on Warsaw. How many minutes do you think it would take those same planes to reach Czernowitz? Would there be time enough for you and your family to escape?"

He held up both hands to stop my words. "My dear young lady, I am not uninformed about the current situation. Will it please you if I say that—I have my plans."

I stood up. "Herr von Anhauch, I can only plead—don't wait too long. Even men like you—men with the golden key—can find the fences up, the gates locked—if you wait too long."

He smiled. "I appreciate your concern."

The same phrase had been said to me by so many men during the past few months. Men who had given money; some grudgingly, some almost willingly, as though appeasing fate. But so far as I knew not one of these men had altered his way of life one whit.

I was often reminded of lines spoken in Warsaw by Ze'ev Jabotinsky as he made a speech to the Jews of Europe:

"It is as if twelve million educated people were put in a carriage and the carriage was being pushed toward an abyss. How do such people behave? One is crying, one is smoking a cigarette, some are reading newspapers, someone is singing—but in vain will you look for one who will stand up, take the reins into his hands and move the carriage somewhere else. This is the mood. As if some big enemy came and chloroformed their minds."

Chloroformed their minds. That was it. One could recite facts; recount what was going on this instant with Jews in Germany, Austria, Czechoslovakia. And now, Poland. What would happen to the three million Jews of Poland? One could shout. One could weep. But to what avail? They nodded. They reassured me that they were taking steps. Some smiled with tolerance at my desperate intensity. Some called me outright a panic maker. Their reactions were different. But their actions were the same. They did nothing. It was, indeed, as if the Germans had a monstrous secret weapon. Chloroformed their minds!

As I left Von Anhauch's office I wondered how long this wealthy and powerful Jew would remain in his present position. It was hard to walk through this splendidly furnished suite of rooms and envision their owner a pauper. Yet, it had happened to the wealthy Jews in Germany. It had happened in a matter of months. The golden key could so easily be confiscated by the conqueror.

I went to Stefan's office. I had never seen it, but he had described it to me and the place felt familiar. He had told me that often when he worked late and was alone in the office he would envision me sitting in the large armchair in the corner. He would come to me; take me on his lap. . . .

I sat in the wooden chair in front of his desk. We were as formal and distant as strangers, or as two lovers after a soul-destroying fight.

But we had not had a fight; unless he had fought it out within himself. Was this what he had decided then; to cut it off, to end it?

He gave me a list of names; contacts he had made for me. I jotted down addresses; notes about each of the men I was to see. Then he handed me a sealed envelope.

"I wish," I said, "that you were buying yourself four berths on the *Hilda* with these thousand pounds."

He smiled as though I had made a mild joke.

"Stefan, I've said it so often to so many people. I don't know what words to use any more. Leave. Get out. Now. While there still is a chance to escape."

"Look!" His voice was curt. "My daughter is still on crutches. It will be months before she can walk. What do you propose, that I take this poor child on one of your nightmare voyages?"

I said nothing. The Mossad had strict regulations. We were not to accept passengers who were crippled, ill or too old to fend for themselves. Even pregnant women were banned.

"My family is quite safe," Stefan went on in a more reasonable tone. "They've been at the mountain house all summer. They'll extend the stay, that's all. I've already told the children that when school starts next week, they won't be going. As a matter of fact, that's the main reason my wife came to town. To see the teachers. Get homework assignments and books. We're well organized. The cook is up there; the maid. We've got plenty of provisions—"

"Stefan, the Jews of Europe are on their way to disaster. And you think you can sit it out in your country house with your cook and your maid!"

His secretary came in with some papers for him to sign.

Stefan looked at me. "Perhaps I can see you before you leave town?" The question was casual, remote.

"Perhaps," I said.

I left his office quickly. I felt I was leaving my life behind me.

The hours that followed were strange and torn, shunting and sliding between past and future and obsessed throughout by thoughts of Stefan.

I went first to the Jewish Community Center, marble-entranced, with daylight seeping in through the white ceiling dome. Stefan had phoned Dr. Weisselberger, president of the Zionist Organization in Czernowitz.

The money was ready; the envelope taped inside a Zionist pamphlet entitled *Palestine: Land of Promise.*

"When are you coming to the land of promise?" I asked Dr. Weisselberger.

This bald-headed, shy, bespectacled man knew what lay ahead for the Jews of Europe. He too had tried to shock people out of complacency, urge them to flee. "Certainly, they see hard times ahead," he told me. "But they look to the far future when life will be again as it is today. No one will admit that he may not be here to see this far future day."

"And you, Dr. Weisselberger? We need you in Palestine. I can help you get there."

"If I left," he said, "I would be a traitor to my people. My job is to persuade others to go to Palestine. I will be the last one to leave."

As I walked to my next appointment, I passed the school to which I had gone. The children were spilling out the front door, on their way home to lunch. The same children, it seemed, who had been my classmates, the same faces.

A few blocks farther on I passed the place where my aunts and my cousin Menachem and I had lived when we came to Czernowitz. I stood staring in the huge front window. Menachem and I used to put on pantomime plays in that window. Sometimes quite a crowd gathered in the street to watch. The place was now a pharmacy; the window was filled with vials and bottles and a pyramid made of talcum-powder boxes.

A small boy and a well-dressed woman came from the pharmacy. The boy was sucking a lollipop. They spoke in a language I did not know. I watched them as they climbed into a parked car, a car with Polish license plates. Refugees; the wealthy could escape. They had cars or could rent them. Our family too had been wealthy in 1914 when the Great War began. After a few days as refugees we were digging in the fields at night for frozen potatoes which we stole to keep from starving.

The past closed in with claustrophobic chains.

I hurried on through the streets of my childhood.

By late afternoon I had raised the down-payment money. But I had not succeeded in impressing a single person with the need to flee from

Europe. Even those who had been among the wandering homeless hordes in the last war had now lost all sense of reality or imagination.

I turned toward the home of my brother David. Would I be any more successful here?

I'd had a letter from my sister-in-law Sophie before I left Palestine. They'd moved, she informed me, into a new flat on Siebenbürgerstrasse. I remembered it as an elegant residential street lined with chestnut trees. But as I entered the street now I saw it had taken on a new luxury. The older houses had been painted; new buildings had gone up. The street had an air of quiet eternal opulence.

Sophie opened the door to my ring.

She screamed.

"What is it?" My brother David hurried from the next room.

When he saw me, he took me wordlessly into his arms.

"Well, come in! Come in!" Sophie exclaimed. "Where did you drop from? My God, why didn't you tell us you were coming? I have nothing ready. Not even a room prepared for you. You could sleep on the new living-room sofa, only it hasn't arrived yet. But don't worry, the boys can stay over with friends tonight. You'll have their room. Where's your valise? You must be exhausted, my darling. Come into the kitchen. Have some cake and coffee. Fresh cake straight from the oven."

I laughed, and let her rushing tide of words sweep me into the kitchen. The smell of fresh-baked cake made me realize that I was famished. I hadn't eaten all day.

David sat down with me at the kitchen table. Sophie hovered about us; a fount of perpetual questions, revolving now around Palestine, Poli and Emmanuel. Fortunately, before I was able to answer one question, the next came.

David and I smiled at each other, and in our silence much was said. He asked only one question: Had I heard from Arthur?

"Not for months," I said. "And you?"

"We had a letter five weeks ago. He was planning to go to Czechoslovakia on business of some sort. Rachel was fine. Little Erika was growing more beautiful every day. He sent us a snapshot of her."

"Yes," I said. "They sent me one also."

I had, in fact, taken the picture with me from Tel Aviv. I kept it in my Bible.

I had stayed with my brother and his wife when I was a student in Vienna. I was there when Erika was born. The baby and I shared the same room. I had come to love her as though she were my daughter.

Sophie held out both hands to me. "Come, Rutichka, if you've finished your cake, let me take you on the grand tour."

With unfettered pride she showed me her new stove and oven; the antique cabinet which contained her grandmother's fine chinaware. The row of copper pots and pans polished to such a shine it seemed they had never been used.

We by-passed the living room; the furniture had not yet arrived. "And we ordered it over three months ago!" Sophie exclaimed in despair.

But David's library was fully furnished. If the kitchen was Sophie's domain, this was his. Three walls lined solid with books. The heavy mahogany desk by the window. The overstuffed armchair with its bright white antimacassar. "I just finished crocheting this yesterday," Sophie said with pride. "In fact, it's my first attempt."

Crocheting antimacassars while Rome burned.

Standing in this room walled with books, a line came into my mind. I said, "When they burn books, sooner or later they will burn human beings."

Sophie stared at me blankly.

David said, "What?"

"A line," I said, "written by the poet Heine in 1853. It was in 1933 that the Germans had their bonfire of books: Jewish books. I wonder in which year they will begin burning human beings. Jewish human beings."

Sophie exclaimed, "Ruth! What a thing to say! You sound like a mad woman!"

"Do I?" I looked at her. "Sophie, David . . . what words can I use? I've come here to try to persuade you to leave Czernowitz . . . to get out of Rumania . . . to get out of Europe. At once. Before it's too late."

"*Leave?*" The word shot from her mouth. "You *must* be mad. Why on earth would we *leave?* We've just bought this apartment . . . ordered new furniture . . . had the whole place repainted!"

David started to speak. His voice was low; the words came slowly.

At first Sophie, in a state of indignant shock, did not listen. Then she turned to him, frowning.

"I was in Berlin in May of '33," David said. "It was May tenth. All afternoon raiding parties of uniformed Nazis went into public libraries and to private libraries. They had long lists of books which Dr. Goebbels had decided were unfit for Nazi Germany. Most of them were by Jewish authors. These books were thrown out of doors and windows, into the street. There, more Nazi squads collected them, carried them off to add to the huge funeral pyre of books on Franz Joseph Platz between the State Opera House on the beautiful boulevard Unter den Linden, and the world-famous University of Berlin.

"I stood there through the afternoon, watching as the pile grew higher . . . higher . . . higher than a house. And the mobs gathered around the mountain of books, howling, jeering. . . . At nightfall they put torches to the books. University students mixed with the mob . . . danced around the bonfire . . . screaming, chanting.

"Then Dr. Goebbels, the new Propaganda Minister of the new German nation, stood before a microphone. I remember his words very well. Six years ago, and still I remember the words as if they'd been spoken six minutes ago. 'Fellow students, German men and women, the age of extreme Jewish intellectualism has now ended. . . . You are doing the right thing in committing the evil spirit of the past to the flames at this late hour of the night. It is a strong, great and symbolic act.' "

For a long moment no one spoke. Then Sophie said, "Come, Rutichka, let me show you the room where you'll sleep tonight."

I stared at her now as though *she* were the mad woman. We were within inches of each other yet stood, I felt, like two human beings on opposite sides of a vast abyss.

"What's wrong with you both?" she said irritably. "The Nazis burned a pile of books six years ago in Berlin. Is that any reason for us to leave our home here on Siebenbürgerstrasse? We're in another country, hundreds of miles away! What would happen to humanity if, at every catastrophe, everyone in every country picked up and started running somewhere else? You *stay!* That's how you help the world keep its balance. You stay in the place where your children go to school . . . where their friends are . . . where your friends are. You stay on the block where your house is . . . You stay in the neighborhood where you know the shopkeepers . . . where your doctor is . . . your dentist is . . . your beauty parlor is. . . . You STAY!" She screamed the word at us in anguish and fear.

"Last week," I said, "a new police regulation went out to Jews of Berlin. They are now forbidden to enter a beauty parlor. Or a barbershop. Or to buy a newspaper. Or to own a pet. Do you," I asked Sophie, "own a pet?"

"A pet?" Her voice was soft now, but it had a screamy quality. "Yes, we own a pet. A Siamese cat. What are you suggesting, that I flee the country to save the life of my cat?"

"I mentioned the beauty parlor and the pets," I said, "because I've found that sometimes when I recount horror stories to Rumanian Jews they close their ears and their minds. But the small details which they can relate to their own lives—these things they will listen to. With these I can make an opening wedge."

Sophie had backed against the wall of books. She was staring at me with hatred.

I sat down in the armchair with its newly crocheted antimacassar. "If I believed that this would be a matter of beauty parlors and Siamese cats, I would still be in Palestine. I am here now because I believe that we will soon be knee-deep in Jewish blood and disaster. I believe that the Nazis are, right now, carefully working out means and methods for the total destruction of all the Jews in all the countries the Germans will conquer. I believe that the Jews of Europe are already on their march of death. Without even knowing it."

"*You* believe!" Sophie shrieked at me. "You come here and threaten our home, our happiness, because of your own nightmares."

I understood her; beneath my desperation I felt a searing compassion. "I know," I said, "the idea is so monstrous that anyone who believes it is looked upon like some sort of brutal monster himself. How *could* such things happen. After all, this isn't the age of the Inquisition when people were put on the rack and pulled to pieces because they were not Christians. Or the age of ancient Rome when people were devoured by lions because they *were* Christians. This is twentieth-century Germany we are talking about. Germany, land of philosophers and poets! Germany, which is at this moment overrunning our neighbor Poland.

Germany, whose armies overran Rumania within days after the last war was declared."

I stood up. "A week ago at the Zionist Congress I met a young man who had visited Berlin and was coming home to Austria—when it still *was* Austria. The dining-car steward gave him his change in German marks, and when my friend—his name is Ehud—protested, the steward said, 'Keep the marks. You'll need them soon enough.'

"Ehud kept the marks. He'd seen enough in Berlin to convince him that the steward was right. On the day he got back to Vienna he told every Jew he met, 'Get out. Somehow. In three weeks they'll be here.'

"But no one believed him. It can't happen here! But it did. In three weeks exactly the Germans marched in. The nation of Austria ceased to exist. And you know what happened to the Austrian Jews—the Jews who were so very certain that it couldn't happen. Not to *them!*

"David." I put both hands on my brother's arm; perhaps the pressure of my fingers would reach him if my words did not. "Oh, God, please, listen to me. Sophie!" I turned to her. "I can help you get on a ship to Palestine if you'll let me. Poli will be there to welcome you. You can stay on his kibbutz until you get settled. Look, if nothing happens, you can always come back. But now—have the courage to lock up the house and walk away from it. Don't risk your lives for the sake of some newly crocheted antimacassars and shining copper pots and pans."

Sophie's green eyes were narrowed in fury. I could hear her unspoken words: *Get out of my house. Leave us alone!*

I turned to David. "For God's sake, let me help you. Now, while I still can. Now, before all the gates are closed."

He was an imposing-looking man. He stood tall in his neat, gray pin-striped suit. His voice was always calm. He emanated a sense of security and well-being. "Well," he said, "I suppose we should at least hear what you have in mind."

"First," I said, speaking very softly, "you must believe that it can happen here. Otherwise, you won't have the strength to leave now while your lives and your street are still peaceful."

"What kind of spineless cowards do you think we are?" Sophie shouted the words at me. "Running away—from what? The Germans may never set foot in Rumania. They need this country as neutral territory. Everyone knows that!"

"Even if you're right," I said, "just remember, it needn't take an invasion. We have our own home-grown Iron Guard."

"They have no power! They're illegal!"

"Yes, Sophie. And Hitler was illegal too when he founded the Nazi Party. In fact, he was on parole from prison—forbidden to make political speeches. Nevertheless, he succeeded—starting from scratch, you might say. Don't forget, when *he* started out German Jews were—assimilated! They were Germans! Proud citizens. Anti-Semitism. In the Weimar Republic. Ridiculous!

"But here! Just remember, Sophie, before the last war Rumania was called the most anti-Semitic country in Europe. Jews weren't even allowed to be citizens—until the peace treaty. And then only because the Allies insisted on it. Just remember, the Iron Guard has flourished here since 1924. The Iron Guard—which was *founded* on anti-Semitism. The Iron Guard—which very nearly took over this country less than two years ago. Next time, they may succeed."

She said nothing. She looked down at her fists which were clenched in her lap. I felt some hope. Perhaps my words were drilling through her wall of resistance.

I turned to my brother. "In Germany it took five years. Here it could happen in five days. Look back. Remember what happened in Germany. Remember what the German Jews said. Exactly what you're saying now. David, if you were a Jew in Germany today, wouldn't you give anything to get out? But you'd have nothing left to give. And there would be no way out."

They *were* listening. They *would* come with me. Impelled and encouraged by their silence, I went on. I recalled the facts of those five years. And the reactions of German Jews which, in retrospect, seemed so incredible.

"Remember the first year Hitler came to power, all Jews in the civil service fired. Jewish teachers fired. Jewish actors, singers, directors, producers—the whole entertainment industry, *judenrein*.

"The second year, Jews excluded from journalism. From radio. From the stock exchange. From farming. Jews forbidden to practice law. Medicine. Forbidden to apply to a university. Forbidden. *Verboten*. The sickness spreading.

"The third year, the Nuremberg Laws—making every Jew an official outcast. Subject to all German laws. But with no legal rights at all. By the fourth year, half the Jews in Germany—unemployed. And the signs. You remember, David. You traveled through Germany in 1937. You told us about the signs. Hanging above hotel doorways . . . in shop windows . . . at the entrance to public parks. No Jews Allowed. Even above the kindergartens, signs: 'Jewish Scum.' You told us yourself, David, in some towns a Jew couldn't buy milk for his children. In some towns it was impossible for a Jew to buy food. Or medicine. Because of the signs at the doorways of dairies . . . pharmacies . . . groceries. *No Jews.*

"And what did the Jews of Germany do about all this?" I turned to Sophie. "Make every attempt to get out? Yes, of course, some of them did. Especially the famous—since there were committees organized in other countries to rescue famous Jews. And many of the young people left. If you have a short past, it's a lot easier to face a new future. But most of the others—the vast majority—talked just like you, Sophie. We'll stay. Stick it out. After all, Jews have endured persecution before. For two thousand years, in fact. This too will pass. Life is difficult now, yes. But to move might be more difficult."

"Right!" Sophie shouted. "Exactly! Don't you know there were Jews who did emigrate to America. To Palestine. To other countries. And they came back to Germany! It was too hard to learn a new language. To build a new life. So they came back home. Even last year—bad as things were—I heard of some Jews who came back to Germany."

"That was before the Kristallnacht," I said. "No Jews came back after November Tenth. Right now, Sophie, right this minute there are long lines of Jews in Berlin, Vienna, Prague; Jews waiting in front of the embassies and legations of every country in the world. Jews desperate to get out. But now it's too late. Now they're trapped. Now they know they waited too long."

"David," I turned to him, "for the sake of your two sons, leave Europe now. Come to Palestine."

Sophie uttered a shrill sobbing cry. She ran from the room.

David started after her.

"Wait!" I said sharply.

"But she's crying," he said.

"I want to talk to you alone."

He hesitated.

"Please, David. I can't tell you in front of her."

He frowned and closed the library door. "All right," he said. "What are you really doing here in Rumania? Is that what you want to talk about?"

I nodded and told him then about the Mossad.

He asked many questions about our mission, about the *Hilda*, about the dangers of the voyage.

He *was* listening. He *would* bring his family to Palestine.

Presently Sophie returned carrying a tray of cups, coffee and small cakes. Her eyes were red. But her voice was controlled. "How long will you be in Czernowitz?" she asked me.

"I plan to leave tomorrow night."

She nodded. "Will you stay for dinner?"

"I'm sorry," I said. "I want to see Bertha and my aunts." Then I looked at David. "I can—come again tomorrow."

David took a cake, broke it in half, set the halves back on the plate. "Ruth," he said, "you tell me that by staying in my own home I may be responsible for the murder of my wife and my sons. But—" He picked up his coffee cup. Then he set it down again. "You and I start from different premises. So we come to different conclusions. You see, I cannot believe that the Nazis are some new species of psychopathic murderers. I cannot believe that they plan to kill all the Jews. And, as you yourself say, they may never come here. The worst we may have to deal with is our own Iron Guard. And in this blessed land of baksheesh, there is always a way out. I have a good business here. The boys go to a good school. And Sophie—" He smiled a little. "Can you imagine my Sophie on a kibbutz?"

"Yes," I said evenly. "I can."

"I may change my mind, of course," David said. "But right now, weighing the scales, I think we're better off in our own beds, in our own home, on our own street than we would be on one of your ships. Since the war started those journeys will be more hazardous than ever. The Mediterranean will be heavily mined. If we went on your ship, you might turn out to be our unwitting murderer."

"Oh . . . God . . ." I whispered. I stood up. Then I looked at him. "I wonder whether Arthur would agree with you—or with me?"

David walked with me down the block to the tram stop.

As we waited he asked hesitantly, "Does your organization have anyone in Vienna now?"

"For the time being, yes. If you're thinking of Arthur—our Mossad man will do his best to get them out."

David nodded.

"Tell me," I said, "do you think Arthur was right to stay in Vienna as long as he did?"

"Vienna," David said flatly, "is not Czernowitz."

The tram was coming now. I embraced my brother.

"You have my address, in Bucharest," I said. "If you change your mind, let me know at once."

"Yes," David said. "Well, we'll see. We'll wait for a while and see how things go here."

I looked at him. "David. Don't wait too long."

He smiled a little. He kissed me on the forehead.

The tram came. I climbed aboard, sat down, looked out the window and watched my brother's figure recede slowly into the gray evening.

TWENTY-EIGHT

I WENT THEN to the Jewish Quarter to visit my sister Bertha and my aunts.

Czernowitz had a large Jewish population and an ancient one. Walking now at sunset through the narrow cobbled streets of the Quarter was like walking back in time through the special civilization Jews had built for themselves in hundreds of cities and rural villages throughout Eastern Europe: a civilization with its own language, Yiddish; its own style of dress, its own style of life.

Small boys with sidelocks and *yarmulkas* walking home from evening services with their bearded, black-frocked fathers. Long-skirted married women with kerchiefs covering their wigs or shaven heads, hurrying home to make dinner. Small shops lining the sidewalks. I noticed that there were no cars with Polish license plates parked in these narrow streets. Were any Jews escaping from Poland?

All at once I was walking into a nightmare vision of my own creation. I saw buildings blazing . . . heard the cries of playing children turn into terrified screams . . . saw people running, stumbling down the street. And black tanks lumbering along the cobblestones spewing death from their gun turrets.

I reached the house of my sister Bertha, climbed a flight of unlit stairs, stumbled to my knees in the darkness. Did they never have light in the hallway? Or had the light gone out? Everything suddenly seemed frighteningly symbolic; even so small a matter as a burned-out bulb.

Takor, my brother-in-law, opened the door to my knock. He grasped my hand, pulled me into the room, kissed me soundly. My sister Bertha screamed, just as Sophie had done; then hovered about me asking for news, recalling memories . . . scurrying back and forth to the kitchen to make me dinner, which I did not want.

I asked about my cousin Menachem. He had married recently, she told me. He was a certified accountant now. But he rarely came to visit them. He lived in another part of town and was very tied up with his new wife and his new life.

I asked when she had last heard from Arthur. She too had received a letter five weeks ago. She too had received a snapshot of the little girl Erika, which she had put in the frame of her dresser mirror.

When I finally mentioned the matter of Palestine, it was Takor who responded as though I had thrown a lifeline. He was a Christian, an Armenian. The Armenians, he told me, like the Jews, know the meaning of persecution.

But Bertha was adamant. She was a respected costume designer here in Czernowitz. She loved her work at the Opera House. Exactly how many opera houses did they have in that land of desert and swamp called Palestine? Bertha had never been a Zionist. Quite the contrary. It was, perhaps, part of her old rebellion against my mother.

"A Jewish state in Palestine!" She fairly screamed the words at me. "*That* is the road to annihilation, can't you see? Gather all the Jews together in one vast ghetto in the Middle East—so that they can be wiped out in one grand massacre by the Arabs. You can see it beginning right now. Arabs massacring men, women, little children in the kibbutzim. Ambushing buses and donkey carts on the roadways. Mutilating bodies. You think we don't know what's going on in that Holy Land of yours? We know! How dare you come in here and suggest that we leave our home; that Takor give up his candy factory—for what? To move to a country where we wouldn't be safe in our beds at night. You must be mad!"

For a long moment we stared at each other.

I wanted to run to her, to embrace her. To forget the present. To find the past. To ask forgiveness for all the unhappiness I had brought to my older sister. I wondered suddenly about the lover she had left long ago in Prague, to come to Czernowitz because of me. I felt again the aching pangs of childhood guilt.

How could I dare to suggest that once again she disrupt her life? Perhaps she *was* right. Perhaps she was better off here in the Jewish Quarter of Czernowitz than she would be in Palestine.

I did go to her. Our arms went around each other. We stood in silence.

When we moved apart there were tears on her cheeks and on mine.

I left after dinner.

Takor accompanied me to the door. "Perhaps," he said, "if I can at least get her to move to Bucharest—we would be closer to some way of escape. If it should prove necessary."

"Yes," I said. "I have an apartment. You could stay with me, until we see where to go from there."

He wrote my address on a bill of lading.

"God bless you," he said. "Perhaps we will see you very soon."

But as I left, feeling my way down the dark staircase, I wondered whether I would ever see either of them again.

I went then to visit my aunts.

They encased me in an ebullient bubble of surprise and joy. I did not want to slash into it with words about escape to Palestine. But how could I leave here without at least having tried?

Finally, I spoke the words. They merely looked at me. Three elderly ladies; they barely knew what was going on in the world outside this Jewish Quarter of Czernowitz.

"What do you mean, come to Palestine?" my aunt Shaindl inquired sweetly. "Do you still need us to take care of you? You have your own husband now; your own life. What use could we be to you any longer?"

What use could we be?

The answer was stark and simple.

The unspoken understanding among Mossad members was that preference be given on our ships to those who were young and strong. If one day the Jews did have to fight for their right to exist in their historic homeland, it would be the young and strong who were needed.

What right did I have to offer space on our ship to my three beloved elderly aunts?

I said no more about Palestine. We chattered on recalling old memories, restoring them once again to life.

At last I said it was time to leave.

"Come back very soon," Aunt Bertha exclaimed. "Next time don't stay away so long. And next time bring your handsome husband with you!"

As we embraced at the door I wondered whether she still thought of Colonel Gregori Nikoliev who had been shot to death before her eyes.

I returned to the hotel, locked the door of my room. I was exhausted; yet filled with desperate energy. I went to the window, opened it wide. I wanted to scream out the window, to shake this city from its complacency.

Of all the members of my family, only Takor had responded. And only Takor would be safe if he stayed.

I threw my suitcase on the bed, opened it and started to pack.

I would take the night train to Bucharest. I had accomplished my mission for the Mossad. I had raised the ten thousand pounds. There was no reason to stay here the extra day. There was every reason not to.

If Stefan came to my room tonight I had neither the strength nor the will to resist him. Yet, I knew that what I had told him this morning was true.

I thought of Ehud. His fiancee was in Palestine. He could have chosen to go there. This very day could have been his wedding day. Instead, he had headed back to Vienna.

Each man in the Mossad had, in some way, set aside his private life.

I could do nothing else but to leave this city, to leave Stefan.

The desk clerk at the Schwarzer Adler thanked me profusely when I turned in my key and told him I was checking out a day early.

"There are now," he said, "over three hundred Poles waiting here in the lobby and outside in cars, desperate for a room."

In the station waiting room I met one of the Poles, a little girl with curly dark hair and large dark eyes. I sat next to her. I had a packet of sweets and offered them to her.

She looked at me; shook her head.

I smiled at her, but she turned away.

The woman next to her said, "She's just come from Poland. She rang my bell this morning. She gave me a note from her mother. I barely know the mother. I met her once on vacation. I'm Polish myself. But I moved to Czernowitz when I married. Her mother and I exchanged New Year's cards. That's how she had my address. She asked if I would put her child on the train to Bucharest. Of course, I'm taking her there myself. I can't send this little one off alone. She speaks no Yiddish. Only Polish. She'd never find her way."

"Where will she go in Bucharest?" I asked.

"Oh," said the woman, "she has a great-aunt living there."

I looked at the child, who sat staring straight ahead like one hypnotized by an inner vision.

The woman beside her kept talking in a rush of words, telling me what had happened to this little girl named Dasha.

"She comes from a good family. A well-to-do Jewish family in the town of Bendzin. That's near the German border, you know. Well, the parents were afraid the German Army would overrun the town. So they put this poor child on a bus and sent her off to stay with relatives in central Poland. People she had never seen."

The woman described with eloquence how Dasha had arrived in the town of Szczekociny with a small suitcase and a letter of introduction pinned inside her jacket.

Her relatives took her in, made her a bed of straw and a blanket, and were kind to her. That night she was awakened by screams. She looked out the window. The street was in flames.

"Get dressed," her aunt told her. "The Polish Army is retreating. They've set fire to the town. Get dressed. Run." Then the aunt forgot about Dasha. She had eight children of her own to attend to.

Dasha did not need to get dressed. She had never undressed; she wanted to be ready at any moment to return home.

She went to the doorway. Because of the flames and the smoke she could not see the sky. Everyone was running. She started to run. Through the burning town. Into the forest. German planes were flying low, above the treetops. Strafing. People fell down; screaming, wounded. She ran on. Her suitcase grew heavier. But she did not leave it behind. Her mother had packed this suitcase for her.

All night and all the next day she was in the forest. There were many others there, running. But she spoke to no one. Finally, at the edge of the forest she met a man on a motorcycle. He was going east. Dasha asked him to take her back to Bendzin.

When she got home she found her mother in the garden, sobbing. The German Army had come. They had locked all the Jewish men they could find into the synagogue. Then they had burned it down. Dasha's oldest brother and her cousin had been burned alive.

The mother put her little girl to bed. But late that same night she sent the child off again with a Christian family heading by car for Rumania.

I wanted to take the child on my lap. To hold her, to comfort her. But she sat staring out as though she had turned to stone.

"Her mother?" I said. "Will her mother be coming to Bucharest to be with her?"

The woman shrugged. "This is just one of the children. The mother has three others. They were sent off to other Polish relatives, each with a letter of introduction and a label on his coat. And her husband fled when the Germans came. The poor woman must wait there to see whether anyone comes home."

I took down the address of Dasha's great-aunt in Bucharest. Perhaps when the *Hilda* was organized I could help the little girl get to Palestine.

The train clanged into the night station and I joined the surge of people shoving aboard. I tried to stay near Dasha, but we were separated.

The corridor was stifling hot and so crowded it was virtually impossible to move. After what seemed an interminable time the train started. Soot and cinders swept in through the open windows, together with a cooling breeze.

As the lights of the city were smothered by night, and the train plowed its way between the darkness of fields and sky I found that I was weeping.

For the little girl? For my brother, my sister, my aunts?

Ashamed, I realized that I was crying for Stefan.

I tried to fasten my thoughts onto the job which lay ahead. I would return to the city by early morning, visit the Shamen, make the down payment, contact Alexander, Orekhovsky, Cotic, Solomonides—

A hand gripped my shoulder.

I turned my head and cried out.

Stefan was standing behind me. He moved so that he could hold me. I raised my face and we kissed, clinging together. People were pressing tight around us, yet we had never been more alone.

He said something, but his words were blotted out by the noise of the passengers and the clattering train wheels.

"What?" I said.

He lifted me off my feet, held me so that his lips were close to my ear. "I want to marry you," he said. "Will you marry me?"

"Yes," I said.

He kept holding me, against him and off the ground. "I came to your hotel room with flowers and a fine speech. The door was opened by a fat Pole with a black mustache."

I laughed and again we kissed.

He set me back on my feet, but his arms were around me holding me hard against him.

"Will you come to Palestine?" I said.

"If I must."

"You must. With your wife and children."

He nodded.

Perhaps his wife would one day forgive me if, because of me, she and her children were safe.

"We'll come," he said, "as soon as Viorica is able to travel. In the meantime, I'll try to sell my house, my business. As a matter of fact, I have an appointment tomorrow morning with a man who might be interested in the business."

The train was slowing. The lights of a station glowed through the darkness.

He took a gold signet ring from his finger, pressed it into my hand. "Keep this. Our engagement ring."

We clung, kissing.

The train drew to a stop.

"I'll get off here," Stefan said. "I'll phone you at the apartment tomorrow night."

He made his way through the corridor to the door.

I leaned out the window waving to him until the train started to move, pulling us apart.

TWENTY-NINE

AT NINE THE NEXT MORNING I returned to my apartment on the Strada Rosetti.

When I entered, David Arnon was in the kitchen making breakfast. Alexander was sprawled in an armchair making telephone calls. And Yitzhak Hecker was kneeling by a valise, unpacking submachine guns.

He greeted me with a chagrined smile. "We didn't expect you back till tomorrow," he said. "But everything will be out of here by this afternoon. We've made all the arrangements."

I was then invited to take part in this operation. David explained it over breakfast. They had rented a large car. We would drive out to a forest near Bucharest and bury the arms. If someone happened along, we would quickly spread a picnic tablecloth over the hole. "It's lucky for us that you did come back early," he said. "After all, who would really believe a picnic in the woods—without a girl?"

I exploded. "The Mossad has enough worries without becoming involved in smuggling *guns!* As it is," I cried, "the British are after us. Plus the police of Bucharest. Plus the Iron Guard. Plus the—"

David held up both hands and blocked me with a word: "Wait!" Then he explained that he and Yitzhak were, in fact, here on several missions. True, by securing arms to smuggle into Palestine for the Haganah, they were working against the British. At the same time, however, they were working with the British. They were, in fact, agents in Section D, a division of British Intelligence devoted to sabotage and demolition.

"Therefore," said David buoyantly, "the arms you help us bury can, in fact, be used for your own protection. If, one day, you're thrown into prison we merely go to our fellows in Section D. We offer them maps of our buried arms—in return for your release from jail."

"And if your fellows in Section D wonder why you've been so busy burying arms?"

"For *their* use, of course—if Rumania is overrun by Germans. For the use of British tommies who parachute behind enemy lines. Or for the Jews of Bucharest. To help fight the Germans."

His logic seemed rather strained. I could not see that British Intelligence agents would have much influence in securing the release of a Palestinian national from a Rumanian jail. Nevertheless, I agreed to go with them, provided they found other arsenals for their arms in the future.

About six that evening we loaded the car. My landlady happened along just as David was hoisting a suitcase of grenades into the back seat.

"I'm—driving my friends to the airport," I said.

Mrs. Schecter gave a long look at the cases and cartons piled high in the back seat. "I doubt they'll let you take all that in the plane," she remarked. "I understand they're very strict about excess baggage."

"We'll store most of this stuff," David told her, "until we come back to Bucharest."

I introduced Yitzhak and David. They shook hands. Mrs. Schecter then looked down at her palm which was overly greasy. The boys had spent all afternoon coating pistols, grenades and light machine guns with a heavy layer of grease, to protect them against the earth's dampness.

My landlady was frowning as we drove away. I could not blame her. Times were perilous enough for the average Jew in Rumania. No one needed a tenant whose actions might invite suspicion and investigation.

As we drove down the broad Sosea Boulevard David asked, "How did you get on with your fat friend this afternoon?"

I had of course visited the Shamen at once. He accepted the envelope with our ten thousand pounds as though its contents were repugnant to him. "If I'd leased the ship to a legal company," he grumbled, "I would not only keep out of trouble, I'd have made a handsome profit."

Over coffee and cognac I tried to persuade him that the satisfaction he would derive from saving lives could not be measured in pounds and pence. As I left his apartment he suddenly embraced me and I felt I was being smothered and crushed by mounds of fat encased in white silk shirting. I gained my release only by gasping out a promise to have dinner with him one night very soon.

However, I reported none of this to David or Yitzhak. I somehow had the feeling that the less they knew about the Mossad's affairs the better off we would be. I merely told them that things were going as well as could be expected with the Shamen.

The drive to the Băneasa Forest took thirty-five minutes. When Stefan and I had come this way in a horse-drawn carriage it had taken over an hour; yet that magical, sunlit hour seemed to telescope into minutes. I wondered whether we would pass the restaurant by the lake where Stefan and I had lunch that first day.

I touched his ring. It was too large for my finger; besides, I wanted no questions about it. It hung on a chain, beneath my blouse.

When we reached the outskirts of the Băneasa, David followed a dirt road deep into the forest. The road ended in a lane, paved with white pebbles, and the car ground to a halt.

Yitzhak and David went out to locate a suitable spot for the burial, leaving me in the car as nursemaid to the munitions. Finally they returned. They had found a well-hidden glade close by; had mapped it out carefully by paces. Now I was told to come along as lookout, while they dug.

We were a strange procession. David carried two shovels wrapped in a bright tablecloth, plus a suitcase of explosives. Yitzhak carried a guitarlike instrument called a *tambal,* a tarpaulin, a broad board and a carton of pistols. I followed along with a picnic basket, a bottle of wine and a kerosene lamp. David had insisted we start our operation in the daytime. To venture out for a picnic at night would be too suspicious. Yet, if we were interrupted, it might well be dark before we finished.

My job was an easy one. While the boys dug, I strolled around the periphery of the area they had selected. The woods were deep; silence broken only by the silvery sound of birds chirping, calling.

As I walked my rounds I came suddenly upon two lovers lying in a grassy glade. Their bodies, close, moving in unison, were covered by the soft warmth of afternoon sunlight which fell through a space in the branches overhead. I walked on, filled with longing for Stefan.

By the time I returned the boys had dug a trench almost four feet deep. They stopped for a refresher of bottled water, and I started off in the opposite direction.

I heard them before I saw them. The spangled laughter, the loud male voices speaking a language I recognized as Romany. Gypsies.

I hurried back to our picnic site. Quickly Yitzhak shoved the munitions and tarpaulin into the hole. David spread the board on top. I flapped the tablecloth over the board, spread out our cheeses, our wine, our fruits, our loaf of bread, picked up the *tambal* and started singing a new Rumanian love song which was being played in the cabarets and over the airways.

> "The train left the station,
> In the train was my love.
> Tonight, to whom shall I say goodnight?"

The gypsies burst upon us, singing, laughing. We suddenly seemed beseiged by small, dirty, near-naked children. Chattering, pleading, they pointed to our food. We gave it to them, all of it, hoping they would then depart. But, in heavily accented Rumanian, one of the men promised us a special treat in return for our generosity. He hurried off into the woods and returned shortly leading a huge brown bear on a chain.

"Hey, Martine," he called to the bear. "Start dancing!" The bear lumbered about as the gypsies stamped and sang and clapped for accompaniment. One of the boys grabbed up the *tambal* and started strumming.

I wondered how many more gypsies were in this troop; whether even now another contingent had discovered our car and was busy unpacking the munitions.

When the bear had finished, her master demanded we pay five lei for the privilege of having seen Martine perform. "For another five lei," he said to David, "Martine will walk on your body and get rid of your backaches."

Since David and Yitzhak did not speak Rumanian, I translated this generous offer.

"Tell him," said David, "I don't have a backache."

"Well," said the gypsy, "the bear will walk on your back in case you get one."

"Listen," said David, "give them ten lei to leave us alone!"

I did, and the gypsies departed, laughing and prancing like bright-colored creatures of the woods.

Hitler, I reflected, cast these gay carefree people along with Jews as the earth's scum. They were often thrown into prison for the sole crime of being gypsies.

I made a quick reconnaissance trip to the car. The trunk and the doors were still locked.

It was past nine o'clock when we left the woods that night; the precious munitions safely buried. Upon David's suggestion we had kept out several pistols for our personal use.

David and Yitzhak were quiet on the drive back to Bucharest; too exhausted, perhaps, to speak.

I stared out the window, alone with Stefan, humming the haunting melody of the song; our song.

The train left the station. . . . In the train was my love. . . . To-night, to whom shall I say good night?

The days then jarred into the nights. Hands on the clock spun crazily. As with the *Tiger Hill*, time was split by an overlapping series of appointments to be met, decisions to be made, all the minutiae of details jamming into one all-encompassing word: *Hurry*.

When we were organizing the *Tiger Hill* there was no time to sleep, no time to eat. But at least there were some snatched moments each day when I could return to my hotel room, lock the door, kick off my shoes and lie down for an hour or so between appointments. The phone might ring; it often did, incessantly. But at least my door was locked. I was alone.

The apartment on the Strada Rosetti was a different matter altogether.

After my return from Czernowitz I never called it *my* apartment. Nor did anyone else. It was The Apartment. It belonged to the Mossad. It became straightaway the gathering place for Mossad members and for information. There were some thirty other Palestinians in Bucharest at that time: representatives from kibbutzim, from political groups, from religious groups, from the Histadrut, the Haganah, from the Jewish Agency for Palestine. The Apartment became their meeting place as well. It was a kind of clubhouse; a fine place to drop in for coffee, a drink, a chat.

As a result, if I tried to relax in a hot bath, the doorbell would ring. If I tried to lie down for a nap, the doorbell would ring.

As the only woman in the operation, I was expected to serve as non-stop hostess. And all too often my uninvited guests arrived desperate for something to eat or for a drink.

During the *Tiger Hill* operation I had often felt encased in a cocoon of loneliness. Now there was neither time nor place in which to feel lonely. Except at two or three in the morning when my visitors had left and I went to bed, and thought of Stefan.

Since his family was still in the mountains, we could now phone each other in the nighttimes. I would lie with the phone beside me on the pillow, his voice in my ear. In these dark private minutes we made love and we planned for our future in Palestine.

He also sent flowers. I arranged them in vases, coffeepots, milk containers. They were on the window sills, the bed table, the bookshelf. And they occasioned a good deal of comment from my constant visitors.

But the flowers served a function which Stefan perhaps had not envisioned. Or perhaps that was why he sent the bouquets with such regularity.

It was far easier to forestall an advance when I could indicate that my love and my loyalties were elsewhere. The flowers gave credence to my claims, and acted in a way as chaperones and sentries.

Aside from the fact that I was now completely responsible for the Mossad's Rumanian operation, and aside from the fact that I was now going about in a state of perpetual exhaustion, there was a third element which made the organizing of the *Hilda* a totally different operation from that of the *Tiger Hill*. That, of course, was the war.

The news from Poland became more ghastly day by day. Never before in history had one country so brutally decimated another in so short a time. The Jews in Poland were trapped. And the Jews in Rumania were stunned, but there still were no particular attempts at an exodus. Almost all the Rumanian Jews I met would "wait and see." Yet, each realized that he might, indeed, have to leave in a desperate hurry. Each seemed to feel that money provided his only security. Rumania was still the land of baksheesh. But as the gates closed the exit fees went up. No longer would Rumanian Jews pay for another Jew's passage to Palestine. Each felt that he might very well need every last lei to pay for his own family's escape. Raising money, therefore, became more difficult than it had ever been.

Whenever I entered the apartment, the radio was on. David, Yitzhak, Alexander—sometimes some stranger I'd never set eyes on—would report the latest news. On those rare occasions when I came into the apartment and found it empty, the first thing I did was to turn on the radio.

Although I knew no Polish, I spoke Russian, and the languages were sufficiently akin to enable me to follow what was happening. At times no words were needed. My short-wave radio transmitted clearly the whine of bombs being dropped, the muffled boom when they exploded.

There were, of course, newspaper reports. But it was the radio which brought the war directly into the quiet apartment on the tree-lined Strada Rosetti. It was the radio which propelled us to overcome impossible obstacles regarding our ship.

Late one night a call came through from Shmarya Zamaret. His jubilant "you sees" were peppered heavily through the Hebrew and code. And his excitement was so contagious that when I'd hung up David Arnon said, "Well! What's happened? You're glowing!"

"Just—something about a ship," I said, trying hard to be casual.

"You can't share the good news? We could all use a small dose right now."

I wanted to tell him. But, although we were often together, our missions were far apart. We had an unspoken agreement to keep the details of our operations to ourselves. If one of us were arrested there was no point in being burdened with more information than we needed to know.

That night, however, I was alone when Dani Shind called from Bulgaria. And, in careful code, I told him the incredible news.

We owned a ship! We, the Mossad, had managed to purchase—not merely lease—but purchase a ship. She was small; three hundred and ninety-eight tons. She was old; built in 1892. But she was sturdy. A salvage ship into which a strong submarine motor had been installed. We could build a structure on her decks which would house three tiers of wooden berths. When reconverted she could hold five hundred passengers. She could ply back and forth, carrying load after load of illegals from Europe to Palestine.

"How did it come about, this miracle?" Dani wanted to know.

"Through a drunken captain Shmarya met in a waterfront cafe in Piraeus. The fellow owned this ship. And he was in some sort of trouble. Needed thirty thousand American dollars in twenty-four hours' time. Shmarya persuaded him that *he* was Mr. Rich American. Kept him there drinking, while he put through a call to Saly Meyer in Switzerland. And—can you believe it—Saly came through. Shmarya had a bank draft in a matter of hours. Went with the captain to the American Express. And now Shmarya owns a ship! He's renamed it already. The *Darien*. After a gulf in South America—since she'll be flying under some South American flag."

"Maybe," said Dani, "this will be the beginning of a little good fortune, for a change."

Dani Shind was not an effusive man. But underneath the dry words I could hear excitement.

And perhaps there was truth in his prognostication.

The following night a call came through from Ehud in Vienna.

It was the first time he had been able to contact us since his return.

His coded message also held hope. There was nothing certain, of course. The operation was still built on a wobbly bridge of ifs and buts. However, there was a distinct possibility that by late October one of the plans he had told us about in Geneva would become a reality. The Mossad might be running its own pleasure cruises down the Danube to the Black Sea.

We spoke for several minutes. Then the line was abruptly cut.

From the first moment I had ached to ask him one single question: My brother Arthur, his wife, his daughter—have you any news?

Now the connection was broken. I could not call him back. Perhaps, if he had news, he would have told me at the beginning of the conversation. Though if it were bad news he might have hesitated; waiting to prepare me.

I lay awake, hoping that Ehud would telephone again.

But the call never came.

The next day, September eighth, when I switched on the radio I heard for the first time the voice of Warsaw's Lord Mayor, Stefan Starzynski. He announced that German forces had reached the outskirts of the city. The capital was not only under bombing attacks night and day; it was now also being besieged.

The Lord Mayor came on the air often during the horrific days which followed. David, Yitzhak and I adopted him as our hero. The boys called him Stefan. I could not say the name. I called him the Mayor.

Day and night he walked the streets of his city, dodging bombs and falling debris, surveying the block-by-block decimation. Then he would come to the microphone to report, to reassure, to give directions.

"The fire department cannot get around the city because of the barricades, so you yourselves must help extinguish incendiary-bomb fires. . . . Citizens are asked to give all spare beds to hospitals which have been bombed. . . . Citizens are asked to report any cases they know of wounded horses, as their flesh is needed—for food."

Often he aimed his words at the Allies. "We ask our friends to come to our aid. We are counting on your air force and fleet. Victory will still be ours."

By September twelfth, British forces were landing in France. And British planes were flying low over Germany. However, they did not drop bombs. They dropped paper. Millions of propaganda leaflets.

The Poles fought on alone.

Three highly mechanized German armies attacked from three directions. And the German air force pulverized the cities of Poland. A new word for a new kind of warfare was invented: *Blitzkrieg.* Never before in history had a country been overrun so cruelly and so quickly.

How long could the Poles hold out?

Sometimes when we switched to Radio Warsaw we heard only four musical notes: a phonograph record which played over and over. Four musical notes to let the world know that Poland's capital city had not been taken.

As the days passed, the Lord Mayor came to the radio station more often. Whatever his message, he always ended the same way: exhorting his people to continue resisting. But often his voice belied his words. We could hear the desperation and the frenzy.

"German bombs have no effect on us. . . . We are accustomed to them. . . . I have ordered all shops to remain open. . . . Warsaw in victory will save Europe!"

Some of the Radio Warsaw announcers tried to emulate their Mayor in his dredged-up optimism. One proclaimed: "We are accustomed now to air raids . . . German bombs are being badly aimed . . . Our cellars are safe . . ."

Sometimes Polish newscasters spoke in English, as if insisting that the world be witness to their city's demise. I wrote down their words. I used them, like weapons, to try to pry help and money from people so that the *Hilda* could sail.

"Warsaw is drowned in the noise of roaring airplanes and explosions of heavy bombs. High flames are leaping from many buildings against the jet-black sky."

It was the nightmare I'd had when walking through the Jewish Quarter of Czernowitz; the nightmare which, within a week, had turned to horrendous reality.

On September sixteenth, a BBC newscaster announced that Russia had just signed an armistice with Japan. David Arnon, who was sitting by the radio, frowned and said, "Well, now Russia has neutralized her enemy to the west *and* her enemy to the east. I wonder how soon her troops will move into Poland?"

At 6 A.M. the next morning I woke suddenly; perhaps because the four musical notes had gone off the air. Those four notes had become for me a kind of eerie lullaby.

I twisted the radio dial. Turned to a Rumanian station. A voice crackling with intensity, announced that at this moment Russian troops were invading Poland. The Russian Government had proclaimed it was sending in the Soviet Army to defend the interests of Russian nationals in the Republic of Poland. Then the newscaster added: "The Rumanian Government has received assurance from the USSR that this troop movement will in no way affect Russia's relations with Rumania or with any other bordering countries." The announcer said nothing more, but his brittle tone indicated how much faith he put into such promises.

It was Sunday. My day was crowded with appointments. But Yitzhak Hecker remained by my radio, monitoring the news. When I returned that evening he informed me that Russian troops had invaded along the whole length of the frontier. Poland's President, her Foreign Minister, the Commander in Chief of the Army, along with fifty-six other important government officials, had landed in Rumania.

"The Mayor of Warsaw?" I asked.

"No word about him. But he wouldn't have fled." Yitzhak repeated the words with insistence. "He wouldn't have fled!"

I went into the kitchen and made some coffee. After a time I tried to get Czernowitz and Rădăuţi. The lines were tied up.

Suddenly, sharply, Yitzhak called me.

I ran into the next room.

The four musical notes were sounding again from Radio Warsaw. Then an announcer reported, "Mayor Starzynski rides around the city exhorting the troops and civilians to hold out."

Mayor Stefan Starzynski had remained with his beleaguered people.

By the following day the Russian troops had reached Vilna.

Two days later they had entered the southern city of Lwow, a mountain range away from Czernowitz.

Over and over I tried to reach my brother, my sister, Stefan and Emmanuel's sister in Rădăuţi. I could get no calls through. Finally, at 4 A.M., the morning of September twentieth, a line was clear. I heard the phone ringing in Stefan's room. It rang and rang . . .

Had he gone to the mountains to be with his family?

I asked the operator to try the home of my brother David. The connection was cut abruptly. I was unable to get through again.

That afternoon I got into a taxi. But when I gave the address, the driver shook his head. "Impossible, mademoiselle. That whole area has been cordoned off."

"But why?" I asked.

He turned, stared at me. "You have not heard? Calinescu has been assassinated."

"*Assassinated?*"

He nodded. "At a quarter of two, when the Premier was returning home from the Ministry of War—he was killed. On St. Elefterie Bridge. He was shot. That is all I know. Except that it is the beginning of the end. The end of Rumania."

I returned to the apartment. Alexander was there; the radio on. He had the details.

As the Premier's limousine came to the bridge, it had stopped—for a cart was blocking the way. A policeman got out of Calinescu's car to investigate. Another car drove up. Six young men jumped out of it with drawn revolvers. They killed Calinescu; wounded his *Directeur de Cabinet* and the policeman. Then they drove off.

"They went straight to the radio station," Alexander said. "There was a music program on. They wounded three people at the station. Then they grabbed the microphone. They yelled into it that Calinescu had been shot—by the Iron Guard. In retribution for the murder of their leader Codreanu."

By nightfall, the men who murdered Calinescu had been caught by the police. They were taken to St. Elefterie Bridge to reconstruct the crime. When they boasted of what they had done, they were shot by the police. Their bodies were left lying on the bridge—as warning.

The body of Armand Calinescu lay in state in the high-domed Aetheneum, a splendid building opposite the Royal Palace. The funeral took place four days after the murder. It was an affair of pomp and circumstance, attended by the King and Crown Prince Michael, who followed the cortege to the cemetery.

Three days after Calinescu's funeral there was another wake. A city died.

We heard the death throes over Radio Warsaw at two-fifteen in the afternoon. The announcer's words were slow and stunned.

"Shells and bombs tear and burn the ruins of our once beautiful city. . . . Fires rage unchecked. . . . Anything left of Warsaw is burning. . . .

"Three thousand civilians have died so far today. . . .

"The water supply has failed. . . .

"There is fear of plague. . . .

"Our food situation is tragic. Our last hospital was destroyed by shells today. The dead and dying are lying in the streets. . . .

"The city is razed," the announcer said. "But we live on."

Then Radio Warsaw went off the air. The four notes sounded no longer. Only silence.

At nine-ten that evening of September twenty-seventh, we heard a gloating communiqué from Radio Berlin.

"Warsaw has surrendered."

The announcer went on to declare that a hundred thousand Polish soldiers would deliver their arms to the Wehrmacht the following day. Mayor Stefan Starzynski would hand over the ruins of the city to the Third Reich.

Exultant music then burst forth from the Berlin station, "Deutschland über Alles."

Germany over All.

I switched off the radio.

Two days later Foreign Minister Joachim von Ribbentrop arrived in Moscow at the head of a large German delegation. Their mission was not revealed, but it was obvious. How to divide up the conquered country of Poland.

Within a week Russia had occupied two thirds of Poland including the industrial regions around Lwow and most of the oil fields. The German and Russian forces met in Brest-Litovsk—the place where the same two nations had signed a peace treaty twenty-one years ago.

Polish refugees were now arriving in Bucharest by the thousands. Their mud-splattered cars were often riddled with bullets. Sometimes the passengers crowded inside included a dead body.

The Rumanian Red Cross issued constant radio cries for help. Help with housing, with food, with clothing, with money for the refugees.

The Rumanians responded. Doors were opened, larders were opened, purses were opened. There were, however, numerous complaints that the Poles did not know how to act like refugees. It was still mainly those families of some influence and wealth who managed to escape; those families who had, or could muster, a car. They arrived for the most part starving and penniless, but encased in the aristocratic mien and manners which they had always known. Stories about the proud and stiff-necked Poles circulated throughout Bucharest. Particularly prevalent were tales concerning Marshal Edward Smigly-Rydz, head of the Polish Army. He was, it seemed, highly incensed that he had not been received by the Rumanian Government with full military honors.

One could only wonder how wealthy Rumanians would react were they hurtled into the role of penniless refugees within a few weeks' time.

The Jews, however, seemed attuned to the role of refugee. Even those who had lived in luxury for years adapted abruptly to their new circumstances. Perhaps the blood of the eternal wandering Jew flowed through their bodies. I met many of them as they crowded into the Palestine Office. They expected nothing: not beds, nor clothes, nor money. They asked for nothing, except the impossible: Get us out. Get us to Palestine.

The Palestine Office was now so glutted with refugees that it was difficult to make one's way in and out of the building. When I passed them I felt simple shame. I had an apartment, an address, a bed to sleep in. I had a passport. I could re-enter Palestine.

Despite the fact that the Palestine Office grew more crowded every day, relatively few Polish Jews were escaping.

In Germany, the Jews had comprised less than one per cent of the population. In Austria and Czechoslovakia, Jews had made up less than three per cent of the population. But one out of every ten Poles was a Jew. In almost every large town and city in Poland, Jews made up twenty-five per cent of the population. Some small towns were virtually one hundred per cent Jewish.

Yet, a survey made by the Associated Press in Rumania and Hungary revealed that a scant two per cent of the Polish refugees streaming into those countries were Jews. What of the other three million five hundred thousand Polish Jews? Would they all be trapped in the country which was now being divided by its two conquerors?

Of the three million five hundred thousand we had saved five hundred and one on the *Tiger Hill.* To compare the two figures was terrifying. Immobilizing.

We could go on with our work only if we thought in terms of saving hundreds. The waiting trapped millions we must try to shove from our minds.

One hot night in early October, the telephone rang. Ehud was calling from Austria. The sound of his voice alone was like a blaze of hope in the darkness.

His words also held hope.

The Donau Dampfschiffahrts Gesellschaft had agreed to lease their Danube pleasure boats to the company Ehud had organized, starting November first.

"Now," said Ehud, "the question is, can there be a Mossad ship waiting at Sulina to take these pleasure cruise passengers to Palestine?"

"The *Hilda* should be ready to sail on December first," I told him. "Until that time, can your passengers live on the riverboats?"

"They'll have to," Ehud said.

Then I asked, "Will you be one of the pleasure cruise passengers?"

He changed the subject; asked about the political situation in Rumania since the murder of Calinescu.

I told him that the new Premier, Constantin Argepoianu, was known as a scholar in law, economics, literature, philosophy. He was also known as an unscrupulous strong man.

We spoke for five minutes. During all that time I ached to ask him one single question. But I held back. When we'd parted in Geneva, Ehud's last words to me had been: "I'll look up your brother Arthur when I get home."

Why was he saying nothing now about that meeting?

There was a long pause.

Then I heard Ehud's voice again.

"Ruth, listen—as soon as I returned to Vienna I went to see your brother Arthur. He—wasn't there. Someone else was living in the apartment. As I was going downstairs a neighbor told me—Ruth, your brother is in a concentration camp. Theresienstadt. His wife and the little girl have disappeared."

THIRTY

THE DAYS OF FALL sank quickly, hurtled into a bitter cold winter.
Despite all Ehud's efforts he had learned nothing further about the
fate of my brother Arthur in Theresienstadt. Nor had he found any
slightest clue as to what had become of Arthur's wife and child.

Ehud always telephoned at three or four in the morning. When I
hung up and pulled the chain on the bed-table lamp, the darkness was
swollen with silence; the terrible screaming silence. I would press my
hands over my ears to shut it out. And to shut out the flooding memories . . .

Walking the floor with the infant Erika when she cried . . . coming
into the small room we shared to discover the baby at a precocious five
months standing in her crib . . . the feel of her fist grasping onto my
finger as she tried her first staggering steps . . . the sound of her first
recognizable words, Mama . . . Papa . . . and Ruti.

I tried to use the news of Arthur and his family as a lever, to pry my
family in Czernowitz loose from the false security of their familiar
streets. The *Hilda* was now a reality; a twelve hundred-ton cargo ship,
built in 1925, currently being reconverted in secrecy at the Danube
port of Brăila. My pleas to leave Czernowitz were accompanied, therefore, by practical plans for escaping to Palestine.

My sister Bertha did arrive in Bucharest, accompanied by her husband, Takor. It was he who insisted that she at least come to hear what

I had to say. Bertha borrowed a neighbor's sewing machine; made me several new dresses. And heard nothing of what I had to say. Naturally, she told me, if Czernowitz were Vienna, she and Takor would leave at once. But no one was threatening their security in Rumania. Why should she undertake the hazards of a voyage on the *Hilda?* Such a trip was for young, brave pioneers. Her arthritis was far worse now. She probably would not even survive the voyage.

After a week Bertha and Takor went back home to Czernowitz.

I phoned my brother David as often as possible. Pleaded with him. Even wept on the telephone. His responses were pained and noncommittal. "We'll see, Ruth. . . . I'll talk it over with Sophie. . . . There's a lot in what you say."

But he never even came as far as Bucharest.

Stefan needed no persuading. However, Viorica's recovery was slow. If his daughter were unable to travel by the time the *Hilda* was ready to sail, he of course would have to pass up this opportunity. But perhaps on one of our future ships . . .

I informed him somewhat bitterly that we were not in the travel business running scheduled cruises to Palestine. There might not be another ship after the *Hilda.*

Although the borders of Poland were irrevocably closed, Ehud's Danube riverboat scheme was now in full operation—rescuing Jews from Germany, Austria and Czechoslovakia. On October eleventh, some three hundred and fifty refugees had been brought out of Berlin. They sailed down the Danube, past Budapest, Belgrade, to Brăila. But conversion on the *Hilda* was far from completed and could not be carried out with passengers aboard. So the Berlin Jews proceeded to the Black Sea port of Sulina, where they waited on their pleasure boat.

Meanwhile, more riverboat passengers, bound for the *Hilda,* were on their way from Prague and Bratislava. They too reached Sulina, to wait.

A third group—the largest—ran into trouble. In early November they arrived at the Yugoslavian border town of Kladovo, on the Danube. But they could not proceed to a seaport. They had no transit visas.

We tried desperately to secure the necessary visas so that at least some of the people trapped at Kladovo could sail on the *Hilda*. Kladovo was directly across the river from Rumania. But we dared not approach Rumanian authorities, since to acquire a transit visa it was necessary for a Jew to prove that he had some place to go—outside Rumania. The *Hilda*, which could offer such proof, was being reconverted in Brăila. We could not risk letting officials in the visa office know of the ship's presence in Rumania.

We tried, therefore, to acquire Bulgarian transit visas. If this proved possible, the *Hilda* could pick up the refugees at a Bulgarian Black Sea port. But the officials we approached seemed to turn deaf at the mention of transit visas for Jews.

There were, however, two packed boatloads of refugees waiting, restless, at the Rumanian Black Sea port of Sulina. And there we faced a new nerve-racking opponent: the weather. We must complete the conversion of the *Hilda*, take her down the Danube to Sulina, transfer the riverboat passengers to the *Hilda* and return the riverboats to the Donau Dampfschiffahrts Gesellschaft—all before the Danube froze.

On that steaming hot summer night in Geneva when Ehud first told us of his Danube riverboat negotiations, this part of the agreement seemed hardly to merit consideration. But now the "weather clause" in the contract hovered as a daily threat.

The Rumanian section of the Danube often froze solid by mid-December. Yet, this November of '39 was one of the coldest in memory. The Danube might start to freeze any day now. Ehud's contract with the Danube Steamship Company stated specifically that if the pleasure boats were not returned to the company before the river froze, the Mossad must pay an astronomical fee.

Aside from the fee, failure to return the ships would mean this last rescue route from Germany, Austria and Czechoslovakia would be shut off. In addition, failure to return the ships would mean Ehud's immediate arrest.

Finally, by late November, the reconversion work was finished. The *Hilda* left the port of Brăila, sailed down the Danube to Sulina. There she was boarded by the refugees from Berlin, Vienna, Prague and Bratislava. There was also one Polish Jew: the beautiful six-year-old child named Dasha whom I had met at the train station in Czernowitz.

The riverboats were on their way back to their Austrian owners. The *Hilda* was supplied, manned and ready to sail for Palestine. Except that the Kladovo people—as we came to call them—had not yet received their transit visas.

There were frantic calls from Sima Spitzer, the head of the Jewish community in Belgrade, and the man in charge of the refugees stranded at Kladovo. There were now eleven hundred of them, living on three riverboats in the Danube. The *Hilda* could not sail, Spitzer would shout at me, not until he had managed to secure transit visas for the Kladovo people. He could get the visas only if the authorities were convinced that there was a ship waiting to take them away from Europe.

Naturally, the *Hilda* could not hold all of the Kladovo refugees. But it could, Spitzer insisted, be used to gain them all transit visas to a Black Sea port. And once in a port it would be far easier to make their way somehow to Palestine.

The Kladovo Jews were halutzim; young, dedicated and well trained. They were a very special group. Special for a grim and ominous reason.

After the fall of Poland the Germans had announced the creation of a new "Jewish national home." They selected an empty, swampy stretch of land where the water was polluted, and where nothing grew. It lay in the province of Lublin between that part of Poland annexed by the Germans and that annexed by the Russians. Jews were locked into cattle cars and shipped to the deserted, frozen "homeland" where, in these bitter-cold months, the temperature hovered around zero and sometimes sank to forty below. There the Jews were told: "You will be unloaded into the open fields, and you will take care of yourselves."

Through a contact in the Gestapo, Ehud had learned that by February 1940 the Nazis planned to deport one million Jews into this area.

Eichmann, however, had made a pronouncement: "We don't care if the Jews emigrate or die out, as long as we get rid of them."

Using Eichmann's words to bolster his arguments, Ehud had approached his contacts in the Gestapo who opposed the Lublin

Deportation Plan. He had succeeded in winning permission for one single, swift emergency operation in which the few Zionist training camps near Vienna, Danzig and in Czechoslovakia were emptied of young pioneers. They were now in Kladovo trapped, waiting.

But how long could *we* continue to wait?

Sima Spitzer's telephone calls to me became ever more frantic. He had new contacts now. He was certain he could secure the transit visas. After all, the Bulgarians had never been an anti-Semitic people. At least not so far as their own Jews were concerned. It was simply that they wanted to make very certain they would not have to take on eleven hundred more Jews from other nations. "Don't you see," Spitzer cried out at me, "we can only get the Bulgarian transit visas if the *Hilda* is there, waiting. Without the *Hilda,* we have no chance at all."

We decided that our ship should leave Sulina and put in at the small Black Sea village of Balchik, close to the Bulgarian border. There the *Hilda* would wait for the Kladovo Jews.

If a twelve hundred-ton ship could be hidden anywhere, Balchik seemed an ideal port for the purpose. The town was known for one reason only; King Carol's mother, Queen Marie, had built one of her summer homes on the white cliffs overlooking the village and the bay. Indeed, the Queen so loved this site that when she died her will directed that her heart be buried there. The royal heart was, therefore, removed from the Queen's body and it lay now in a casket of gold in her little church at Balchik.

Since the Queen's death the village had sunk back into isolated oblivion. It was highly unlikely that any of the peasants in this remote area would be aware of governmental policies concerning illegal shipments of Jews. In any case, the snows and ice which caked the roads to town had virtually cut off Balchik from communication with the outside world.

All this had been reported to us by our advance man Alexander, who traveled to Balchik to see whether it would suit our purposes.

The ship, with all its passengers hidden down in the hold, made its way at night past the port authorities at Sulina, through stormy waters of the Black Sea, past the port of Constantza, and in late November, anchored at the small deserted dock in the bay of Balchik.

The Black Sea village was so isolated that even we in Bucharest received no word of or from the ship.

But we heard from Sima Spitzer every day. Yes, the transit visas for his people were almost a certainty now. If the *Hilda* would just wait for one more, two more days.

One more, two more days dragged into three weeks.

Then, late one afternoon Orekhovsky entered my apartment. He hung up his coat on the hook, he took off his gloves, placed them in his coat pocket. Then he sat down. His maroon-colored scarf was still wound tight round his neck. His black hat was still on his head. His face seemed even paler than usual.

He took a cable from his pocket and handed it to me. It was addressed to the Palestine Office in Bucharest. It came from the *Hilda*. It was signed: *Ship's Committee*.

In terse words, with no attempt at coding the message, it informed us of five facts.

1. The *Hilda* was now frozen to the pier in Balchik and therefore could not sail.

2. Most of the crew had left the ship. Those who remained, including the captain, were always drunk. Some had threatened women passengers with knives.

3. All the fresh water was frozen. The food supplies were almost gone.

4. Two of the women passengers were about to give birth.

5. The *Hilda* passengers planned to send cables to Jewish institutions in Jerusalem, England and New York, as well as to newspapers in those countries, to inform the world that they were being held in bondage under inhuman conditions. And to plead that the world should take notice of their plight.

I stared at Orekhovsky. Finally I said, "Please God, they have not yet sent those cables. That's all we need. Stories in the press!"

I wrote out a message and handed it to Orekhovsky. "Go to the post office. Send this to the ship."

He read the words aloud. "Essential you withhold all telegrams. Top personality in organizing committee arriving tomorrow in Balchik."

He looked up. "Who is this top personality?"

I said, "I am in charge of the ship." My words sounded very faint.

"You—a hundred-and-ten-pound girl—are planning to handle a crew of drunken sailors and—"

"Please!" I cut him off. "Send the cable. I will phone the Shamen. He'll come with me. He'll handle the crew. Please. Go. Send the cable. That's the most important thing right now."

He stood up. He took his coat from the hook by the door, and he left.

My first frantic call was to the Shamen. The phone rang and rang. I tried Arkadi. No answer. I placed a call to Kadmon in Palestine. I must ask for instructions. I placed a call to Saly Meyer in Switzerland. We would need money. That was always the decisive essential. Money and more money. We had the equivalent of two thousand pounds, almost ten thousand dollars, in the safe of my landlord downstairs. But that was money for the Shamen, when the ship sailed. If I took it now to Balchik could we get more for the Shamen? I placed a call to Shmarya in Greece. What of the ship he had bought, the *Darien*? Was there any chance that she could come to Balchik?

To each call the answer was the same. "I'm sorry, mademoiselle, all lines are tied up. Will you try your call again after midnight?"

I ran out to the post office. I sent coded cables to Kadmon, to Saly, to Shmarya. I asked that they send replies to Orekhovsky. I might be on the way to Balchik before the answers came.

Back in my room I telephoned Alexander but, as usual, only reached his querulous mother who, as usual, had no idea where her son could be found.

I ran downstairs, knocked at the landlord's door, tried to sound calm as I asked whether he could open the safe. He was a gentleman. He sat in an armchair and paged through a book as I removed the sealed envelopes of money: Swiss francs, pounds sterling, lei and dollars. I put the money in my oversized pocketbook and informed Mr. Schecter that I would be away for several days. "If my friends wish to use the room," I said, "that's all right with me. So long as you have no objection."

He shrugged. "No objection."

I wondered how much he knew of what was going on. He never asked questions. A gentleman. A good Jew. He must know at least that

333

he placed himself and his wife in danger by retaining me as a tenant in the upstairs flat.

"Have a successful trip," he said as I left the room.

It was night by the time I finally reached Arkadi at his hotel. "You must find the Shamen," I said. "It's urgent."

"Look," said Arkadi. "How do I know where he is? I can't find him. Wait till morning."

"I can't wait. Morning will be too late."

Somehow I persuaded Arkadi to make a round of restaurants and nightclubs in search of the Shamen. "When you find him," I said, "have him phone me. I'll be here waiting."

Shortly afterward Alexander showed up. I showed him the cable from the Ship's Committee and sent him out to try to hire a car.

The phone which usually jangled incessantly after midnight was now ominously silent. I could get no calls through to Kadmon, to Saly, to Shmarya or to Spitzer. Nor could I reach Solomonides. Some lines were overloaded. Some were out of order. I felt imprisoned by a wall of silence.

Finally, the Shamen called. "Well, what is it? Arkadi says it's urgent."

"Your crew," I said, "is on the point of mutiny. Most of them have already left the ship."

"Well!" the Shamen announced. "I don't blame them. Sitting in that god-forsaken place for almost a month. Take your people off the *Hilda*. Give me back my ship. The sailors will be fine as soon as they know they're on a regular ship, doing a regular job. You've broken the agreement. I can't be responsible for—"

"Please!" I cut into his speech. "I'm leaving for Balchik in a few hours. Please! Come with me."

"Me?" he exclaimed. "Impossible! Besides, how do you propose to get there?"

"I've hired a car."

He snorted. "How far will *that* take you? Once you're into the countryside the roads will be rivers of ice."

"Then we'll continue by sleigh."

"Well, good luck to you," he said.

"Wait! Please. Don't hang up. You've got to help. I can't handle drunken Greek sailors. I don't even know the language. You were the one who hired them. It's only you they'll listen to!"

After a long moment he said, "I'll send Arkadi with you. He speaks Greek."

"But he doesn't have the authority!"

"He'll have the authority. However, it's not Greek the sailors will listen to. It's money. More money. Have you got that?"

"Yes," I said, faintly.

"Good. I'll send my man over to you at once." Abruptly then the Shamen hung up. I had no idea where to reach him.

I packed all the sweaters and socks I owned into a suitcase. I put on heavy socks, boots, slacks. I stuffed the envelopes of pounds, lei, dollars and Swiss francs into my brassiere. I pulled a loose Russian blouse over my head. And, beneath it, I strapped on a holster containing the two loaded Browning pistols David Arnon had given me.

There was a knock on the door. When I opened it, a furry figure entered. Arkadi, usually so dapper with well-pressed suit and high-shined shoes was now encased in a huge fur jacket and oversized fur hat and gloves. His boots were far too big for his small feet. He seemed to be dressed for an Arctic exploration.

I watched him as he divested himself of his coat and several layers of sweaters. "Are you dressed warmly enough?" I asked.

Arkadi smiled. "Don't worry. Sitting next to you I'll be warm enough."

He was rather put out when I informed him that Alexander would be coming with us.

We left Bucharest at dawn.

Like everything else, cars were at a premium now. The one Alexander had succeeded in renting was so ancient it seemed unlikely we would make it past Bucharest. Alexander drove. Arkadi and I sat in the back seat. He was in high good humor and regaled us with stories about his career as a ship's captain in Russia and in Greece.

When he inquired as to why I was so gloomy, I replied that I was tired. I was afraid that if I told him of all the catastrophes awaiting us, he would demand to be returned at once to Bucharest. Better to wait until we neared Balchik before he was apprised of the details.

Around noon we arrived at the Danube town of Oltenitza, and drove down to the river ferry. The boatman informed us that it would be foolish to pay passage for our car. All roads on the other side of the Danube were blocked by snow and ice. Better to leave our car here in Oltenitza, and rent a horse-drawn sleigh in Turtucaia across the river. As a matter of fact, he had a brother-in-law in Turtucaia who would be happy to oblige us.

"Will he take us to Balchik?" I asked.

"Balchik is a long way," the boatman said. "Especially in winter. But my brother-in-law will take you on to the home of his cousin. There you'll change horses and sleigh. And our cousin will take you on another twenty miles. We have a system well worked out. You'll reach Balchik. However, you may be frozen solid by the time you arrive."

The ferry had walls and a roof, but this did little to keep out the cold. The winter wind careened down the river and knifed through every crack and crevice. I huddled into my landlady's old fur coat. The good woman had insisted I borrow it when she learned I was taking a trip into the countryside.

I was the only woman aboard. The passengers, all peasants, sat on a bench across from us and stared at me. Some smoked on strong, stinking pipes. Others munched raw onions and black bread. Some carried live chickens and geese with feet tied together. The raucous squawking of the frightened fowl was strangely orchestrated by the sibilant winter wind.

When we finally reached Turtucaia, the boatman went off to find his cousin while we remained aboard, waiting.

Arkadi, who had started off like a tourist on a holiday, relapsed now into glum grumbles about the Shamen. "He should have come himself! At least he has his fat to keep him warm."

"Pity the poor horses," I said, "if they had to pull *his* weight in the sleigh."

Arkadi did not even trouble to smile.

The boatman's cousin looked like a hill of rags. Scarves were wound around his head, face, neck. Only his eyes were visible. His two horses

336

were also well covered with blankets. Their breath hung on in the frosty air.

I sat between Arkadi and Alexander. The driver buried our feet and legs in straw, then wrapped horse blankets around us, and encircled our faces with heavy rags which smelled strongly of onion and sweat.

The padding was of little avail against the piercing frozen winds which swept across the open fields.

In the car and on the ferry when I'd thought of the problems awaiting us in Balchik fear churned within me. Now it seemed that even the fear froze. My thoughts fastened on a single vision: stopping at a pub, thawing out before a roaring fire.

But when we finally stopped—at the home of the cousin's uncle—it was only to change sleigh, horses and driver. We each had a cup of scalding hot tea, some black bread, dried ham and a glass of *tuica*. Then we moved on. We had to, the uncle said, or we would never reach Balchik by nightfall.

We drove past snow-blanketed fields and occasional clusters of small mud-brick houses, their thatched roofs hidden by snow. We drove over streams and small rivers, each frozen solid as a road. The sun glinted sharp on the white stretches of ice and snow. But even the sunlight seemed frozen.

We went on for another one hundred kilometers. This time there was a chance to thaw out before proceeding. Alexander had to argue vehemently with the uncle's great-nephew before the young man would agree to take us on the next lap of our journey. Finally, after demanding twice the sum the uncle had asked, the great-nephew nodded. At which point the uncle asked why he should not receive the same as the great-nephew was getting. When we complied, a look sped between the two. It was obvious that the same maneuver would be tried at our next changeover.

It was. And this time Arkadi too had a maneuver.

We had stopped at a village pub. Arkadi inquired and found there were two rooms available. He flatly refused to go on. "It will take us at least twelve hours to thaw out," he said. "So we'll let our sailors have one more night of drinking, and we'll arrive tomorrow. What's the difference? What's the big rush?"

It was obviously time to break the dismal news. I told him about the situation aboard the *Hilda*.

He stared at me. "What are you talking about," he said. "I will commit suicide."

He kept exploding in such anger that specks of spittle shot out of his mouth.

Finally I said, "I will never forget what you told me the first time we met. You thanked us—Kadmon and me—you thanked us for making you remember that you are a Jew. You told us, 'If I can help—you know where to find me.'"

"Sure!" said Arkadi. "It's easy to make fine speeches when you're sitting in the back seat of a chauffeur-driven limousine on a beautiful spring day in Bucharest."

At least he remembered the scene and the promise.

"In any case," I said, "Alexander and I must reach Balchik as soon as possible. If our passengers start sending those cables we are lost. They and we and all the others we still may be able to save."

"Well," said Arkadi, "since I am concerned only with the crew, and since the ship is frozen in, there is no big rush about *me* getting to Balchik. We'll let the crew have another night of carousing. It'll do them good."

When the new driver announced that his horses and sleigh were ready, I stood up. Arkadi did too. I thought he was going upstairs to his room. But he was the first to take his seat in the sleigh.

THIRTY-ONE

WE ARRIVED IN BALCHIK late that night, and were welcomed by a snarling, yapping pack of dogs who followed our sleigh down to the pier.

The *Hilda* loomed like a dark monster, caught in the ice. The ship was indeed imprisoned. How many years had it been since water at the shores of the Black Sea froze? Even the forces of nature seemed to conspire against us.

Moonlight cast a faint, chilled brightness which shimmered on the ice. We could see a few dark shapes on deck. They aimed their flash-light beams in our direction.

We sat in the sleigh, immobilized by the wind which came hurtling in from the wild blackness of the open sea.

"Well," said Arkadi, "I may as well have a look for the captain." He climbed from the sleigh, screamed and fell to his knees.

"What's wrong?" I cried.

"Nothing at all," he replied. "But wait till you try walking on frozen legs." Muttering a stream of Russian curses he stumbled and crawled through the ice-crusted snow till he reached the gangplank. Several of the dark shapes on deck descended to help him aboard.

Alexander told the driver how to reach the mayor's house. We'd ar-ranged that I should wait there while Alexander boarded the *Hilda* and sought out members of the Ship's Committee. He would bring them to see me.

Alexander got out of the sleigh. He too fell, and started crawling, cursing, toward the ship as the driver pulled at his reins, and we took off.

The mayor's house was on top of a small hill. The horses seemed to expend their last vestige of energy pulling the sleigh upward. When we halted before the house the driver turned to me. "Well," he announced, "you are lucky, mademoiselle. At times I thought we never would make it. It is a dangerous matter, driving these roads in the night-time. Naturally, if one of my horses had broken his leg you'd pay for a new horse. As it is, I will merely charge you double the price we agreed on."

I nodded. Usually, we at least argued, bargained, bartered. It was expected. And, for us, it was absolute necessity since the lack of money was our most constant crisis.

But now I felt incapable of arguing. Indeed, I felt that I could not even move. "Please help me inside," I said. "Then you will be paid."

He carried me in his arms; kicked at the front door.

It was opened by a portly man with a very red nose.

"What's wrong with her? Is she dead?" he inquired, as the driver strode into the room and placed me in a chair by the fireplace.

I unwound the scarves which covered my face and asked to see the mayor.

"I, mademoiselle, am the mayor of Balchik. Can I be of service?"

I told him that I had come from Bucharest to take charge of the ship.

The mayor uttered a shout of laughter. "They say they are sending a top man from Bucharest. A man who will solve all our problems. And what do they send? *You!*"

"Monsieur," said the driver, stamping the snow from his boots, "we're half frozen. Can you let us have something hot to drink?"

The mayor opened his mouth wide and uttered a bellow. "Anna!"—whereupon a fat woman in a heavy nightgown shuffled in from the next room.

"Madame," I said, "I hope you will forgive us for troubling you at this time of night."

She said nothing, regarded me with a glower of suspicion.

I turned to the mayor. "I am told it is not safe for a woman to stay the night at the pub. I have come to ask you for help. Where in Balchik can I rent a room?"

"Here, of course," said the mayor. "There is no other place. We have a guest cabin out back. The cost," he added, "is a thousand lei a night."

It was far more than I'd paid at the Ambasador Hotel. But, again, I did not have the strength to bargain. I nodded.

The mayor raised his voice to a lordly shout, though his wife stood but a few feet away. "Anna! Get the guest room ready. But first, something to eat and drink for our visitors!"

As we sipped the steaming hot soup, the mayor regaled me with complaints about our ship, its passengers and crew. "This is a peaceful village, mademoiselle. Suddenly a thousand strangers descend upon us. Your sailors stagger drunk through the streets. They fight with each other. And with our men. Our women and children are terrified. And your cursed ship! There for a month, like a house of evil in our peaceful bay. The noise. And the smell. I was on that ship, mademoiselle— for ten minutes! It was all I could take of the stink. They throw their droppings into our fine, blue bay. And now, that the waters have frozen, onto the ice. It is a miracle that plague and pestilence have not yet swept through the ship. And through our town. As mayor of Balchik, mademoiselle, I must demand that as soon as the ice thaws, your ship leaves our port. You can buy my silence no longer. If your ship does not sail, I will notify the authorities in Bucharest."

I assured him that the ship would have been gone by now had the ice not made this impossible. "And you must admit, sir," I said, "none of us imagined that the Black Sea would freeze!" I apologized for the inconvenience our ship had caused his people. "But," I pointed out, "perhaps some good comes along with the bad. We have, after all, paid well for the supplies we bought in your town."

"Supplies!" he exploded. "You have stripped us bare like a horde of locusts. Now we must journey to Bazargic for the things we need. And you have seen yourself, mademoiselle, what it is like to travel these roads in the wintertime."

I had seen, indeed. Some feeling was now painfully returning to my hands and feet.

I told the mayor that I had not slept for thirty-six hours and asked whether I might go to my room.

Again, he bellowed for his wife. "Anna! Is the guest room ready?"

"It is!" she called back. "As ready as I can make it."

I paid the driver, who said that he would spend the night in the pub. "If you wish, mademoiselle, I can take you back with me in the morning."

I smiled at him faintly. I had no idea what the morning would bring. Only one thing was certain. I would not be returning to Bucharest.

The guest room was a storage shed. It had no window. It had no heat. It was not attached to the main house. There was a straw-filled mattress on the floor. This was covered with a dirty quilt and a horse blanket. There was a small bench which held a kerosene lamp. Burlap bags and crates were piled against the wall.

"The outhouse is in the back," the mayor said. "And here is your private towel." He presented it to me with some pride. "My wife will heat you some water in the morning." He turned to leave. "Sleep well, mademoiselle. The door, I'm afraid, has no lock. But don't worry. No one will trouble you. Not here in the house of the mayor of Balchik."

The door not only had no lock, it did not even close properly. It was like sleeping in the bitter cold open air, except that one could not see the stars.

I wound the scarves about my face and crawled under the quilt wearing all my clothes including boots, six sweaters and my landlady's fur coat.

As I fell into a cavern of sleep I imagined booted, bearded men shoving open the door of the shed, yanking me up from the straw mattress, ripping off my clothes to find the thick envelopes of money hidden in my brassiere.

I was, in fact, awakened by booted, bearded men.

Alexander knocked at the door of the shed; then entered, leaving the door ajar. I could see a huddle of men, backed by the thin, gray light of early morning.

"My God," Alexander exploded. "This place is like sleeping on an

342

iceberg. Are you all right?" Without waiting for an answer he informed me that the Ship's Committee was outside. "They wanted to meet with you last night. I managed at least to keep them off until the crack of dawn."

I got out of bed. My nose felt like an ice cube, my fingers like ten stiff icicles. But otherwise, I was warm. The layers of clothing had retained my body heat. And I had slept like one drugged.

I thanked Alexander for holding off the meeting until this morning. I now felt better able to cope with problems.

But when the Committee had crowded into the shed and started flinging the problems at me, my fleeting moment of self-assurance fled.

There were thirteen men on the Ship's Committee, all halutzim. They took seats on boxes, crates and on the bed. Some stood leaning against the wall. As Alexander made introductions, the men stared or glared at me. Each seemed as dismayed to see me as the mayor had been.

There were five medical doctors. It was they who stood against the wall, like a separate contingent: Dr. Szekeles, Dr. Sand, Dr. Adler, Dr. Zentner, Dr. Grubler. There were two lawyers, Dr. Willi Thein and Dr. Fritz Weisskopf. There was Arthur Loewy, a restaurant owner. And a textile sales representative, Hans Klein, who was now manager of the ship's provisions.

Before Alexander had finished naming the others, they all burst out, simultaneously and vociferously, with complaints.

"Please!" My word was sharp as a shot.

It was followed by silence.

"We'll get nothing done," I said, "if you all speak at once. Tell me first about the passengers."

"All right," said Willi Thein. "In a sentence: They are by now completely impossible to control. We've had to let them off the ship to get at the snow. The snow has kept us alive, since we have no water to drink. Each night we try to count those aboard. But we can't. The ship's too crowded. There's too much confusion. For all we know a few may have taken off already. Tried to make their own way to Bucharest. To inform the world of what's going on here."

Alexander uttered a volley of curses.

Willi Thein looked at him. "Oh, it's fine for you, my friend. You

343

come, give some suggestions, some orders. Then you take off. Back to your flat in Bucharest. Tell me, do you have a bathtub in your place? Hot and cold running water? It's been over six weeks since any of us had a bath. You sleep in a bed with a mattress and sheets? Not on a board with sixty-five centimeters of space between it and the board above your head where someone else sleeps. Or tries to."

I broke in. "Let's hear all your problems, point by point. We'll see if we can find some solutions."

"*You!*" said Klein, bellowing the word. "You are the first problem. We've kept our people in some sort of control since the cable came from the Palestine Office. We've told them that a top man is coming here. By now they expect some sort of Messiah. When they see a woman the explosion will come."

"They won't see her," Alexander said. "None of the Mossad people are ever seen by the passengers."

Klein nodded, mollified. "That's a relief in any case. But the real question is, how can *she* solve our problems?"

They spoke to each other above my head, as though I were not in the room.

"Look," I said, "we'll try to solve the problems together. Just set them out, one by one."

Each member of the Ship's Committee had a different matter he regarded as top priority.

Loewy, the Czech restaurant owner, claimed that passengers and crew were at the point of starvation. "At first it was fine," he exclaimed, "we had three kitchens. Well stocked. One for the crew. Two for the passengers. Kosher and nonkosher. We still have our three kitchens. Each with the same menu. Frozen bread. Spaghetti. Beans. And sauerkraut. In the kosher kitchen we announce it's kosher sauerkraut. But it's all from the same tin cans."

"He's right," Dr. Sand broke in. "Now you can say the passengers are suffering from severe malnutrition. Another week of this and you'll have to call it starvation."

I told them I had brought money: that we'd muster all the sleighs we needed, journey to Bazargic and buy out the town.

"Fine!" Dr. Zentner exclaimed. "And the first two people on those sleighs must be the two pregnant women we have on board. There's a hospital in Bazargic."

"How pregnant are they?" I asked.

"They may both be giving birth this minute," the doctor replied.

"I thought," said Thein, turning on me, "that you did not allow sick people or pregnant women on Mossad ships. We have enough problems and enough passengers without the addition of two new ones."

"The Mossad can't be blamed for this," said Dr. Adler. "Both women told me they had swaddled themselves in scarves and smuggled themselves aboard. They were well aware of the hazards of giving birth aboard an illegal ship. But they felt the risk was worth it. To remain home, they were certain, would mean eventual death for them and their babies."

I thought of my sister-in-law Sophie, waiting in her Czernowitz apartment for the new living-room furniture to be delivered.

Would that every Jew in Europe had the clear sight and the courage of these two pregnant women.

I knew that we could not take these two women to the hospital in Bazargic. The risks were too great. Bazargic was not a village like Balchik cut off from civilization by high white cliffs and by winter roads. Bazargic was a town with telephones and a cable office. It would be too dangerous to allow any of the ship's passengers to reach Bazargic where the story of the *Hilda* could spark a conflagration which would not only mean the end of this ship, but the end of our operation in Rumania.

I turned to the doctors. "As I remember the plan of the ship, the captain's cabin is the only private place aboard. Can the women be delivered there?"

"I'm afraid," said Dr. Adler, "that the captain has other uses for his cabin."

"But if he could be persuaded to co-operate?"

No one answered. Instead, they got onto the subject of the turkish bath. Some of the passengers had climbed the hills behind the village; had explored the deserted villa of Queen Marie, and had come across a turkish bath which had not been used for decades. Now it seemed a dream and a determination had settled in the mind of each of the *Hilda*'s passengers. To have a bath. It was more, Klein explained, than getting clean. And ridding themselves of lice. To have a bath would mean, somehow, a renewal of hope, of courage.

I understood. How many times, frayed with fatigue, had I lain in a tub of soothing warm water while some of the tensions seeped away? "I'll speak to the mayor," I said. "I promise you, if humanly possible, everyone on that ship will have a hot bath."

"And what about the crew?" said Loewy. "We've all carefully said nothing about the crew!"

They proceeded then to regale me with tales of the sailors—the pirates, as everyone called them.

The crew was comprised of Turks and Greeks. They were rarely sober. Each argument between two crew members seemed to flare into a knife-flashing brawl as Turks and Greeks rushed to the aid of their countrymen. The crew furthermore delighted in terrorizing the women passengers aboard the ship. And the girls of Balchik were afraid to leave their homes unescorted. "What about the captain?" I asked. "Can't he do anything to control his men?"

"The captain," said Klein, "spends most of his days drinking in the pub or recovering in his cabin. Does that sound like a man who can control such a crew? As for the sailors—well, for example, one of them told me last night he could never go home to Greece. He was wanted for murder."

"We're at their mercy," Loewy exploded. "We're in fear of our lives. The men you've hired are more like a pack of thugs and thieves than licensed seamen."

I saw no point in telling the Committee that no licensed seaman in his right mind would sign onto an illegal ship. Why should he, when discovery would mean the revoking of his license. It was only the seamen whose licenses had already been revoked for drunkenness, for thievery or for worse crimes whom we could sign on as crew members.

I pointed out that we had one potent weapon for dealing with the crew. I had authorized Arkadi to offer a bonus of one hundred pounds sterling to every sailor who agreed to return to the ship at once, to submit to discipline and to sail to Palestine. Half the money would be paid when the ship sailed; the other half when the *Hilda* returned to a European port.

"All right," said Willi Thein, "money may help to bring some of the sailors back to the ship. But the others—the thieves and the murderers, the drunkards lurching around the village streets—we'll need a better weapon than money to bring them back and keep them in line."

I unfastened my fur coat, undid the holster. "Would a pair of pistols help you?"

"Yes!" said Thein. For the first time his voice sparked with enthusiasm. He held out his hand for the holster.

"I gather you know something about guns?" I said.

"I was an officer in the Czech Army."

I gave him the pistols.

"Perhaps," said Hans Klein, "you've also brought us a few secret weapons for handling the passengers. We can't bribe *them* with an offer of a hundred pounds a head. Or with extra rations. Or even a hot bath. A few of the women are at the point of hysteria. One girl already tried to commit suicide. Some are talking of returning home. The Czechs, especially. No hell, they say, could be worse than the one they're living now. We've got a boatload of intellectuals. Lawyers, chemists, engineers, professors. Each one is used to thinking for himself. These people are not easily led. There are meetings all over the ship to decide on plans of action. They won't listen to us any more. The Committee! They spit on the word. Or laugh. Have you brought us any solutions on how to handle over seven hundred rebellious and desperate passengers?"

"They must be made to understand," I said slowly. "They must realize their position. And our position. And that of the Jews we still hope to save."

"They understood!" Klein exclaimed. "When they boarded the *Hilda* at Sulina, they understood. When they reached Balchik and sat waiting for the Kladovo Jews they understood. But now, after five weeks, now at the point of starvation and no nearer to Palestine, now they're forgetting how to understand. We're not the same people we were when we boarded the *Hilda*. We want to get off. We want to make our own way to Budapest or Bucharest or Sofia. We'll be safe enough there. We've escaped from the Reich. And that's enough. That's enough."

After a long moment I said, "Tell your people that at nine this morning a member of the Mossad will come aboard to speak to them."

"Impossible!" Alexander exclaimed. "It's against all the rules."

347

"Perhaps," I told him, "each emergency creates its own rules." I turned to the Committee. "Ask them all to meet in the hold. How dark is it down there?"

"Like eternal night," said Loewy. "The generators aren't working, so there's no electricity. Only oil lamps for light. And candles."

"Have what light you need for the passengers," I said. "I'll stand on a box or a table. In the dark."

"It all sounds most dramatic," said Fritz Weisskopf, his words clipped with sarcasm. "The bodiless voice. But what can you tell us?"

A shattering blast exploded.

I screamed.

A bullet had ripped through the shed, leaving a neat hole in the wall.

"Oh," said Willi Thein, "sorry. I haven't handled a Browning before."

"If you're any example of a Czech officer," Loewy remarked, "no wonder the country fell without a shot being fired."

The door was flung open. The mayor entered, apoplectic. "What kind of maniacs are you? Shooting holes in my guest room! You could easily have shot me—the mayor of Balchik."

The Committee beat a diplomatic retreat as Alexander and I discussed with the mayor the amount of damages we must pay for the hole in the wall, and for the fright the mayor had received.

We settled on a figure of two thousand lei, and somewhat mollified, the mayor invited us into his home for breakfast.

I asked for a few moments of privacy, and Alexander stomped off behind the mayor through the snow which had fallen fresh during the night and was now knee-high.

I scooped up some of the white frosty softness, washed my face and hands, brushed my hair. I wanted desperately to change my clothes and tried to imagine how it must feel to sleep in the same set of clothing day and night for weeks like the passengers on the *Hilda*.

I also wanted to rid myself of the scratching envelopes of money which bulged out my brassiere. But I could think of no better bank.

How idiotic I'd been to give both pistols to Willi Thein. The only weapon we had was the money I carried with me. I'd been warned that the women passengers and the peasant women of Balchik had been threatened by drunken sailors, armed with knives.

I went outside.

Icicles hung like daggers from the eaves of the storage shed. The early morning sun was still swathed in gray clouds. The small houses of the village seemed half buried by snow. Beyond spread the vastness of the Black Sea. She was well named; black, except at her shores. Alexander had told me the ice trapping the ship was six to eight inches thick.

"Please, God," I said. "Help us."

My words turned to smoke in the frosty air.

THIRTY-TWO

THE MAYOR'S HOUSE seemed a sudden rustic paradise. The warmth of the blazing fire. The table with its plate of white caşcaval, its mound of homemade thick-crusted bread, its ceramic pots of preserves and its mugs of steaming tea.

As we started to eat, four small figures came hurtling from the back room. Two wore ankle-length woolen skirts, two wore trousers. Aside from that they were almost identical, each clothed in jackets and scarves, each carrying schoolbooks.

They stopped, stared at the early-morning strangers, then plummeted on their way out the door.

The mayor sat down on the bench beside me. "It is not often that my table is graced with such beauty," he said as his wife put a platter of eggs and bacon on the table.

She gave me a strange look, a blend of servility and resentment, and returned to the kitchen which was separated from the rest of the room by an armoire.

Alexander wolfed down his breakfast, then announced that he had to return to the ship.

We understood each other. I had one small weapon which sometimes proved effective with men somewhat past their prime. It worked best, without an audience.

When the mayor's wife had also departed, to feed the animals, I turned to him and I smiled.

Sex, I had found, was a tool or weapon which created more problems than it solved. As an alternative, I had developed a father-daughter approach.

As we ate our cheese and bread and sipped at the hot tea, I asked the mayor's advice. I let him know that I was grateful to have such a wise and experienced man to turn to. And I mentioned parenthetically that I could offer a small amount of money to any of his townspeople who understood our plight and had sufficient heart to want to help us.

However, when I mentioned the turkish bath, his response was a single explosive word. "Impossible!" He repeated it in separated syllables for greater emphasis. "That turkish bath has not been used for decades. We could never heat it. And the wells up there have been dry since the death of the King's mother, God rest her soul. What do you propose, mademoiselle, that we carry water up the hill in barrels? Have you seen where that villa sits? Practically on top of a cliff! Your passengers have gone without a bath for weeks! Let them stink for a few weeks longer."

I tried to make him understand that our people were at the point of desperation. "I believe," I said, "that this turkish bath can do more to restore their spirits and their sense of responsibility than any other single thing. Except lifting anchor to sail to Palestine."

"And just when *do* you plan to sail?"

"As soon as the ice breaks, monsieur."

"No more waiting for more passengers who never arrive?"

"No more waiting."

The mayor nodded. "I make no promises. But if you have plenty of money to pay for it, I will do what I can to get the turkish bath into operation."

By the end of breakfast the mayor had also agreed to organize a group of men who would drive empty sleighs into Bazargic to buy all non-perishable foods the townspeople would sell us. Alexander and I would go along as purchasing agents.

For this too the mayor had his warning. "You must know, mademoiselle, that this area—the Dobrudja—is known for its thieves and smugglers. You drive off into that wilderness of ice and snow carrying more money than any of our people will make in a lifetime. I can't guarantee that there won't be an—accident before you reach Bazargic."

"Would it help if Alexander and I each carried a gun?"

He raised his brows. "Help? If you handle a gun as well as your friend in the cabin, yes it would help. It would help those who may attack you and take your gun from you."

I left the mayor's house with his assurance that he would try to select his most honest townsmen for our sleigh safari to Bazargic.

At nine o'clock I walked up the ice-slick gangplank of the *Hilda*. Alexander was waiting on deck. Otherwise the ship seemed deserted.

"They're all below," Alexander said, taking my arm. "The stage is set. But I don't envy you your audience."

We bent into the harsh sea wind; made our way to the entrance of the hold. Alexander disappeared into the darkness. I followed him down the ladder.

It was like climbing into a cesspool. The stench of sweat, excrement and vomit was unbearable.

Alexander led me through the crowded darkness; lifted me onto a packing case.

Waves of bodies swelled before me. Some sat, squatted, stood; the rest lay on tiers of wooden berths. The portholes were open; circles of daylight fell upon some of the faces. Others were lit by the pale glow from kerosene lamps which hung throughout the hold. I saw contempt, bitterness. I heard ironic laughter.

"What's she like?" someone called out. "Did you see her?" The words were sharp with scorn.

Voices rose, hostile, demanding. Then subsided.

"*Shalom*," I said.

Their silence seemed alive with hatred.

It was like waking suddenly to find the people of your nightmare massed before you. Women with matted, uncombed hair. Dark-bearded men, sullen, menacing.

My mind blanked. There were no words.

Their voices rumbled and rose, in anger, disgust, despair.

"For God's sake, talk to them," Alexander said.

"Haverim . . . comrades . . ."

"Louder," Alexander said.

"Haverim." My voice rang out through the stinking, choking gloom.

"I have been sent here by the organization. We will try to help in every way that we can. We have met with your Ship's Committee. We know of your problems. But you must understand our problems as well. Because you, also, are responsible. Responsible for those who may come after you. On ships like this one. Or worse than this one. Their fate is in your hands. You must continue to bear your hardships in silence. Not only for your own sakes. But for their sakes."

I paused. No one laughed. No one spoke. But I felt their rejection, their resentment.

I must try to make them partners with us.

I told them all that I could—perhaps more than I should—about our struggles to secure ships, to supply those ships, to smuggle Jews aboard, and to see that the ships set out from Europe on the perilous sea-mined voyage to Palestine.

I tried to make them understand why there must be no more talk and no more thought of exposing the plight of the *Hilda*'s passengers to the world press. "Yes, certainly, you're perfectly right. Your story would make good newspaper copy. A shipload of men and women guilty of nothing, yet forced to flee for their lives—trapped on an illegal ship. Desperate. Starving."

"The story would be splashed across the front pages!" someone shouted out. "*That's* what we want! To open the eyes of the world. Let them know what's going on here. What's happening to the Jews of Europe."

"The front pages?" I said. "Yes, that's where the story should appear. But would it? What happened to the story of the Évian Conference when representatives of thirty-two nations—statesmen of the highest rank—met to discuss the plight of the Jews of Hitler's Reich. Reporters from the thirty-two nations were there at the opening session. And they filed stories far more dramatic than yours. It was, after all, a highly historic occasion. Yet, not one report about Évian appeared on a single front page anywhere. On the opening day of the Conference, the great New York *Times* devoted a half column to the story. On page thirteen. They gave a full column that same day to the momentous news that Adolf Hitler had opened an art show in Munich. On the final day of the Conference when each of the thirty-two nations declared that they could or would do nothing to help the Jews—that story rated another half column in the New York *Times*. On page twenty. And the *Times* was one of the few newspapers that printed any Évian stories at all!"

They were listening now. The silence was heavy.

"The story of the *Hilda*," I said, "might also rate a half column on page twenty of the New York *Times*. Will that make the people of the world rush to help you? Welcome you to their countries with valid passports? I'll tell you exactly what would happen. Rumanian officials would come at once and confiscate our ship. You would all be sent back where you came from. And, in all likelihood, the Mossad would be unable to function any further. Is that what you're after?"

This time silence was an answer; the answer I wanted.

Then someone shouted: "When will the ship sail?"

"When the ice breaks."

"And the Kladovo people? If we hear they're coming?"

"You will all help us make the decision," I said, "as to whether or not we should wait."

"We can decide right now!" The woman who spoke was squatting close to me in the darkness. "There's no room for anyone else on this ship. Look at the way we're living now. It's unbearable."

I turned to her. "Do you know the tale of the man who went to the rabbi complaining that he could not go on any longer? His wife, his eight children, his parents crowded together in a one-room house. The conditions were unbearable, he said.

"So the rabbi advised him to take his goat into the house with the family. The man protested. But the rabbi said, 'Do as I tell you. Then come back to see me in seven days.'

"The next week the man came back complaining to the skies. The goat stank. It ran about butting the children. It bleated all night. No one could sleep.

"'All right,' said the rabbi. 'Now take the goat out. And come back to see me tomorrow.'

"The next day the man returned. 'Thank you, Rabbi. I took the goat out. The house is quite comfortable now.'"

No one laughed. But it was not laughter I asked for.

"If the Kladovo Jews don't come," I said, "I can only promise you that we will do our best to bring more Jews from Bucharest to board this ship. The *Hilda* can hold more passengers. We know this because

354

other Mossad ships have been far more crowded than this one. And those passengers survived. They are now members of the Yishuv in Palestine. Say that to yourselves. Let those words be your rabbi's goat. I must endure this so that I too can reach Palestine."

I told them we would try to heat the turkish bath. That we would try to buy supplies in Bazargic. That we would try to get the sailors back on the ship.

"And get the pregnant women off!" someone shouted from the back. "If you don't, you'll be murderers. No infant could survive in this hellhole."

A roar of assent went up.

Then a woman got to her feet. A kerosene lamp hung close to her. Her swollen body was silhouetted in the flickering light.

Silence fell around her.

"And if you put us off the ship, will my baby live? Or will he one day soon be killed by strangers?" Her voice rose. "I take the responsibility for the life of my child. If he dies I would rather have him die on this ship of Jews. Heading toward the homeland." She turned to me. "Please. Don't put us off the ship. Please God, let us stay!"

Words came into my head. *I will gather them from the coasts of the earth . . . the woman with child. . . .*

Words I had seen when I opened the copy of the King Carol Bible given to me by Father Gala Galaction. I had learned the passage. Perhaps for this moment. I spoke the words aloud.

"The Lord said to his prophet Jeremiah, 'Arise ye, and let us go up to Zion . . . Behold, I will bring them from the north country and gather them from the coasts of the earth, and with them the blind and the lame, the woman with child and her that traveleth with child together; a great company shall return thither. They shall come with weeping, and with supplications will I lead them; I will cause them to walk by the rivers of waters in a straight way, wherein they shall not stumble.'"

The stillness in the hold was broken now by the muffled sound of weeping.

"We do stumble," I said. "Those who organize the ships. And those who sail on them. We stumble and pick ourselves up and go on. Because this may be the last road to survival. The last escape from a terrible death."

355

I paused for a long moment.

"You will receive no world acclaim," I said. "No medals. Yet, you must look upon yourselves as heroes. For you are. Every Jew who struggles and suffers to escape . . . to keep alive . . . is a hero. Every Jew who endures the kind of conditions you find on this ship is a hero. It is because of people like you that Jews have survived through twenty centuries of pogroms and persecution. It is because of people like you that Jews will always survive. You are the—the receivers and the creators of our tomorrow."

I climbed down from the wooden crate on which I stood. Hands reached for me; led me to the ladder.

Someone started singing "Hatikvah." In a moment the hold swelled with the sound of voices singing the fervent words of our national anthem. The national anthem of a people. A people without a country, except one given to them by God. *Hatikvah*, the ancient Hebrew word meaning hope.

I climbed up the iron ladder into the blinding brightness of the morning.

THIRTY-THREE

A FEW HOURS LATER we set out for Bazargic, a strange cavalcade. There were ten empty sleighs, each with its team of heavily blanketed horses and its driver swathed like a hillock of scarves and blankets. Alexander and I were equally wrapped against the freezing winds. Only our eyes showed.

As we drove through Balchik it seemed that every dog in the village came bounding through the snow to snarl and snap at the horses. In addition, our procession was observed by honking geese, squawking chickens and pigs who wallowed about in the snowbanks.

The houses we passed were made of mud brick or stone, or both. Most, Alexander informed me, had only one room, with an outhouse in back and a shed for the animals. A man's wealth—or degree of poverty —could be determined in some measure by the number of windows in his house. But whether there was one window or five, each that we passed was crowded with faces.

"In a village where nothing ever happens," said Alexander, speaking loudly through layers of scarves, "we must seem quite a spectacle."

In the distance tiny figures, like miniatures in a Brueghel painting, inched their way up a snow-crusted hill which sparkled in the sunshine. Each carried a wooden barrel of water on his back. *Was* this a mad endeavor, trying to clean and heat a turkish bath which had not been used for decades? Alexander certainly thought so. He was an account-ant and kept strict debit-credit columns in his mind. Never before had the Mossad used its limited funds for so frivolous an item as this: a bath. He had stormed at me in protest. And I agreed with him. I also knew very well that Kadmon would agree with him. Yet, I'd persisted for I felt that in the case of the *Hilda* passengers, a hot bath had become a necessity for both body and soul.

Since the peasants of Balchik had little work to do in the wintertime they had proved amenable enough when the mayor proposed the project. If the crazy ship people wanted to spend their money on such madness, it was fine with them.

The mayor had also found it easy to round up horses, sleighs, and drivers to go to Bazargic. He had, however, taken the precaution of telling the drivers that they were picking up more passengers for the ship.

"This way," he assured me, "there's not so much risk. It may not enter their heads that you're traveling to town with all that money. Leave them at the pub while you do your buying. And on the way back —well, at least all the money will have been spent. You're not so likely to be murdered for a sleighload of sausages and frozen bread. They can't be hidden so easily as money. Furthermore, each driver has been told that he won't be paid until he gets back to Balchik."

As we left the village our spirits were a good deal higher than they had been when entering Balchik the night before.

The *Hilda* passengers were now co-operating. The Ship's Committee had decided that the pregnant women should remain aboard. Arkadi had persuaded—or bribed—the captain to allow his cabin to be turned into a hospital room. Within a matter of hours the place had been scrubbed clean by a contingent of passengers. Some collected buckets of snow to be boiled. Others scoured the cabin. At least we had no shortage of doctors. There were over forty aboard, several of whom specialized in obstetrics.

Committees had started to function once more: a Work Committee, a Sanitation Committee, a Lecture Committee, and a Hanukkah Committee to prepare a program for the forthcoming holiday.

The crew, however, was proving far more difficult than the passengers. Though Arkadi had won the captain's co-operation regarding the cabin, it was evident that we could expect no great leadership from that quarter. The captain retired to his favorite seat by the fireplace in the Balchik pub. Arkadi and the Ship's Committee were left with the job of trying to round up the twenty-two crewmen. Some roistered through the village streets, drunk in the middle of the morning. Some were sleeping off last night's drinking bouts in a shed or a cow's stall. Some were in bed with a village girl. No matter where he was found, no matter what his state of mind and inebriation, each swore that he would not return to the cursed ship.

Our hope was that a hot bath, a hot meal, newly stocked supply shelves, a sobered-up captain, plus the promise of a hundred additional pounds might serve to change their minds.

We reached Bazargic by late afternoon and, as the mayor had suggested, we drew up at the pub. The horses were unhitched, taken off to the stable. And the drivers disappeared in swift procession through the pub door. Alexander and I could have done with a hot drink, but time seemed to be nipping at our heels like the half-wild village dogs.

Within two hours we had, quite literally, bought out Bazargic. Each of the ten sleighs was piled high with sacks and boxes of food: cheeses, sugar, coffee, tea, smoked meats, sausages, breads, sweets, biscuits, cereals, rice, candles, soap and carton upon carton of canned goods. We'd also visited the Bazargic pharmacy; had emptied the shelves of aspirin, rubbing alcohol, and various mixtures and elixirs for coughs, colds, nausea, diarrhea and other ailments from which passengers and crew members were suffering. We tried to buy diapers and other clothing for infants. But to no avail.

Then we entered the pub to muster our drivers. We were somewhat concerned as to what they would say when they learned they'd been tricked; that we had come to buy supplies, not to pick up more passengers. On our trip into town our anxiety about these men had mounted. They seemed to grow more fearsome as the hours went by and the warming sun was muffled by winter-gray clouds. They spoke in a dialect we could not understand; threw long sentences of frosty words from one to the other, and speared us with dark, malevolent looks.

But now when we entered the pub we found the drivers encased in a drunken glaze of camaraderie. The blazing fireside and blood-warming *tuica* had wrought a transformation.

I announced that we would pay their pub bill. This action seemed to dispel all antagonism. When they came from the pub and saw their sleighs stocked with provisions they broke into lusty laughter. Indeed, they sang and laughed all the way back to Balchik and somehow managed to keep their sleighs from sliding into snowbanks or tipping over on the ice-glazed roads.

Incredibly, this laughter and camaraderie persisted through the hours to come.

That night passengers and townspeople watched and cheered as the supplies we had bought in Bazargic were brought aboard the *Hilda*.

And that night two babies were born in the captain's cabin; a boy and a girl. They named the little girl Hilda. The boy was called Yehuda, the Hebrew word for Jew.

The birth of these infants, which had been regarded with such dismay and anger, now seemed a kind of miracle. Though no one spoke the words aloud, it was clear that, for the passengers on the *Hilda,* the baby boy and girl had become a symbol of hope and life. They were the true receivers of our tomorrow.

The new mothers were now treated with deep respect and concern. Indeed, some of the orthodox Jews looked upon the women with a kind of awe.

The crewmen, more superstitious than religious, were convinced that the babies were an omen of good luck. Miraculously, the drunken brawls ceased. The men returned to their stations. The generators were put into working order. The ship had electricity once more. The frozen water was heated. For the first time, and for one day only, passengers and crew were allowed to drink as many tin cupfuls of water as they wished. By noon the three kitchens were back in operation, and the hot lunch served that day seemed to the passengers like a banquet.

When I returned to the house of the mayor a peasant woman was waiting for me. She presented me with a pile of hand-stitched, folded diapers. She had learned, she said, that we had been unable to buy diapers in Bazargic. She had also been told that our passengers were able to bring aboard only a cup, a plate, eating utensils, a blanket and a single change of clothing. "I was sure that the babies would not have enough diapers," she said with a shy smile. "So I made these." Then she added, "I made them from sheets and a tablecloth that I was saving for my dowry."

I looked at her, then could not see her for my eyes clouded with tears. When a peasant woman was past her twenties it was often hard to tell her age. Was this woman giving away her final hopes of marriage by cutting up her dowry sheets? Or had those hopes been packed away long ago with the unused linens?

"It's very kind of you," I said. "Perhaps you would like to go on board yourself and give your gift to the babies?"

She shook her head. "No, please. I don't want that. Just tell the two mothers—I wish them well." Then she pulled her dark shawl around her, and before I could stop her she had hurried out the door.

As I stood, staring after her, I wondered why her simple human gesture had moved me to sudden tears. I had not cried at the situation I found on the *Hilda*; human beings forced to live under conditions of stench, filth, airlessness unthinkable even for animals. Human beings half starved, often half frozen. Each allotted the amount of sleeping space he would get in a grave. I had not cried at the many horror stories I'd heard about the *Hilda* passengers; the terrors they had endured in Germany, Austria, Czechoslovakia. I had not cried at their reports of the sundering of families as a father, a brother, sometimes a mother, even a child was rounded up with hundreds of other Jews in a school auditorium, a concert hall, an empty warehouse; then marched to the railroad station to be shunted into boxcars, and taken off—where? No one knew where. To Poland, perhaps. We'd heard from our Mossad man in Poland that the Germans were setting up a new ghetto in Nisko, another dumping ground for Jews shipped out from the German Reich. But none of the *Hilda* passengers had heard what had happened to their family members who were taken away. There were no reports at all.

To function one had to cut oneself in half; encase one's emotions inside an impenetrable wall. When it came to the subject of Jews one could not cry. Yet, to continue as a human being, one must let other emotions flow. Therefore, one could cry at this gesture of a peasant woman who had brought a pile of diapers.

But could one love? I realized then that I had not even thought of Stefan since leaving Bucharest. It all seemed another lifetime away. Yet, if Stefan's daughter had recovered in time he might be on the *Hilda*, with his family, sailing for Palestine.

A few hours later I left Balchik for Bucharest. This time I traveled alone. Arkadi must remain, do his best to see to it that the captain and crew stayed sober and kept the ship in condition so that she could sail when the ice broke. Alexander must remain to try to ensure that order was kept among the passengers, and that the new arrivals—from Kladovo or elsewhere—would be allowed aboard, and allotted their own coffin space of room in the hold.

But I had to return at once to Bucharest. I had to return to our hub of communications: the telephone in the apartment on the Strada Rosetti. I had to learn what had transpired about the Kladovo Jews. If the transit visas were not forthcoming, I had to work at once with Orekhovsky to send perhaps fifty more Jews to the *Hilda*. Again the most ghastly job of all, that of *habchira*—the choosing—would fall upon us.

Before I left I asked Alexander whether he could find on board a little Polish girl named Dasha. According to Mossad regulations I had not spoken personally to any of the *Hilda* passengers. But what harm to greet a six-year-old child? To hold her on my lap. She would know me only as the lady who had sat beside her at the Czernowitz station. This little girl who had run terrified all night long through a burning forest—to me she symbolized our people now, even more than the newborn infants aboard the *Hilda*. She had survived the inferno. She was on her way to a place where she would be welcomed, if she ever reached the shores of Palestine.

But when he came to see me off, Alexander came alone. Dasha, he said, could not be found. He insisted that I leave at once. Since I was traveling alone, I must reach Bazargic before dark. These roads were dangerous enough for a woman traveling unescorted—no matter how heavily the sleigh driver had been bribed. But the danger increased tenfold in the darkness. I would stay overnight at the Bazargic pub, then proceed in the early morning to Oltenitza where we had left our rented car. From there I could make my way in relative safety with only normal hazards to concern me: the icy roads coupled with the fact that I was a totally inexperienced driver.

I left Balchik to the incredible sound of singing: a Hebrew song of the Hashomer Hatzair. The words carried clear through the frosty afternoon.

They were singing because they were clean. As one line of passengers made their way up the steep hill toward the turkish bath, others descended, singing. They had soaped and soaked themselves, and washed their clothes—some of which were already hung out on lines strung up on deck, flapping in the winter sun and wind. Indeed, I had the feeling that these drying skirts and shirts and trousers were waving me an exuberant good-by.

That, as it turned out, was the *Hilda*'s happy day; the Day of the Turkish Bath.

In some of the days which followed it seemed that the ship had plunged not into a sea which could be seen on any map, but into hell.

Alexander reported the events to me upon his return to Bucharest.

On the afternoon of December twenty-ninth, someone mistakenly filled the kerosene lamps with benzine. When one of the passengers lit a lamp it blazed up. Unthinking, he threw it from him. The benzine splashed on the clothes of a woman passenger. And the fire licked at the straw which served as a mattress. In a few instants flames climbed to other straw mattresses and the hold became an inferno. Panic broke out, wild as the flames. Passengers ran for the ladder, shoving, screaming. The woman with benzine on her clothes was pushed accidentally into the blaze. She became an incendiary torch. They tore off her clothes.

Somehow the well-organized fire brigade aboard managed to put out the flames. Many had been severely burned. The woman who had been set afire was carried, moaning, off the ship. Two days later, she died.

Her name was Irmagard Levinstein. She was a member of the halutz movement in Germany. For years she had been training for the life she would lead on a kibbutz in Palestine.

The day after the fire the ice started to break up, and spirits soared because it seemed that the *Hilda*'s six-week siege at Balchik was finally ended. But still the ship could not depart.

The transit visas had not come through for the Kladovo people. I informed Spitzer that we could wait no longer. The mayor of Balchik had promised that he would notify the authorities in Bucharest if our ship continued to wait for the people who never came. I had no reason to doubt that he would see his threat through.

Orekhovsky therefore had chosen fifty more passengers from among the thousands of applicants in his files. He had done this alone and on his own; relieving me of a nightmare involvement.

The fifty men and women were en route to Balchik, when a violent winter storm broke out on the Black Sea.

Alexander was aboard the *Hilda* during that night.

"It was horrible," he told me. "We had the feeling that all the forces of hell came together to toss our miserable ship from side to side."

The anchors were torn loose. The wind cracked the ship against the pier; then started driving the helpless vessel out to the open sea.

"We rang the distress sirens," Alexander said. "But no one on shore heard us. The noise of the storm drowned out the sound of the sirens.

"We were afraid of fire. So we put out the fire in the ovens and in the lamps. There was no electricity. We were in pitch blackness. All those people imprisoned in that black hold. Everyone violently seasick. The shrieking wind and the moaning and vomiting and the stinking darkness—I could never in any dream concoct such a nightmare. We were all certain the ship would sink."

The next morning the storm had abated. Fishermen found the ship's anchors. The *Hilda* returned to Balchik. She had been damaged in the storm. She was leaking. Repairs had to be made.

Hanukkah arrived. The Hanukkah Committee had built a huge candelabra made of wood, with electric candles. And the *Hilda* passengers joined with Jews throughout the world as they celebrated the Feast of Lights. They sang the traditional songs. And they told stories; stories from the centuries of the Jewish past. Then a young man and a girl who had met on the ship stood up and announced their engagement.

A few days later, the *Hilda* sailed from the port of Balchik into the open sea.

For twenty-four hours we heard no word at all. Then, finally, a telephone call from our Mossad man in Istanbul.

364

The ship had to put in to port to take on more coal; one hundred and forty-two tons of it. That was according to plan. And, according to plan, all the passengers had been asked to hide in the hold while the ship was in port. Except in cases of emergency like this one, there were always several hundred passengers on deck in a carefully rotated system, for the simple reason that it was impossible for all the seven hundred and twenty-nine people to be jammed into the hold at one time.

But in Istanbul, the impossible became necessary. If British observers saw the illegals, the ship might just as well turn around and head back to Rumania. And British observers came in all nationalities, for the network of spies proliferated every day.

So our people were confined to the hold, while goats roamed free on deck; goats which we'd put aboard in Balchik for milk and for camouflage.

That night in Istanbul, dysentery suddenly ran rampant among passengers and crew. The toilets were all on deck.

Believing themselves to be protected by the darkness, men and women crept up from the hold, stood in long lines at the toilets; leaned on the rails to vomit into the sea.

They were seen.

As the ship left Istanbul, she was suddenly flooded in light. She was flanked by two British Royal Navy vessels. A British officer and two crewmen boarded the *Hilda* and took command.

That night one of the passengers, a young girl, jumped overboard. They brought her back, screaming and sobbing. It was the same girl who had tried to commit suicide in Balchik.

Then the *Hilda* sailed through the Dardanelles, escorted by the British ships.

There were more agonizing days of silence.

We made frantic calls to Turkey, to Greece, to Palestine. Could a ship simply disappear? Where had the British taken her?

On January twenty-fourth, a cable came. The *Hilda* was entering Haifa harbor!

The news was incredible. Had the British suddenly adopted a new policy? Now that the war was five months old, had they decided to accept the full co-operation the Yishuv wanted to give?

At the start of the war, David Ben-Gurion had declared: "We shall fight the war as if there were no White Paper, and we shall fight the White Paper as if there were no war."

Perhaps the British had finally understood the difficulties of our position; trying desperately to fight side by side with a nation we were also forced to fight against.

During the first week of the war most of the young men and women of the Yishuv had volunteered to fight with the British Army. They were rejected. Why, said the British, should they train and arm Palestinian Jews who might, at a later date, make trouble for them in Palestine? They did, however, allow some Palestinian Jews into service units. They permitted others to volunteer for virtual suicide missions. And their secret service worked closely with men like David Arnon, Yitzhak Hecker and Yehuda Arazi.

Perhaps the British had finally decided that it was folly to pander any longer to the Arabs' demands that the Jews be kept out of Palestine. How many Arabs had volunteered to fight with the British Army? The Grand Mufti Haj Amin el Husseini, the most important leader in the Arab world, the man the British were trying hardest to please, was now living in Berlin as the personal guest of Adolf Hitler.

Perhaps the British were using the *Hilda* as a symbol, to show us that they would henceforth disregard the White Paper. Perhaps that was why they had not sent the *Hilda* back to Rumania. Perhaps that was why they had escorted our ship to Palestine.

Orekhovsky had gloomy doubts about these optimistic theories. "They'll let our passengers in all right," he declared gloomily. "But they'll send them to Atlit Detention Camp. Also, they'll deduct seven hundred and twenty-nine legal certificates from our lists. Our *Hilda* passengers will therefore cause the eventual death of seven hundred and twenty-nine European Jews."

I argued with him. Could he not understand that a government might realize its wrongs; change its policies?

The next day another cable came from Palestine.

We translated the code and sat then, stunned, unable to believe the message. The British Mandatory Government had decreed that our ship set sail at once for Paraguay.

Paraguay!

366

The passports which we'd distributed to our passengers had Paraguay designated as the destination. Subterfuge like this was essential. No port authorites could be bribed to let one of our ships through if its official destination was Palestine.

But our leaking hulk of a cargo ship was barely fit to make the voyage across the Mediterranean Sea. To send her into the Atlantic was to issue a death warrant to the ship, its passengers and its crew.

The next day a call came through from Kadmon, filling us in on developments.

The *Hilda*'s captain had persuaded the British that the ship could not put out to sea at once. She was leaking badly. She needed repairs.

Overnight, the Yishuv plastered the city of Haifa with posters demanding that the passengers of the *Hilda* be permitted to land in Palestine.

When no action was forthcoming, a hunger strike was planned.

On January twenty-eighth, we received another cable. The passengers on the *Hilda* had painted four words in huge white letters on the side of the ship. WE WILL NOT LEAVE.

The following day, the British Mandatory Government met with a delegation of the Council of the Jewish Community of Haifa. The delegation was threatened. They must bring the Jews of Haifa into line. They must stop all talk of hunger strikes and retribution.

David Hacohen, a member of the delegation, answered with a question. "Do you believe that there will be a single Jew who will not seek revenge if this ship is sent away?"

The passengers were taken from the *Hilda*. The men were sent to Atlit Detention Camp; the women to a *Beit Olim*—an Immigrant House. They were all informed that they would soon be returned to Europe.

But they were not sent back. Within six months they were all released by the British.

The seven hundred and twenty-seven men and women and two infants named Hilda and Yehuda became members of the Yishuv in Palestine.

PART THREE

February 1940 to June 1941

THIRTY-FOUR

THREE WEEKS LATER on a chilly afternoon I entered the apartment on the Strada Rosetti and found a stranger asleep on my bed.

I stood looking down at him. He was tall, handsome in an irregular sort of way. He looked to be about thirty years old, yet his hair was graying.

Suddenly I knew who this was. David Arnon had mentioned that his chief might be coming to Bucharest. But when I asked why, David changed the subject abruptly. To my further queries he had answered with a shrug. He knew nothing. Yehuda Arazi was not a man to discuss his moves or his motives with anyone.

Even Yitzhak, ordinarily so open and frank, merely cast his eyes down when I asked about the forthcoming visit of Yehuda Arazi. "If he gets here," Yitzhak said, "he'll tell you himself why he's come."

I knew something of Yehuda Arazi. A swashbuckling adventurer—with a mission. It was said that he spared neither himself nor anyone else to fulfill each separate undertaking. And it was said that no one crossed Arazi and got away with it. Even in sleep his features expressed determination.

I remembered hearing that Arazi had started his career as a secret agent at age nineteen when—on orders of the Haganah—he joined the British police force in Palestine. He was thus able to supply the Jewish underground army with the names of police informers, the whereabouts of Arab arms caches, and other such interesting information.

Arazi rose in the ranks, became an inspector in the British secret service. Then the British discovered his extracurricular activities. They fired him. And he had since become one of the top men in the Haganah.

Why had he come here to Bucharest? What did he want of me?

There was one thing I imagined he *would* want when he awakened. I went into the kitchen, made a large pot of coffee.

When I looked into the room again he was sitting up, putting on his shoes. He glanced at me, stood up. "Well," he said, "so you're Ruth." He smiled a little. "There are few things nicer to wake up to than the smell of hot coffee, made by an attractive woman. Perhaps," he added, "I should introduce myself."

"Yehuda Arazi. Alias Yehuda Alon. Alias—"

"You were told I was coming?"

"David said you might be passing through." I felt wary of him, though I did not know why.

"I apologize for making myself at home. David let me in. And since I hadn't slept for a day and a half, he suggested I use the facilities."

I wanted to ask where he'd come from; where he was going. But perhaps if I asked him no questions, he would ask none of me. I somehow did not feel like giving any information at all to this tall and undoubtedly charming stranger.

However, it was not that simple.

As he ate breakfast and downed a pot of coffee, he plied me with questions about the *Darien*. Our miracle ship. The ship owned by Shmarya Zamaret. The ship which was now being reconverted at Piraeus under Shmarya's direction. She was a salvage ship, but we were building a structure on her deck which would hold tiers of berths. All this was, incredibly, being done with no bribes to port officials. The American could do what he wished with the ship he had purchased from a drunken sea captain in a waterfront cafe.

Arrangements had already been made with Spitzer. As soon as the *Darien* was ready, she would be used to rescue the eleven hundred refugees stranded at Kladovo. We would not need to worry any longer about transit visas. The *Darien* was small enough to make her way up the Danube to Kladovo.

Furthermore, since we owned the ship, she would sail where and when we ordered. And I had promised Spitzer that the *Darien* would return three times to Kladovo, rescuing every last refugee who remained there.

All this I told Yehuda Arazi. But I told him only because I had the strong feeling that he knew these facts already. He kept nodding with sympathetic interest.

"Is her name the *Darien?*" he inquired finally. "Or the *Darien II?*"

"Shmarya chose the name *Darien,*" I told him. "Then Lloyd's Register informed him there was another ship by the same name. So Shmarya said, okay—ours will be the *Darien II.*"

Yehuda nodded. Then he leaned back in his chair and said, "Ruth, my pet, I'm afraid I've come with orders you won't like. As soon as the reconstruction work on the ship is finished, you must turn the *Darien II* over to us."

I stared at him. "Who," I said finally, "is—us?"

"You know," he replied, "that we're working with British Intelligence. Well, we've come up with a plan. And they're most enthusiastic."

He pulled a map from his pocket, spread it on the table before me, pointed to a spot on the German section of the Danube. "At this point," he said, "the Danube is narrow and shallow. We tell the Germans this American-owned vessel has come to collect Jews and bring them to Palestine. The British will let it be known to the Germans that because of Anglo-American relations they will carefully ignore the existence of this particular ship. The Germans will undoubtedly follow suit. How, after all, can they do otherwise?"

There was some logic in the plan. If the Germans refused to let Jews board this American ship, bound for Palestine, statesmen might actually begin to believe what we in the Mossad had believed for months: that the Nazis' "solution" to the "Jewish problem" was not immigration, as they so vociferously claimed, but extermination.

"So," said Yehuda, "our plan is this. As the *Darien II* comes up the Danube, she'll appear to be empty. However, she'll be carrying several thousand boxes of dynamite and a quantity of depth bombs. When she comes to this spot—" again he pointed to the tiny mark on the map —"she will blow up. The Danube will be blocked, perhaps for months. The Germans' oil route to Rumania, for example, will be cut off. That

373

single fact alone could do a great deal to bring the war to an early end."

I stared at him, so stunned that I felt nothing at all.

As he watched me, his blue eyes turned piercing cold. "It's been decided," he said, and stood up.

"Who?" I cried out. "Who has decided such a thing? No one has the right to decide! This is *our* ship! A Mossad ship! We are independent of everyone. We operate on our own. Our ships are for saving the lives of Jews. That is our mission. We have no part in sabotage. *We* are not working for the British. We're working against them. The *Darien* will first save the Jews at Kladovo. And then return to Europe for more refugees. And still more. If you want to block the Danube, that's your business. Not ours. Find some other ship. Not ours."

"Look," said Yehuda easily. "Please. Not the hysterical woman act. If the Mossad had a fleet of ships, fine. We could take another. But since you have only one—and one which by great good luck can traverse the Danube—that is the one we must use."

"You say it's been decided. By whom? Our leaders? Berl? Eliahu? Saul Meiroff?* They would never agree to such a plan!"

"The Yishuv has many leaders."

"Name one who approves of taking our ship—to destroy it."

"David Hacohen."

David Hacohen! The man who had pleaded the *Hilda*'s case so eloquently before the Mandatory Government. Only yesterday I'd received a transcript of Hacohen's full and moving testimony before the commissioner. With it Kadmon had enclosed a copy of the letter sent by the illegals on the *Hilda* to His Excellency, the Right Honorable High Commissioner of Palestine.

I took this letter from my bed-table drawer. "These are the kind of people who will sail on the *Darien*. Let them speak to you—if you won't listen to me!"

I read the letter aloud.

" 'We, the undersigned, more than seven hundred passengers of the S.S. *Hilda*, who were only because of our Jewish origin imprisoned in German concentration camps, and then compelled to leave our countries, submit to His Excellency the urgent supplication not to prolong

* *See* Appendix Seventeen.

374

our wandering which has lasted now for more than a quarter of a year and caused the death of two women. We hope that the petition to allow us to enter the country of our ancestors, the only refuge we have, will not be done in vain. On board S.S. *Hilda*, January 27, 1940. Haifa port.' "

I looked up. "Suppose," I said, "that this letter had been written to you by the eleven hundred Jews at Kladovo. 'We the undersigned beg you to allow us to enter the country of our ancestors, the only refuge we have.' "

"Look," said Yehuda, "if I weren't working with British Intelligence, I'd be working with the Mossad."†

"Why then do you work against us?"

"I'm not." He walked to the armchair. He was very tall, but his shoulders were stooped and he bent slightly to one side. I noticed for the first time that he had a slight limp. He sat down, turned to me, all patience and understanding. The man changed his mood and his mien like a chameleon. "Ruth, I truly believe, and Hacohen believes, and many other of our leaders believe that the *Darien II* can save more lives—far more—by helping to shorten the war."

"But your plan is all made of *ifs!*" I cried. "What makes you think the Germans would let the ship through without searching it? They'll find your dynamite and depth charges. They'll confiscate the *Darien*. And we'll have lost on every front. Even the little co-operation the Mossad has won from some Gestapo officials—even that will be destroyed."

"It's quite true," Arazi said. "We may be discovered. The plan may blow up and the *Darien* with it. But it's not true that we'll lose on every front. Whether the plan succeeds or not, we will gain a great deal."

He lit up a cigarette. "We have excellent reason to believe that through this one dramatic maneuver we can show the British how important it could be to them to allow us—the Yishuv—to co-operate as fully as we want to. I'm talking about the possibility of a Jewish Brigade in the British Army. I'm talking about sabotage schemes I'm not even permitted to talk about. Schemes which the secret service are now merely considering. But they're afraid to move ahead with us. Or to let

† *See* Appendix Eighteen.

us move by ourselves. They're blocked by government policy. Even those officers who want to work with us need an exploit like the *Darien* plan to prove to the government what can be gained in allowing the Yishuv to co-operate with them in every way that we can."

"Surely," I said, "if the British are so stupid as to require proof in order to allow us to be their allies, surely you in your brilliance can come up with some other Machiavellian scheme. And leave us alone. Leave the Mossad ships alone!" I handed him a story from the Danish newspaper *Politiken*, sent me by a haver in Copenhagen. Attached was a typed translation in French. "Read this! A description of the deportations to Lublin. And this is just the beginning! You know that as well as I. We must fight the war *two* ways: with the British and against them—at the same time. *That* was Ben-Gurion's directive. Not that the Mossad should be subservient to the British secret service. Even Weizmann, look!" I took another paper from my bedside folder. "You heard him at the Zionist Congress. Tepid. Mealy-mouthed. Never so much as mentioning illegal immigration. Even *he* has made an about-face! Look what he wrote last week." Again I read aloud. "'We must not acquiesce. We must not accept the lot that is meted out to us as refugees. Acceptance of such a lot would mean the destruction of our state and the end of our existence as a people . . . At this very moment ships bearing our young immigrants are making their way to Palestine through mined and submarine-infested seas, and they will reach their destination in spite of all the dangers that lie in wait for them.'"

Arazi was smiling a little.

"The words of Weizmann amuse you?" I said.

"*You* amuse me. You have a fine file of clippings, I'll say that for you. Printed words for every occasion."

"Yes, I save clippings," I told him. "These are *my* ammunition. When things are printed in a paper they often have more reality for people from whom I must try to get money. Read that story of the deportations to Lublin. The *Darien* can save thousands of Jews who might otherwise be making another voyage—a hundred and fifty human beings crammed into each cattle car."

The story was a graphic one. It described how thirteen thousand Jews from the Polish city of Stettin had been unloaded into the desolate fields in the Lublin district. The temperature was twenty-two degrees below freezing. The S.S. forced them to march. For fourteen hours they staggered and struggled on. Some were left on the road to freeze to death. Among the frozen corpses was a mother clutching her small child. A little girl of five was found with a piece of cardboard attached to her coat. Her name was printed on it: Renate Alexander. She was frozen, but not quite dead. A Polish farmer took her to a hospital in Lublin. Both hands and both legs were amputated. The child said that she had been sent to visit relatives in Stettin. When the S.S. came and ordered her relatives to go at once to the railway station, she, Renate, went along with them. Now she would live the rest of her life as a stump of a human being. If she lived at all.

The report concluded that each deportee had been allowed to bring with him only a single piece of hand luggage and twenty zloty, about five dollars. Even those who had survived the march were now slowly dying.

"Read it!" I said to Arazi. "Read it and remember that some of the passengers on the *Tiger Hill* were from Stettin. They are now safe in Palestine."

He handed the newspaper clipping back to me without glancing at it. "I don't need to read clippings. I've just come from Poland. I know very well what is going on there. As a matter of fact, I was born there."

"Then," I cried, "how can you dare to demand our ship?"

He stood up, stubbed out his cigarette, and said a single word: "Priorities."

"Priorities!" I screamed the word back at him. "What can have priority over saving lives?"

He made no answer, started for the door. Then he turned. "In any case, I came here to give you warning. Get another ship for the Kladovo people. I understand you're negotiating for the *Dora*."

"That fell through long ago. We have no chance at all for the *Dora*."

"Well," he said, "I'm sure you can turn up some other ship if you try hard enough. I have great faith in you." He smiled. "Thanks for the coffee and eggs. I'm leaving for Palestine tonight. Any message for anyone?"

I said nothing.

He shrugged and left.

I stood, staring at the closed door; stunned, sick.

Then, finally, I went to the telephone.

Within twenty-four hours I had received corroboration from Kadmon in Palestine, and from all the Mossad members I could contact in Europe: Ehud, Yulik Braginski, Dani Shind, Zvi Shechter and, most important, Shmarya Zameret. We all agreed that no matter what happened, no matter what orders we received to the contrary, we would proceed with our original plans for the *Darien II*.

That night when I spoke to Sima Spitzer in Belgrade, the connection was exceptionally clear. I told Spitzer that the *Darien* would be ready to sail in a few months' time. And he told me that two shipments of clothing, food and medicine had just arrived for the Jews at Kladovo. One shipment came from the Joint Distribution Committee; the other from the International Red Cross.

His voice, which usually ranged from glum to desperate, now sounded almost cheerful.

THIRTY-FIVE

WE PROCEEDED WITH OUR PLANS for the *Darien II* as though the visit of Yehuda Arazi had never occurred.

It was a strange kind of limbo time. As the winter months thawed, the mood in Bucharest brightened. One could feel it in the cafes; see it on the streets. People seemed more relaxed. The inherent Rumanian optimism bubbled to the surface once more.

But the reason for the city's renewed sense of hope and springtime *joie de vivre* was a grim one. German and Russian troops were heavily engaged on other fronts. Rumania could therefore pursue her chosen course of fence-sitting neutrality. Indeed, both Germany and her Soviet bedfellow had promised to protect Rumania's borders. And certain political pundits were claiming that Rumania's precarious status quo would remain throughout the war. Rumania was already supplying Germany with what the Reich most needed from her: agricultural produce and crude oil. So why should Germany trouble to send her army into the country? As for Russia, her troops were engaged, rather incredibly, in fighting Finland.

This side war gave the Rumanians food for jokes and food for hope. If the forces of tiny Finland could successfully fight off the massive might of Russia, the Soviet might think more than twice before trying to invade another small nation.

Furthermore, a Balkan Federation was in the works. Discussions were held between the governments of Rumania, Yugoslavia, Bulgaria

379

and Greece. A Balkan block of seventy million people could surely withstand Russia and Germany. Or so the feeling went. Hungary, of course, was not asked to join the Balkan Federation. She had been pro-German from the beginning—since Germany had promised to see to it that Hungary got back Transylvania, the territory she had lost to Rumania after the Great War.

Then, at Federation meetings, Bulgaria started insisting *she* wanted back the territory she had lost to Rumania after the war. King Carol stated vehemently that not one kilometer of his country would be ceded to anyone. And the Balkan Federation quickly foundered.

In early March—after three months of fighting—Russian troops broke the Finnish resistance. And the balloon of hope, blown up by the cafe sitters in Bucharest, suddenly burst. A sense of reality began setting in.

Rumania was now on full wartime footing. She had one million five hundred thousand soldiers in uniform. Fortifications were being built in frantic haste along the borders.

The sudden enormous expense resulted in sharp devaluation of the currency. And funds for the Mossad became even more impossible to obtain.

The Shamen was working on three ships which he had hopes of acquiring, so that he could lease them to us. He had by now graduated in our minds from "a good goy" to a haver: a comrade. I carefully showed him all the clippings I could gather about the ever-worsening conditions for Jews in Hitler's Reich and in Poland. And they had an accumulated effect. He finally began to realize that the wild-sounding statements I had made to him at our first meeting might in fact turn out to be true. Every Jew we were able to crowd onto a Mossad ship might indeed mean another life saved.

It was the reports of individual tragedies which moved him the most, especially when they concerned children. I showed him a clipping which stated that within a single week seventeen hundred Austrian Jews had committed suicide. He read the story, handed it back to me. "Reports," he said. "Who can believe such things?" But when I showed him the story of an Austrian-Jewish girl of twelve who had died with a gas tube in her mouth, the Shamen frowned. He read the story again and again. When he handed it back to me he said once more, "Who can believe such things." Only this time the words were not a dismissal, but an expression of horror. This time he believed.

The Shamen no longer spoke about exorbitant sums of money when he discussed the three ships. He grew irritated if I even mentioned the matter. "What do you think of me?" he said. "I'm a profiteer in human lives? The ship will cost what it will cost. But no more."

The trouble was, however, that the three ships were like phantoms; slipping in and out of his grasp. Since every country's need for ships increased drastically as the weeks of war went by, it became virtually impossible to secure any vessel of any type for purposes of illegal immigration. If a ship did loom on the horizon, it was virtually impossible to hire a captain. Every captain knew that he would be subject to eight years' imprisonment in a British jail if he was caught bringing his ship of illegals within Palestine's three-mile limit.

We of course did not limit our ship-securing efforts to the Shamen. We tried every source we could. For a brief hopeful span of weeks it seemed that the *Dora* might again become a possibility. But then we learned from the ship's North African owners that they would never allow us to lease their ship again. Negotiations were abruptly ended. They would respond to no further communications.

Only the *Darien II* remained a reality.

During these days of early spring my telephone rang incessantly. The calls came, in the main, from Jews who had fled from Poland and the Reich; Jews who begged me to help them get to Palestine.

Orekhovsky's office was now so swamped with refugees seeking legal certificates that their desperation had settled inside him like a madness. I had asked him not to give out my telephone number to anyone. Yet, he became increasingly more unable to face the despair he met when he informed an applicant that there was no hope of a legal certificate. In order to avert what he was certain would become a suicide, he gave my telephone number and with it some slight information about our illegal ships. And how could I blame him for doing so? I knew full well that throughout this city there were thousands of homeless, stateless Jews living on the shreds of hope the Mossad was able to offer.

Now when I phoned Czernowitz, the answers I received were different from those given me only a few months ago. Yes, my brother David was definitely coming to Bucharest. Yes, he agreed, the situation was serious. He and Sophie and their boys would take advantage of my contacts.

When was David coming? Well, as soon as he could persuade Sophie of the necessity of leaving their home. And when would that be? Well, perhaps in a few weeks. Or, without any doubt, within a few months.

My sister Bertha echoed the sentiments of my sister-in-law Sophie.

As for Stefan; yes, as soon as his daughter was able to travel he and his family would leave for Palestine. In the meantime, he was coming to Bucharest to see me. I kept putting him off.

Alone in the nights I would long for him. Sometimes when he phoned I would simply sit, my eyes closed, his voice rushing through me, unable to speak at all.

This was what frightened me. With Stefan I was a woman in love, beset by all the turmoil which comes with this condition. If he were in Bucharest could I deal competently with the constant crises which arose? I did not know, and I dared not try to find out.

One day we would be together in Palestine. Until then our love must exist on the memories we had already made, and on the plans and dreams we had for our future.

On April ninth, the newspapers blazoned surprising and frightening news: GERMANY INVADES DENMARK.

Within twelve hours thousands of German troops had swarmed across the country. The army was aided by the fierce bombardment from air and sea. They met little resistance. Denmark fell beneath the black shadow of the swastika.

The following night the German forces entered the fiord of Oslo. Within hours they had taken the capital city of Norway without a shot being fired—and with the help of the head of the Norwegian Nazi Party, Major Vidkun Quisling who had, it turned out, worked efficiently and secretly to prepare his country's swift defeat.

The Allies had, once again, been taken totally unaware. But this time, at least, they started fighting in earnest. The so-called phony war was over.

They started fighting. And they continued losing.

On the morning of May tenth, Radio Bucharest was playing patriotic music. It was the national holiday, commemorating the date that the first King Carol had arrived in Rumania. His voice puffed with pride, the broadcaster described how King Carol II stood on his draped reviewing stand, looking imposing in his most picturesque uniform as troops and tanks paraded past the Royal Palace.

Crown Prince Michael stood before his father, looking—said the announcer—extremely handsome and—

The broadcaster's voice broke. There was a long pause. Only martial music was heard. Then in quite a different tone he spoke again. The words he used were short and stunned.

At 3 A.M., German troops had marched into Belgium, Holland and Luxembourg.

The days which followed were torn with contradictions. Springtime Bucharest had never been more beautiful. But it was like the last vivid remnants of a world which was sinking all around us into doom. Gypsy orchestras played still in the restaurants and open-air cafes. The song they seemed to play most often was "Avant de Mourir"—"Before Dying."

The trees of the city had burst into greens and were splashed with color; flowering almond, quince, plum and cherry trees. The flower stalls on the Boulevard Brătianu lined the street with the bright fresh colors of spring. And well-dressed ladies and gentlemen, girls and soldiers, nursemaids and children strolled as they had in springtimes past along the tree-lined boulevards and down the Calea Victoriei, and through the city's green and flower-planted parks.

Many Bucharestians admitted to a guilty feeling of relaxation and relief. At least when the furious fighting continued to be elsewhere, no one would pay much attention to the Balkans. Perhaps, as Hitler was loudly proclaiming, the war, indeed, was in its last phase. Which meant that Rumania could remain self-contained and neutral. And life could go on more or less unchanged.

Only in the Jewish Quarter of Văcăreşti was the mood visibly different. There too all windows were open to let in the springtime. But through these windows Jews could be seen sitting by their radios, listening to the newscasts, mesmerized by horror and by hopelessness. Millions of human beings—among them hundreds of thousands of Jews—only hundreds of miles away were being sucked and swallowed into the greatest nightmare known to mankind. And the Allies were in full retreat. It seemed that nothing could stop the onslaught of Hitler's tanks and troops and dive-bombing Stuka planes.

The apartment on the Strada Rosetti became more of a gathering place than ever—because of the short-wave radio. No matter what time of the day or night I returned home I was certain to find at least two or three men gathered around the radio which was usually tuned to the BBC. But sometimes we turned to Radio Berlin.

We heard the shrilling voice of Adolf Hitler. "Soldiers of the West Front! The hour for you has now come. The fight beginning today decides the fate of the German nation for the next one thousand years."

The fate of the German nation and the fate of the Jews of Europe and the fate of the civilized world.

The news reports became a crescendo of horrors. And the new term of modern warfare was heard again and again: Blitzkrieg. German mobile units stormed across the lowlands, their way paved by the desecration caused by thousands of their low-diving bombers.

The Dutch and the Belgians fought back fiercely. But on May fourteenth, the Netherlands fell. On May twenty-eighth, Belgium surrendered—and six hundred thousand French and British soldiers were suddenly trapped in a small triangle of land. We listened aghast to reports of German tanks and troops pressing onward inexorably, shoving the Allied forces back to the sea.

Then there came stories of the small boats. Fishing boats, sailboats, yachts, manned by British civilians. Crossing the British Channel beneath an overcast sky. On their way to try to rescue the soldiers of Britain and France. There were larger boats too; destroyers, cruisers. Back and forth across the Channel they went, carrying thousands upon thousands from the port of Dunkirk and nearby beaches to safety on

British shores. For a time the Luftwaffe was grounded by bad weather. And when the fog and rain cleared, British Spitfires and Hurricane fighters did their valiant best to keep German bombers from destroying the strange and hastily improvised armada.

In four days it was over. Most of the British Expeditionary Force had been rescued. Or so the communiqués announced. But now it was an army without arms. For there had been no time and no room for the tanks, trucks and guns to be carried back home.

The operation was called a miracle. The Miracle of Dunkirk. "Perhaps," said Kadmon, "this experience of desperation and small boats will make the British more understanding of what the Mossad is trying to do."

"First worries first," said Orekhovsky. "What we must pray for now is that Britain herself should survive."

That afternoon, June fourth, we heard Winston Churchill's eloquent answer. "We shall defend our island, whatever the cost may be. We shall fight on the beaches, we shall fight on the landing grounds, we shall fight in the fields and in the streets, we shall fight in the hills; we shall never surrender."

But German bombers were now based a mere five minutes away, directly across the English Channel. And France—Britain's sole remaining ally—had lost most of her armaments as well as her best troops in the fighting in northern France and Belgium.

On Friday the twenty-first of June, I returned from Brăila. The railway porter who took my suitcase was weeping.

"Can I help you?" I said.

He looked up at me. "No one can help us now, mademoiselle. Our sister has died."

"Your sister. I'm sorry," I said.

Tears ran from his bloodshot eyes down along the furrowed wrinkles of his face. "Not my sister. Our sister. You have not heard? France has fallen."

France signed her surrender to Germany in the same spot, indeed in the same railroad car, in which the Germans had signed their surrender to the Allies twenty-two years ago.

And Rumanians went into shocked mourning. Bucharest had long been called the Paris of the Balkans. Rumania for over a century had felt far closer to France in culture and spirit than she did to any other nation. A newspaper editorial expressed the feelings of most Rumanians: "It becomes an almost physical pain, the thought of Nazi troops marching down the Champs Élysées; the thought of Nazi brutality tramping upon so many centuries of shining culture, of luminous intelligence and creative liberty."

The fall of France ended the myopia of Rumanians. It had happened there. It could happen here.

Perhaps the city was no more silent than it had been, but one felt that a hush of dread had descended. One passed a stranger on the street—and felt a kinship. For each of us knew that the other was filled with the same unspeakable sense of horror.

It was like standing helpless before some natural disaster over which human beings could have no control; a raging flood, a hurricane, an earthquake which sundered the continent of Europe.

King Carol reacted like an ant trying frantically to tread water in a raging river. His eyes were glued to Germany. Try to propitiate the Reich. Show them that they have no need to concern themselves about Rumania. We have our own home-grown Nazis. No need to send in German gauleiters.

On June seventh, Foreign Minister Gafencu "resigned." He was far too liberal, far too much a Francophile. Neutrality meant a pro-German, Premier Gigurtu. Tatarescu became Minister of Foreign Affairs.

But perhaps the entire government was not noticeably enough pro-Nazi. So the Renastere Nationala was transformed and reorganized into the Nation's Party. Completely totalitarian. With the King as its supreme chief. And with many important positions filled by members of the Iron Guard.

Horia Sima, head of the Iron Guard, was invited to come home from exile in Germany. He was made Minister of Education and Enlightenment. New anti-Semitic decrees were announced. There was a nationalization of industry. There were new party salutes. And new party uniforms.

Carol also issued a strange proclamation: "Those who by their own wish or by their actions place themselves outside the party discipline will be condemned to a vegetable existence."

This sounded, in any case, far less ominous than directives being issued throughout the nine Nazi-conquered countries. And we could only pray fervently that Hitler would consider King Carol sufficiently obedient and would not feel it necessary to divert troops into Rumania.

Then, to further clarify his position, the King made a speech declaring that he no longer wanted British guarantees or her friendship, and stressing his devotion to the Greater German Reich.

On June twenty-seventh, Radio Bucharest crackled with electrifying news. Another catastrophe was to be inflicted upon Rumania from another enemy.

Moscow had delivered an ultimatum to Bucharest. The whole of Bessarabia was to be returned to Russia at once. Russia had taken this province from Rumania in 1812. It was given back to Rumania in 1918. Now, said the Soviets, as "compensation for damages of Rumania's twenty-two-year occupation of Bessarabia," the USSR also demanded Northern Bukovina—which had never been part of the Russian Empire.

Czernowitz lay in Northern Bukovina.

I immediately placed four calls: to David, to my sister Bertha, to my aunt Bertha, and to Stefan's office. All lines were tied up. I tried again and again. To no avail. I sent four telegrams. *Come to Bucharest at once. I can arrange accommodation for all.*

The city of Bucharest was flooded with refugees from Poland. Every available room in the city had been rented by Poles. The hotels were crowded with Germans: so-called tourists, businessmen, government officials.

Accommodation in Bucharest was now an impossibility. But the first problem was to get my family, and Stefan's family to come. When they arrived I would worry about where and how to put them up. And then I would worry about how to get them out of the country.

At noon the radio reported that King Carol was meeting with his Crown Council and military authorities to consider the Russian ultimatum.

Then we learned that German and Italian ministers had arrived at the Royal Palace. On June tenth, Italy had officially joined the Axis and entered the war. Now the Reich was considerately allowing her ally to sit in on certain negotiations.

Would the visiting ministers advise the King to fight against Russia? Was the ultimatum as much of a surprise to the Axis as it was to Rumania? Or was the Russian ultimatum, in fact, only part of a Nazi-Soviet secret plan: to divide the entire continent between them just as they had already divided Poland?

The next few hours might bring the answer.

We sat by the radio in an anguish of anxiety, Orekhovsky, Alexander, Cotic and I. We all had family and friends in Northern Bukovina and in Bessarabia. Would they soon be cut off by a new national boundary line?

It was obvious that King Carol and his Crown Council could make no independent decisions. They must do what the Reich ministers decreed. Rumania was surrounded on three sides by enemies. England—the only remaining nation still fighting Hitler—seemed as far away as the moon.

The music which came over Radio Bucharest that afternoon was horrible, ludicrous. Waltzes and operettas when we waited for words, for news.

Then, at last, the report. King Carol had sent word to Moscow that he was appointing plenipotentiaries to negotiate the conditions put forth in the ultimatum. The King also announced that he had signed a mobilization decree to go into effect at six o'clock that evening.

It seemed that the Germans *had* been taken unawares by the Soviet ultimatum. Did they plan to use the Rumanian forces to inflict a few punishing punches at Russia's belly?

In any case it was made very clear that neither Germany nor Italy would help Rumania. If she fought Russia, she would fight alone.

That night all phone lines out of the country were cut. It had always been possible to at least reach an overseas operator. But no longer. At dawn my phone went dead.

When the post office opened the next morning I sent more telegrams to Czernowitz and Rădăuţi. I was told there was no guarantee they would be delivered.

That evening at 5 P.M., Radio Bucharest reported that Moscow had refused to negotiate about anything. The province of Bessarabia—would have four days to be evacuated. Then Russian troops would move in. But the cities of Czernowitz, Cetatea and Alba must be evacuated at once. By midnight.

I became frantic. They had seven hours in which to escape. How to reach them? How to make sure they would come?

My phone still was dead. I ran out, took a cab to Mandel's office. Perhaps he could get a call through. I must get to them, speak to them somehow. Before this became impossible.

Mandel had gone when I reached the bank. But his first secretary, Mr. Feuerstein, allowed me to use the phone. The line at least was not dead. But it might as well have been. There was the same infuriating refrain: "The circuits are tied up. Please try again later."

Feuerstein told me about the new official regulations for foreigners. "I'd advise you to get all your visas in order," he said. "It's not going to be easy to get out of Rumania quickly."

He showed me the sheet. The regulations might have been lifted from a Kafka novel. There were eight of them. One involved getting a permit to enter the Bureau for the Control of Foreigners in order to apply for permission to make out a form for permission to travel to a frontier. Another involved the purchase of an army stamp and an aviation stamp to place upon one's application. Still another stated that one must have the Secret Police certify that there was nothing of a prejudicial nature in the applicant's dossier.

I thanked Feuerstein for the information and promised to get my visas in order. It was obvious, however, that we must now acquire such documents through means other than the official sources.

I slept little that night, and my sleep was torn by terrifying dreams. I was a child again watching the Cossacks gallop across the fields toward me, their sabers flashing in the sunlight. . . . Then I was climbing up a steep, rocky mountainside, calling for Stefan. I came to the edge of a cliff and looked over. His body lay far below, a tiny figure sprawled on the rocks. Vultures swooped down to land on his dead body.

I woke up crying.

Over and over Stefan had said he was coming to Bucharest. And I had said no.

At dawn the sound of the telephone ripped through the stillness of my room.

It was my sister Bertha. She had received my wire. She had been trying all day and all night to get through to me.

They'd had a family conference; she and Takor, David and Sophie, my cousin Menachem and the aunts. They had all decided to remain in Czernowitz. "Don't you see, darling," she explained, "it's the best thing that could have happened. We'll be safe now under the Russians. They'll protect us from the Germans. It's you who have to worry, Rutichka. We all beg you to get out of Bucharest. Go back to your husband in Palestine. You must leave at once!"

For a moment I was so stunned that I could not speak. Then I started to shout at my sister. "*Safe?* The Russians will *protect* you? Protect! How can you use such a word! What about Proskurov?" I shrieked the name at her.

Proskurov was a town in the Ukraine. My father's family came from a village nearby. We had heard the stories often. One Saturday afternoon in February, Russian soldiers had been told by their leader Samocenco: "The town is yours. Take three hours off. Enjoy yourselves. Kill the Jews."

By sunset they had massacred some two thousand Jews; men, women and children. Eighteen hundred were maimed. Many of these died later. All had been slain or wounded with sabers. Not a bullet was wasted.

"Proskurov!" Bertha sounded incredulous that I should even mention the name of this town and this pogrom. "That was in 1919! This is 1940. It's a different world!"

"Is it?"

"Those were Cossacks who came to Proskurov! These are the people who fought the Cossacks—who fought the Czar!"

"These are the people allied with the Germans! These are the people—"

The line went dead. We had been cut off.

Once again I tried, over and over, to reach my sister or my brother David, or my aunts or Stefan.

Over and over the same refrain: "I am sorry. The circuits are tied up. Please place your call again later."

Maps were published in the newspapers; maps issued by the Russians showing how far their troops would advance each day. This, it was explained, was done to assure orderly evacuation.

But the evacuation was far from orderly. The papers and the radio reports were filled with tragic descriptions as hundreds of thousands of sudden refugees clogged the roads; Rumanians fleeing from Bessarabia and Northern Bukovina before the Russian troops marched in. So far as we could learn from those who poured into Bucharest, only a tiny per cent of the refugees were Jews. Ten per cent of the population of Bessarabia were Jews. Yet they did not flee. It seemed that the reasoning of my sister Bertha was prevalent throughout the province of Bessarabia and Northern Bukovina. And, perhaps, after all they were right. In this world, the lesser of evils could appear in the guise of a savior.

Then we heard other reports. The Rumanian Army was in full retreat. Yet, they took time out along the way to indulge in furious attacks on the Jews, whom they blamed for Russia's invasion. Communistjew. They made the term into one word; a violent curse as they tossed boulders into Jewish shop windows. As they chased and beat up Jews who ran before them down the narrow streets of the Jewish quarters.

The retreat of the Rumanian troops began on June 30, 1940.

Early the following morning I sat by my open window staring out at the leafy treetops of Rosetti Square. Sunshine spilled over the greens, highlighting colors. The sky above was a wash of pale blue. In a few hours mothers and nursemaids would bring their small children into the protected square to play.

A cable was slid under my door. I heard footsteps walking away down the hall.

The cable was in code. From Shmarya Zameret in Greece.

Shmarya had been ordered by the Haganah leaders to sell our ship the *Darien II* to the British. There must be no more delay. The British would pay us fifteen thousand pounds.

THIRTY-SIX

SELL THE DARIEN II to the British.

There were no undertones to these orders; no hidden suggestions—play along, pretend. Yehuda Arazi had won his case. He had even succeeded in splitting the Mossad. Most of our own men seemed now to believe that the *Darien* could indeed play a more important role if she were used as Arazi had directed. But Yulik and Shmarya and I did not believe this. Eleven hundred people were waiting at Kladovo. Waiting to be rescued by the *Darien*. This was the reality. All the rest were plans, proposals, politics. So the three of us agreed to proceed alone. We could do this, or we thought we could, for the ship was in Shmarya's name. We could do this, but it meant defying the direct orders of men who had been our father figures; men we respected more than any others in the world.

Sell the *Darien* to the British.

To Great Britain, our implacable enemy.

To Great Britain, our valiant hero.

Listening to the news reports, or looking at the newly drawn maps which were constantly being printed in the newspapers, it was not difficult to see why our leaders had issued the orders. If there was anything we could do to help; anything anyone could do—that must be done.

For Britain fought alone.

Within the past eleven months most of the countries in Europe had either been conquered by Germany or had joined with her. Austria. Czechoslovakia. Poland. Norway. Denmark. Holland. Belgium. France. Each had fallen within a matter of days or at most, weeks. Hungary, Italy, obedient Axis partners. Spain ruled by Hitler's friend, the dictator Franco. And to the east, Russia; now joined to the Nazis by political pact. Russia and *her* conquests: Estonia, Latvia, Lithuania and Finland.

Opposing all this massive weight of manpower, raw materials, farm produce, factories to make the machinery of war and German armed forces which had been preparing for this Blitzkrieg of a continent for more than a decade—opposing all this was one island, utterly unprepared for war. Great Britain.

While German youth were being taught that they were a superrace with a destiny to rule the world by force of arms, British youth were brought up to be ardent pacifists. The other countries of Europe had compulsory conscription between the two wars. Not Britain. Indeed, most Englishmen regarded their tiny regular army as an escape career for young men who couldn't get a decent job.

All political parties in Great Britain had vigorously espoused a policy of disarmament.

Chamberlain, the peace-in-our-times Prime Minister, had not fallen from power until May 10, 1940, nine months after Britain declared war on Germany. And our haver in London had told us that when Prime Minister Winston Churchill walked through certain sections of the city, epithets were still shouted at him—particularly the word "warmonger."

Great Britain. The only country in the world fighting the greatest menace the world had ever known.

The United States? Concerned citizens had organized a Bundles for Britain campaign. They sent food packages to the British, who were on near-starvation rations. On July fourteenth, the United States State Department announced a simplification of procedures so that a certain number of British parents who wanted to ship their children to safety could send them to the States on a visitor's visa "for the duration." Some American animal lovers wrote to British newspapers offering to adopt dogs and cats which might otherwise be killed in the bombing raids.

As for military aid, there was none. Not even the firm promise of aid which would be forthcoming should Germany dare to invade the British Isles.

Britain fought on, totally alone.

It seemed that simple statistics were enough to sound her death knell.

The combined population of the United Kingdom—England, Wales, Scotland and Northern Ireland—was 48,188,000. The population of Germany alone was 80,000,000.

The Reich could bring Britain to her knees by air raids and a sea blockade; it seemed inevitable.

In normal times Britain produced only three fifths of the food her people needed; the rest was imported. In normal times Britain lived by exporting manufactured goods abroad; and she produced only twenty per cent of the raw materials she needed for making those manufactured goods. Import and export were her veins and arteries; her lifeline. But now her sea lanes were mined and patrolled by German ships. Heavy cruisers. Battleships. Destroyers. And submarine packs which could berth and refuel in the neutral ports of the Republic of Ireland.

How long could Britain survive?

France, with her well-fortified Maginot Line, with three million well-trained, well-armed men in her fighting forces; France, reputedly the best-prepared nation in Europe—France had fallen in thirty-eight days.

Britain? We had been told the date of her demise: August fifteenth. On that day, said Adolf Hitler, Germany's conquest of the British Isles would be complete.

In the meantime, the people of Britain would be bombed into submission.

We listened with horror to BBC news reports.

The blackouts in London were useless, for the city was illuminated every night by raging fires which turned the skies red. Docks, wharves, installations, railroad stations, utilities; targets of nighttime and daylight bombing. Strategic bombing preparatory to invasion. And nonstrategic bombing, preparatory to invasion. Low-diving Stukas shrieking down from the skies.

The noise was a weapon. We could hear it sometimes on our shortwave radio. The distant drone and throb of bombers—swelling ominously as planes approached their targets. The scream and whistle of the falling bombs. The thud—and the shattering explosion.

And we heard the speech of Sir Hugh Ellis, chief of Britain's Civil Defense, as he put the matter plainly before his countrymen: "As sure as God made little apples, we are going to get a lot more bombing. It's the noise that frightens. Don't be frightened. Be angry. It's a good cure."

"Anger," Orekhovsky said very quietly. "Yes, indeed, that is certainly a powerful weapon against bombs."

The British had other notable weapons. Stirrup pumps, for example. Men and women on rooftops armed with buckets of water and a foot pump—to fight the roaring blazes of thousands of incendiary bombs which, in addition to the high explosives, were dropped on the cities every day and every night.

And the British had balloons! Barrage balloons attached to trucks by long steel cables; balloons which made huge, clumsy potshot targets for Luftwaffe air gunners.

And Boy Scout staves. There were not enough rifles to go around so thousands of men in the Home Guard went into training to repel the invasion using mop handles and staves.

Britain, of course, was covered by a taut blanket of censorship. But we learned some of the dismal details through coded messages sent us by our haverim in London.

August fifteenth arrived.

Somehow none of us had made appointments on that day. We gathered in the apartment on the Strada Rosetti, as if attending a wake.

Hitler kept to his promise. The bombing England had thus far endured was but a foretaste of the havoc which struck on Britain's predicted day of demise: August fifteenth.

The radio reports were horrible. It seemed that every bomber in the Luftwaffe had been mustered to blacken the skies above London and other cities. And every bombing squadron was surrounded by a host of protective fighter planes which made the carriers of death almost invincible.

Hour after hour they came, waves of German planes sheering in. Flying at different heights. At different speeds. Making defense an impossibility. Turning entire sections of the cities into masses, mazes of flame and rubble.

It was impossible to think that the British could endure this day.

Yet, around teatime we heard the impossible and the incredible. Britain's Overseas League had planned a mammoth tea party on August fifteenth for His Majesty's forces from overseas. And the party was being held. In London. The target of most of the bombs.

In the midst of the terror, destruction and death, the British were serving tea.

The German planes kept coming. All that night. All the next day. And the next. There was no cessation. No letup in intensity.

Yet, there was no talk of surrender. Nor were there any reports of German invasion barges or massing of troops on the seacoasts of France, Belgium and Holland. When *would* the invasion begin? Had Hitler been bluffing? Was he not ready? Was it possible that the anti-aircraft guns on British commons and rooftops, and the persistent British fighters in the RAF had given the Germans cause to reassess their invasion plans?

We knew that the Royal Air Force had prototypes of some excellent planes; most of them still on the assembly lines. We knew that thousands of boys in the RAF had been shot out of the skies while still in training schools.

Yet this skeletal air force seemed to be engaged in constant dogfights with bombers. RAF planes soared up to ambush German Stukas returning home empty of ammunition. And, most incredible of all, RAF planes—fifty or more a night—would sally forth from their home base to bomb German cities.

It was the first time victory-logged Germans had felt the war on their own soil. Was this what stayed Hitler's invasion orders?

Day after day went by. Germany kept up her massive air raids. Fleets of bombers . . . four hundred . . . five hundred planes every day. Every night. Bombarding British cities. But the British held out. With simple, stoic, plodding heroism they refused to give up.

By the end of August the invasion still had not come.

And by the end of August I had still heard nothing from or about my family in Czernowitz or Emmanuel's family in Rădăuţi. Again and again I tried to get word to them. But there was no telephone service. No mail service. No cable service. Czernowitz and Rădăuţi had not only been swallowed up by another nation; it was as though they had fallen off the map altogether.

There were many reports from the Rumanian soldiers who had fled before the invading Russian Army; reports of roads clogged with refugees fleeing into Greater Rumania. But not Jews. Jews had fled the other way. Thousands upon thousands of Jewish families from Czernowitz, Rădăuţi, Jassy, Galati had run toward the Russians.

And more and more reports came of slaughtering and pogroms as Rumanian soldiers in a morass of humiliation turned with fury on the Jews. Why would the Jews be running toward Russia if they had not collaborated? The Jews were responsible for Rumania's ignominious loss of her provinces! Kill the Jews!

Were members of my family among those on the roads; among those slaughtered in the streets? Or was Sophie still sitting in her new apartment on Siebenbürgerstrasse waiting for the living-room furniture to be delivered?

And my brother Arthur in the concentration camp at Theresienstadt; was he still alive? His wife and little Erika? There still was no word of them at all.

And Stefan.

Somehow I felt certain that he would find a way to get a message to me. Love finds a way. Those worn words; leftovers from another world. But I still believed them.

Yet, there was nothing. Day after day, nothing.

Then, at the end of August, another totally unexpected event blackened Rumanian headlines.

Rumanian Premier Gigurtu returned from the Reich. He had been summoned there by the Axis powers to attend a so-called Arbitration. As a reward to the Hungarians for siding at once with the Nazis, the Italian and German representatives at the Vienna Arbitration, had forced Rumania to cede half of Transylvania to Hungary.

The afternoon that the news came out I passed by the Palace, at least as close to it as I could get.

The Palace Square was dark with mobs of enraged citizens. It was a Sunday. But it seemed that no one had gone to church; no one was strolling in the parks. Bucharestians were drawn as if by a magnet to the Royal Palace. And the magnet was hatred. Hatred for their King. They shook their fists. They shouted for his head! And their chant grew and swelled down the city streets. "We will never give up Transylvania! We will never give up Transylvania!"

Suddenly gendarmes appeared in gas masks, and two armored cars with revolving turrets. From the turrets came streams of ice-cold water, which sufficed to disperse the crowds. But it did not extinguish the anger.

Orekhovsky was in the apartment when I returned home.

"Have you seen the new map?" He held it up, a newspaper drawing of the newly diminished Rumania. "Do you realize that when the Vienna decree was signed yesterday, the death warrants of one hundred fifty thousand Jews were also signed. One hundred fifty thousand Rumanian Jews who now can be handed over to the Nazis as further proof of Hungary's loyalty to Herr Hitler."

The revulsion of feeling and the revolt against King Carol did not die out as he, perhaps, had anticipated. Indeed, it spread like a series of separate fires throughout the land. In Bucharest, day and night, on this street or that, crowds would suddenly materialize to march and shout. Some were anti-Axis. Some were anti-Hungarian. Some were anti-Jews. The cries crescendoed into a strange contradictory chorus. Down with the Germans. Down with the Jews. But the chief rage seemed to be against the King who had handed over so much of his kingdom, first to the Russians, then to the Reich.

"What could the poor fellow do?" Orekhovsky said. "He is just pulling another Chamberlain. Trying to keep his country out of war. Or—what he has left of his country."

But I heard few such sympathetic comments during those days. Everyone in his own private fear and fury seemed to gain some inner relief by using the King of the land as whipping boy.

Then, in what was undoubtedly a Machiavellian scheme to throw the country into civil war—thereby making its conquest far easier—the Reich demanded that King Carol fulfill *Bulgaria's* territorial requests. At a conference held at Craiova, Rumania was forced to give Southern

Dobruja to Bulgaria. (She had held the territory since 1913.) In this swift move Hitler assured himself of the end of King Carol, who had publicly cut all ties with Britain—but who, nevertheless, could not be considered completely "reliable" in Nazi terms.

When the outcome of the Treaty of Craiova was announced, it was as though benzine had been hosed onto the fires of indignation alight already throughout the land. A bitter joke made the rapid rounds of the Bucharest cafes. "King Carol is the kind of man who would sell his own mother's heart—and did!"

Balchik was in Southern Dobruja. Queen Marie's heart lay in its casket of gold in the chapel at her Balchik villa.

Hostile crowds now massed day and night in the square before the Royal Palace. In two months King Carol had given away one third of Rumania. King Carol must go.

On the evening of September fourth, a car drove into the Palace Square. Leaflets were tossed out the window; leaflets headlined: "AB-DICATE: THAT IS THE CRY OF THE NATION!" Then shots were fired at a lighted window in the Palace. And the car sped away.

At noon the next day it was announced that Prime Minister Gigurtu had resigned. The King had appointed General Ion Antonescu as the new Prime Minister.

Antonescu! Just three weeks ago the King had placed the general under house arrest. Antonescu had been confined in a convent at Bistritsa because of his outspoken insistence that Carol should have fought to keep Bessarabia.

Antonescu, the short, red-faced, hot-tempered strong man whom they called Red Dog. He was not a Guardist. But he was a man the Iron Guard might listen to. Perhaps that was why the King called upon the general to save the chaotic situation. For it was the Guardists who led most of the anti-Carol demonstrations.

The general did save the situation. By kicking out the King.

By the following afternoon Rumania had a new king. Antonescu read the short precise proclamation into the microphone of Radio Bucharest, and performed the swearing-in ceremonies as eighteen-year-old Prince Michael became King of Rumania.

But it was clear that henceforth the real ruler of the country would be the pro-German general, who had given himself the title *Conducator*, the Rumanian term for *Führer*.

Suddenly Bucharest turned green. Shopkeepers, tram drivers, waiters, postmen, street sweepers, hotel porters, office workers; men we knew and spoke with every day and had never suspected of being Guardists came to work wearing green shirts, the uniform of the Iron Guard. Guardists seemed to have taken over the city. The Green Revolution, people called it.

At 4 A.M. on the morning of September eighth, the former King Carol, his mistress Lupescu, their dogs, several servants, the commander of the Royal Guards, and the Court Chamberlain left town in the royal train. On the train, according to newspaper reports, were three or four automobiles (with bullet-proof windows), many of the ex-King's valuable oil paintings, his stamp collection, trunks full of clothing and, it was surmised, as much gold coinage and jewelry as Carol and his consort could lay their hands on.

Then, as a final dashing ending to his colorful royal career, came the chase at Timisoara, the last town before the Rumanian-Yugoslav frontier. The royal train had been scheduled to stop there to take on water. But the stationmaster at Timisoara, a loyal King's man, received word that a group of Guardists planned to ambush the train and kill the King. The stationmaster wired to the train's engineer.

Instead of stopping, the train raced through Timisoara. The Guardists opened fire with machine guns, then climbed aboard a locomotive in the Timisoara railway yards, held a pistol at the head of the engineer and forced him to give chase to the royal train.

Carol, however, with something of a head start made it in safety across the border.

One of the royal servants later returned to Bucharest and gave the newspapers a vivid report of the flight. Before the train reached Timisoara, he said, Lupescu had been put into the bathtub in the bathroom of the royal sleeping car. Here, they told her, she would be protected against bullets. When the train reached Timisoara and a hail of bullets smashed the windows of the royal private car, ex-King Carol II jumped into the bathtub too.

In less than a month, without a bullet wasted or a regiment deployed, the Reich had, in effect, taken over Rumania. The Guardists were efficient stand-ins for Nazi storm troopers. Endlessly the Guardists marched through the city streets shouting their slogans and their songs and carrying high the placards of their dead leader, Codreanu.

The Iron Guard was also known by the poetic title Legion of the Archangel Michael. On September fifteenth, Antonescu announced that Rumania was now a National Legionnaire State. He appointed the fanatic Guardist Horia Sima as Vice-Premier, and installed thousands of Guardists in government posts. Antonescu himself donned the green shirt, the riding breeches, the shiny black boots, with spurs; uniform of the Iron Guard. And he proclaimed himself official chief of the Legion of the Archangel Michael.

The Legionnaire salute was suddenly seen everywhere. Once Bucharestians had laughed at this strange calisthenic (pat chest with right hand, slap forehead with palm of right hand, followed by straight-armed Nazi salute). They laughed no longer. It was as though Antonescu had turned the country over to an organization of madmen, who fed on terrorism, anti-Semitism and mysticism. In the initiation ceremony a new Guardist member had to suck blood from a slash in the arm of every member of his "nest." He was then required to write, in his own blood, an oath that he would commit murder whenever ordered to do so. And before starting out on an expedition which might involve murder, each member of the nest had to cut his own wrist, let an ounce of his blood flow into a goblet, mingling with the blood of the other members. Then each man drank from the goblet.

Under King Carol, the Iron Guard had been illegal. Most of the top-ranking Legionnaires had spent time in prison. Now the lawbreakers were suddenly the leaders of the country and the law of the land.

As might be expected, most of the new laws passed were anti-Semitic decrees. They came thick and fast, as though Rumania must catch up in a month to all the anti-Semitic decrees passed in Germany during the eight years of Adolf Hitler's reign.

No Jew could sign a legal document. No Jew could drive an automobile. No Jew could employ a Gentile woman under forty. A business that employed so much as one Jew would be classified as a Jewish establishment. No Jew could buy food from a peasant. A Christian who married a Jew would be classified as a Jew. Only the oldest son or daughter in a Jewish family was permitted to marry. And on and on.

Suddenly, all over the city—all over what remained of the country—Jews who had thought themselves situated for life were unemployed. This, coupled with the certainty that they could not be rehired anywhere, brought about a state of near panic.

It can't happen here. How many times, in how many varying words, had I heard that refrain when I pleaded with Rumanian Jews to get out. While there still was a way. While there still was time. Now it was happening here. Now there was no more time.

We had only one ship, the *Darien.* Or did we have it? And even if we did, the space had been promised months ago to the eleven hundred Jews trapped at Kladovo.

Spitzer telephoned almost every night. With increasing desperation. He needed money. More money. It was costing the equivalent of two thousand dollars a day to support the men, women and children at Kladovo. I must send him money, at once. Unless I wanted them all to starve.

I tried to tell him that money was almost impossible to come by in Bucharest. "What about the Joint?" I asked several times. I'd been told that the Joint Distribution Committee was sending money regularly to the Kladovo Jews.

Each time he gave the same incomprehensible answer. "Joint? *Was ist das?* What is that?"

When I pressed him further he would shout at me; it seemed that the telephone wires must quiver with his frenzied passion. *"Fragen Sie mich nicht! Fragen Sie mich nicht!* Don't question me!"

Sometimes he sounded like a man who was losing his mind.

Spitzer's one question—which came over and over—was *"Wann kommt das Schiff?* When is the ship coming?" I dared not tell him of the conflict concerning the *Darien II.*

At the end of October, Italy declared war on Greece. Six waves of Italian bombers roared over the country; bombed the Athens airport and the port of Piraeus. The *Darien* was being reconverted at Piraeus. Did our ship still exist?

Communications to Greece had been cut. I could not reach Shmarya. Again and again I tried. By phone. By cable. Nothing.

Nothing except dismal news reports. The Greeks were fighting back. They had one hundred airplanes, most of them obsolete. It was reported that Greek men and women were climbing into the mountains, dragging cannon behind them.

The Greeks were fighting valiantly. But how long could they hope to hold out? And how long before the Germans came in?

We had at least expected that Antonescu's new Iron Guard regime would keep the Germans out of Rumania. Indeed, we were certain that this was why the Red Dog—who had never been a Guardist— now so loudly and proudly proclaimed himself leader of the Legion of the Archangel Michael. And why, on September thirtieth, he had signed a Tripartite Pact; formally tying Rumania to Germany and Italy. But it seemed that Hitler did not sufficiently trust Antonescu, though the general had been an ardent pro-Nazi from the start of Hitler's regime.

On October seventh and eighth, two motorized divisions of thirty thousand German soldiers occupied the oil wells in and around Ploesti. By mid-October the first contingent of a German military mission arrived in Bucharest, headed by two generals and a number of high-ranking officers. Suddenly, the German businessmen and tourists who filled the city's hotels donned their military uniforms. Everywhere one went there were German soldiers and officers.

Most Bucharestians seemed to polish up their rose-colored glasses and continue on with their lives in an unconcerned manner. Their capital city had now been visibly taken over by a foreign power, yet they did not appear to notice.

Late one night I was on the telephone, talking to Spitzer. He informed me that many of the Jews had been taken off the riverboats at Kladovo and had been moved to tents and huts on land near Sabac. The Yugoslav Government had allocated this land to the refugees until such time as a ship was readied to transport them out of Europe.

When I asked what living conditions were like in the new camp and why the people had been moved, he answered in the sentence which had now become a frenzied refrain from him. *"Fragen Sie mich nicht!*" He followed with his second refrain, asked always with high-pitched tension: *"Wann kommt das Schiff?"*

Suddenly the line went dead.

This was not unusual. Then I noticed that the chandelier was swaying gently. This was unusual. It was a warm Indian summer's night. The windows were open wide. But there was no wind.

There came a crash from the kitchenette. Dishes falling, breaking. Then a terrible thunder. The room shook. The bed in which I sat started moving across the floor.

The lights went out.

I heard screaming from the hallways of the house.

Hunks of plaster fell from the ceiling.

Should I get under the bed? But the bed kept moving. Sliding.

Someone was pounding on my door. "Ruth, are you there? Are you all right?"

It was the landlord, Mr. Schecter.

I ran across the room in the shaking darkness, unlocked the door.

He stood there, in his pajamas, holding a candle. "Hurry!" he shouted at me. "An earthquake. It's safer to be in the street!" He grabbed my arm. Pulled me down the hallway behind him.

We gathered in the street, tenants from our building and from other buildings. All in nightgowns or pajamas. Mrs. Schecter carried a little boy in her arms. The child was crying. Everyone else was quiet. In soft voices we asked each other, "Where should we run to? Which place is safe?"

Since there was no answer, we stayed outside in the street, hearing the screams, the sirens, the clanging bells of fire engines. The quaking of the earth had stopped. Would it start again? Was it safe to go inside?

It started to rain. Still we stood there; no one even mentioned the rain.

Finally, faint rivulets of dawn started to streak the night sky. This somehow offered reassurance. We said good night to each other in a polite half-embarrassed manner. We returned to our rooms and our lives.

I went into the kitchen, and in the dull light of the early morning, I started to sweep up the broken dishes and the fallen plaster.

Shortly after seven there was a knock on my door.

David Arnon entered. Ordinarily his voice was full of vigor, his manner charged with strength and ebullience. Now he sat slumped on a kitchen chair. His face was pale. His voice was pale.

I'd heard no reports. The radio was dead. The phone was dead.

David Arnon gave me reports. Told me what he had seen.

He had come down the Boulevard Brătianu, past what had been the Carlton Building, the proud skyscraper of Bucharest. The first three floors housed a theatre. There were ten floors of apartments above the theatre. On top of the ten floors was a lookout tower, from which one could see all over Bucharest.

"The Carlton Building," said David, in his strange soft voice, "now reaches only to the second floor of the building next door to it. The Carlton just collapsed in the quake. Three hundred people in the apartments. Dead. I was helping to pull out the bodies. We found a mother who had thrown herself over her baby's crib. The mother was dead. The baby was alive. We pulled out bodies of German officers. Each one was with a girl. A half hour ago the German Army came in with anti-aircraft searchlights, bulldozers. They told us all to go away. They took over the job of pulling out bodies."

"Was it just the Carlton? Just that tall building?"

David shook his head. "Hundreds of people are dead. All over the city. Thousands are wounded." Unconsciously he used the battle term. "Private homes . . . public buildings collapsed. Or damaged. It's not safe to walk in the streets. The place is like a realm of rubble. All over the city chimneys have fallen off. Balconies have fallen down. Walls of buildings collapsed." He looked up at me. "The world isn't blowing to bits fast enough. We had to have this too. You look at the destruction—the death. And there's no one to hate. Hatred at least is a little release. But this—an Act of God. You have nobody to hate."

I made breakfast. Then I left. I had an appointment to see the Shamen at his apartment. If his apartment still stood. If the Shamen were still alive.

THIRTY-SEVEN

THE SHAMEN was very much alive. He greeted me with open arms, then a crushing embrace, in relief and delight at the fact that I had escaped harm.

Indeed, all our haverim had escaped unhurt.

The filing cabinets at the Palestine Office had, however, been flung across the room, their contents disgorged all over the floor. Orekhovsky, Alexander and I spent hours that night trying to put the files back in order again. There were thousands upon thousands of applications. Each with its own separate story of desperation. Each name, each family was living somehow, somewhere in Bucharest. Each waiting, day after day, for a way out. Only to be told day after day that there were no legal certificates. No illegal ships. Nothing. Not yet. Be patient. Perhaps tomorrow. Perhaps next week we can offer you some hope. Your name is on file. Your case will receive every consideration. Try to hang on.

We told each applicant of course that if he could find any possible way out of the country he should take it. But the answer was always the same. Escape, yes. But where? Who will have us?

Though millions of Jews were now in dire peril, immigration restrictions around the world had not lessened. Indeed, the ever-swelling numbers of Jews frantic to get out of Europe had served only to further terrify nations that might have offered a haven, even nations suffering from underpopulation. Many countries had hastily passed even more stringent immigration restrictions. The diplomatic language differed. But the reading was always the same. No Jews wanted. No Jews allowed.

Still the only spot on the entire globe which had no restrictions on immigration was the international city of Shanghai. But it was almost impossible to get there. And the city was already bursting at the seams with some twenty thousand European Jews, most of whom were unemployed.

Still the only spot on the entire globe in which Jews were actively welcomed was Palestine. Welcomed by the Jews of Palestine. Welcomed and needed and not allowed to enter. Because of the British. To dwell on this situation also brought one brinking to madness.

The British were so desperate for ships that, in mid-September, they had acquired fifty overage destroyers from the United States—at an extraordinarily high price. They had given the United States naval and air bases in Newfoundland and Bermuda. And they had leased to the United States further air and naval bases in the Bahamas, Jamaica, St. Lucia, Trinidad, Antigua and British Guiana.

Yet, despite their all-too-obvious critical need for ships, the British were still deploying a destroyer and patrol boats to police the coastlines of Palestine—in order to make very certain that no fishing vessel or ancient cargo ship jammed with Jewish refugees should succeed in landing on the night beaches.

Why?

With our heads we could even make some answer to this question. Some of the Arab nations were actively pro-Axis. But others were still, in a manner of speaking, neutral. There was Egypt, which held the key to the British lifeline to her empire: the Suez Canal. And there was the strategic matter of Arab oil. Yes, all right, if she felt it a diplomatic necessity let Britain officially bow to Arab pressure. Fly the White Paper high.

But with our hearts we could not understand why Britain was so bulldoggedly diligent about enforcing these White Paper restrictions. Could not her tommies who patrolled the night beaches sometimes just look the other way? Must Britain assign her speediest patrol boats to ply the seas off Palestine's shores? We certainly made no announcements about the number of illegals who entered Palestine. Why could the British not keep silent? Why must they close, bar and bolt this last entryway to survival?

For two weeks after the earthquake Bucharestians were busy clearing away the piles of debris from crumbled walls, fallen balconies, shattered window glass. Meanwhile, as if spurred on by the sight and the smell of destruction, the Guardists began rampaging through the city at unexpected hours. They would knock on doors, burst into private homes, confiscating whatever pleased them. The homes of Jews, of course. But also the homes of non-Jews. People were terrorized and afraid to protest—for to whom could they protest? The Guardists were demanding resignations of functionaries high and low; the vacancies were filled with their own incompetent members. A policeman who tried to arrest a plundering Guardist ran the very real risk of being fired at once.

So complaints of terrified civilians went unheard.

What had happened to the Red Dog, the powerful General Antonescu? It seemed that he, like everyone else, feared the Iron Guard; did not know how to control them. So the country was ruled by lawbreakers, governed by anarchy.

On the evening of November twenty-seventh, I returned to my apartment; heard the telephone ringing as I unlocked the door. I ran to answer.

"Ruth. Thank God, you're safe. Don't leave your apartment. Bolt your door."

It took several moments for me to recognize the strange, taut voice. George Mandel.

He described to me then the death of his friend. The murder of his friend Dr. Nicholas Iorga. Dr. Iorga, former Premier of Rumania. Dr. Iorga, world-renowned scholar. Dr. Iorga, beloved and adulated throughout Rumania. Known as "The Teacher of the Nation."

Dr. Nicholas Iorga, one of the few important men in the country who had dared to speak out against the Iron Guard.

They had come—Mandel could barely get out the words—seven Guardists. They had pounded on the door of Iorga's home. They had ordered the seventy-nine-year-old man to come with them. They all

408

had guns. They had walked him at a fast pace toward Jilava Prison at the edge of Bucharest. After three hours they reached their destination, a spot in the forest near Jilava, where their leader Codreanu and thirteen other Guardists had been shot and buried two years ago. There they tortured the old man. They killed him. And they left him lying in a ditch.

When Mandel stopped talking the telephone line went dead or seemed to. I could not speak, nor could he. But we were still connected.

Then Mandel said, "They have also killed Dr. Virgil Madgearu. My source did not know the details of that death."

Madgearu was one of the leaders of the Peasant Party; another of the very few who had dared to speak out vehemently against the Iron Guard.

Neither Dr. Madgearu nor Dr. Iorga were Jews.

"You must leave the country at once," Mandel said. "Are your papers in order?"

"I can't leave," I told him. "I saw the Shamen last night. He thinks he has his hands on a ship. We must start to work on it at once. Besides—have I told you—the *Darien* is safe. She escaped the bombing. She'll be sailing soon for Kladovo. I can't possibly leave here. There's suddenly so much we can do. I've got to—"

He cut me short, sharply. "You can work from Bulgaria. Or Turkey. Listen to me. I have information. You have got to believe me. You must leave at once. Take the two boys with you. And Alexander. You've got to get out. Tonight. I'm trying to arrange for a car. God knows what will happen here in the next few days."

"What sort of information do you have?" I asked.

"Just trust me and believe what I say. Destroy what you don't want to be found. Are your papers in order? Did you take Feuerstein's advice? Did you get your visas?"

"Look," I said, "when do *you* plan to leave?"

There was silence.

I repeated my question. The question I had asked since I first met Mandel fifteen months ago.

He inevitably answered with some evasive statement.

Now I said what I had never said before. "I won't go unless you come with us. Why should we take your advice when you don't follow it?"

"I can't."

"Why can't you?" I flung his words back at him: "God knows what will happen here in the next few days. You may be next. If they learn how you have helped us—"

"My wife," he said, "is an invalid. She can't leave the house—much less leave the country."

He had rarely spoken to me of his wife. He had never mentioned this.

One could not say: Leave Rumania, leave your wife. I said nothing. But I felt with dread certainty that my silence was speaking with certain prediction: Mandel and his invalid wife would be murdered in the home they could not leave.

That evening I spent destroying papers; tearing them into the toilet bowl, flushing them into extinction. I kept only my contact book; during the hours ahead I would have to commit hundreds of names and telephone numbers to memory. And I kept all of Stefan's letters. But I burned the envelopes, and I cut up pages which contained passages through which Stefan might be traced.

There was still no communication between the so-called Old Kingdom of Rumania, and the section which now was part of Soviet Russia. But if Stefan somehow got across the border, if he came to Bucharest, I did not want his life endangered because of a sentence in a love letter.

As I read through the letters once more . . . and still again . . . memories twined with daydreams of the future. The unexpected telephone call . . . his knock on the door. Over and over I lived the moments of our reunion. At first we would not speak because we could not speak because he was holding me. He would hold me in his arms until we could not stand up any longer.

Was it possible that we had been alone in peace and privacy in a hotel room in the Schwarzer Adler, and I sent him away?

Mandel had made me promise not to go out, not to unlock my door to any stranger. He was arranging for a car to drive me to the border. In the meantime, I must sit and wait.

I waited with two companions, the radio and the telephone.

Orekhovsky was at home. I tried to persuade him to come with us, if indeed we did have to leave Rumania. He was adamant. His work was here. Finally, in answer to my frantic pleas, he hung up on me. I rang again and again, but he did not pick up the telephone.

I tried to reach Alexander. I could not find him. Nor could I locate David Arnon or Yitzhak or Cotic. The Shamen. Arkadi. No one answered the telephone. Where were they all? I began to feel like a prisoner in my room.

Yet, as I listened to the radio I saw no point at all in disobeying Mandel's orders.

Throughout that night and the next day horrific reports filled the airways. Radio Bucharest was stifled by censorship. But somehow foreign correspondents were getting the story out. I learned what was happening in Rumania from stations in France, England, even Germany. The newscasters on Radio Berlin seemed delighted to report the full details of Rumania's self-massacre. As if to authenticize the veracity of its news reports, Radio Berlin kept quoting American press dispatches.

The murders of Iorga and Madgearu had served as incendiaries to the Iron Guard. During the next twenty-four hours several hundred more Rumanian intellectuals were killed by Guardists.

Civil war exploded throughout the country. The Regular Army vs. the Iron Guard. It was reported that the Guardists held the strategic Danube town of Turnu-Severin, the town which topped the treacherous Iron Gate Rapids and which, therefore, could control river traffic. It was reported that the Army had taken the city of Brasov.

The government buildings were split, as was the country. Guardist machine gunners were stationed on rooftops and in courtyards of some of the buildings. Non-Guardist government officials had taken refuge in the Department of the Interior.

Guardists were also warring among themselves. One faction had formed around Vice-Premier Horia Sima, another around the father of the Iron Guard's founder, hero and official martyr, Corneliu Codreanu. At the Green House, Bucharest headquarters of the Iron Guard, the two sides shot it out. Two priests were killed, as well as the brother of the dead Codreanu.

Then came a grisly announcement, fraught with explosive danger.

The Guardists had discovered and had disinterred the body—the remains—of Corneliu Codreanu. Their hero. Their leader. Their *Capitanul.*

And they had dug up the bodies of the thirteen Guardists who had been shot and secretly buried with Codreanu two years ago, on the orders of Premier Calinescu.

The Legion of the Archangel Michael. Mystical. Hysterical. With the drinking of blood as part of their initiation ritual. What havoc would now be wrought in the name of the disinterred bodies already being hailed as the Fourteen Martyrs?

The answer came almost at once. The Radio Bucharest newscaster reported that Guardists had stormed into Jilava Prison where sixty-four important Rumanian officials were behind bars. They included a former Premier, a former Minister of Justice, three other former Cabinet members, three generals, and the former police chief of Bucharest. All sixty-four had been locked up on orders of Antonescu who had been given his orders by the Iron Guard. The sixty-four, the Guardists had claimed, all played some part in the murder of Codreanu. They had, therefore, been sent to Jilava Prison to await trial.

But there was no trial. The Guardists broke into the prison. They shot and killed all sixty-four.

Then, within minutes, came a further announcement on the radio. It was obvious that a Guardist had shoved aside the station broadcaster. His voice held the hysterical jubilance I had heard so often in the speeches of Adolf Hitler.

Tomorrow, he screamed, Saturday, would be two years to the day since their leader Capitanul Codreanu had been murdered. The Legion of the Archangel Michael would make certain that the nation revered his memory in a fitting way. The fourteen coffins would lie in state at the Church of Ilie Gorgani. At this very moment, all over the country, Guardists were on special trains, heading toward Bucharest for tomorrow's ceremonies. Thousands upon thousands of the Capitanul's loyal followers would mass in the city. All offices, shops, public buildings were to be closed for the day. All public buildings in Bucharest must be draped with green flags. All newspapers throughout the country must print a memorial edition in green ink or on green paper. In every church throughout Rumania masses must be said for the martyrs from sunrise to sunset. And at ten-thirty in the morning every church bell in the nation must toll for half an hour in memory of the Fourteen Martyrs.

Was this the information Mandel had received? Was this why he insisted we leave the country at once? What else would happen on the Day of the Fourteen Martyrs?

Again and again I tried to reach my haverim in Bucharest. The unanswered ring at the other end of the telephone line began to sound like a death rattle. Where was everyone? In hiding? Arrested? Or merely afraid to answer the phone.

During that long night came the reports I had been expecting. Throughout the country loyal members of the Iron Guard who had been unable to board a train to Bucharest decided to celebrate the Day of the Martyrs in a traditional manner which would please the dead Capitanul. Nor did they even wait till dawn before starting their rampages through the Jewish sections of towns and cities; looting, burning, killing.

Always before in this apartment I had longed for a bit of privacy. Now that I desperately wanted someone, anyone, with me I was totally alone.

The air in my room crackled with fear. Fear emanating from the radio and, it seemed, from my very soul. In action I felt no fear. But here, confined, trapped, unable to do anything at all, fear settled in like a debilitating disease.

The telephone was ominously silent. Only Mandel rang up several times to warn me over and again not to go out. To keep the door locked. Had I destroyed incriminating papers? Was I packed and ready to leave at a moment's notice? He was still trying to arrange for a car. It appeared that every hired car in Bucharest had been booked up for the funeral parade. To use the car of any private person would of course put the owner in immediate jeopardy were we apprehended on the road.

The radio announcer who reported on the funeral services was eloquent. He seemed determined that those who could not get into the Church of Ilie Gorgani would be carried along to the ceremonies through his vivid words.

Over one hundred fifty thousand people pressing into the church and the public square facing the church and the streets leading to the church. People weeping, screaming and cheering.

The fourteen green caskets trimmed with gold atop a new-built wooden altar in the public square. On the hundred steps of the altar funeral urns issuing smoke and the strong scent of burning incense. And in the hastily built reviewing stand, the officials. Antonescu in his Iron Guard uniform. Vice-Premier Sima. The international delegations. Hitler Jugend. Italian Fascisti. Spanish Falangista. There was even a delegation from Japan. And, turning the streets and the public square green, thousands upon thousands of loyal followers of the Legion of the Archangel Michael.

The church service took two and a half hours. Then at dusk the funeral cortege began. First came church dignitaries in their long, black robes. Then the fourteen caskets carried by one hundred and sixty-eight green-shirted pallbearers. Followed by Rumanian officials, government men and generals. Then a colorful parade with bands spewing out Guardist songs and religious music. German Brown Shirts. Italian Black Shirts. Spanish Blue Shirts. Surrounded by the endless seas of green.

Down the boulevard they marched, singing, chanting. Overhead German planes flew low, dropping wreaths of flowers through the soft-falling snow.

The procession of pallbearers reached the Green House Courtyard. The coffins were carried into the mausoleum. Outside masses of people knelt in the snow and the sharp wind. There was a sudden stillness.

I found myself listening, taut, waiting. For what?

Then the voice came clearly, eerily. High-pitched. Amplified. The words were drowned out by a swelling roar of cheers and shrieks.

"It is the voice of Codreanu! The Capitanul speaks to us!" The broadcaster was swept up in the religious ecstasy of the event he was reporting: the reinterment of fourteen murderers.

"Listen!" he shrieked over the airwaves. "Quiet!" he commanded his audience.

Silence fell once more. And once more we heard the recorded voice of the dead man. We heard his shrill commands:

"Many of us must expect to sacrifice our lives for our movement. You must await the day to avenge our martyrs."

414

Late that night someone knocked on the door of my room.

"Yes, who is it?" Mandel? Was the car ready?

"It's Alexander."

I opened the door. He entered. He stared at me; stared through me as though I did not exist.

"What is it?" I whispered.

He sat down. His face was haggard. He took out a cigarette, tried to light it. He could not. His hands were shaking.

"What's wrong?" I cried out. I knelt down beside him. "What's happened?"

"I was there in the apartment when they came. When they came for him. His wife was there and I was there and they came. They hammered at the door and then they knocked down the door and they came in with guns. They all wore green shirts. They were drunk and laughing and cursing. They took him away."

"Who?" I screamed the word.

He looked at me. "Orekhovsky. I have just seen him. Orekhovsky."

"Where? Where did you see him?"

"In the slaughterhouse."

Alexander's eyes, first glazed, now turned into wells of terror. "The kosher slaughterhouse. The police brought me there to identify the body. And the head. There were many of them. Hanging naked. Jews. Men. Circumcised. They had cut off the heads. The bodies were hung on iron hooks along the wall. Meathooks. The bodies were stamped in Yiddish. *Kosher meat*. The bodies—I couldn't identify his body. I never saw him without any clothes. Then they showed me a basket of bloody heads. I saw his head staring up at me. The eyes were open. The open eyes staring at me. 'Yes,' I told them. 'That's Mordechai Orekhovsky. That is my friend Mordechai Orekhovsky. He is a good man. He spends his life helping other people. That is what he does. That is Mordechai Orekhovsky, head of the Palestine Office in Bucharest. Yes, I identify him. My friend Orekhovsky.'"

I lit the cigarette Alexander held in his trembling fingers.

He sat, holding the lit cigarette, staring straight ahead. I stayed on my knees beside him, frozen.

Night snow made small flicking sounds against the window pane. And there was the sigh of the winter wind.

THIRTY-EIGHT

THE TELEPHONE.

It rent the screaming stillness.

Horror was replaced by terror.

"I can't answer," I whispered.

It kept on ringing.

Alexander got heavily to his feet. He stubbed out his cigarette. He crossed the room. He lifted the receiver.

"Spitzer." He held the receiver out to me.

"I can't," I said again. "Not now. You talk to him." To cope with Spitzer's querulous complaints. His desperate demands. Not now. Not yet.

I did not even look at Alexander. I heard him exclaim. First he said, "What?" Then, later, softer, he said, "No." And once again, "No."

Presently he hung up.

Then I did look at him. But I could not see his face in the faint dawn light which sifted through the room's dimness. He was like a standing shadow figure.

"Have you heard the news of the *Patria*?" he said. His voice sounded like someone speaking from a far distance.

"The *Patria*?" I said. "A ship? No. I never heard the name *Patria*. Whose ship is it? What happened?"

He remained there in the shadows. His words came flat, slow, relentless.

"The *Patria*. A passenger liner. Owned by the British. It was in Haifa harbor. They put eighteen hundred illegals on board. Illegals who'd come in on other ships. Three small ships. But the British wouldn't let them land. Wouldn't even put them in a detention camp. They've got a new plan now. Have you heard about their new plan? Have you heard about Mauritius?"

I shook my head.

"Mauritius," Alexander said. "It seems that the Mandatory Government announced their new policy last week. All illegals will henceforth be deported to the British colony of Mauritius. There they will be locked up in an old fortress prison. Till the end of the war. And then they will not be permitted into Palestine. They will be sent back where they came from.

"It was announced that the eighteen hundred illegals on the *Patria* would be the first to be shipped off to Mauritius. But—they didn't want to go. After months of the hell they had lived through to get to Palestine, they did not want to be sent off to a fortress prison on an island in the Indian Ocean. So—they blew up the ship."

I asked the question because I had to. But I knew the answer. "Did they—get the people off first?"

"Just where would they get the people off to?" Alexander asked. "They were forbidden to land. The only place open to them was the water. The ship sank in twelve minutes. Over two hundred and fifty were drowned. Those who were finally rescued, yes, they were allowed into Palestine. They were sent to Atlit Detention Camp."

He crossed the room. He sat in the chair. "Among those who drowned were children," he said. "One had been born on the *Patria*. As a matter of fact, he was born November twenty-first—the day after the British announced their new deportation policy. A baby one day old, already an outcast. And three days later, dead. Drowned—in protest."

I stared at the wall. I saw bodies. Headless bodies lacerated by huge meathooks. Hanging lifeless against the wall. And I saw bodies floating face down in the water. Why? Because they were Jews. But *why*? Because they were Jews. The answer did not fit the question. Yet, it *was* the answer. Just because they were Jews. It could not be the answer. There was no answer. There was only the question. *Why?* It was a dead-weight question thrown into the sea. But instead of subsiding the sound reverberated out. In concentric rings, filling the room. Louder and louder.

"Why don't you make us something to eat?" Alexander asked. "Then I must go. I haven't been home all night. My mother will worry."

It seemed such a wildly incongruous thing to say. My mother will worry. I felt like laughing crazily. I felt more mad than sane.

"Would you like your eggs scrambled?" I asked him. "Or fried?"

He said that he would like to have scrambled eggs.

As I stood in the kitchen stirring the eggs my mind was filled with the vision of the drowned infant, four days old.

The two hundred and fifty dead bodies in Haifa harbor, who were they? One day perhaps the list would be compiled by our people. Name. Age. Place of birth. Profession. I had seen such lists. Too many such lists. But the *Patria* Jews were the first who had killed themselves—in protest.

Had they meant to kill themselves? Perhaps only a small explosion had been planned. A delaying tactic. A hole in the ship which required repair. But the Jews on board must have had help from the Haganah. And the Haganah knew a great deal about dynamite. The illegals on the *Patria* had risked death by drowning so that the explosion would be heard far beyond Haifa harbor.

But would it be heard? Who was listening to our cries for help?

Alexander walked into the kitchen as I spooned the eggs onto plates. He sat down. I poured coffee.

"How does Spitzer know all this?" I asked. "From where does he get all his information? Sometimes he sounds to me like a madman. Perhaps it's not true. It never happened."

"He had a call from his cousin in Haifa," Alexander said. "This cousin was in a motorboat helping to haul people out of the water. One of those they saved was the mother whose four-day-old baby had drowned."

The telephone rang.

Alexander sat staring at his eggs, not eating.

We both acted as though we did not hear the phone. If we paid no attention, perhaps the ringing would stop.

"Eat," I said. "You wanted eggs. They're difficult enough to get now. So eat them."

"You sound like my mother," Alexander said. He put his fork into the eggs. But made no further move.

The telephone stopped ringing. "I should have answered," I said. "I always answer the telephone."

It started again, and I jumped up. I ran across the room.

It was the Shamen, calling to find out whether I was safe. He had heard about the Jews who were murdered in the slaughterhouse.

"Look," he said then. "I have a ship for you. A Turkish ship. The *Vatan*. Can I come to you? To discuss the details."

I had never given him the address on the Strada Rosetti. For many reasons.

"I will come to you," I told him. "I will be there in half an hour."

"It's not safe on the streets."

"I'll be there in half an hour," I said. And I hung up. To keep busy. To keep trying. This was the only antidote. The Shamen knew this. Was the *Vatan* another phantom ship? How had it materialized so quickly? Perhaps he had been planning to sell it elsewhere. Perhaps the news of last night's massacre had made him change his mind. Perhaps he would almost give us the ship in his private attempt to atone for the unspeakable crime which he had not committed. The *Vatan*. Her image was clear in my mind. A sleek, sturdy ship. How many tons? How many passengers could she hold? Where would we send her for reconversion? Varna, perhaps. Or Brăila.

I went back to the kitchen. "Well," I said to Alexander, "we have another ship to work on. The *Vatan*. I'm to meet the Shamen right away. Do you want to come with me?"

"You're not going into the street," he said. "It's not safe."

"Safe?" I looked at him. "What does that word mean to any of us now? Orekhovsky was sitting at home, you told me. Eating his dinner. Was he safe?"

There was a knock on the door.

We stared at each other.

"For heaven's sake, eat your eggs," I told him. "They'll get cold."

Someone rattled at the door handle. Then I heard the voice. "Ruth, are you there? Are you all right? It's David."

I opened the door.

Yitzhak Hecker entered first. He seemed shrunken in size. He was a short, slender boy, no more than five feet two or three. But when he walked into the room he looked shorter, thinner, more haggard than I had ever seen him.

David Arnon was equally grim, equally pale. He walked over to the radio, switched it on. "I wonder," he said, "whether they'll have it on the morning news reports." He sat down. He did not ask us whether we had heard about the death of Orekhovsky. He told us. He and Yitzhak had been to the slaughterhouse. They had heard the story from an eyewitness.

"She knows all about it," Alexander said. "She doesn't want to hear any more."

But David spoke on. As though the words had to come out. And Yitzhak sat, staring. And the radio played its pleasant popular song.

"After they stripped them naked," David said, "they forced each Jew to get down on his hands and knees. Like an animal. Then they drove the animal Jews up the wooden ramp. And as each Jew on his hands and knees entered the slaughterhouse he was hit on the head with a wooden mallet by a member of the Iron Guard. Then another Guardist slit the jugular vein with a long, sharp knife."

"Shut up, can't you?" Yitzhak screamed out the words.

"Some of the Jews tried to fight back," David went on. "With sticks. Thank God, we have guns buried here. We will go today and dig up the guns and—"

The shrill of the telephone cut his words. He kept on speaking. To himself. To the room. To God.

I answered the phone. It was Mandel.

"You must leave at once. I'm sending a car. It will be there in a few minutes."

Alexander crossed to the door. "I'll see you this evening," he said to me. He unlocked the door and went out.

"Wait!" I cried after him. "Alexander! Wait! Don't go!"

But he left, closing the door behind him.

"Don't take anything with you," Mandel said. "Just your passport."

"I can't possibly go," I told him. "The Shamen has a ship. I'm to meet him in—"

"Can a corpse negotiate for ships?" Mandel said. "I have contacts, don't you understand! I've been told that they are coming for you. Don't use the front door. The car I'm sending will go into the back courtyard. You must leave at once. This minute. Do you understand?"

"David and Yitzhak are here," I said.

"Take them with you. You must all leave."

"And you," I cried at him. "Carry your wife into a car. Come with us!"

He hung up.

There were heavy voices from the downstairs hallway.

Yitzhak went to the door. Opened it slightly. Listened. Quickly then he closed the door. Locked it. "Is there any way out of here?"

I pointed at the bathroom.

David ripped sheets from the bed. We locked the bathroom door behind us. Yitzhak flung open the window.

"Do you see a car in the courtyard?" I said. "Mandel said he was sending a car."

"There's no car."

David tore the sheets. Yitzhak tied them together. He secured one end of the hot-water pipe. "I'll go first," he said. "If I don't get shot, you follow, Ruth. Then David."

I watched him as he went out the window, and slid down the sheet rope. He landed and crouched behind a hedge.

I unlocked the bathroom door.

"Where the hell are you going?" David said.

"If we're leaving, we've got to have money. Passports." My pocketbook had been packed for many hours. I put on my coat. Then I heard my landlady's voice. Shrilly crying. "Ruth Klüger. I told you. She's not here!"

The angry voices of men.

I ran back to the bathroom. Again I turned the key in the lock. A pitiful lock, meant only to assure privacy.

Alexander. What had happened to him? Had they taken him?

I stood on the toilet, climbed up on the narrow window sill. Then I leaned far out, clung onto the rope of torn sheets. Lowered myself. Hand over hand. My arms ached. One shoe fell off, fell with a small thud to the cobblestones below.

I landed. Crouched with Yitzhak behind the hedge. Watched as

David came down, hand over hand. He was heavy. The sheet rope broke. He crashed down. Then picked himself up, limped toward us.

There was no car. We could not wait here. We started walking down the narrow street from the courtyard.

"My shoe!" I ran back. Searched for it. How could I walk casually down the street wearing one shoe? I found it, on top of the hedge.

David and Yitzhak were waiting. We walked on for several blocks past the small park with its statue of the statesman C. A. Rosetti. Later small children would come here to play if the weather did not turn too cold.

Where was Alexander? Where were we going? Should we try to get out of the country?

A car drove by. The men inside were singing. They wore green shirts.

The car pulled up before the courtyard from which we had just come. We turned the corner.

"Well," David said, looking down at me. He smiled a little. Then he added, "Why don't you come back to our hotel?"

It seemed a sensible suggestion. If, indeed, we had to leave the country they too would need their passports and visas. Besides, the hotel had a telephone in the lobby. I could phone Mrs. Schecter, find out what had happened to Alexander. And I could phone Mandel.

The hotel lobby was lit only by the bare light bulb which hung above the front desk. The night concierge was still on duty and he was asleep. I welcomed the solitude and the dimness; a place to hide.

David and Yitzhak went upstairs to pack. I went to the telephone and called Mandel at home, praying that he was not yet on his way to the office.

He answered the phone himself, at the first ring. "Where are you?" he said.

I told him that the car had not come; that the Iron Guard had. I gave him our address.

"A car will be there in five minutes," he said. "Don't move from that lobby. Do you understand? The driver will come in and get you."

"Please," I begged. "George, please, come with us."

He hung up.

I could not get through to my landlady. Perhaps the Guardists had ripped out the telephones.

I phoned Alexander's home; awakened his mother. She was more suspicious and irritable than ever. "No, he hasn't been home all night. I'd have thought *you* knew where he was."

"If he comes within the next ten minutes," I told her, "ask him to wait in the street, with you. And your papers. We are leaving Rumania. All of us."

"What are you talking about?" she exploded in vehement Yiddish. "I am not going anywhere. Nor is my son. Leave him alone, can't you! Ever since you came to this city he's been—"

I cut short her speech which I had heard too often. "You must both be downstairs in ten minutes' time with your passport and papers. Take no more than one valise."

This time it was I who hung up.

Yitzhak had come down to the lobby. I had many telephone calls to make. But so had he. And at the moment his seemed the most pressing. I stood guard outside the telephone booth and heard him give instructions to locals as to the whereabouts of suitcases, trunks and hidden caches of light machine guns, pistols, explosives and grenades.

Mandel's chauffeur entered the lobby.

Surely George Mandel had not sent his private car for us! If we were caught, he would be arrested at once for giving aid to foreign agents.

I knocked at the door of the telephone booth; heard Yitzhak say, "I'll leave my room keys at the desk for you. There are two more suitcases under my bed. Don't fail to pick them up. At once. I'll tell the concierge you are coming. *Shalom.*"

Yitzhak emerged from the booth, hurried across the lobby, awakened the concierge. Meanwhile, the chauffeur had taken my arm, was propelling me toward the front door.

But I refused to leave the lobby. "I'm not going anywhere in his car! Get a taxi, or—"

Mandel strode through the door.

I started to argue. He put his hand firmly over my mouth. Then he leaned down and kissed my forehead. "You must go quickly. Ion has full instructions. Don't ask questions. The danger is very real. You must go at once." He took his hand from my mouth. He was smiling a little. "Thank you for all you have done for me," he said.

"Come with us," I whispered. "Yitzhak and David will carry your wife. We will get her to Palestine safely. I promise. Come with us."

He shook his head. "Don't worry. Please. We have money. In this country, thank God, money can still buy safety. Now go."

David and Yitzhak were hurrying toward us across the lobby.

"And when they take your money away—when they come to your door as they did to mine—"

"For us there is time," George Mandel said. "For you there is none. Get out of here now. Get into the car."

"George. Please."

I saw his tears. "I will come. We will come. Later. But it is you who have no more time. You must leave. Now. Or we will all be arrested."

I was in the back seat of George Mandel's private limousine. I stared out the window. I had not cried. Yet, his tears were my tears.

I gave the driver Alexander's address. "We must pick up two people." But he kept on, straight ahead, down the boulevard.

"Ion," I said, "they are waiting for us outside the house."

"I am sorry, mademoiselle," he said. "I cannot drive into the Jewish Quarter. It is not safe. Besides, Mr. Mandel instructed me to make no stops until we reach the border."

"Look," David said to me, "if we drive into Văcăreşti in this car we may as well issue a warrant for Mandel's arrest."

He was right, of course. Besides, it was highly unlikely that Alexander's mother had been persuaded to leave her small comfortable apartment in order to face the terrors of the unknown. And it was highly unlikely that Alexander would leave without her. If, indeed, he had not already been arrested.

We reached the outskirts of the city. There were few cars on the road. Snowy fields, thatch-roofed houses flicked by as we hurtled away from Bucharest.

Would I ever see any of them again? My brother David, my sister, my aunts. And Stefan.

Through the violent kaleidoscope of memories I kept seeing Mandel's tears.

THIRTY-NINE

"Now, MADEMOISELLE, may I have your permission to—feel you?"

I stared at him. "What?" I said faintly.

The customs inspector shrugged one shoulder. Then the other. "I am sorry, mademoiselle, but at a small border town like this one we have no woman to search you. So—" He shrugged both shoulders. "I must do the best I can by myself."

I glanced helplessly at David.

My brassiere was lined with over five hundred pounds sterling. Smuggling foreign currency across the border was dangerous. We could be arrested on the spot. Furthermore, on this single matter, customs inspectors were diligent—for when they discovered foreign currency they were entitled to a hefty per cent of it. The inspector had already taken twenty minutes going through the scanty belongings of David and Yitzhak. He had even slit a toothpaste tube to see whether it contained a wad of foreign currency.

"Look," David said loudly, "you lay a hand on my fiancee and I'll knock your head off."

"Monsieur," said the customs inspector. "Please. I do it quite without emotion, I assure you. It is part of my duty, that's all. The girl has no suitcase. She comes—she says—to see you off on the train to Sofia. Why can't she kiss you good-by here in Giurgiu? Why must she go all the way to Bulgaria to say good-by? You must admit, monsieur, the story sounds a little strange." He turned back to me. "Now, mademoiselle, if you will kindly remove your coat—"

"My friend," said David, "I am a young man with old-fashioned ways. I cannot stand by and see the girl I plan to marry—*felt* by—" He broke off for a strategic moment. He glanced around. There was no one in the small customs shed but ourselves. Yet, he carefully lowered his voice. "You know how much money I have, since I emptied my pockets before you. It would be worth it to me, to save my fiancee the shame and the humiliation—"

The customs inspector frowned and shook his head.

"One—feel," said David incredulous, "is worth more to you than four thousand lei?" He spread the contents of his wallet on the counter. The inspector pocketed the money and waved us through.

"Thank God," said David as we stood on the pier which jutted out into the Danube, "another good goy."

Yitzhak had gone off to find a boatman who would take us across the river. An icy wind blasted up from the water. I shivered. David put both arms around me; held me close to him. "It is not only warmer," he said, "but safer. Our friend the customs inspector is watching us from the window." Then he added, "It is also in line with our —*amitié amoureuse*."

He had told me more than once that what he felt for me was more than friendship. I had told him more than once that I was in love with another man. Standing on the pier with David's arms around me Stefan seemed at one and the same time close and another lifetime away.

Yitzhak returned with a boatman who claimed it was his lunch hour. We must either pay double or wait until he had eaten and rested himself.

"Look," David exploded, "my fiancee is freezing to death here!"

"Let her wait in the customs shed," the boatman suggested.

"We have to get across," said David. "We must catch the train to Sofia."

The boatman shrugged. "My price is my price," he announced.

After a suitable span of arguing and gesticulating we agreed to his price and climbed down the icy ladder from the pier into the small boat. All the while the customs inspector watched us from the window. If we had dispensed with the expected ritual of bargaining with the boatman, he would certainly have grown suspicious. Why were we in such a hurry to get away?

We were perhaps two hundred yards from the Rumanian shore when the customs inspector did, in fact, emerge from his shed. He ran to the end of the pier, shouting and waving his arms frantically. The boatman was, fortunately, turned toward the Bulgarian shoreline, tending his motor.

David burst suddenly into song. We all joined him, singing at the top of our lungs. Between our singing and the winter wind the words of the customs inspector went unheard.

Then, as we continued singing, David scrambled to the back of the small boat, engaged the boatman in conversation.

More men had joined the customs inspector on the pier back at Giurgiu. Shots rang out.

Were they shooting at us, or shooting merely to attract the boatman's attention? Was it the Iron Guard? Rumanian police? Yitzhak and I sang frantically, an old Russian boat song.

The boat suddenly sped toward the Bulgarian shoreline with a new and unsuspected burst of energy.

"I told him," David shouted to us in Hebrew, "we'd double his fare once again if he got us across in time to make our train."

Then, a tiny miracle, we saw a train. It slithered like a gray snake along the distant shoreline. David stood up, pointing and screaming with excitement.

The boatman unleashed another burst of speed. His eyes were drilling straight ahead to the pier at Ruschuk on the Bulgarian shore. He did not look back. As we neared the pier, however, he cried out in agony and pointed. The train had reached the station, had stayed there for perhaps ten minutes, and was now departing.

When we stood safely on the pier David shook the boatman's hand and paid him double. "After all," he said, "you did your best. And one's best deserves double."

David had not learned much Rumanian during his weeks in Bucharest. But he always seemed to muster up the right words for the occasion.

We sat in the small restaurant opposite the station waiting for the next train to Sofia. From the window one could look out across the gray winter river and see Rumania.

Yesterday, at about this same time, Mordechai Orekhovsky had been forced to crawl naked on all fours up the ramp into the slaughterhouse where he was hit with a mallet, his jugular vein slit, and his head chopped off.

The waitress came. The soup she set before us steamed hot.

"I forgot to turn off the radio," I said.

"What radio?" said Yitzhak.

"The radio in the apartment on the Strada Rosetti."

"What apartment?" David said. "I never heard of the Strada Rosetti."

We looked at each other.

Then we started to eat the steaming soup.

I had planned to go on to Sofia with the boys. To remain a week with Dr. Berger and Dr. Baruch, our locals in Bulgaria. And then to visit Spitzer and the people in Kladovo and Sabac.

However, as we sat in the restaurant, David made a casual remark which caused me to change my plans at once.

Arazi was arriving in Istanbul to take over the *Darien II*.

I choked.

David, full of solicitude, pounded me on the back. When I'd recovered my breath and my senses, I apologized. Something had gone down the wrong way.

Something most certainly had.

I asked no further questions about the *Darien* or Arazi. It was strange. Working together and at the same time at sharp cross-purposes. Strange, yet completely understandable, for David, Yitzhak and Yehuda Arazi worked directly with British Intelligence under Section D. It was the British who had supplied the arms we hid in Băneasa Forest. David had already invited me to have drinks with his contact in Sofia, a high-ranking British officer.

Yet, in Palestine I was in danger of immediate arrest—by the British. They had, I'd been told, raised the price on my head to a flattering five thousand pounds.

A confusing situation. But somewhere a clear line must be drawn. And for me that line stood firmly at the *Darien*.

David's chance remark put him, in my mind, on the other side of the line.

After dinner I excused myself on the pretext of looking for a ladies' room. Instead, I crossed the street to the station.

The night train to Sofia, I learned, was due in half an hour. There was no through train from Ruschuk to Turkey. I must detour to the capital, remain several hours, then board the express to Istanbul. I booked a seat—a meaningless procedure these days. Then I cabled Yulik at the Park Hotel, Istanbul, that I would be arriving at Sirkeci Station the following afternoon about four o'clock. I also cabled Dr. Berger and Dr. Baruch to meet me at the Sofia station at dawn.

David, Yitzhak and I had a single seat on the train to Sofia. We sat in shifts and dozed, or tried to. The carriage was brittle cold, and our compartment included as passengers several roosters in a wooden-slat crate. Their timetable had obviously been upset by their travels for they crowed nervously at irregular intervals, punctuating the darkness with their announcements of dawn, which it seemed would never arrive.

It did, however. Soft snowflakes fell from a bleak sky as we pulled into Sofia.

When we descended from the train I stumbled and fell. David picked me up. I was shivering with cold. My knee was bleeding. "You," he informed me, "are one sorry-looking sight. You're going to sleep for at least twelve hours. Those are orders. We're booking into the Grand Bulgarie. Price be damned."

I told him I was already booked—on the next train to Istanbul.

David exploded. Yitzhak insisted: I must remain in Sofia and rest, for a day at least.

Then I heard my name reverberating through the station. We stared at each other in horror.

Coming from Rumania where secrecy was the byword, where suspicion and imminent danger were omnipresent, the sound of one's name resounding in a public place brought instant fear.

But this was Bulgaria. Still a land of relative freedom. If a man wanted to contact a passenger unknown to him by sight, he could avail himself of that simple device left over from a peacetime world: the station loudspeaker.

Dr. Berger was a figure from that peacetime world. He was waiting for me at the information booth; an elegantly dressed gentleman in his late thirties. Soft-spoken, courteous. He kissed my hand in a courtly manner and greeted me with quiet appreciation as though I had just alighted swathed in furs and perfumes from a luxurious compartment in the first-class carriage.

I bade a hasty good-by to the boys, told them to look me up at the Park Hotel if they came to Istanbul, and was swept off by Dr. Berger to his waiting car, leaving an astonished David and Yitzhak in my wake. I wondered, as I looked back at them, whether and when I would ever see them again. Life, these past months, had been a series of sudden relationships, made abruptly close by the intensity of circumstance. Relationships sundered with equal abruptness, leaving one with the constant feeling of falling into an abyss. Yet, I knew that the road directly ahead meant direct conflict with Yehuda Arazi, from whom these two boys took their orders. I knew that our triumvirate must be broken, here, in Sofia.

Dr. Berger drove me to his home for breakfast. I was so tired I could barely speak. I tried to pretend I was giving careful consideration to his comments. But I was merely fighting off sleep.

Scenes of the city flicked by. In these early-morning hours, hazed by winter mist and falling snow, Sofia seemed an unreal place. The wide cobbled streets were virtually empty. We passed stone-arched arcades of a shopping center. Neither shopkeepers nor customers had as yet arrived. We passed a Greek Orthodox church, its golden domes seemed to float against the gray sky. In the distance were mountains framing the city and fading off into the mist.

Then we passed a building with a heavy black swastika painted on the wall.

I asked Dr. Berger about the strength of the *Ratnizi*, the home-grown Bulgarian Fascist movement.

He shrugged. "Of no importance. Not in numbers or in influence. Yes, they paint a few swastikas here and there in the night. But they're

430

no Iron Guard, I assure you. And never will be. Not so long as Boris remains King."

I asked about the political pressures on the King.

"There are many," said Berger. "The place is overrun with Nazi wolves in sheep's clothing. They come in ski clothes. In business suits. Tourists with cameras and spyglasses. They say there are twenty thousand Germans here, waiting for the day they can don their uniforms and go into action. But at the moment they're quiet. At the moment the King rules the country. The King and the Parliament."

He turned down the side street, stopped the car before a splendid stone mansion.

"Of course," he commented then, "the King has many pressures coming at him from all countries. And from within Bulgaria as well. His subjects are Slavs. His wife is the daughter of the King of Italy. And the King himself—" Dr. Berger shrugged. "He puts it like this: 'My wife is pro-Italian. My ministers are pro-German. My people are pro-Russian. I am the only neutral in the country.'"

"And the Jews?" I asked. "How much danger is there here?"

Dr. Berger smiled, and told me in other words what I'd heard before but still found hard to believe. "If it were left to the King and his countrymen, Bulgarian Jews would be safe. Oh," he said, "they're starting to pass decrees, of course. But what decrees! They've mobilized men for work brigades—no Jews allowed. So what's happening? All over the city Christians are converting. Becoming Jews overnight so they don't have to go in the work brigades."

I stared at him. Across the border Rumanians were beheading Jews, impaling their bodies on meathooks. And here, at the same moment in time, Christians were becoming Jews.

We went into the house.

The soft carpets, the fine paintings, the antique furniture spoke to me in one insistent chorus. A fine home like this must have a bathtub with hot running water. When Dr. Berger summoned his servant and asked what I wished for breakfast, I answered, "Please, a bath."

I had it. And emerged refreshed and fortified, to find a sumptuous breakfast awaiting me.

As I drank my first cup of *kafe Amerikanski*—American-style coffee, with cream—Dr. Berger told me of the matter troubling him most:

431

There were men operating out of Bulgarian ports, men selling space for exorbitant fees on illegal ships headed for Palestine. "But these ships!" Dr. Berger exploded. "You must see them! Some of them old sailing vessels without a motor. It would be a miracle if they made it to Istanbul. Much less across the Mediterranean. There's one being organized now, in Varna. They're selling space to refugees who've escaped from Germany, Austria, Poland, Rumania. It's a suicide ship. Dr. Baruch is in Varna, trying to see to it that the sailing is held up until the ship is made seaworthy. We must go there. When you've finished your breakfast, we will start for Varna. I've heard about you. If you can arrange for a ship to sail, as you did with the *Tiger Hill* and the *Hilda,* you can surely see to it that a ship does *not* sail."

There were many such ships. Some of them had managed to make it to Palestine. The passengers were well aware of the hazards of the voyage. But those who boarded the vessels believed that here at least lay a chance for escape. To remain in Europe meant death. They were convinced of this. And who was I—who was anyone—to weigh one grim chance against another? Some called the speculators dealers in death. But the men who organized the vessels often heralded themselves as heroes, and claimed that the vast sums they charged for passage did not nearly defray the huge expenses involved.

I had dealt with several of these speculators. There was almost no way to stop them. They would eagerly accept advice. Promise to invest in a brand-new motor. Draw up elaborate plans to make their ships more habitable with such minimal conveniences as boards for berths, an adequate food and water supply, a basic stock of medicines. Then the ship would slip out at the dead of night, crowded with more passengers than possible, with none of the plans and promises fulfilled.

Perhaps if I went to Varna today with Dr. Berger, I could succeed in stopping one of these ships. Perhaps not. And perhaps if the ship did sail it might—as others had done—manage to land its passengers in Palestine. And perhaps—as others had done—it might sink en route.

But there were no such ghastly scales to weigh concerning the *Darien II.* Not in my mind.

I told Dr. Berger that there was a matter even more vital which made it imperative that I proceed to Istanbul at once.

After a further briefing about the Jewish Community in Bulgaria, he drove me back to the station and I boarded the Istanbul Express.

It was late afternoon by the time the train reached Istanbul. The tracks edged the old city. On the right spread the broad sun-sparked Sea of Mamara, with ferries plying the waters between Stambul and Scutari. On the left were the crumbling fourth-century sea walls; the original walls of ancient Byzantium.

There was the swift glimpse of a palace, and within minutes the train pulled into Sirkeci Station.

I felt a sudden lift of excitement. I had never been to Turkey before. I had read about it; had studied maps of the Bosporus, Mamara, the Golden Horn. I knew the names, the shapes, the depths of the harbors and inlets. But the country, its people and particularly the history-layered Istanbul were all completely unknown to me. I had come to a city which spanned two continents. I had come to a city where the sun was shining. I had come from a world where horror raged, into a land which still lived at peace.

And Yulik would be at the station. I had not seen him since the Zionist Congress. But with all we had lived through together via long-distance telephone, I felt him to be a lifelong friend.

He was not, however, at the station.

Had he received my wire? Should I wait? Should I proceed to the hotel?

As I stood, uncertain, a crowd of porters descended on me, pleading for my patronage—despite the fact that I had nothing to carry but a pocketbook.

I was rescued by a short round-faced man with reddish hair and a pot belly. "Ruth. You're Ruth." He did not ask it; he announced it. "I have a car outside. Jacob will drive you to your hotel. I will see you soon." And he rushed off.

I asked the young man named Jacob, "Was that Simon Brod?"

"Of course," said Jacob.

At the far end of the waiting room Brod was erupting; shouting, gesticulating at some railway official who looked both pompous and nonplused. Then the official shrugged and walked away. Brod followed him.

433

"Watch," said Jacob.

Presently Brod emerged like a sheep dog yapping at his flock. He herded a bedraggled-looking lot of men, women, children of all sizes, across the waiting room toward us. *"Geh schoin! Geh schoin!"* he yelled at me in Yiddish. "What are you standing there? Go! Go!"

We went.

I followed Jacob from the station. Brod's huge black limousine was waiting.

"He meets every train that comes from Europe," Jacob said. "He can always spot the refugees . . . the ones without papers . . . without money . . . without anywhere in the world to go."

We climbed into the car and started down the broad street which bordered the entrance of the Golden Horn.

I'd heard of Simon Brod, of course. A one-man Jewish rescue committee who accomplished more than many organizations. He got rooms for the refugees; certain hotels and private apartments were filled always with "Brod's people." He got them transit visas, dressed them well, and sent them on their way, usually traveling in a first-class carriage.

He had come from Poland to Turkey as a boy; had made his money in textiles. And now was spending it fast on refugees.

It was said that he knew every stone in Istanbul, and how to turn it for the aid and benefit of his people. He shouted and cursed, stamped and stomped; was constantly running from the waterfront to meet passenger vessels and fishing sloops, to the railway station, to banks, government offices and back to the station to meet the next train. Many who watched him in operation considered him half mad. But he resurrected dozens of penniless, homeless, hopeless Jewish refugees every week. And sent them through Syria to be smuggled across the border into Palestine.

We crossed Galata Bridge which spanned the Golden Horn. The afternoon had mellowed into sunset. The sky was shot through with molten gold. When I looked down my breath caught at the beauty of the expanse below. The water was layered over by gold. Small boats with rusty-red sails skittered around the harbor. Ships flying flags of all nations were berthed at the docks.

434

I looked back and saw the slender minarets of mosques piercing the sunset sky.

"This is the best time to arrive in Istanbul," Jacob said. "At sunset you don't notice the garbage, the beggars, the smells. Have you been here before?"

Because I had not, because I wanted to cling onto the brief limbo time before plunging once more into Mossad operations, and because I had no idea how much Jacob knew of our work, I asked him to be my guide as we drove to the Park Hotel.

It appeared he knew a little about our work. As we reached the end of Galata Bridge he pointed down a steep hill to the right. "I imagine you'll be spending a good deal of time down there," he said. "Offices of the shipping companies."

I said nothing.

He smiled a little. "You've been warned not to tell your business to anyone in Istanbul. Well, that's right. This city's certainly the spy capital of the world right now. You can't say a word in front of a waiter, a taxi driver, a porter that you wouldn't want your enemies to hear. You'd better assume that everyone in your hotel is in the pay of one side or another. Some spy for two sides. Or three."

"And you?"

"I'm in the pay of Simon Brod. You don't need to tell me anything. Because Brod tells me everything. And somehow he seems to know everything that he wants or needs to know."

"One question," I said. "If this is the cloak-and-dagger capital, how much—dagger is there?"

"According to what's reported in the paper—not much. After all, this country is fighting as hard as it can to stay neutral. And one important way to do that is to carefully overlook anything which might be classified as political murder. But—if you judge by the number of dead bodies one hears about being fished out of the Bosporus, or slumped at the back of a cafe or a railway compartment—" He let the sentence hang.

I had read that Istanbul was built on seven hills. They swelled before us; hills of houses. We entered a narrow, cobbled street lined by gloomy stone buildings, four to six stories high.

435

"Karaköy," Jacob said. "The business district. Banks. Offices. Merchant houses. This side of the bridge is the European section."

There were no mosques or minarets to enchant the skyline. Nor had there been any transplantation of the charm of European cities. The cobbled streets were gloomy and drab narrow canyons, climbing upward between the walls of old stone buildings which were lined by long narrow windows, most of them painted dark for the blackout.

There was, however, one landmark which rose above the stolid skyline; a tall column on top of a hill.

"Galata Tower," Jacob said. "Fourteenth century. One hundred fifty feet high. It's used for fire watching. And, believe me, they need it. All the older houses are made of wood."

We traveled slowly, for the streets were not only precipitously steep, but they were perilously crowded. Then we entered what Jacob informed me was the main street of Istanbul, Istiklal Caddesi—Independence Street. It was well named, for each individual vehicle and pedestrian seemed bent on being independent. Taxis darted along, dodging trams, ponderous buses, ladened donkeys and pony carts. The sidewalks were equally crowded. There were dark-suited businessmen hurrying by with briefcases . . . peddlers with panniers of fruit and vegetables balanced from the ends of a shoulder pole . . . well-dressed women shoppers . . . porters bent almost double by their heavy loads . . . maimed beggars . . . black-smocked schoolchildren . . . countrywomen in kerchiefs and pantaloons . . . pushing . . . honking . . . shouting . . . shoving.

"Is this the rush hour?" I asked Jacob.

"Every hour is the rush hour on Istiklal," he answered.

Finally, we drew up before the Park Hotel, a sprawling stone building lined with french windows which opened onto broad balconies.

My eye was caught then by the flag which flew from the rooftop of the building next door. It stood out stiffly in the winter wind: a swastika.

"Yes," said Jacob, who seemed to hear my thoughts before I spoke them. "Your neighbors. The German Embassy."

A uniformed doorman opened the car door.

"I must report back," Jacob said. "Your friend Yulik has reserved a room for you. He asks that you wait for him there. I'm sure we will be meeting again." He smiled. "Enjoy Istanbul," he said, loudly enough for the doorman to hear.

I got out of the car.

The doorman asked for my luggage; eyed me suspiciously when I said that I had none. I followed him into the lobby.

It was crowded with well-dressed gentlemen and their ladies. The double doors to the restaurant were open; I glanced in at another opulent era. Soft music, chandeliers, tuxedoed waiters.

I went to the reception desk, filled out the required forms, handed in my passport, followed the bellhop up a flight of carpeted stairs which were lit by elaborate turkish chandeliers.

Where *was* Yulik? Because catastrophe had now become a commonplace, I wondered whether his failure to meet me was somehow a dire portent.

The bellhop unlocked the door to Room 39. There was a small corridor with a bathroom on the left. He presented it to me with a flourishing gesture, said something in a lilting Turkish, and showed me how the hot water faucet and stopper worked. I gathered from his manner that rooms with a bath were something of a luxury at the Park Hotel.

I wondered if Yulik knew of my weakness. Members of the Mossad had often commented on my ability to keep and to spread calm. I was able to do so, if I could soak out my own fatigue and tensions in a hot bath.

A milk-glassed door from the corridor opened onto the room, which was large and furnished with a huge brass bedstead, a handsome wardrobe closet, a long table and heavy brocaded window drapes. The air was heavy with a chill dampness.

I tipped the porter in Rumanian lei, for I'd not yet had the chance to acquire Turkish pounds. He was obviously used to a variety of foreign currency, for he recognized the fact that my tip was a generous one. Then he left the room.

I went, automatically almost, to the telephone.

In the Continental, the Ambasador, the apartment and now here in Istanbul only one item in my room had remained the same: the telephone. Once again it stood black, long-necked, imperious on the bed table.

I put through two calls to Bucharest; one to Alexander, the other to

437

Mrs. Schecter, my landlady. Had the Guardists harmed her when they found I was gone? Had she been imprisoned for harboring an enemy agent?

And Alexander? If the Guardists knew my name and identity, they might well know his. This dedicated man with the doting mother, what had happened to him?

The hotel operator informed me that long-distance calls usually took hours to come through. If I went to the restaurant would I advise her, so that she might have me notified.

I pulled back the drapes, opened the french windows, stepped out onto the balcony. The wet dark wind wrapped around me. I shivered and pulled my coat closed. The soft glow of sunset had muted into the smudged gray of oncoming night. The vista of Asia could no longer be seen. Small dark shapes moved slowly on the water. I reflected that the blackout might ease the way for Mossad ships traveling through the Bosporus, for at night all vessels looked like secret ships.

Then I thought of Stefan. Memories and dreams of him broke upon me often. But I was most vulnerable when I was lonely. And standing here on the balcony overlooking a strange city, brinking on a new life which I had not yet entered, I felt I had stepped into a void of loneliness.

"Where are you?" I said the words into the wind. "When will you come to me?"

There was the far-off eerie blast of a foghorn; a mocking answer.

I stepped back into the room; the presence of Stefan followed me. A knock on the door.

I opened it, and with relief saw Yulik standing there.

He greeted me with effusive shaloms, grasped my hands, then we embraced.

"Come in." I laughed and closed the door behind him.

Dear Yulik, with his bushy head of blond hair, his round, pleasant face, his soft gentle voice. He was like a harbinger of good tidings.

Instead he told me, "Forgive me for not being at the station to meet you. Shmarya and I have been down at the docks, negotiating with Yohanis Pipinos."

"The captain of the *Darien?*"

He nodded. "We've directed him—or persuaded him—or overpaid

438

him—what you will—to take his ship away from here tonight. He's to go to Sulina. To wait there for the Kladovo people. We had to move quickly. There was no other way."

"Why? What's happened?"

"We've had word that Yehuda Arazi is arriving tomorrow. With directives from David Hacohen, and Shertok. We're to sell our ship to the British at once. No more delay." He peered at me. "You agree, don't you? We had to send the ship away."

"Of course I agree. And of course we don't have to obey their directives. The Mossad's independent. Of everybody. Even the heads of the Haganah. It was set up that way."

"They seem to have forgotten that," Yulik said.

"Hacohen? Shertok? What have they to do with us? What about Berl? Eliahu? Haven't *they* sent directives about the *Darien?*"

"Nothing. The worst of it is," said Yulik, "this issue may even split the Mossad. Kadmon's still in Palestine. But he's coming here. And I understand he's siding with Arazi. At least for the moment. Dani Shind is coming here tonight. He refuses to take sides—until he hears both sides." Yulik hesitated. Then he said, "If it turned out to be the three of us, Shmarya, you and me, against the directives of all our leaders and against the rest of the Mossad—would you still stick to our course?"

"You know I would."

Yulik smiled. "Let's celebrate that by going down to dinner."

"We don't indulge ourselves often in here," Yulik said, as we entered the luxurious dining room. "Most of our meals are illegal. Smuggled into the hotel. Cooked on a kerosene burner. But there's someone who'll be here tonight that I'd like you to meet."

As we followed the headwaiter to the table I heard snatches of conversation which seemed to span the globe: Turkish, Arabic, Russian, French, English and heavy guttural German.

When we were seated Yulik remarked, "They say that eighty per cent of the people who eat here are agents of one sort or another. Most of the others are diplomats. It's because of them that we're headquartered here. If we can't get to see a man in his office we can always happen to run into him in the lobby or the restaurant."

"Who is it that we're here to meet?"

"A man named Eddie Goldenberg. He was the director of a bank in Dresden. When the Nazis came he fled to Turkey. Now he's the director of a bank in Istanbul. We had hopes he'd be our Mandel in Turkey. But so far we haven't been able to get to him. Inside, I mean. Oh, he's polite. He's sympathetic. But—" Yulik broke off. I saw him stiffen.

"The party being seated," he said quietly. "Ambassador von Papen."

They were at the next table. Franz von Papen was a slender, dapper, gray-haired man with a small gray mustache. His bow tie matched his pocket handkerchief, which protruded in a careful corner from his breast pocket. He spoke with seeming courtesy to the two women who were with him.

"Frau and Fraulein von Papen," Yulik said softly.

It was hard to believe. Sitting in an elegant restaurant in Istanbul directly across from one of Hitler's top-ranking henchmen. Von Papen was one of the men who bore chief responsibility for Hitler's rise to power. The impoverished baron had married the daughter of a wealthy industrialist—the skinny horse-faced lady who was now divesting herself of her furs. Baron von Papen had subsequently seen to it that Hitler met most of Germany's biggest industrialists—who backed him. Von Papen had then been made Vice-Chancellor in Hitler's first cabinet. And a year later was appointed Special Minister to Austria—where he spent his time preparing the Anschluss. Now, as Ambassador to Turkey, he was presumably assigned to see to it that this country joined the Axis and opened the door to Germany's *Drang nach Osten*.

"Von Papen eats most of his meals here," said Yulik. "In case you're interested, he always orders the same thing. Boiled beef and sauerkraut. And Amstel beer. According to the head waiter Grigori, the Ambassador spends most of his time away from the Embassy. He's afraid it will be bombed."

We were handed a long and elaborate menu. I had suddenly lost all desire to eat.

"We follow a certain policy here," Yulik said. "It is good for the stomach and for the purse. Shmarya and I have told Grigori we're under doctor's orders. We can eat only boiled eggs, fish, pilaf, goat cheese, yogurt and hot tea. The cheapest items on the menu. The hardest part is watching other people stuff themselves with Turkish delights. But—" He broke his sentence short. "Here's Goldenberg."

Grigori led a couple to our table. The man, I noted with surprise, was a hunchback. Small, misshapen, like an elegantly dressed Toulouse-Lautrec. The woman with him was tall, olive-skinned and astonishingly beautiful. She had high cheekbones, huge gray eyes, soft dark hair. I assumed she must be Goldenberg's mistress.

Introductions were made. They sat at our table. Her name was Sophie. She was Goldenberg's wife.

Within minutes I had forgotten that the grim Von Papens sat across the way.

And within minutes I had forgotten that Eddie Goldenberg was deformed. He exuded an easy charm and warmth; his brilliance and wit glittered and sparked through the conversation.

We spoke German. And we spoke of the days when we both had known Vienna; the early thirties when life was *gemütlich,* and the Danube meant students and singing, romance and Strauss waltzes. Not a river used as a highway of war, and a last roadway out for desperate Jewish refugees.

Eddie Goldenberg waved the menu away, ordered caviar and champagne. This was followed by *mezés,* a host of exotic Turkish hors d'oeuvres, each in its separate dish: stuffed mussels, eggplant salad, shellfish, fish roe salad, vine leaves stuffed with rice.

By the time we had finished tasting this and sampling that, I felt I had found a new family. There was a rare warmth between us; an unspoken kind of deep communication.

Like her husband, Sophie was charming, gracious, intelligent. It was obvious that she made the ideal hostess for the many parties the Goldenbergs gave.

When I mentioned that I'd arrived in Istanbul with nothing more than the clothes I had on, Sophie made delighted plans to take me shopping the next day. We would visit her couturiers. We would—

Here, for the first time, Yulik interrupted as if to let me know that he had given Goldenberg some idea about our endeavors in Istanbul. "In our work," he said, "we must operate on a strict budget. I'm afraid—"

But Eddie cut off his words with a gesture. "For her work she must be well dressed. Let that be part of my contribution. Besides, she's coming to a dinner party at our home tomorrow night. She can't show up in a plaid wool dress. I forbid it."

Grigori stopped by our table. "Miss Klüger, telephone. Long distance. Will you take it in the lobby booth or in your room?"

I excused myself. Hurried through the restaurant. Up the stairway. Ran down the corridor to Room 39. The phone was ringing as I entered.

For an hour with the Goldenbergs, caught up in their golden life, I had half forgotten my escape from a land ruled by evil, rampaged by terror. Yet I had left there little more than twenty-four hours ago. The telephone bound me back.

It was the call to my landlady which had come through.

I could hear her voice clearly. I could even hear the fear in it. "Yes," she told me. "Your—friends who came here looking for you Sunday morning were disappointed not to find you at home. I said that you'd moved. I didn't know where. Even so, they—they—" She broke off. Not knowing a code.

"I understand," I said quickly. The apartment was being watched. Her phone was being tapped.

I asked about the weather in Bucharest.

"It's snowing," she answered.

"The—storm," I said. "When I left—"

"Oh. Yes. Well, that's quieted down. At least for the time being."

"Have there been any calls for me?"

"Calls! Yes! The phone never stops ringing. But no one would leave his name. Except one called Alexander. And a gentleman called Stefan Meta. He was very insistent on leaving his name. He left a message too. He said his family is now on the orange grove. He came to Bucharest to tell you this. He seemed disappointed to learn you'd gone away."

Disappointed. Oh, God, Stefan. Disappointed. Stefan, my love.

"Listen," I said. "Mrs. Schecter, it's very important. If anyone calls—anyone—you may tell him I'm at the Park Hotel in Istanbul. I will be here for weeks, for months. Anyone may call me here, or write me here or visit me here. Don't be afraid to give out my address. Even those—friends who came on Sunday morning. Tell them you've heard from me. That I've left the country. Then I think they won't trouble you any more."

"Yes," she said. "Well, let us hope that's true."

I ended with a few amenities. She should sell the clothes I had left in the closet; keep the money in payment for this month's rent. She should give my short-wave radio to the man named Alexander, if he came by. She should—

I interrupted myself.

"Mrs. Schecter, did he say where he was staying? Where I should contact him?"

"Alexander? He said nothing."

"Not Alexander. Stefan Meta. Did *he* say—"

"Nothing. Except that he would call again."

"And when he *does* call, you will surely tell him—"

"The Park Hotel, Istanbul. Shall I forward your mail there?"

"Please. And Mrs. Schecter—thank you. Thank you."

I hung up.

He was in Bucharest. He would surely call Mrs. Schecter again. The next time the telephone rang, it might be Stefan.

FORTY

YEHUDA ARAZI ARRIVED the next morning.

We met in my room.

He arrived full of grace, charm, smiles and good wishes from friends in Palestine. Also, he informed us, he arrived with official orders to take over the *Darien II*. After breakfast Shmarya would accompany him to the ship; explain the situation to the captain.

"Impossible," said Shmarya. He lit a fresh cigarette from the stub of his old one, a habit I remembered from our meetings at the Zionist Congress. He was a chain smoker. It was said that he used only one match a day.

"Why impossible?" Arazi inquired, still using guarded gentle tones.

"The ship's not here."

"No?" The knife edge was coming now into his words. "May I ask, where is she?"

"On her way to pick up refugees."

I had heard the expression "pale with rage." Now I saw it.

"You had your orders months ago," Arazi said. "The final arrangements have been made. Plans been drawn up to the last detail. You will cable your captain at once. Tell him to bring the ship back to Istanbul. British Intelligence will take possession in—"

"Excuse me," Shmarya broke in, his voice as gentle as Arazi's was harsh. "You say you have drawn up plans to the last detail. You seem to have forgotten one detail." He took a document from his pocket, handed it to Arazi. "The bill of sale for the S.S. *Darien II*. A ship that I

444

found. A ship that I bought. A ship that I renamed. I hired the captain and crew. I procured the flag. I, my friend, am the owner."

"We are well aware of all those facts," said Arazi, each separate word stiff with anger. "This is exactly why the *Darien* is unique for our purposes. The Germans will allow an American-owned ship up the Danube to—"

"As owner," Shmarya continued blandly, "I say where the ship should sail. And what cargo she will carry. I choose human beings over depth charges."

"Am I to understand," said Arazi, "that when you received your orders, you completely disregarded them?"

Shmarya's silence spoke clearly.

"You were told," said Arazi, "to prepare the ship as if it were to carry refugees. You were told to bring the reconverted vessel to Istanbul. You were told that I was arriving to—"

"You seem to forget something else, Arazi!" This time it was Yulik who broke in. "The Mossad was set up by the Haganah as an independent organization. We make our own rules."

"Not when the head of the Political Department of the Jewish Agency issues orders!"

"What orders?" Dani asked. "We've seen no orders."

"Shmarya's seen them," Arazi said abruptly. "He's been receiving orders from us for the past three months."

"Who is 'us'?" said Dani. "You?"

"The cables were sent by me, yes. But the initial decisions were made by Shertok and Golomb."

Dani said nothing.

Perhaps sensing a foothold Arazi remarked smoothly, "I find it strange that you, Shind, one of the founders of the Mossad, should have been kept in the dark about this matter."

"Dani arrived in Istanbul late last night," Shmarya said. "This is the first time the four of us have been together in one country since this *Darien* matter arose."

"Look," said Arazi reasonably, "if you still lived in America, Shmarya, and a direct order was issued to you by the Secretary of State and the Commander in Chief of the Armed Forces, and your country was at war—fighting for its life—would you disobey the directive?"

"We don't have a country," said Shmarya.

"And we never will!" Arazi slapped the sentence at him. "If we don't obey our leaders." He opened a battered leather briefcase, extracted four typed documents. "You were right, Zameret. There is one detail we still need. Your signature on these papers—officially turning the ship over to its new owners. And now, if you people will excuse me, I have another meeting. I'll pick up the papers this evening. And I'll expect the *Darien* back here within twenty-four hours at the latest."

He left quickly, closing the door hard behind him.

"For Christ sake," Dani said. "I didn't know the top men in the Jewish Agency were involved in this. I didn't know Shmarya had been receiving orders—and doing the opposite. Who are we here? Four nobodies. We have no country. All we've got is a government and leaders. How can we cut ourselves off from them? Maybe they're right. Shertok doesn't make decisions without a lot of thought behind them. Disobeying government orders in wartime! If our government was an official one, we could be strung up for treason."

There followed then a harsh word battle between Dani and Yulik; a battle made all the more terrible because these were the two men who had founded the Mossad in the summer of '37.

"We're illegal enough as it is," Dani shouted. "We can't be doubly illegal."

"We've been doubly illegal from the beginning."

"Have you heard from Berl?" Dani asked. "From Saul Meiroff? Are any of them behind you?"

We'd heard nothing; only that David Hacohen would be arriving in Istanbul. Hacohen who fully backed Arazi. Hacohen, one of the top members of the Executive Committee of the Jewish Agency.

"Whatever they say, the Mossad has always had its own goal. We've always played our own game." Was Yulik trying to convince Dani—or himself? "If we try to play everyone else's game as well, we are lost. We achieve nothing. There are eleven hundred men, women and children at Kladovo and Sabac. They've been waiting over a year for this ship. It's finally on the way. That's what we've got to think about. Nothing else. Rescuing refugees. Saving Jewish lives."

"Look," said Shmarya, "it seems to me what we've got to try to do is convince Hacohen that we're right. Arazi—when he gets an idea—especially if it's his idea—there's no other way. He's like a bulldog. But Hacohen, if we can persuade him to have those orders rescinded—"

"And until Hacohen gets here," said Dani, "exactly what do you propose to do?"

"I plan to proceed with our plans," said Shmarya. "And I plan to get some breakfast. A fried fish sandwich for fifty krus. Will anyone join me? Under the bridge."

Wordlessly we followed him to the door.

Arazi, I reflected, played upon men's feelings like a skilled musician. Sensing that Dani was not in accord with the rest of us, yet knowing that he would not contradict us while Arazi was in the room, he had made a rapid and dramatic exit. Divide and conquer; it was as good a strategy as any.

Another phrase came into my mind; a warning uttered by one of the biblical prophets: *respect and suspect*. A phrase we should bear in mind regarding Arazi.

We all respected him. His role was unique. His courage was legendary. His accomplishments were formidable. Yet, we must suspect him as well. He was dedicated to this idea of his. And we all realized that the plan had valid and vitally important merits. Perhaps it could shorten the war. Perhaps it would—as he insisted—help the Political Department of the Jewish Agency in their negotiations for a Jewish Brigade of Palestinians within the British Army.

But Arazi's plan was larded with "ifs." Our need for the ship was a certainty. To use the *Darien* for sabotage—or to save lives. In my mind there could only be one answer to the equation. And it was equally clear that in Arazi's mind there could only be one answer. His determination was as legendary as his ingenuity and his bravery. He'd never been known to give up on a project he believed in—or to lose out. He was one of our heroes; yet in the matter of the *Darien* we must regard him as an enemy.

"Perhaps," said Dani as we walked out into the hall, "we can find another ship to sell to the British. Some old wreck of a boat which would never make it to Palestine in any case."

"I've been in Greece over a year," said Shmarya, "negotiating for ships. Deal after deal fell through. There are no ships. I got the *Darien* through a pure fluke. Victor Meyers's still in Greece. Trying to find a ship. Results: zero."

As we started down the stairs I wondered uneasily about this open conversation. Even walls have ears. Did walls know Hebrew?

"The situation in Rumania's exactly the same," I said. I had also spoken to the Shamen last night. The ship he'd mentioned before I left Bucharest—the *Vatan*—a coal barge, it too had proved to be unavailable.

The *Darien* was not only the first ship we had ever owned. It might also be the last ship available to us while the war went on.

"Miss Ruth!"

I looked back. Elana the chambermaid stood at the top of the stairs, a thin little woman with black hair pulled back in a bun. We'd had a long conversation last night in a patchwork of languages. She knew some words in French, German, Arabic. We understood each other well. She commuted each day from a village on the Bosporus, two hours away. She was a widow with four children. She worked six days a week from seven in the morning till nine at night. For the equivalent of seven dollars a month. Plus tips. I'd given her a large one.

"Telephone, Miss Ruth."

Stefan!

I had placed many calls last night. To the Shamen. To Alexander. To Cotic. To Spitzer. To Dr. Berger. To Kadmon in Palestine.

But somehow I was certain that the voice at the other end of the line would be Stefan's.

"Look," I said quickly to the others, "I don't really want breakfast. You go have your fish sandwiches. I'll meet you later in the room."

Before they could protest that they'd wait for me I fled back up the stairs, down the hall, and I locked the door of Room 39 behind me. I had even forgotten to thank Elana. I would explain later. She was a woman. She would understand.

I sat on the bed, picked up the receiver. My throat was dry, my heart thumping.

"Hello."

It was Sima Spitzer.

For a moment my mind blanked with disappointment. I completely forgot why I had placed the call in the first place.

"Yes? Who is it? Who's calling me? Who's there?" Spitzer's querulous voice was loud in my ear.

I told him that at last, after all these months, I had the news he'd been waiting for. The *Darien II* would reach Sulina during the day.

It would wait there for eight hundred of the Kladovo people. It would transport them to Palestine, and would then return at once for the rest.

Silence.

I could understand it. Perhaps he was weeping with relief. Perhaps hearing the news after all these months upon months of waiting for it left him speechless with emotion.

Then he said, "They can't come."

"*What?* Why not?"

"The river," said Spitzer. "It's frozen."

I did not believe him. I'd heard no reports that the river was frozen. And if it were—"They won't be coming by river!" I said. "You have the transit visas. Didn't Alexander inform you? Somebody in the visa office must be trying to atone for what's been going on in Rumania. Your people can cross the country. As soon as the Rumanian port officials at Sulina send word that the ship has arrived, your transit visas will be issued."

"How do I know that the ship will arrive? I may bring my people to Sulina and no ship will be there."

"Go to Sulina yourself!" I said. "See the ship. Count the number of berths. Inspect the food supplies. But you must choose your people to-day—and get them ready to move!"

Once the ship had its full cargo of illegals, even Yehuda Arazi could not demand that these men, women and children, who had already suffered so much and so long, should be thrown off—to be replaced by high explosives.

Then Spitzer said, "I've decided that the Kladovo people should stay where they are."

This time it was I who was struck into silence.

Finally I said, "I cannot have heard you correctly."

But this phone connection between Belgrade and Istanbul was a good one. He might have been standing in the next room. Indeed, his voice was so clear that I felt I could see him. Shmarya had described him to me: small, sharp featured, with a large red birthmark smeared down half his face.

"The situation has changed," Spitzer said. His words coming fast now. "The government—the Yugoslav Government—they've been very

449

kind. They've built huts for our people. Yugoslavia's a safe place. Not like Rumania. It will never be like Rumania. I've given a lot of thought to this matter. Now that Italy's entered the war, the whole situation has changed."

"Italy!" He sounded like a madman. "That was seven months ago! What has Italy to do with it?"

"Mines!" he shrieked at me. "Mines in the Mediterranean. I should ask my people to leave security here. For what? To be blown up by mines? They've made a life for themselves here. They have committees. They put on plays. Poetry readings. There are Hebrew lessons."

"Spitzer!" I was shouting back at him. "Listen to me. What does a dead man need with Hebrew? The Germans may march through Yugoslavia next week, next month. Certainly by next year."

"And they may not! Hitler can't disperse his troops so widely. I tell you my decision has been made. The day I heard about the *Patria*, I decided."

"*You* decided! Who are you to decide? Put it up to the people at Kladovo. And Sabac. Let them decide. It's a matter of life and death, Spitzer. Their lives and their deaths."

He went ranting on as though I had not spoken at all. "What am I to do? Take them away from everything they've built up here? Send them on a precarious voyage. For what? Even if—by some miracle— they should survive the trip, what then? They'd be shoved into prison at Atlit. Or locked up in a fortress in Mauritius. Or maybe they'd choose to drown in Haifa harbor."

"Spitzer, listen to me." Perhaps he had not heard my words because I'd shouted them. I repeated them now as calmly as I could. "You have no right to make this decision yourself. Ask the people at Kladovo and Sabac. Put it before them. Tell them there's a ship waiting to take them to Palestine. Tell them there may not be another chance at another ship. Tell them the transit visas have come through. Tell them about the mines in the Mediterranean. Tell them about Mauritius and the *Patria* and anything else you want. But let each one of them make his own decision for himself. For God's sake, you must do this. Spitzer . . . listen to me. Will you do this?"

Again, the grueling silence.

"Spitzer," I said. "Listen, maybe you're right. Maybe they'll all decide to stay where they are. Maybe half of them will want to come. Then we'll make one trip for your people. Not two. But Spitzer—you have got to put it up to them. Right now. Will you promise me this?"

Finally he said, "I will think about it."

"Think about it!" I was shouting again. "You have no time to think about it! *We* have no time. We must get the ship loaded and on its way to Palestine. This must be done in a day or two at the most. Spitzer! You must put it to your people. At once."

He flung his sentence back at me. "*I will think about it!*" Then he hung up.

I sat on the bed. I was shaking. I started to cry.

There was a knock on the door.

I said nothing. I could not stop crying.

Elana entered carrying a pail, mop and broom. She stared at me, disconcerted. "Miss—can I do something for you?"

I shook my head.

"You prefer that I return at a later time?"

I nodded.

She drew back the window drapes. Sunlight fell in. "You see, it is a so beautiful day. Go you out, miss. Enjoy on this beautiful day. *Keyif* we say in Turkish. It mean relax yourself. Enjoy. It is what to do in Istanbul on a so beautiful day."

I managed to smile at her as she left the room.

Then I put through a call to Spitzer. I told the operator we'd been cut off; insisted she reconnect us at once. She informed me icily that there was nothing she could do. All circuits to Belgrade were tied up. I should expect a twelve-hour wait, at the least.

Twelve hours.

I could only pray fervently that Spitzer would do as I'd suggested, demanded. I regarded him now as half mad, incapable of making correct decisions. Yet, in a world half mad who could be certain which decisions were the right ones? Perhaps Arazi *was* right. Perhaps Spitzer *was* right. One day, if we lived, we could be wise with hindsight. But now no man could claim to have foresight. We were living through days which had no parallel. One could not act with logic. One must proceed by instinct.

I put through a call to Alexander. If the *Darien* was not filled with

Jews from Kladovo and Sabac, we must at once board refugees from Rumania. Alexander must organize this exodus; he and Cotic and whoever was left in the Palestine Office.

Yulik returned to my room alone.

For the second time that morning I saw a man go pale with anger.

"You can't mean it?" he shouted when I told him of the conversation with Spitzer. "For months the man begs us, implores us, plagues us. He must have a ship. A ship for his people. Now that a ship is coming to save them—" He sat on the bed. "It's impossible. One of us must leave at once for Kladovo."

"Wait till the call comes through," I said. "Maybe he has done what I asked. If he puts the matter to his people they may be boarding the *Darien* tomorrow."

It was cold in the room and damp. But Yulik took out a handkerchief, wiped his face as though it were a sweating summer's day. Finally he said, "I don't know what to do. I tell you, I don't know what to do. David Hacohen is coming here in a few days' time. It is a fine thing when one must dread the arrival of one's own people."

"Everything will work out." I said the words because he so badly needed to hear them; not because I believed them.

Yulik put his handkerchief away, looked up at me. "When we sat on a bench under the bridge eating our fish sandwiches Dani said something which sticks in my mind like a fishbone sticks in the throat. We were talking about the *Darien,* trying to convince him he must stand with us. Even though Shertok sends official orders that we give up the ship. Dani listened to Shmarya. To me. We talked to him and at him for an hour. But at the end he said, 'We can't go on alone. We Jews are enough alone as it is. We can't cut ourselves off from—ourselves.' "

"Perhaps we won't have to," I said. "Perhaps when Hacohen comes we can make him understand."

He did not answer.

I walked to the window; stood looking out.

Stefan, where are you?

It was, indeed, as Elana had said, a day full of beauty and sunshine. The dense blue of the cloudless sky was mirrored in the Bosporus and

452

the waters shimmered with sunlight. Steamers crossing to and from Scutari were crowded with rush-hour workers coming from their homes in the Asian section of the city to their jobs in Pera and Stambul. Bright-painted sail boats scudded about like bugs on the water. A large cargo ship flying a Russian flag slid by almost directly below my window. I could see the sailors aboard, lounging in the sunshine, taking in the view. When Stefan phoned, as he surely would today, he might well have news of my family. I'd heard nothing, nothing at all, since Bukovina was swallowed by Russia.

David . . . Sophie . . . their sons . . . my sister Bertha . . . Takor . . . my aunts . . . not a word from any of them, about any of them, for months.

And on the other side of the black wall shadowed by the swastika, no news from or about my brother Arthur in the concentration camp Theresienstadt . . . his wife, Rachel . . . their daughter, Erika . . .

Stefan, where are you? When will you call me? Will you bring me some word?

I saw a cluster of birds hovering in the sky. I'd heard there were hawks which flew above this city. But from the distance the birds looked like vultures, wheeling, waiting.

For a week I scarcely left the hotel. More than ever before I was tied to the telephone. Overseas calls had been difficult enough to make in Rumania. In Istanbul they verged on impossibilities. If one went out for a five-minute walk to break the smoke-filled tensions of the room, one might miss a vital call from Spitzer . . . Alexander . . . Berl . . . Solomonides . . . Cotic . . . or Stefan. (Had he left Rumania without troubling to check back with Mrs. Schecter who now had my forwarding address? *Stefan, where are you?*)

To make matters more impossible, we had to keep from Yehuda Arazi the news that the *Darien* was in Sulina waiting for the Kladovo people—who might not come.

I had not been able to contact Spitzer again. I'd been informed by some man who worked with him in Belgrade that Spitzer had gone off to Kladovo. It was impossible to reach him there. The nearest telephone was at the railroad station, thirty-three miles away. Kladovo itself was locked in by ice and snow. One could reach it only by sleigh.

Arazi was often in my room when the telephone rang. When Alexander or Solomonides called I had to try to get and relay information by meaningful silences and a noncommittal kind of double talk.

Solomonides was handling negotiations which concerned the supplying of the ship. Alexander was arranging papers, transport and other details for a stand-by list of illegals who would crowd onto the *Darien* if the Kladovo people did not come.

But we had to wait. Wait for word from Spitzer. For months his people had been promised this ship, the *Darien II*. How could we take it from them before we knew of their decision? But how long could we wait? Hacohen was expected any day. If the ship were still empty could we resist his official demands that the *Darien* be taken from us?

Kadmon had come from Palestine. He and Dani kept a considerate silence when we tried to combat the implacable arguments of Arazi. But when Arazi left the room, they took up the battle for him.

We had thought that nothing could break the solidarity of the Mossad. The *Darien* was doing that.

In addition to the countless torturing decisions concerning this ship, there were the local problems brought to us by Simon Brod. The more we could help him, the more people he could help. And the number of refugees arriving in Istanbul every day seemed to increase by geometric proportions.

As a counterpoint to the agony of waiting for phone calls, arguing about the *Darien,* and listening to individual stories of desperation transmitted to us by Brod, there were meals in the dining room with Eddie Goldenberg and Sophie.

Eddie was, indeed, turning into another Mandel. He helped us with funds, but even more, with contacts. Because I did not want to leave the hotel, he invited dinner guests whom he thought might be useful to us.

He introduced me to Arthur Whittal, the British consul in charge of visas. If the immigration policies had been put in the hands of this tall and gracious gentleman, the White Paper would have been torn to shreds. That much was clear. It was also clear that Whittal and important Turkish officials to whom Goldenberg introduced me were under ever-increasing pressure from the British Mandatory Government in Palestine. Do not allow Turkey to become a refuge or a stop-over spot for Jews attempting to reach Palestine.

How could Britain bother with such cruel incidentals when her cities were raging with flames?

She was still fighting totally alone.

Once again we sat appalled before the short-wave radio listening to transmitted reports of the bombing of Coventry: the city they called Britain's Detroit. Strategic bombing might have limited the destruction to the factories, all on the city's outskirts. But the Germans were also bent on destroying the men and women who worked in those factories. Mile after mile of homes, shops, offices, even the historic St. Michael's Cathedral became a realm of rubble in a single night. And a new word entered the world's vocabulary: Coventrizing.

Then Birmingham, industrial center of the Midlands, was Coventrized.

Yehuda Arazi was in the room as we listened to reports of the two mass burials held in Coventry. Unidentifiable bodies interred in a vast grave.

"These are the people you are refusing to work with," he shouted at us. "To win a war, you must take a long-term view, can't you see that? If the Arab countries cease being neutral, Britain can lose the war. Don't you see that? If Britain loses, we all lose. Don't you understand?"

We did understand. Which made our course of action all the more agonizing.

On the morning of December twelfth, David Hacohen arrived in Istanbul.

His entrance was disconcerting to say the least, for a man whom we had awaited with such dread.

He strode into my hotel room laughing mightily. A tall, lean, handsome, distinguished-looking man. "So," he announced, looking me over, "you are the lady Ruth who has such an admirable reputation." He told us then that he had been given a small room at the back without a bath. When he went down to the desk to ask for a room with bath, he was told there was a severe room shortage in Istanbul. He was lucky to get anything at all in the Park Hotel. When he asked, "Where do I take a bath?" the concierge said, "You will take a bath in the room of Miss Ruth."

"Naturally," said Hacohen, "I expressed some surprise. 'How will that look?' I asked. 'Me taking a bath in a single girl's room?'

"So the concierge told me, 'All your friends take baths in the room of Miss Ruth. And we know it's all right. There are men in and out of her room all day and all night. And we know it's all right. Miss Ruth could walk down the hall naked and we will know it's all right.'"

But after that jocular introduction, Hacohen got down to the reason he'd come. And we saw at once why he'd become a member of the Jewish Agency Executive, the Yishuv's equivalent of cabinet member.

Arazi had given us all the arguments; given them over and again, spelling them out in the finest detail. Hacohen gave the same arguments in a way which brooked no argument. The Political Department of the Jewish Agency had decided. They understood, of course, our immediate concern for the refugees. But the political ramifications of this matter were of even greater importance.

He addressed his speech—it could only be termed that—to all of us. But at the end he turned straight to Shmarya. "I haven't come here with a request, Zameret. I've come with an order. From Shertok himself. You must sign the papers Arazi brought. You must turn the ship over to the British. I assure you, Shertok would not have given the *Darien* so much time and consideration if he did not feel that the matter was one which came into his realm of operations. He feels, we all feel, that the plan proposed for the *Darien* will, without doubt, end the war sooner. And the sooner it ends, the more lives will be saved. Including Jewish lives. Furthermore—and this point I can't stress enough—if we co-operate with British Intelligence in this matter, one in which they happen to be vitally interested, we have every reason to believe—" he repeated the words slowly, *"every reason to believe* that they will co-operate with us in matters in which we are vitally interested. Arazi has mentioned a Jewish Brigade in the British Army. But I can tell you, Zameret, that is just one example. There are many others which I'm not permitted to go into at this point. But I *can* say this, Zameret, the matter of the *Darien* is one which might even have bearing on our postwar future. Whether or not we Jews ever have our own nation may be in the laps of the gods. But it's very definitely in the hands of the British. If we go back on our promises to them and use the ship in direct contradiction to British law—if they see that the man who would be, in all likelihood, our first Foreign Minister has no control over his countrymen in so vital a matter—" Hacohen let the sentence hang, like a noose around our necks.

The winter wind lashed raindrops in a sudden frenzy against the french windows.

At length Shmarya took the stub of a cigarette from his lips, lit another. "It's true," he said, "my name is down as owner of the ship. But I don't own her. She is owned, you see, by the Mossad. So I can't give you a decision. I must consult with the other members of the Mossad."

David Hacohen stared at Shmarya, his face reddening. He had told us, specifically, that he had not come for our decision. He had come with orders. Nevertheless, he nodded. "I have appointments in Ankara this afternoon," he said. "I'll be back here in a few days to pick up the papers Arazi brought you. With your signature on them, Zameret."

He left.

But his presence remained.

Kadmon and Dani were silent.

Yulik spoke, Shmarya and I. Spoke to them. Spoke at them. But for the first time our words had lost their fervor.

Suddenly Shmarya said, "My country right or wrong! I think they're wrong. But Hacohen is right—if we ever hope to have a country, we've got to begin by obeying our leaders. How can we put ourselves above them?" He looked straight at me.

I felt broken inside. I whispered, "We can't."

Shmarya turned to Yulik.

"I too go by a simple saying," Yulik said. "First things first. The ship is in Sulina. Ready to sail. There are refugees ready to board her. You all talk of our people. Cutting ourselves off from our people. Are *they* not our people? The ship can hold eight hundred. If you sign that paper, Shmarya, you might well be signing eight hundred death certificates."

My country right or wrong. First things first. The agony was that both sides were right. And everything came first.

457

They did not leave my room till late that night.

As I lay in bed in the darkness it seemed that my body was pervaded by the constant, slashing rain. An incessant kind of universal weeping. Backed by the gloomy omnipresent foghorns.

I remembered the file cards on the floor of Orekhovsky's office. Picking them up, sorting them out after the earthquake. Each card a symbol of a life. Each card someone's son or sister or wife or child. Or husband.

That night it was clear to me what we must do. Shmarya must not sign the papers. The *Darien* must be kept as a rescue ship.

But in the daytime the other voices took on more strength. How could we, Yulik, Shmarya and I, refute the direct orders of our leaders? They had much information we did not have. Information relating to the Yishuv's future role with the British—in the war effort, and perhaps even beyond that. I kept remembering Dani Shind's words. *We can't go on alone. We Jews are enough alone as it is. We can't cut ourselves off from—ourselves.*

The next three days were a new kind of hell.

Hacohen had not yet returned from Ankara. But we expected him any hour. And no decision had been made. Kadmon and Dani believed we must sign the papers.

Yulik held to his position: The ship had been bought, reconverted and sent to Sulina to save lives. That was the stark and simple purpose of the Mossad. We must stick to it.

Shmarya and I were torn between. Both sides had irrefutable arguments. Both sides were right.

We five stopped talking to each other. We avoided each other. I spent most of my time with Brod and his people. They knew nothing of the conflict of the *Darien*.

Yulik spent most of his time in his room, the door locked.

But a decision had to be made before David Hacohen returned.

Late on the third night I received a telephone call from Alexander. He had followed orders. He had prepared a list of refugees from Orekhovsky's files; men, women and children who would board the *Darien* if the Kladovo people did not get through. But some of the refugees had not obeyed orders. Though they had been given no details, they made their way to Sulina. They had boarded the ship. One hundred eighty men, women and children were now living in the hold of the *Darien II*.

"I told them," Alexander said, "that I had no authority to let them stay on the ship. One of them asked me if I had authority to murder one hundred eighty Jews. That's what I'd be doing, he said, if they were sent back."

"You've heard nothing from Spitzer?"

"Nothing," Alexander said. "Should I—"

The telephone connection was suddenly cut. It was an occurrence which happened frequently. But this time, for the first time, I was glad of the interruption. Alexander did not know of the conflict concerning the *Darien*. And I did not know what to tell him.

Presently I went to bed, but not to sleep.

Would his call come through again? Perhaps I should instruct him to take the *Darien* out to sea, so that more refugees could not force their way aboard. Perhaps the ship should proceed to Constantza. Since the Kladovo people now had transit visas, they could travel to Constantza to board her.

If we heard from Spitzer.

If we kept the ship.

The turmoil of arguments clashed again.

One of them asked me if I had the authority to murder one hundred eighty Jews. . . .

One hundred eighty men, women, children living now in the hold of the *Darien II*; waiting for our rescue ship to take them to Palestine.

Not names on Orekhovsky's file cards. Human beings, in the hold of the *Darien II*. Who would be the one to tell them to get off the ship?

After a while, I sat up. I reached for the telephone, asked for Yulik's room.

He answered at once.

"Were you asleep?" I said. "I'm sorry."

"I wasn't asleep."

"May I—come up?"

"Of course."

It was four in the morning. But Yulik was dressed; his bed was made. Had he been to sleep at all? His face looked haggard.

459

I told him about the hundred and eighty men, women and children who had forced their way on board the *Darien*.

After a moment Yulik said, "Are you ready to give the order that they must get off the ship?"

"No."

"Are you ready to side with me?" Then he added, "With the understanding that you won't change your mind."

I hesitated.

His eyes burned into me.

I said, "Yes."

"Good." He turned from me abruptly. He stared out the open window, into the darkness. After a time he repeated the word. "Good," he said several times.

Then we sat together and tried to determine what to do next.

There were five of us here in Istanbul; five Mossad members who were apprised of all the arguments. To contact the others by telephone would be meaningless now. How to describe, half in code, the tortured conflicts of this case? The decision must be made by the five who were here. Kadmon and Dani had taken their stand. Yulik and I now stood together. Shmarya had the deciding decision. Shmarya who legally owned the ship.

"Well, we'll meet him for breakfast," Yulik said. "We'll try. Go back to bed now. Get a few hours' sleep."

As I was about to leave the room, his telephone rang.

"Shmarya . . . No, I wasn't asleep."

The conversation was a short one.

When Yulik hung up, he looked at me.

"Well?" I demanded.

"It seems," said Yulik, "that our friend Shmarya has not been sleeping too soundly either these past few days. He tells me he's just remembered an old American saying. Or maybe it's British, he's not sure."

"What saying?"

"Don't give up the ship."

FORTY-ONE

I WAS WRENCHED FROM SLEEP.

I sat up violently.

Someone was hammering at my door.

I ran through the darkness. "Yes?"

"Brod. Open."

He stood there in the hallway. He raised his hands at me, shook them. But for once there were no words.

"What is it?" I pulled him into my room. Closed the door. Groped for the light switch.

In the darkness he shouted the words at me. "A ship of illegals is sinking in the Sea of Marmara. I will wake Yulik. Phone Shmarya. Dani. We must get there at once. My car is downstairs. Hurry, for God's sake." He left.

I ran to the telephone. Shmarya and Dani were staying at the Pera Palace. After interminable minutes the operator put through my call. But there was no answer. Were they together somewhere? Was Shmarya trying to convince Dani to change his mind about the *Darien*? While people—our people—were drowning in the Sea of Marmara.

I pulled on some clothes, raced out of the room, down the stairs, through the empty lobby.

"Miss Ruth," the concierge called out to me. "Is anything wrong? Can I be of assistance?"

It was snowing outside; strong wet sleet, slashing the night. There was a sharp wind.

Brod's black limousine was waiting. It looked like a hearse.

I climbed in.

"Yulik wasn't there!" he shouted at me. "Will Shmarya and Dani be waiting for us?"

"I couldn't reach them."

The car shot off. We plummeted down a narrow street, across Galata Bridge—empty now. Sounds of sirens cut the darkness.

"*Now* they come to help! They commit the murder. Then they come to pull in the bodies." He was crying. Not shouting. Not swearing. Speaking softly and crying.

The road by the edge of Marmara was empty. We careened along, the car lights silhouetting the boulders and the sea walls into monstrous shapes against the snow-streaked night.

"She was a sailing ship," Brod said softly. "Her motor was broken. She asked the port authorities for permission to dock till the storm was over. She did not receive permission. Because the passengers were Jews, and they had no transit visas. The authorities gave them some food and water. And permission to anchor. In the outer Bosporus. This afternoon when the storm let up, they were told to proceed. To cross Marmara. Through the Dardanelles. Into the Aegean. Through the Mediterranean. This ship with no motor and rotting sails."

"How many people were on board?"

"I don't know," he said. "Too many. That is all I know."

"Where was she from?"

"Bulgaria. Varna."

Varna. Dr. Berger had begged me to go there. If I had gone would I have been able to stop the sailing of this ship?

"What was she named?"

"*Salvador*. In Spanish it means Savior."

As we rounded a curve in the road we saw the searchlights, slicing through the blackness. They centered on the specter of a tilted mast. And the sinking hulk of a ship. As we drew closer we heard the piercing wail of sirens. But it was not until we got out of the car that we heard the screaming.

Rescue workers were standing waist deep in the raging waves, reaching for swimmers who had somehow managed to make it to shore. Fishing boats were lurching on the dark sea. Motorboats careened through the storm-rent waters. And everyone—survivors, rescuers and those who were drowning—everyone was screaming.

"You stay in the car," Brod shouted at me. "I'll bring people to you." He climbed down through the wet rocks, into the water.

I followed him. I waded out into the water. A hand. An outstretched arm. I reached for it. A wave lashed against me. I fell into the freezing, seething blackness. I got to my feet. The hand and arm had disappeared. I started to scream.

A man was standing beside me. He was huge. The waves dashed against him, receded, came at him again. He stood, staring out into the darkness, not moving. Staring.

"Come into the car," I shouted at him. "We have a car. Come with me."

Somehow I made my way to him, slipping, again falling. I stood beside him, shouting at him. He did not hear me. He did not see me. I took his arm, tried to shake him. He was like a statue. He would not move.

I saw the limp body of a child being sucked under. I ran to the place. I reached for the body. My hand closed on a tangled mass of hair. I pulled the child to me. A little girl. Somehow I got her out of the water, up the rocks. I put her in the back seat of the car, took off my coat, wrapped her in it. The coat was heavy with sea water. But perhaps the weight would keep her warm. She started to vomit and she started to cry.

"Where is your mother?" I asked her.

She answered in a language I did not understand. I held her as she vomited, then I kissed her forehead. "I'll be back," I told her. Her hands clutched onto me. But I pulled away; ran, slipped, slid down the rocks. The wind was edged with ice. Snow and sleet bit at my skin as I waded out again toward hands, arms stretched from the waves. A man grabbed onto me. Pulled me under. I struggled to the surface, shoved at him with my foot. Then reached for him again.

"Help!" I shouted at the colossus who still stood, knee-deep in water, staring out into the blackness. My word reached him. He looked at us. He came to us. He pulled the half-drowned man from the waves. "Please!" I shouted, "Carry him up to the car. This way."

He lifted the younger, slighter man into his arms. Followed me to the car, sat him gently beside the child who sobbed, gagged, screamed.

Then we went together back into the sea.

I don't know how many we pulled from the raging water. Some were dead. We filled the car. Others we lay on the sea rocks. People had come, with blankets. There were donkeys. A few horses. "Hospital," I shouted at those who had brought the animals. "Take these people to the hospital."

I saw Brod. He had organized a human rescue chain. He called to me, but I could not hear his words over the shriek and blasts of the sirens, the foghorns, the wind.

I made my way to him.

"Drive my car to the hospital. Tell them to send help. Doctors. Nurses. Ambulances. Then come here for more survivors."

He went back to the water.

"I will drive." I looked up at the man. It was the first time he had spoken. Water dripped from his hair. Tears ran from his eyes.

We went to the car.

It *was* a hearse—of living corpses. They were quiet now, except for the little girl who kept crying out words in a strange language. No one seemed to understand what she was saying. No one answered.

After a while the man who was driving spoke again. He spoke in German. "I tried to save my wife," he said. "But I couldn't. I saw her drown. We have a little girl named Gretchen. Three years old. She doesn't know how to swim. I looked and looked for her in the water. But I couldn't see her. She doesn't know how to swim."

"Maybe someone saved her," I said. "Maybe you'll find her at the hospital."

"That is my hope," he said.

The City Hospital was a gray prisonlike building, with long drafty corridors. There were few nurses or doctors on duty at this time of night. Nor were there beds. I helped carry mattresses into the hallways and blankets. I helped serve hot soup. "I can't stay here," I kept saying. "I must go back." Perhaps no one understood. Perhaps they only spoke Turkish. They kept pointing at people, shoving me toward them with a blanket, a hot-water bottle, a vomit pan.

"You stay here," the man who had driven the car told me. "You're needed here. I'll go back." He started down the hallway, then came back to say, "My little girl is not here. Not yet. But if she is brought in—Gretchen, her name is Gretchen Heller. Tell her not to be frightened. Tell her Papa will come for her in the morning."

"I'll be with her," I promised. "I won't leave until you come."

The corridors were crowded. More survivors were carried in. I served more hot soup. I doled out more blankets.

"Were you on the ship?" one of the doctors asked me.

I was shivering. My clothes were wet, my hair dripping.

"Get a blanket," he told me. "Get out of those wet clothes." He hurried away.

A little girl was brought in; about three years old. I went over to her. "What's your name, little one?"

She stared up at me. Her eyes were dark, like wells of terror.

I took both her hands in mine. "Is your name Gretchen?"

She shook her head. "Helga," she whispered.

The faded light of dawn pressed against the windows. The rain and sleet had stopped. The storm was over.

One of the nurses said to me, "You must go home now and get some sleep or you will be back here on a stretcher."

"How many survivors were brought in?" I asked her.

"Over a hundred. But some have already died."

"There were three hundred and twenty-six refugees on the ship," I told her. "Plus the captain. And two men in the crew."

"It's terrible," she said. "It's terrible." She went away quickly down the hall.

"Three hundred and twenty-six passengers." Many of the survivors told me that. They repeated this figure over and over like a grim incantation.

I was kneeling by a thin blond woman, spooning hot soup into her mouth. She ate obediently, like a baby. But she would not speak.

A newspaper reporter came down the corridor. He stopped by each of the survivors. He asked only name, age, country of origin. Some tried to say more. But he cut them off. "The paper goes to press in a few hours," he told them. "I don't have time for all these stories."

He stopped by the woman to whom I was feeding soup.

"Do you speak French?" he asked.

She nodded.

"Could you tell me, please, name, age, country of origin."

"Until last night," she told him, "I had a husband and three children. They were drowned. My husband was drowned. And my children were drowned. A man tried to save two of my children. But he was hit on the head by a plank from the ship. They all drowned."

"Would you tell me your name, madame," the reporter said. "Your age. Your country of origin."

"Austria," she said. "My husband's name is Heinrich Cohen. Age forty-two. Chemist. The children. Bertha, age thirteen. Erich, age ten. And Lisa, the baby, age two. The man who tried to save two of my children was named Stefan Meta."

I did not hear. She had not said it. I kept on feeding her the soup.

"Thank you, madame," the reporter said. "Now if you would tell me your name, your age—"

"Why?" She looked up at him. "It is the names of the dead you should write down in your notebook. It is the dead who need to be remembered."

He nodded and went on to the next survivor.

I heard myself asking her a question. But how could I be speaking? I was somewhere far away.

"This man who tried to save your children, how do you know what his name was?"

"I know his name because I know him," she told me. "We met in Varna. He was very fond of my daughter Lisa. He said she reminded him of his own daughter when she was two years old."

"Did he ever mention the name of his daughter?"

"Veronica. Something like that. Viorica. Why?" She looked at me. "Did you know him too?"

I put the bowl of soup on the floor. I got up. I walked down the hospital corridor. I heard some people call out to me: "More soup, please. Another blanket." Many were sobbing.

"Yes," I said to one, "I will get you more soup."

466

"Yes," I said to another, "I will get you another blanket."

After that, I don't remember. I started again to shiver violently. Everything was gray.

It was a strange room, filled with sunlight. Someone was bending over me. My mother. She had come to find me in Czernowitz. When I woke she would take me away.

"No," I heard a soft voice saying. "I'm not your mother. I'm Sophie. Don't you remember me? Sophie Goldenberg. Are you feeling any better?" Her hand was cool on my forehead.

I slept.

Screams.

Who was screaming?

A hand stretched out. I tried to reach it. *Stefan.* A plank shot through the dark waves; hit him.

I screamed. Woke up screaming.

Shmarya was there. He was holding my hand.

I whispered his name.

"So—you know me," he said.

"Where are we?"

"At the Goldenbergs. Sophie decided you'd never get better in that great gloomy hospital. She had you brought here."

I was in a canopy bed. The room had pale pink wallpaper. The french windows were wide open, framing a soft sky.

It had been winter, with sleet and rain.

"What day is this?" I asked. "What month?"

"Well," said Shmarya, "as a matter of fact, it's the end of March."

Sophie came in. She wore a dressing gown. Her dark hair fell loose over her shoulders.

"She's—back," Shmarya said to her.

Sophie stood by the bed, smiling down at me. I reached for her hand. "Thank you," I whispered.

"It's we who must thank you," she said.

After a few days I knew that I could not remain at the Goldenbergs. The name suited; golden hill. Their home was an isolated oasis of luxury and gracious living. But as memories swarmed at me, I became logged with guilt. The *Salvador* survivors had lain shivering, moaning, weeping on blankets or old mattresses in hospital corridors. And I was here in this pale pink room in an antique canopy bed.

I must leave. I must get back to work.

But the doctor who came to visit me daily insisted that I stay, at least a week. "No one," he told me, "expected you to live."

That evening as Sophie sat by my bedside she said, "It seemed to me that you didn't want to live." After a time she added, "Would it help if you talked about him?"

I looked at her.

"In your delirium you kept calling out for him," Sophie said gently. "I—saw his name listed among those who died in the *Salvador* disaster."

The tears came. Her arms went around me. She held me as I cried.

Memories we had made flooded through me. . . . Visions of the life we might have had; clear as though we had lived them. He sat on the terrace of our Tel Aviv flat; he was reading the morning paper. In Hebrew. I was in the kitchen. I squeezed him a full glass of fresh orange juice. Then I made him scrambled eggs. "How do you like your eggs?" I called out to him. "Soft or—"

I had not even learned how he liked his scrambled eggs.

She wept with me. As she wiped my tears, I saw hers.

"I know," she kept whispering over and over. "I know."

Ten years ago she had fled from Russia with a small child. Who was the child's father? Had she loved him? Was he dead?

I did not tell her about Stefan Meta. If there was a man she had loved, in Russia, she did not tell me. But the tears bound us. The tears helped.

And the tears bound me to the others, all the unknown others, who wept for the victims of the *Salvador*.

I read the newspaper reports. Two hundred and thirty-one had drowned. One hundred and three bodies were recovered. Including sixty-six children.

There were one hundred and twenty-three survivors.

They were now in the detention camp at Atlit. In Palestine. They had been saved by our ship, the *Darien*.

468

The next day Shmarya told me about the *Darien*.

"By December twenty-ninth," he said, "we still had not been able to reach Spitzer. And we were still under pressure from Hacohen, Arazi, from Shertok in Palestine. Where was the ship? They wanted the ship. So we told the captain to proceed to Constantza. He would wait there for the Kladovo people.

"Well, he proceeded. Or tried to. The ship was caught in a terrible storm. Lost her anchor. Was thrown up against the rocks near Agigea. Solomonides got a tug to pull her off. There was sea water in the bunker. Two engines were damaged. But she managed to make it to Constantza, where she was repaired. While we waited for the Kladovo people."

"Had you found Spitzer?"

"We had," said Shmarya. "At least he answered the telephone. We tried everything. We screamed at him. We implored. We begged him, as you had, to present it to his people. Let them decide. It was their lives. But Spitzer heard nothing. He was like a rock. Yulik wanted to go to Kladovo. But we had no time. Hacohen and Arazi were still here. Still demanding the empty ship. On February nineteenth, she left for Varna. With three hundred and eighty refugees aboard.

"We told Spitzer he had one more chance to reconsider. Some of his people could still board the ship. We would wait for them at Varna.

"But at Varna, you see, the matter was taken out of our hands. There were hordes of refugees waiting there on the dock. The captain insisted that the space was being held. But some of them forced their way on board with guns. Then the Bulgarian port authorities said they'd confiscate the ship if we didn't take on some undesirables. And in this case they *meant* undesirables. They unlocked prison cells. Presented us with a crop of prostitutes and thieves.

"At the end of February, the ship landed in Istanbul. By this time, you see, Yulik and I had won our case. Or you might say, the *Salvador* survivors had won our case for us. Arazi and Hacohen visited them in the hospital. Saw them sitting, day after day, at the docks, waiting. We couldn't get visas. The Turkish Government was threatening to send them back where they'd come from.

"Finally, Hacohen came up with a compromise. His British contacts agreed. Shertok agreed. And we agreed. The *Darien* would stop in

Istanbul, take on the *Salvador* survivors. The British would allow the ship into Haifa port. The refugees would be interned at Atlit. The British would confiscate the ship. Use it for their own purposes—after paying us the agreed-upon fifteen thousand pounds.

"Well, you see," he concluded, "we have the money now. We could buy another ship. Except there's not a single ship of any sort to be found. Nothing."

"And Spitzer?" I asked. "The Jews at Kladovo and Sabac?"

"We can only hope," Shmarya said, "that Spitzer was right. They'll be safer in Yugoslavia."

A week later I returned to the Park Hotel. Eddie Goldenberg managed to get me a room; the same room. I immediately asked for my mail, my radio and the newspapers. All three had been forbidden at the Goldenbergs, on doctor's orders.

There was a letter from Stefan, forwarded from the apartment in Bucharest. Postmarked: Varna, Bulgaria.

For a long time I sat, staring at the envelope. His hand had written these words, my name. I heard his voice repeating the words he had written. Then his voice changed; he was calling to me. Ruth . . . Ruth . . .

Did misery lay close to madness?

I carefully opened the envelope.

MY DARLING:

I don't know where you are, but I do know that I'll find you. (Perhaps before this letter does. Since I doubt that it will ever reach you, I'll keep it short. Though I'd like to write on and on tonight. Keeping in touch. Touching you.)

I'd hoped, my love, to find you in Bucharest. Your landlady was uncommunicative, to say the least. She informed me that you had moved. She refused to say when or where or why. I contacted some rescue people, thinking they might know of you. Instead, I was told of a ship leaving Varna for Palestine. It was organized, they said, by a Dr. Confino. A Bulgarian Zionist, a dedicated man, they said. Apparently he's rescued hundreds of people on small fishing boats, sailboats and other such. I had to bear this in mind this evening when I saw the *Salvador!* This old lady doesn't look as though she can make it to Istanbul.

When she does, I, for one, will disembark and—with the few coins I've got left—will make my way, as they so euphemistically put it, overland through Syria, into Palestine. (Which, by the way, is how my wife and children entered the country.)

When I arrive, I'll locate your brother Poli. If he knows where you are (and is more communicative than your landlady), I'll try to join you. Otherwise, I'll wait for you to come home. (Strange that I should use the word 'home'; I've never set foot in the place. God knows I've never been a Zionist. I use the word because it will be home when you and I live there, together.)

Until we are together again, be good, little one. Keep safe. And keep remembering that I love you.

Your
STEFAN.

The tears which came within me were too deep to be wept.

I sat on the balcony staring across at the opposite shore which was hung with the gray of evening. Was it Asia, or was it the place that the dead gathered, to look back, to scream out their terrible "why?" The word which rent the sky and struck the stars. The word which no one answered; which no one heard.

The *Salvador* had been one small ship, searching for a port of safety. A ship crowded with fleeing Jews. Why? What had they done that they must leave their homes, leave the lives they had built as carefully as any man does? What had they done that they must suddenly search for a place in the world where they could land? What had they done that there was no country to stretch out a hand of help, of welcome?

There were only the Jews of Palestine aching to offer them a home. But forbidden to do so.

The newspaper stories about the *Salvador* had brought sympathy for the survivors. Sympathy for the victims. But that was all.

The world was divided into those nations who were killing Jews. And those nations who were allowing Jews to be killed.

What harm would we have done, Stefan and I, had we been allowed to live out our love? Stefan and I and the hundreds of thousands of others?

And I knew that this was only the start. The massacre would spread to such massive proportions that one day in the far distance all the unconcerned countries in the world *would* look in horror at what had

471

been done. But then it would be too late. They might even ask themselves in shame, or shock, *why* they had done nothing. But if they asked the question at all, they would turn away from it quickly. What use to probe or ask questions? It was too late. The Jews were already dead. Hundreds of thousands—perhaps the number would mount into millions—of Jews dead. Murdered.

Why?

That night Elana brought me my radio.

I lay in the darkness, listening to soft music, afraid to fall asleep. Afraid of the ghastly nightmares.

A news and interview program came on. It was one I had listened to often, for its audience was the huge foreign population in Istanbul. There were interviews in French, German, Russian, Arabic, English.

Tonight, a chemistry professor from Bucharest would give some eyewitness details about the pogrom which had taken place in Rumania from January twenty-first to January twenty-third.*

Another pogrom in Bucharest.

Rigid with horror I listened as the professor detailed what he had witnessed in the dry monotones he might use to deliver a chemistry lecture.

"One of my dear friends, Rabbi Hers Guttman, and his two brilliant young sons, Jancu and Josef, aged twenty-five and twenty-seven, were among the hundreds of Jewish leaders and scholars who were taken in wagons to the forest of Jilava, thrown out and machine-gunned in groups of five or ten. As it happened, Rabbi Guttman was one of the few who was not killed. He lay in the snow, bleeding. He held the wrist of each of his sons, counting the pulse beat. When his sons died, Rabbi Guttman, a great and good and compassionate man, my friend Rabbi Guttman crawled through the forest, leaving a trail of blood behind him. Somehow he got back to the city.

"Another group of Jews, businessmen, bankers, were herded together in the confiscated home of Oscar Kaufmann, director-general of the Banque de Credit Roumain."

Kaufmann! One of Mandel's friends and business associates!

* *See* Appendix Nineteen.

"All the older persons in the group were driven in trucks to Jilava at one end of the city and murdered. The rest were taken in the opposite direction to Băneasa Woods. They were beaten and then released. But a few hours later another group of Jews were stripped naked, whipped, then mutilated and murdered in the Băneasa Woods."

Băneasa. Where Stefan and I had eaten lunch in the lakeside restaurant. . . .

"For days naked frozen corpses lay in the snow at Jilava and Băneasa. Relatives went out to identify the bodies. But this was difficult, since many of the bodies had been so mutilated."

Mandel—was he one of the naked frozen corpses?

"A student of mine, Moise Silberstein, was made into a human torch, burned to death on the Jewish street called Văcăreşti."

Văcăreşti. Where Alexander lived with his doting mother.

"Another dear friend—I omit his name out of deference to the way he died—was flogged in a public square while a crowd watched and jeered. His genital organ was exposed to ascertain that he was, indeed, a Jew. It was then cut off. My friend was locked into a pillory. The Iron Guard invited schoolchildren to throw snowballs at him. Which they did. Eventually, he froze to death.

"A friend of my mother's, Ernestine Riegler, was in the synagogue in Calea Mosilor, praying. The synagogue was burned down and all the Jews who had assembled for prayer were murdered.

"There were more Jews killed in the slaughterhouse. Beheaded with the mechanical instruments used for killing cattle. Many of the corpses were then hung on meathooks—"

I switched off the radio. But the voice of the chemistry professor went on and on in my head. Recounting details. Relighting memories.

Orekhovsky.

"*I couldn't identify his body*," Alexander had said. "*I never saw him without any clothes. Then they showed me a basket of heads. Bloody heads. I saw his head staring up at me. The eyes were open. The open eyes staring at me.*"

Why?

The word shattered through the room's darkness.

Orekhovsky had been beheaded and hung up on a meathook because he had tried to help and to save Jews.

Early on the morning of April sixth, Hitler's Luftwaffe stormed the skies over Belgrade. Within three days Yugoslavia's capital was a searing mass of flames.

Hitler's armies smashed across the borders of her new allies: Hungary and Bulgaria. Into Yugoslavia.

The Yugoslavs resisted fiercely.

They were defeated in twelve days.

We later learned that when the Germans arrived at the Kladovo camp they had gone on a sporting spree. They allowed the Jews to scatter and run, for as much as two miles. They then pursued the men, women and children, shot them down, one by one. There was not a single survivor.

The death race was played again at Sabac.

Spitzer, too, was murdered.

In early June I received new orders.

Though the need for illegal ships increased drastically day by day, it was impossible to procure ships. And even if a few ships did somehow become available, there was little likelihood that we could smuggle out enough Jews to fill them. The walls of the ghettos were rising. New concentration camps were being built. Starvation and disease had joined grim forces with Hitler's *Einsatzgruppen*—massacre squads—to murder Jews.

The last road of escape had closed for the Jews of Europe.

But there were Jews we still could reach. Jews who might soon face similar disaster. Hundreds of thousands of Jews in the Arab countries. My assignment was to proceed to Cairo. There I would raise funds and help organize a rescue operation to bring Jews from Egypt, Lebanon and Syria across the borders into Palestine.

Shmarya, Yulik and Dani had already left Istanbul.

I did not tell the Goldenbergs or Brod about my orders. I did not want them to see me off. I had said enough good-bys.

When I turned in my key at the Park Hotel desk the concierge remarked politely, "I trust you've enjoyed your stay, Miss Ruth. And that you'll be back with us soon."

How many times had he spoken these words to the guests checking out of the Park Hotel? Ritual words. But I could not bring myself to make a ritual reply. I hoped I would never have to return to this place where Stefan had died.

As I crossed the crowded lobby I thought of the day I had arrived in Bucharest to join the Mossad. A morning in June. 1939. It was, I remembered, a hot and muggy day, full of sunshine.

It was again a morning in June. 1941.

Two years.

I walked out into the street. The day was the same. Hot and muggy, and full of sunshine.

EPILOGUE

Ruth Klüger's work in the Mossad continued throughout the war years, and in the postwar Paris days.

She became such a vitally important figure in the Aliyah Bet that when the State of Israel was born, and its citizens were encouraged to take Hebrew surnames, Ben-Gurion suggested the name which he said was suitable: Ruth Aliav.

A brief account of the work she did in the Mossad from the summer of 1941 through 1948 is related by two men who worked closely with her during those years: Roger Itzhak Oppenheim and Ehud Uiberall, who later took the Hebrew name Ehud Avriel.

Ruth Klüger in Egypt

AN ACCOUNT BY ROGER ITZHAK OPPENHEIM

ROGER OPPENHEIM *was born in Egypt in 1907. His father was president of the Zionist Organization in Cairo, and Roger began working in the movement at age thirteen. He completed his studies in Paris, returned to Cairo at twenty-four, and resumed his active participation in the Zionist Organization. He became secretary of the Organization in 1939 and president of the Hehaloutz Hatzair. During World War II and afterwards he worked with the aliyah bet.*

On May 14, 1948, the day the State of Israel was declared, Oppenheim was arrested by the Egyptians. He was put in a concentration camp. Finally, in 1956, he was allowed to leave the country. Oppenheim, his wife and young son went to Israel. In Tel Aviv he organized the Union of Jews from Egypt, and is presently working on a history of Egyptian Jews and Zionist activities in Egypt for the Hebrew University. He is also manager of the shipowners division of the Chamber of Shipping of Israel.

I first met Ruth in Alexandria early in 1942. The "flag" under which she was working was raising money. But I soon discovered she was involved in many other enterprises—concerning all facets of the aliyah bet. For instance, I had several flats in Egypt. Ruth used to tell me: "We need your flat in Cairo or Sidi Bish or Aboukir." I'd give her the key. I wouldn't ask why. I'd just say, "For how long do you want me to stay away?" I knew that the flats were used for hiding weapons, making weapons, having secret meetings, hiding illegals we were transferring from one place to another. My flat in Alexandria was used for making illegal passports and documents.

My wife was secretary of one of the departments of the Alexandria police which was in the hands of the British. She was kept busy typing up secret reports. But whenever anything looked as though it might be of interest to the Jewish Agency, my wife would keep me informed. I'd get the report to Ruth. And she would get it—I don't know how—to the proper people in Palestine.

But Ruth was in Egypt primarily to raise money. And this she did! Before she came, it seemed that every Jewish Palestinian organization—sporting clubs, religious organizations, university and whatnot—had its fund raiser in Egypt. They all approached the same rich Jews. And the pickings for every one of these groups grew slimmer and slimmer.

Finally, the Jewish Agency made an agreement with the Mossad. All other money raisers would be called off. Only Ruth would have the responsibility for raising money in Egypt. I was told that half the money she raised would go to the Jewish Agency, half to the Mossad.

In her first year Ruth collected eighty thousand pounds (about four hundred thousand dollars) which was much more than the money previously collected for the Jewish Agency. The money Ruth raised in Egypt was used primarily to bring Jews overland across the borders of Egypt, Lebanon and Syria, into Palestine.

During those years, 1942–44, there were eighty-five thousand to ninety thousand Jews in Egypt. At that time they had no problems and lived an easy life like the Jews in Germany before Hitler; they were an accepted part of the European communities. So the majority of the Jews of Egypt had no pressing reason to take very much to Zionist activities. Most of the wealthy Jews had one concern: their coffers. Money, they felt, was their only security.

Ruth was determined to throw the flame in; she told them what she had seen in the Balkans. She made them understand that they had a responsibility to help.

And she did reach people. She broke down barriers of nonchalance, ignorance, apathy.

What is more, she turned many of these wealthy Jews into ardent, working Zionists; Jews who before had gone to the synagogue Friday night, and that was it; Jews who didn't want to hear about Zionism. She made them realize they were part of the Jewish nation. She used to tell me, "The best way to bring people into the movement is first to get them to pay for it. Then they think it must be worthwhile, because they've already paid so much."

Ruth's contacts extended far beyond the Jews of Egypt and the highest representatives of the Jewish Agency in Palestine. She also knew many high-ranking Egyptians, senators and other men of influence.

What was her special appeal to all these diverse types of people?

481

She had, you might say, an ensemble of qualities: her sincerity, her reliability, her way of speaking to people, of drawing out the best that was in them. The fact that she was a woman may have played a part, but other women had come before her and had not succeeded to any notable degree in, for example, raising money. So Ruth's success must have been due to her own very special personality.

She remained in Egypt until 1944 when she left for France.

Ruth Klüger in Paris

AN ACCOUNT BY EHUD AVRIEL

FROM 1938 TO 1948, Ehud Uiberall (Avriel) worked as a member of the Mossad. He was in Austria from 1938 to January 1940. In '43 and '44, he was based in Turkey; in '45, in Yugoslavia and Greece and in late '45, '46 and '47, in Paris.

On May 17, 1948, three days after Israel gained her statehood, Ehud Avriel became the first ambassador to be appointed by the new nation: ambassador to Czechoslovakia. In 1950, he was made Israeli ambassador to Rumania. He was then appointed director general of the Prime Minister's Office under Ben-Gurion. He became a member of Parliament, served as ambassador to Ghana, Liberia and the Congo. He was director general of International Co-operation and African Affairs in the Foreign Office; served as ambassador to Italy until 1968, when he was made president of the World Zionist General Executive Council, the supreme elective body of the World Zionist Organization.

At the end of the war, Ruth was sent to Europe as the first official representative of the Jews of Palestine. She was the first Jew from Palestine to enter the concentration camps a day or so after they were opened by the Allies. She was like the Israeli Joan of Arc.

At first Ruth was entirely on her own in Europe. Later, when others were sent and the operation grew, Ruth still had only one immediate superior, Ben-Gurion. She took orders only from him.

Ruth never regarded herself as an agent of some underground operation. She, of course, acted according to the rules of our organization with all the rigid disciplines of conspiracy necessitated by our work which was still politically classified as "illegal." But Ruth had the approach of a great humanitarian, rather than of a secret agent.

Because of this attitude she had, for instance, no inhibitions, no hesitations about speaking to General Eisenhower or to Guy de Rothschild or to General de Gaulle on a completely equal basis because she felt: "The equality between us is that we're both human beings and that I have a job to do for human beings which is more important than anything this fellow can have on his hands at this moment. Therefore, I feel perfectly entitled to approach him."

None of the men in the Mossad would have even considered trying to talk directly to General Eisenhower in 1946—to ask him to give us ships for our illegals. We would all have thought: "Eisenhower is the greatest political figure in Europe at this time. He must take into account all sorts of political considerations. Why should Eisenhower want to help us?"

But nothing of this nature ever occurred to Ruth. Her attitude was: "Look, the fellow who can give orders is General Eisenhower. The man who can get ships is General Eisenhower. And if we can get General Eisenhower to help us, every soldier in the occupation armies will work with us; or at least will not work against us. I'll phone General Eisenhower. I'll speak to him. To whom else should I go?"

We argued with her. "Don't make a fool of yourself. You'll never get General Eisenhower to work for the illegal immigration."

But Ruth's feeling was: "I'll be doing him a favor. I'll be giving him a chance. He doesn't know about these things because he's been too busy with other things. But he's a good man and he will want to help us."

I don't know how she got to General Eisenhower. And I don't know what she said to him. But I do know that he was impressed by her approach. And he gave her what she asked for.

I am certain that if I, for example, had managed somehow to get to General Eisenhower he would have said, "Well, for a matter like this, you know, Sergeant Smith is the fellow to see. So go see him and don't bother me."

But with Ruth, it didn't happen like that. Somehow he would be proud and happy to say to her, "If there's anything else I can do for you come again, and don't hesitate."

This was the difference. This was her approach. This was her impact: this instinctive, warm, human decency which characterized her perhaps more than any other person in the Mossad. It was her absolutely innocent, absolutely nonpolitical outlook which enabled her to operate in this simple, direct way. And this was the way that brought dramatic results.

She lifted our organization out of what it could have become, a fantastically efficient secret service operation. (We had at this time, for instance, the kind of facilities for forging documents of which even some rather efficient secret service operations of powerful nations were rather envious.) We could easily have become just another operation doing a secret job, a political job.

But Ruth always saw the Mossad—and helped us to see it—as a great model human endeavor.

This is the most important thing about her. This is the starting point from which you must judge everything she did. This is the way she operated. This is her chief contribution to the magnificent history of the Mossad le Aliyah Bet.

In addition to this, of course, she was a perfect agent; a highly skilled operator, for she knew all the tricks of the trade. And she knew all the right people and places, so vital for our efforts.

I first met Ruth at the Zionist Congress in 1939.

I met her next when I was sent to Paris in 1945. Paris had become the center of our operations. Ruth's headquarters were in the Claridge Hotel. At that time the Claridge was a very highly restricted place with rooms given only to the most important political figures who came to Paris in order to make preparations for the future of Europe.

From the way she was treated by the concierge and by everyone else at the Claridge it seemed clear to me that they regarded Ruth as one of the most important people in the world, and anyone connected with her was also treated with great respect. They also felt there was something very mysterious about this lady who commanded so many young men, a number of them in uniform because they were in the Jewish Brigade of the British Army (but—unknown to the British—were also involved in the smuggling of illegals).

Many strategic meetings were held in Ruth's room at the Claridge—meetings often interrupted by telephone calls to and from, it seemed, everybody who was somebody in Paris. And she spoke to these people on a completely equal level.

She also knew the three or four most elegant dining places—which was a very important thing because there were few high-level restaurants in Paris at that time, and they were the places where important people met.

If we had not been with Ruth, none of us would have been accepted at these restaurants. But she swept in like a great lady. And they all seemed proud to have her.

At that time the French were not completely stabilized on a normal and functioning governmental basis. They were still in the mood of the war and the underground and the adventure and the political irregularities. Everything was in flux.

A lesser person than Ruth would never have been able to make use of the fantastic opportunities in France at this time. But Ruth fitted admirably into the spirit of the French revolution of 1945, and her great imagination was never more active and boundless than at that time in Paris.

She was regarded with great respect by the French authorities, by De Gaulle and by his entire staff—all of whom were political activists, very interested in all sorts of co-operation with other people who were doing things.

Despite the fact that the nation of Israel had not yet been born or named, I sometimes heard Ruth referred to in Paris as Lady Israel. This, in effect, is what she was.

APPENDIXES

Appendix One

FROM CHAPTER ONE

(Berl Katznelson, one of the founders of the Histadrut.)

The Histadrut was perhaps the world's most unique labor union. When founded in Palestine in 1920, the problem was not how to get higher wages for industrial workers. There were no industrial workers. There was, in fact, no industry. So Histadrut set about to create some. It used the dues of its first five thousand members to make work for another five thousand; it set up small factories of its own.

By 1937, the Histadrut had become virtually a second government in Palestine. The world's only "capitalistic union," it was the country's largest employer and biggest business operator. It formed co-operatives and corporations, sponsored a chain of kibbutzim—many of which began to build factories on their farms.

The union owned so much industry that it was able to set wage standards and working conditions by example, rather than by strike.

In addition, the Histadrut had its own "womb to tomb" health insurance; an important daily newspaper, *Davar*, a book publishing firm, a theatre, youth organizations, adult education classes and sports clubs. (The sea scouts who aided in the Mossad's ship-to-shore operations were drawn from the Histadrut's Sailing Club.) And, from the beginning, Katznelson and other leaders of the Histadrut backed the Mossad.

Appendix Two

FROM CHAPTER ONE

(Eliahu Golomb, commander in chief of the Haganah.)

Haganah is the Hebrew word for "defense." It was the word chosen by the Yishuv—the Jews of Palestine—for their underground army; an army organized to protect its people from the Arab massacres which started in 1920, repeated in 1921 and again in 1929, and which developed into a continuous, organized, country-wide campaign of terror in 1936—with the destruction of Jews in Palestine as its holy mission.

In this year, and in those which followed, Arab bands by the hundreds attacked Jewish settlements at night, killing men, women, children. It was perilous to travel on the roadways, for Arab attacks upon buses and trucks, even donkey carts, were aimed at disrupting communications between the Jewish communities. The terror was also turned against many Arab villagers and businessmen who were too friendly with their Jewish neighbors.

The Haganah was a secret army—whose existence was well known by Arabs and British. It was a part-time army, with only a handful of paid "staff officers," yet every village and farm settlement had its Haganah setup.

Appendix Three

(RUTH: *"It was the* kibbutz *I've been training for since I was a child. My mother always said you could milk cows better with a university degree."*)

Almost all of the Mossad members—and most of the Yishuv leaders—came from a kibbutz; often one which they had helped to found. The kibbutz was a unique form of communal living. The concept was born out of necessity. In general, the only land in Palestine which Arabs would sell to the Jews was malarial marshes, rocky eroded hillsides or other land where traditional-type farming was virtually impossible. Men working alone did not have the finances or the idealism necessary to redeem this soil. But groups of dedicated young Zionists, working together, might be able to achieve their goals. Kibbutzniks worked without pay; without thought of personal profit. Their earnings went into a common fund, from which food, clothing, supplies, farm equipment etc. was bought. Each member received clothing and supplies according to his needs. The kibbutz took care of all such matters as housing, schooling, insurance, doctor bills, taxes.

Equality was one of the bywords. Women worked in the fields along with men. Life was run by various committees—with rotating secretaries. Through a combination of dedication, idealism and hard work kibbutzniks managed to transform soil, where nothing had grown for centuries, into flourishing farmlands.

Most of the Mossad members were typical kibbutzniks; the "intellectual tractor driver" rather than the urbane and sophisticated European. Ruth, however, with a seemingly inborn elegance, was outstandingly untypical.

As an organization, the Mossad itself had many qualities of the kibbutz. Chief among these was the absence of a hierarchy or leader. Ruth, in speaking of her *haverim* in the Mossad, often expressed another typical kibbutz characteristic: "We were close, like one large family."

Appendix Four

(KADMON: *"After the* Anschluss *last March there were one hundred and seventy-six thousand Jews desperate to get out of Vienna."*)

On March 12, 1938, German troops swarmed into Austria. Two days later an ecstatic Hitler made his triumphal entry into Vienna—the former capital of the former country which was now a province of the German Reich. The Anschluss was over.

Within a few weeks tens of thousands of Austrian Jews were locked up in concentration camps. Men, women, even small children were cornered on the streets; beaten and kicked by black-booted S.S. men, while Austrians gathered round to jeer. A Jewish housewife on her way to the store might find herself on her hands and knees scrubbing the gutter, as an S.S. man stood above her armed with dagger and revolver. Contingents of elderly rabbis were sent to clean the S.S. toilets.

Jews had represented only one per cent of the total German population. Yet, they were condemned as the scourge of the country; the cause of all its troubles. Austria had even more Jews—one hundred and ninety-one thousand—three per cent of the total population. Therefore, Austrians were told the danger was even greater.

The Austrian S.S. were eager to prove what they could accomplish. The result was a sudden explosion of terror and sadism which excelled anything that had yet been seen in Germany.

And throughout the country, civilians "co-operated" by breaking into Jewish shops and homes, carting out anything and everything of value. Automobiles owned by Jews were confiscated by Nazi officers or party members. (But the Jewish owner had to continue to pay for fuel, garage, tires and repairs.)

Most Jewish workers were dismissed from their jobs. And a new concentration camp was set up on the banks of the Danube, since it was proving too expensive to ship Austrian Jews all the way to the German camps Dachau and Buchenwald.

Appendix Five

(KADMON: *"Now, how many legal certificates do you suppose were available for the Jews of Vienna? Thirty-two! And that, of course, was a year before the British White Paper with its new restrictions on legal certificates."*)

The White Paper was issued on May 17, 1939. In it the British decreed that for the next five years a total of seventy-five thousand Jewish immigrants would be allowed into Palestine; after which time Jewish immigration into the country would cease.

The seventy-five thousand were not to be allowed immediate entry. The certificates of entry were given out twice a year; five thousand at a time. In addition, the White Paper stated: "As a contribution towards the solution of the Jewish refugee problem" twenty-five thousand refugees would be admitted "as soon as the High Commissioner is satisfied that adequate provision for their maintenance is assured."

Jewish land buying in Palestine was also to be severely curtailed.

This British White Paper was a final statement of government policy which had, in fact, been operating for years: that of squeezing down the number of Jews permitted immigration certificates to enter Palestine.

Paradoxically, it was the British who had originally sponsored the Zionist dream of a national homeland for Jews, giving it for the first time a hope of reality. The British Balfour Declaration was issued in 1917. "His Majesty's Government views with favour the establishment in Palestine of a national home for the Jewish people, and will use their best endeavours to facilitate the achievement of this objective."

In that same year, 1917, the Balfour Declaration had been approved by

494

the League of Nations. And a declaration seconding the League's approval had been unanimously adopted by both houses of Congress, signed by the President of the United States. Amid all this welter of approval, Britain, as "Mother of the Declaration," was given a mandate over Palestine.

However, with Suez and with Arab oil of increasingly strategic importance, Britain had, through the years, taken increasingly sharp recognition of Arab pressure to limit the number of Jews entering the country.

In 1935, sixty thousand Jews were allowed legal certificates of entry into Palestine. A year later the British halved that figure to thirty thousand.

Appendix Six

(KADMON: *"And if we do somehow get the ship, and if it does somehow manage to make the trip undetected by British patrol boats and planes, we have the final impossibility of landing our illegals in secret on the beaches of Palestine."*)

Davidka N'meri was the kibbutznik selected to head the Mossad's landing operations. He organized a group of sea scouts. They knew the coast, knew how to handle small lifeboats. And they developed their techniques so well that they could take three hundred people from a ship in an hour on a moonless night; tow them to shore in lifeboats.

N'meri also organized a security unit to warn the scouts and the ships if police were approaching. They used recorded folk songs as signals to the ships. One song meant *Attention: British ambush on beach.* Another: *Sea too rough for landing.* Another: *All is safe. Approach shore.* Songs and codes were changed with each new ship.

N'meri organized medical aid units. And guides who led the illegals to a sheltered place upon landing; an orange grove, a packing house. There a Receiving Group interviewed them, registered them, gave them false identity cards. Then a Dispersion Group decided which kibbutz to send them to. And a Transport Group waited with cars and trucks to bring the illegals to their new homes.

Prior to the setup of these operations, landing in Palestine had been almost as perilous as the trip itself.

With no ship-to-shore signals to guide them to safety on the night-black beaches, passengers were sometimes unwittingly set ashore close by an Arab village. The seasick, half-starved men and women who had managed to cross the Mediterranean in a fishing skiff or a leaky sailboat found their initial introduction to their new country was a fierce hand-to-hand battle with Arabs.

Sometimes the would-be immigrants were able to bribe their Arab captors to grant them freedom. However, the Jews often landed stripped of any valuables they might have brought with them. Some of the boats were manned by waterfront toughs who made their living as smugglers. They did not object to smuggling Jews. Nor did they have any compunctions about robbing the passengers of all their possessions before allowing them to land.

Those Jews who, as a consequence, were unable to bribe their way free from the Arabs were promptly turned over to the British.

And since either avenue proved remunerative for the Arabs, they had organized vigilant beach patrols for the express purpose of tracking down Jewish illegals.

The British too were highly efficient in capturing would-be immigrants. Many small boatloads were caught by His Majesty's patrol boats within Palestine's three-mile limit. At other times the Jews attempted to disembark on a beach where British tommies were walking night patrol.

Appendix Seven

FROM CHAPTER FIVE

(RUTH: "Aliyah aleph—*immigration A—is the so-called legal immigration*.")

In the 1880s, the first large wave of Jews started "returning" to the homeland they had never seen. For the most part they were idealistic and very poor; small shopkeepers from pogrom-ridden Eastern Europe. One group called itself BILU, from the first letters of the Hebrew words of Isaiah: "Children of Jacob, let us go up!" Between 1880 and 1900, some twenty-six thousand European Jews had made their way to Palestine, and they were called the "First Aliyah," or "going upward" to the Holy Land.

The "Second Aliyah" came from 1904 to World War I; thousands of young Zionists who left universities, professions, city jobs to found agricultural settlements in the ancient homeland. They also founded Tel Aviv: the first all-Jewish city to be built in two thousand years.

The "Third Aliyah" was the new wave of Jews who came from Europe to Palestine, encouraged by the promise of the Balfour Declaration.

There were, in all, five distinct aliyahs. But when the illegal immigration movement was started in 1937, the Yishuv switched from numbers to letters. *Aliyah aleph* (A), those who came with legal certificates. And *Aliyah bet* (B), those who came illegally.

Appendix Eight

(MANDEL: "I *understand the old tubs you sail are often unseaworthy. They sink in mid-ocean. Death by drowning is not very pleasant.")*

Since the *Velos*—the first of the illegal ships—sailed for Palestine in 1934, an unknown and unrecorded number of small boats had landed at night on the shores, each discharging some ten to twenty passengers. Those boats which landed successfully were little heard about (even among the Yishuv, the Jews of Palestine). The illegals were quickly spirited away to an outlying kibbutz where they quietly became new citizens of the country—citizens with false papers.

In many cases, however, the small boatloads of immigrants never reached their destination. Their passengers died en route of starvation or were drowned when their boats overturned in a storm.

These boats were usually organized by racketeers who speculated hopefully on the chances of their passengers ever reaching Palestine in the ill-equipped, often unseaworthy craft.

There were also individually organized groups of Jewish "tourists" who secured a visitor's visa to Egypt or Lebanon, then boarded a cruise ship or freighter scheduled to pass close to Palestine. Their passage money included not only transport for themselves, but for an unusual item of baggage—their own personal lifeboat. This was—for a substantial additional sum—lowered into the sea at night, and the Jews then attempted to row their way to the shores of the Holy Land.

Appendix Nine

(Sudden disappearance, and no one to turn to. No one to make an official inquiry. Not the leaders of the Jewish Agency. Not the British rulers of Palestine. Not the officials of any country in which we operated.)

Although the British had been given the mandate to govern in Palestine, Article 4 of the Palestine Mandate established the Jewish Agency for Palestine to represent world Jewry in their relations with the British Mandatory Government. The Jewish Agency for Palestine became, in most respects, the *de facto* government of the Yishuv (the Jews of Palestine). David Ben-Gurion, as chairman of the Jewish Agency Executive, was, in effect, Prime Minister of the Yishuv. The Jewish Agency Executive was the Yishuv's Cabinet. But, of course, the Jewish Agency had no power or rights to protect its "nationals" abroad.

Appendix Ten

(The Revisionists were led by a militant, middle-aged Russian-born Jew named Ze'ev Jabotinsky.)

Jabotinsky started his career as a journalist, poet and sketch writer in Odessa. When a pogrom threatened Odessa the young writer turned fighter; organized a Jewish self-defense corps.

During World War I, he organized a Jewish battalion, the 38th Fusiliers, which fought with General Allenby in the 1918 Palestine campaign to free the country from the Turks (who had held the land under their oppressive rule since the sixteenth century).

In 1920, when an Arab riot broke out against Jews in Jerusalem, Jabotinsky organized a Jewish militia to repel Arab attackers. He was promptly arrested by the British, along with nineteen of his men, and a number of Arabs who had raped Jewish women and murdered Jewish men. Attackers and defenders were all allotted the same sentence: fifteen years in jail. There was, however, such an outcry at this injustice that Sir Herbert Samuel, the first British High Commissioner (and a Jew) granted amnesty to the imprisoned Jews—and to the Arabs connected with the affair.

Jabotinsky returned for a time to the literary world, took up the translation of poetry into Hebrew. But the defense corps he had founded grew. It is said that it was Jabotinsky who gave the name to this "underground army": Haganah—which in Hebrew means, "self-defense."

By 1936, Arab unrest had spread into country-wide violence. Jabotinsky and his followers rebelled against the Haganah's policies of self-defense and self-restraint. They set themselves up as a separate organization, dedicated to retaliation and reprisals and, on occasion, terror tactics. The group was called the Irgun Zvai Leumi.

The Irgun had a three-fold aim; to fight the Arabs to a standstill, to force the British out of Palestine; then to declare Palestine an independent Jewish state.

In July 1937, a British Commission headed by Lord Peel proposed that Palestine be partitioned. The greater part of the territory—to the west of the River Jordan—would become an independent Arab state. A small part would be constituted as an independent Jewish state.

The Jewish Agency accepted the Peel Commission's proposal. The Arabs did not. Nor did Jabotinsky and his followers—inside and outside of Palestine. They wanted to fight for a Jewish homeland which would encompass more of the territory that had constituted the historical biblical area of the Jewish national homeland—on both sides of the river Jordan.

Appendix Eleven

(*The man across the hall from me at the hotel; handsome, affable, always smiling; Levi Skolnik, member of the Jewish Agency Executive.*)

Levi Skolnik later took the Hebrew name of Levi Eshkol. He was Prime Minister of Israel from June 1963 until his sudden death of a heart attack, February 26, 1969.

(*Moshe Shertok . . . who held the second most important position in the Jewish Agency. As head of the Political Department he was, in effect, the Yishuv's Foreign Minister.*)

Shertok later took the Hebrew name Sharett, which means "servant." (He saw his mission in life as one of service to his people.) His brother-in-law was Eliahu Golomb, commander in chief of the Haganah. In 1948, when Israel became an independent country, Shertok stepped into the role of the new nation's first Foreign Minister—but it was a position he had held unofficially since 1933. He was Foreign Minister until 1956. From 1953 to 1955, he also served as Prime Minister. Thus, during these years, he held the nation's two top positions simultaneously.

Appendix Twelve

(The order was signed by Adolf Eichmann, head of the Central Office for Jewish Emigration in Vienna.)

Adolf Eichmann grew up in Hitler's home town of Linz. Indeed, he and Hitler had the same history teacher, Dr. Leopold Poetsch. Hitler paid high tribute to this teacher in *Mein Kampf*: "He was decisive for my whole later life . . . He used our budding national fanaticism as a means of educating us. . . . There we sat, often aflame with enthusiasm, sometimes moved to tears."

But, despite the inspiring Dr. Poetsch, Adolf Eichmann was not interested in studies. Indeed he—the eldest of five—was the only child in his family who did not get through high school. Nor could he manage to graduate from the vocational school to which his father sent him.

In fact, it was not until the age of twenty-two that Eichmann managed to make any mild success of himself at all. He finally got the first job he was able to hold down: that of traveling salesman for the Vacuum Oil Company of Austria.

He obtained the position through family connections. The cousin of his stepmother was married to a Jewish girl. They knew a Mr. Weiss—another Jew—who was general director of the Vacuum Oil Company. And Mr. Weiss had been prevailed upon to give Adolf a job.

For a time Eichmann did quite well. He liked his work. He had numerous girl friends. And—though it was a time of depression in Austria—*he* had money to throw around—for he had no expenses. He lived at home with his family in Linz.

Four years later, however, the firm transferred him to Salzburg. Where-upon, Eichmann complained he lost his *Arbeitsfreude*—joy in his work. And, a year later, he was fired.

He had, however, found a new interest. In April 1932, he joined the Nazi Party and was invited to become a member of the *Schutzstaffeln:* the S.S.—who accepted only the most obedient party members. Their badge was a skull and crossbones, a symbol of their *Kadavergehorsam*—the obedience of a corpse.

Within a year Eichmann joined the *Sicherheitsdienst,* the S.D.—the elite corps of the S.S.

He was elevated to the rank of *Scharführer*—sergeant. And early in 1935—for no particular reason—Adolf Eichmann was assigned to the Jewish Department. Suddenly, for the first time in his life, he began to show real initiative. His *Arbeitsfreude* was unbounded. He applied for a special salary bonus so that he might take Hebrew and Yiddish lessons from a rabbi. When he was turned down by his commanding officer, he set about learning the languages by himself. He became proficient enough to read a newspaper in Yiddish. And he put out the fiction that he had been born in Sarona, the German Templer colony in Palestine.

Within two years he had so impressed his superiors with his "compre-hensive knowledge of Jewry: the enemy" that they made him a lieutenant. And shortly thereafter he was sent to the Middle East to report on conditions in Palestine. He traveled to Egypt; interviewed several people on Palestine. Then he went home and prepared a comprehensive report. Palestine, he summed up, was an economic chaos where Jews were busy cheating each other because they had no Gentiles to cheat.

A year later, on a Monday afternoon—March 14, 1938—Hitler followed his goose-stepping troops into Vienna, the city in which he had once lived as a tramp. And Austria became part of the Greater German Reich.

Some of Austria's one hundred ninety thousand Jews had already fled the country. But the vast majority believed "it can't happen here." And they had remained in the country.

After the Anschluss, however, Austrian Jews wanted only one thing: To get out of this country which had suddenly become a seething and terrifying ocean of anti-Semitic excesses. Arrests. Looting. Street beatings. Murders.

But *how* to get out of Austria?

"A planet without a visa." This had already become a well-worn phrase.

In addition, the very process of *trying* to emigrate was a Kafkaesque hor-ror. Every Austrian Jew was forced to assemble a prodigious amount of docu-ments before he obtained permission to leave the country. But each document was valid only for a limited amount of time. It frequently hap-pened, therefore, that the first document had expired before the final one had been acquired. The would-be emigrant, consequently, spent his days trying to amass the necessary sheaf of papers within the required time period. And before he was arrested.

Four days after the Anschluss, Lieutenant Adolf Eichmann—specialist on Jewish affairs—was sent to Vienna to help in the process of driving out the Jews.

The skinny, bespectacled, innocuous Eichmann had become a new man, with new confidence—acquired along with his new specialty. He now could snarl, sneer and shout obscenities at Jews in a manner which befitted his new position.

For several days he studied the situation. Then he suggested his plan. The S.D. would open an efficient document factory, with representatives of the Ministry of Finance, the police, the income tax bureau and other officials, all under one roof.

A Jew could start at one end of the assembly line and emerge at the other, with all his necessary papers, plus his passport—each page duly stamped with the large red letter "J".

He was also to be given a small sum of money: *Vorzeigegeld,* sufficient for fulfilling the monetary requirements necessary to pass the immigration controls of a foreign country. This *Vorzeigegeld* would come from a collective Jewish bank roll. Rich Jews would, therefore, supply the money for poor Jews.

Eichmann's superiors decided his plan was worth a try. The *Zentralstelle für Judische Auswanderung* was set up in the former mansion of Baron Leopold von Rothschild. (The baron himself was a prisoner in the cellar of the Hotel Metropol.)

The system worked with admirable efficiency. A man started at one end. He might own a shop or some securities. He probably had a bank account. As he proceeded along the assembly line he was speedily and legally stripped of all his assets—which were turned over to the Greater German Reich. At the end of the line he received his dole, his *Vorzeigegeld.* And he received his passport, which was stamped: *You must leave the country within a fortnight. Otherwise, you will go to a concentration camp.*

Three months later the German financial authorities, the Treasury and the Ministry decided to eliminate the *Vorzeigegeld.* Despite the fact that much of the money for this fund came from Jewish organizations outside the country, they were appalled at the fact that Jews should be *given* anything at all.

A year and a day after his triumphal entry into Vienna, Hitler made another triumphal entry—into Prague. Newsreels showed der Führer screaming with pride: "Czechoslovakia has ceased to exist!"

However, when it came to the question of making their country *judenrein* the Czechs completely lacked the "revolutionary zeal" shown by the Austrians. For example, when a rabbi entered a tram, Czechs often stood up to offer a seat to this symbol of Jewish "scum."

Because of this, and because of the new influx of Jewish refugees from the Reich, *Hauptsturmführer* Eichmann was sent for. Czechoslovakia now had some three hundred and fifty-eight thousand Jews—to get rid of.

Eichmann set up a Central Office for Jewish Emigration in Prague.

A similar office was set up in Berlin, based on Eichmann's blueprints, and run by Eichmann's boss, Heinrich Müller.

Early in 1942, when Germany officially inaugurated her "Final Solution" for the Jews of Europe—*vernichtung*—the complete extermination of the Jews, Adolf Eichmann was one of the "generals" in charge of this operation. Six million Jews were systematically murdered by torture, mass shootings, gas chambers and cremation ovens.

Appendix Thirteen

(Yulik who—with Dani Shind—had founded the Mossad le Aliyah Bet in the Polish town of Kazimierz in the summer of 1937.)

That summer there was a convention of halutzim in Kazimierz. The delegates represented over twenty thousand young Poles. They had also invited two kibbutzniks from Palestine: Yulik Braginski and Dani Shind. The two were appalled at what they found: thousands of Polish Jews living on training farms in the most arduous conditions. Sleeping on wooden shelves. Often going hungry because they lived on what they could make doing day work at the nearby farms. (And local farmers were not rushing to hire "Jew workers.") In the night the pioneers met for lectures and lessons on life in Palestine. A life only handfuls of them would ever be able to lead—for many of the farms had hundreds of members. But only one or two legal certificates for entry into Palestine were available to each farm each year.

Furthermore, these well-trained and dedicated young men and women were desperately needed in Palestine. They were needed to work in the fields by day, and in the night to help hold off attacks of Arab terrorists.

Until 1936, relations between Arabs and Jews had been, on the whole, friendly in Palestine. The Jews raised the living standards of much of the Arab community; taught Arab villagers new techniques of irrigation, fertilization, crop rotation, sanitation. King Feisal of Syria, then generally regarded as leader of the Arabs, stated frequently in letters and speeches that continued co-operation between Arab and Jewish communities was one of the basic keys of development of the Middle East.

However, the wealthy Arab *effendis* (landowners) were growing worried. An Arab peasant who worked for a Jewish farmer could make three times more money in a single season than he did working for an Arab landowner an entire year as a tenant farmer. What if the peasants, inspired by the example of their Jewish neighbors, started to rebel against the *effendi*-dominated feudal system under which they were kept in complete peonage?

To ensure the retention of their power and prerogatives in Palestine, the effendis played upon the excitability, fear and religious fanaticism of the peasants. In mosques and coffee houses the same theme was pounded: The Jews were invaders, stealing the peasants' land (even though the effendis had themselves sold this land to the Jews—swamps and desert, for the most part). Constant tension was maintained, a careful barrier between Arab and Jew.

Then, to enhance their power, Arab leaders in Palestine made a secret alliance with the Nazis. The Germans would supply them with money and arms for their "holy war" against the Jews. In return, the Arab leaders promised to support Hitler if war broke out between Germany and England. This alliance was particularly inspired by Haj Amin el Husseini, who had returned to Palestine to take over his grandfather's role as Grand Mufti, religious head of the Palestine Moslem community.

In 1936, the carefully nurtured unrest among the Arabs exploded into country-wide violence. Hundreds of Arab bands attacked Jewish communities, killing men, women and children, sometimes mutilating the dead bodies.

Because the Polish pioneers so desperately wanted to come to Palestine, and because these well-trained young men and women were now so desperately needed by the Yishuv—to work and to fight—Dani and Yulik responded to the pleas of the convention leaders at Kazimierz. They promised to organize an illegal ship. But—unlike the *Velos*—this ship would be carefully organized every step of the way. And if this ship was successful, more would follow. Small boats run by the Revisionists had been bringing pioneers to Palestine, a dozen at a time. But Dani and Yulik decided to lease larger ships, which could carry hundreds at a time. They added two more kibbutzniks to their organization: Levi Schwartz, who would accompany the ship, and Davidka N'meri, who would organize the landing operations.

The group became known as Mossad le Aliyah Bet.

When their first ship was organized and the pioneers ready to board her, Dani and Yulik decided that they should not proceed further until they had the approval from top leaders of the Yishuv. The unofficial approval. For what they were doing was in direct opposition to the decree issued by the Jewish Agency Executive after the *Velos* fiasco.

Dani Shind, therefore, traveled to Palestine to discuss the matter with Berl Katznelson, with Eliahu Golomb and with David Ben-Gurion.

He saw Berl first. Berl listened, without seeming to listen; continuing to work on an article at his desk. At the end of Dani's impassioned recital Berl asked a few questions. And then agreed to give his full support to the Mossad; support which would include money from the Histadrut.

Berl not only understood the need for the Mossad in 1937, but saw its vital role in the years to come. "You may be making history in a way you don't yet realize," he told Dani. "If this ship is a success, I hope that your next illegal cargo will come from Germany."

With Eliahu Golomb things had not been that easy. Golomb worked every day with the British. True, the British rulers of Palestine searched Yishuv settlements for hidden weapons which, if found, were confiscated. And, on occasion, Haganah leaders were heavily fined or imprisoned. But, on the whole, the British tended to condone, if not openly accept, the existence of and the need for the Haganah, the Yishuv's army of defense. This semitolerance would, however, change overnight were it ever to become known that Golomb, head of the Haganah, sponsored illegal immigration.

As Dani spoke, presented his case, Golomb's black brows had drawn together in a black frown. However, when Dani finished, Golomb nodded. The young men, he pronounced, should not have proceeded without the sanction of the Yishuv leaders. However, since they had done so, it was essential that the operation now prove a success. If his unofficial approval was wanted, he would give it.

Dani's third meeting was, of course, the most important. Ben-Gurion, after all, headed the governing body of the Yishuv. If he ordered the Mossad to stop their operations, they must do so at once. Otherwise, they would no longer be considered loyal to the Yishuv and its government.

And B.G. had, in fact, exploded in anger when Dani told him about the Mossad. Who had given permission for such activities? What committee, which leaders had been advised of these plans? The operation must be halted at once. It could jeopardize the entire future of the Zionist movement. It was dangerous. It was unnecessary. It was nothing less than insanity.

And Dani shouted back at B.G., "Permission! Did you ask permission of a committee before you came to Palestine? It was illegal then too, wasn't it? All of our leaders—Berl, Eliahu, Ben Zvi—did they ask permission before they came? Sure, it was a generation ago. But it was still illegal. And where would we be today without men like you? And where will we be in another generation if we keep out all these young Zionists who are desperate to come here? What do you expect us to tell them, the halutzim who are waiting now in Warsaw, waiting for word as to when our ship will sail? And the thousands of others who have renewed hope now, because of the Mossad. We're to tell them they're not wanted? Our leaders won't accept them? They must stay where they are? Rot in their own dreams!"

Then, very quietly, B.G. asked, "Your ship is ready to sail?"

And Dani answered, "We await only your unofficial approval. We're not asking for any public proclamations."

Ben-Gurion nodded. Then he said, "You can tell your people that any Jew who can get into Palestine by any means is all right as far as I'm concerned. When your ship comes in, I'll come down to the beach at night and help the passengers disembark. But!" And he started shouting again. "No more ships! We will not tolerate insubordination! Nothing must be done unless it has been decided upon by the movement. Is that understood?"

Dani understood that Ben-Gurion did not wish to be informed about any more ships. At least not by him or by Yulik Braginski or Levi Schwartz or Davidka N'meri.

Nevertheless, Mossad members were certain that David Ben-Gurion knew about each of their ships which had sailed since that summer of '37. And they were certain that he did not disapprove.

Appendix Fourteen

(*Would you speak this way, Rabbi Abba Hillel Silver if you lived in Berlin —instead of Cleveland, Ohio?*)

Although Dr. Silver was a strong supporter of the Legalist position concerning illegal immigration to Palestine in 1939, he shortly thereafter became an ardent advocate for the cause of illegal immigration.

From 1945 to 1947, he served as president of the Zionist Organization of America. And from 1943 through the establishment of the State of Israel in 1948, he was chairman of the American Zionist Emergency Council, the political arm of the American Zionist movement. Under his dynamic and dedicated leadership, the Emergency Council won overwhelming public support for the U.S. endorsement of an independent Jewish state in Palestine.

Appendix Fifteen

(BERL KATZNELSON: *"With what understanding this aliyah is looked upon by the British Parliament. And with what lack of understanding it is looked upon here at the Zionist Congress."*)

On July 20, 1939, a debate on Palestine was held in the House of Commons. Many Members of Parliament spoke out vehemently, factually and eloquently against the British White Paper. They pointed out the dangers and fallacies involved in trying to propitiate the Arabs. And they spoke with understanding about illegal immigration, pointing out that this was the only road left open for the Jews.

Until Berl Katznelson spoke at the Congress, these British M.P.s made far more eloquent statements against the White Paper and for illegal immigration than were heard at the Twenty-first Zionist Congress.

One of the M.P.s quoted from an article by Winston Churchill; introducing it thus: "If I may respectfully say so in this one paragraph the Right Hon. Gentleman the Member for Epping (Mr. Churchill) has set out the case for carrying out the Mandate. He said:

'The Jews have done no harm to the Arabs of Palestine. On the contrary, they have brought nothing but good gifts, more wealth, more trade, more civilization, new sources of living, higher employment . . . a better water supply—in a word, the fruits of easy and modern science.' "

One of the chief British spokesmen against the White Paper was M. P. Tom Williams, who was invited to speak at the Zionist Congress. He said in his speech that he could well understand the feelings of the delegates when they read about the refugee ships being turned back from the shores of Palestine. But there was no need to despair. Their movement could not be destroyed; their constructive work in Palestine could never be stopped. The Colonial Secretary was not the British Parliament. In fact, at the recent debate on the White Paper in the House of Commons the government had been able to secure only a small majority.

Unfortunately, however, it was Sir Malcolm MacDonald's view which prevailed. Never, during the war years and postwar years, did the British slacken in their endeavors to close Palestine to Jews who never in all their four-thousand-year-old history were in more desperate need of a homeland.

Appendix Sixteen

FROM CHAPTER TWENTY-THREE

(BERL KATZNELSON: *"And when I ask myself who is now the natural bearer of the struggle for existence, my answer is—the scattered refugees on the seas. They will not allow the gates of Eretz Israel to close before them."*)

Eretz, in Hebrew, means "the land." The Yishuv generally referred to Palestine as *Eretz Israel*—the land of Israel—as their Jewish ancestors in Palestine had done for almost two thousand years. In 900 B.C., the land of Canaan was divided into two Jewish kingdoms: Israel and Judea. Just before the new nation of the Jews was officially declared in May 1948, there was great debate as to whether the country should be called Israel or Judea. One of the chief reasons it was called Israel was that ever since the Diaspora Jews all over the world and Jews in Palestine had referred to the land as Eretz Israel.

Appendix Seventeen

FROM CHAPTER THIRTY-FOUR

(RUTH: *"You say it's been decided. By whom? Our leaders? Berl? Eliahu? Saul Meiroff?"*)

Saul Meiroff, one of the top men in the Haganah, later became head of the entire Mossad operation. When his son, named Gur, was killed in Israel's War of Independence, Meiroff took the Hebrew name Avigur, which means the father of Gur. Meiroff's sister, Zipporah, was married to Moshe Shertok (Sharett).

Appendix Eighteen

FROM CHAPTER THIRTY-FOUR

("Look," said Yehuda, "if I wasn't working with British Intelligence, I'd be working with the Mossad.")

In the postwar years, Yehuda Arazi did become one of the most daring and dedicated leaders of the Mossad. Many of the exploits of Ari Ben Canaan, hero of the novel *Exodus,* were based upon the brilliant operations conceived by Arazi.

Appendix Nineteen

FROM CHAPTER FORTY-ONE

(Tonight, a chemistry professor from Bucharest would give some eyewitness details about the pogrom which had taken place in Rumania from January twenty-first to January twenty-third.)

This was the last of Rumania's brutal pogroms.

Despite the anti-Semitism which had been part of Rumanian culture for many years, and despite the two pogroms which took so many Jewish lives, the Rumanian Government, under Antonescu, succeeded in saving hundreds of thousands of Rumanian Jews from extermination.

Vernichtung—annihilation, mass murder of Jews—did take place in every other country in Europe where fascists came to power during Hitler's reign. But not in Rumania. The dictator Antonescu was, indeed, a strong man; so much so that he was able to stand up against Hitler's requests for total extermination of Rumanian Jews. Bessarabia and Northern Bukovina became part of Russia, and Rumanian Jews who lived in these sections were put into concentration camps and were put to death. But in Greater Rumania, Antonescu succeeded in protecting and defending Rumanian Jews throughout the war years. During these same years two thirds of the Jews of Europe —some six million men, women and children—lost their lives.